CRISIS IN THE PHILIPPINES

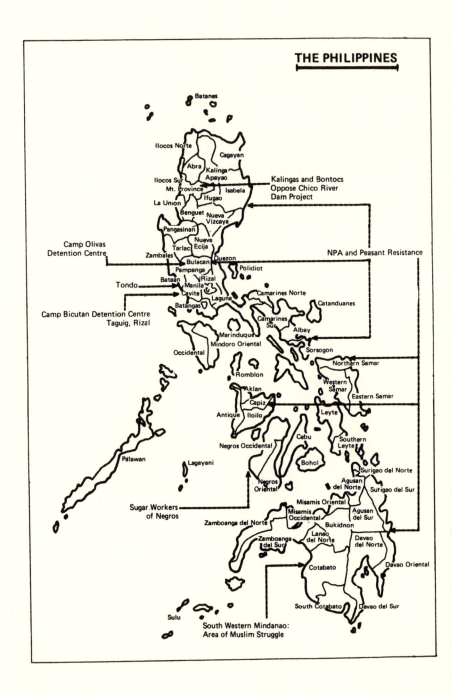

THE PHILIPPINES

Batanes

Ilocos Norte

Cagayan

Abra
Kalinga
Apayao

Ilocos Sur
Mt. Province
Isabela

Ifugao

Kalingas and Bontocs
Oppose Chico River
Dam Project

La Union

Benguet
Nueva
Vizcaya

Pangasinan

Nueva
Ecija

Camp Olivas
Detention Centre

Tarlac

Zambales
Quezon

Bulacan
Pampanga
Polidiot

NPA and Peasant Resistance

Tondo

Bataan
Rizal

Manila

Cavite

Camarines Norte

Catanduanes

Laguna

Camp Bicutan Detention Centre
Taguig, Rizal

Batangas

Camarines
Sur
Albay

Marinduque

Mindoro Oriental

Sorsogon

Occidental

Northern Samar

Romblon

Western
Samar

Eastern Samar

Aklan

Capiz

Leyte

Antique
Iloilo

Cebu

Negros Occidental

Southern
Leyte

Palawan

Lagayani

Bohol

Surigao del Norte

Negros
Oriental

Agusan
del Norte

Surigao del Sur

Sugar Workers
of Negros

Misamis Oriental

Agusan
del Sur

Zamboanga del Norte

Misamis
Occidental

Bukidnon

Davao
del Norte

Zamboanga
del Sur

Lanao
del Norte

Davao Oriental

Cotabato

Sulu

South Cotabato

Davao del Sur

South Western Mindanao:
Area of Muslim Struggle

CRISIS IN THE PHILIPPINES

The Making of a Revolution

E. SAN JUAN

Bergin & Garvey Publishers, Inc.
MASSACHUSETTS

First published in 1986 by
Bergin & Garvey Publishers, Inc.
670 Amherst Road
South Hadley, Massachusetts 01075

6789   987654321

Printed in the United States of America

Library of Congress Cataloging-in-Publication Data

San Juan, E. (Epifanio), 1938–
    Crisis in the Philippines.

    Bibliography: p.
    Includes index.
    1. Philippines—Politics and government—1973–
2. National liberation movements—Philippines.
I. Title.
DS686.5.S256   1986   959.9′046   85–22980
ISBN 0–89789–085–X
ISBN 0–89789–093–0 (pbk.)

PHOTO CREDITS: Joselito Fernandez (pp. 128, 150); Southeast Asia Resource Center (p. 176). All other photos courtesy of the author.

To the memory of all the thousands of victims of the U.S.-Marcos dictatorship, among them: Maria Lorena Barros, Liliosa Hilao, Purificacion Pedro, Zacharias Agatep, Magtanggol Roque, Remberto de la Paz, Juan Escandor, Macli-ing Dulag, Emmanuel Lacaba, Edgar Jopson, Benigno Aquino Jr., Alex Boncayao and Felixberto Olalia.

Contents

Preface   ix

Introduction   1

I. Transnationals: The Watchdogs of Empire   17

II. Strategic Interventions Beyond Class: The Church, Nationalities, Women   29

III. U.S. Hegemony and the Ideology of Neo-Colonial Domination   53

IV. Understanding the Moro People's Struggle: Articulations of Islam, Community, Nation   67

V. Subverting Authoritarian Discourse   81

VI. Unleashing Dreams, Mapping the Space of Desire   105

VII. On the Praxis of People's War   129

VIII. Toward Socialist Feminism   151

IX. Epilogue: Tunnelling Out of the Belly of the Beast   177

Notes   195

Selected Bibliography   235

Index   255

Fear history, for no secret can be hidden from it.

Gregoria de Jesus, Lakambini of the Katipunan
(Association of Sons of the People)

The land is sacred, nourished by our sweat; it shall become even more sacred when it is nourished by our blood.

Macli-ing Dulag,
Igorot Leader murdered by the U.S.-Marcos Régime

Before I joined the New People's Army, I used to say Mass up to three times a day. But it never solved the people's problems. But if you help organize and educate the people so they can stand up for their rights, that means I am offering my life for them. For me, that is the real sacrifice of the mass.

Father Conrado Balweg, S.V.D.

I want very much to have children. But not in the next few years. We are facing a protracted people's war. I have no illusions that this war will be settled in a decade or two. We will become another Vietnam.

Maria Lorena Barros, New People's Army
freedom-fighter killed by the fascist military

Preface

A few weeks before the decisive Congress vote banning aid to the CIA-directed Contras in Nicaragua, a militant of the African National Congress (ANC) from South Africa suggested that were it not for the explosive U.S. crisis in the Philippines , American Marines would already have invaded Nicaragua. Conversely, were it not for the evolving Nicaraguan revolution led by the Sandinistas, the Philippines might have already become (as it did at the turn of the century) the next bloody testing ground where the imperial debacle in Vietnam can be avenged. Could the Filipino-American War (1898-1902) be repeated? This is the grim prospect we Filipinos face in the closing years of this millenium.

Caught unaware and panicked by the massive demonstrations that followed the Aquino assassination in August 1983, the U.S. government immediately convened an interagency task force that met regularly for the next year or so. The task force finally drafted a "secret" report in late 1984 (leaked out in 1985) which uncovered the obvious: that a "growing communist insurgency" leading to a "radicalized Philippines" would endanger U.S. political, economic, and military interests in Asia. In 1984, the U.S. Senate Committee on Foreign Relations issued a staff report entitled "The Situation in the Philippines," which concluded that "polarization in the Philippines has thus reached a new intensity," and many Filipinos are now questioning whether the "democratic tradition" and "free enterprise" system installed by half a century of U.S. colonial rule "can meet the needs of the country as a whole." In the same year, testimony submitted to the House Committee on Foreign Affairs argued for the outright manipulative use of the $900 million rental the Reagan administration pledged to Marcos for the unhampered use of military bases and facilities--the first installment totalled $180 million in 1984, for 1985 $226 million, and for 1986 $275 million of which $102 million is for military purposes. The announced rationale was to send a clear message of U.S. unease about the untenable, unpopular, and obsolescent status of the present dispensation. In his testimony, former U.S. Ambassador William Sullivan bluntly asserted America's principal stake in trying to preserve the status quo in the Philippines (minus Marcos): "One of the consequences of civil and political violence in the Philippines could be the eventual extrusion of the United States from the Philippine military bases, with broad destabilizing effects upon the entire East Asian region." But, one might ask, what about the incalculable sacrifices and aspirations of the Filipino people? Are the Filipinos again going to allow themselves to be treated as dispensable, instrumentalized variables in the cost-accounting logic of empire?

The formulistic invocation of the hallowed phrase "U.S.-Philippines special relations" by bureaucrats and academics can be taken as a symptomatic index of U.S. foreign policy's interventionist syndrome whose genealogy may be traced back to the pragmatic candor of George Kennan, prime architect of Cold War containment strategy: "We should cease to talk about vague and--for the Far East--unreal objections such as human rights, the raising of living standards, and democratization. The day is not far off when we are going to have to deal in straight power concepts. The less we are hampered by idealistic slogans, the better." That belief has been with us for some time now--from the Nixon to the Reagan administration. It has survived in a period when, as Kennan shrewdly anticipated, Japan and the Philippines have emerged as "the cornerstones" of U.S. policy in the region (with the loss of Indochina and the demise of SEATO), making it imperative to "preserve the archipelago as a bulwark of U.S. security in the area." In this ironic impasse, post-"independent" Philippines has become more tightly bound to the now precarious fate of U.S. global ascendancy than when it languished before World War II as the idyllic Yankee trading outpost in Asia.

That fate has now acquired its prophetic and instructive symbol in Aquino's lifeless body slumped on the tarmac of Manila International Airport, televised worldwide, making the Philippines taboo until some demon-scapegoat is exorcised and "business-as-usual" returns. That carnage also sums up fifty years of colonial domination and transnational profit taking. In one dramatic exposure, the creature of U.S. diplomacy for nearly two decades--Marcos's authoritarian state--revealed its inherently repressive character which no amount of U.S. apologetics, weaponry, or influx of military advisers could hide, neutralize, or make acceptable to the Filipino people and the international community. The crying moral issue is: Can the U.S. public continue to allow their money and silent complicity to legitimize the outrageous crimes of a "friendly" dictator who happens to be on the "right" side of the East-West nuclear stalemate?

At this critical juncture when the eagle's claws are bared to strike again, I write to urge an intervention of another kind. Because of the accelerating momentum of disasters--the unrelenting massacre of "hamletted" village folk; the jailing, torture, and killing of civilian dissenters, workers on strike, protesting students, journalists, clergy; and the persistent structural deprivations of hunger, disease, unemployment, malnutrition afflicting millions--brought about by the unimpeded and exacerbated flow of millions of U.S. tax dollars to the Marcos regime, it is necessary to call the attention of enlightened citizens here to the necessity of prevailing on Congress and Washington to withhold or cut off its lifeline of support. This would stave off imminent U.S. direct involvement in a country where, given precisely those "special relations" and the tidal wave of Filipino resistance, fierce confrontations would make Vietnam and El Salvador appear as minor previews and innocuous dress rehearsals. Everyone capable of being "conscienticized" (in Paulo Freire's term) needs, and deserves, to read this book.

On the face of this "clear and present danger" of direct U.S. military involvement against the Filipino people's burning desire for genuine sovereignty and popular, grassroots democracy, I have gathered together the following essays with three purposes in mind. First, to provide a brief background to the crisis using data culled from proscribed publications and out-of-print material hitherto inaccessible to the public. Second, to introduce a mode of theoretical inquiry in the field of U.S.-Philippine relations whose uniqueness lies in its privileging the problematic of "hegemony" (Gramsci); that is, the conjunctural nature of the Philippine formation as product/process of ideological and political struggle, a differential articulation of variable and contradictory discourses traversing religion, gender, class, nationality, spatial (rural/urban), and temporal positions. Third, to open up the space for grasping the complex and dynamic totality of Philippine society conceived as an ensemble of overdetermined, historicized practices; a construct of signifying relations that cannot be reduced *a priori* to an ontological unity (such as that invented by the standard U.S. academic or popular texts on the Philippines), or to a universalized identity based on the traditional mechanistic logic of labor/capital, productive forces/production relations, base/superstructure. All three aims seek to demarcate the space for contesting established dogmas, "common sense" notions, received opinions, and seemingly presuppositionless concepts that merely reinforce the status quo of domination and reification: sexism, racism, chauvinism, and self-reproducing hierarchical practices.

In the last two or three years, the crisis of U.S, hegemony and ruling class legitimacy in the Philippines has catapulted the islands to the foreground of the mass media screen competing with the Soviet "threat", the war in Central America, and other disposable commodities. The consciousness and sensibility of millions vis-a-vis the Philippines have suddenly become the arena of ideological contestation, the theater of warring interests. At this late date, we cannot so innocently accept the ready-made "facts" packaged by CBS, the *New York Times,* or *Reader's Digest* as true or meaningful since they are positioned and framed within a world-view which attempts to conceal rifts and cleavages, flatten out any contradiction into a matter of trivial deviation, and normalize the scandalous for the sake of enabling "free and equal" exchange of ideas and bodies in the global marketplace. However, if we submit to this insidious drive of total commodification--we are not even conscious of this normal habit of everyday acquiescence--then in no way can we ever comprehend, much less learn the existence of, such unprecedented historic developments as the Moro people's fight for self-determination, Filipino Christian "theology of liberation," and the novel expressions of feminism being forged in the Philippine crucible today. This book is an attempt to provide an alternative reading, an oppositional rewriting of the pictures, sounds, and movements filling the gap occupied temporarily by the hyphen in "Philippine-U.S. relations."

Given the metamorphic and continually changing loci of antagonisms in the world today, the multiple points of rupture dispersed everywhere, this discourse whose inside and outside can no longer be neatly separated, is necessarily intertextual. That is, it inscribes itself in the contradictory place of power (hegemonic U.S. culture of government, education, media) and resistances (Filipinos from all sectors and classes), and thus it inevitably registers the effects of such plural wills and efforts at defining the manifold unity of the Philippine formation. Such a mobile, protean unity should be understood as the creation of incessant political and cultural constructions. Finally, besides arousing concern from readers here and abroad, I also hope to contribute to the ongoing collective project of reconstituting the subjectivity of the Filipino people as a protagonist of world-historical changes in the context of Third World anti-imperialist struggles in El Salvador, South Africa, Lebanon, Northern Ireland, and elsewhere. Otherwise, there is no point in the whole exercise.

Most of the chapters in this volume, now revised or complete-ly rewritten, were originally occasioned by specific circumstances and conjunctures--scholars' conferences, seminars, educational projects, etc. They exemplify a mode of theoretical production and intervention that most committed Third World intellectuals, from Mao and Fanon to Che Guevara and Cabral, have felt compelled to engage in as necessary or obligatory moments in the process of holistic subjective/objective transformations. One reason explains the integral, organic rootedness of Third World activists/thinkers in the ongoing political-cultural struggles of their milieu: the heterogeneous, decentered structure of Third World formations. In spite of, and indeed because of, the constraints of exile in which many Filipino progressive intellectuals have found themselves since the late sixties, concomitant with the phenomenal exodus of Filipino labor ("warm body export") into Europe, North America, and the Middle East, a new battlefront has opened up: the Filipino nation-in-the-making outside the archipelago.

Of course there is no denying the priority agenda of mobilizing international solidarity for democratic and humanitarian ends; but in the same process of accomplishing that goal, the chosen responsibility of the Third World intellectual to fight for the justice and freedom and dignity of his/her community aligned with all "the wretched of the earth" (Fanon), with all its personally destabilizing provocations and catalyzing challenges, needs to be constantly affirmed. (Without these mediations, internationalism--where indeed is the phantom vanguard heralding global capitalism's apocalypse?--is an empty shibboleth.) No more eloquent words exist to voice that mandate than those of Jose W. Diokno, Filipino civil libertarian and chairperson of the National Organizing Committee, New Patriotic Alliance (BAYAN): "We appreciate whatever help you may want to give us, but whether you give us any help or not, whether we have to wade through blood and fire, we Filipinos will make of our country, the Philippines, a nation worthy of our children."

Allow me to resituate some of the chapters in their original place of delivery or publication:

The Introduction derives certain ideas from "Comment: The Aquino Assassination and the Challenge to the American People" (*Socialist Politics*) and "Contradiction and Practice in 'New Society' Ideology and Culture, " an unpublished paper read at the First International Philippine Studies Conference, Western Michigan University. Chapter I is an elaboration of "US Imperialism in the Philippines" (*Race and Class*, XXII) a report presented to the Oil Workers' World Anti-Monopolist Conference in Tripoli, Libya. Chapter II is an amplified version of "The Current Struggle Against US Imperialism in the Philippines" (*Our Socialism*, I), first presented at the 1983 Marxist Scholars Conference, University of Cincinnati, Ohio. Chapter III was first delivered at the Southeast Asia Studies Conference, Ohio University, and will appear in *Contemporary Marxism*. Chapter IV was first read at the Southeast Asian Studies Conference, University of Michigan, Ann Arbor, and will soon be published in *The International Journal of World Studies*. Chapter V is based on a paper given at the 16th International Congress of the International Federation for Modern Languages and Literatures (FILLM), Budapest, Hungary. A slightly different version will appear in *Minnesota Review* of Winter 1985. Chapter VI is an expanded version of "From Intramuros to the Liberated City: Salvaging the Aesthetics of the Polis" (*Philippine Social Sciences and Humanities Review,* XLVI); another version can be found in *Jadavpur Journal of Comparative Literature,* Calcutta, India. The last three chapters are original essays appearing here for the first time.

I would like to thank the following friends and colleagues who have helped directly or indirectly in the struggle of the Filipino people for freedom, justice, and national liberation, and for their share in enabling the writing of this book: Peggy and Boone Schirmer, Steve Thornton, Tim McGloin, Jane and Bruce Franklin, Doug Allen, Roger and Mary Bresnahan, Nancy and Norman Chance, Sam Noumoff, John Beverley, and Rufus Blanshard. Without the advice and support of Delia, Karin and Eric, and numerous comrades engaged in various frontlines in the Philippines and elsewhere, I would not have successfully negotiated the perilous passage between the Scylla of voluntarist idealism and the Charybdis of eschatological materialism. Finally, I want to express here my deep gratitude to the Catholic Mass Media Awards, (Manila, Philippines) and the Manila Critics' Circle for honoring my book *Toward A People's Literature.* Let us all continue the struggle until final victory.

E. San Juan
Storrs, Connecticut

Postscript: After an exile of almost eighteen years, my short visit (2-22 August 1985) in Manila provided confirmation to certain views and reflections expressed in this book. I want to record here my deep appreciation and gratitude to the following who made my brief sojourn instructive and pleasurable: Cynthia Nolasco, Fe and Roger Mangahas, Marra Lanot, Noli and Lita Santos, Joseph Lim, Lulu Torres-Reyes, Nicanor Tiongson, Ave Perez Jacob, Grace and Abdulmari Imao, Doreen Gamboa-Fernandez, and Bienvenido Lumbera. My brothers Benjamin and Victor San Juan ferried me to all the venues and meeting places. I had brief but rewarding exchanges with Raquel Edralin, Remy Rikken, Jurgette Honculada, Maita Gomez, Princess Ronquillo-Nemenzo, Julie Delima-Sison, Rose Torres-Yu, Ester Dipasupil, Alfredo N. Salanga, Raul Segovia, Pete Daroy, Ed Maranan, Pete Lacaba, and Ricardo Lee; with members of *Kalayaan* and *Gabriela,* participants of the *Palihang Amado V. Hernandez* at the University of the Philippines (Diliman); with members of *Pluma*; with faculty members of the Development Studies Department at U.P. College (Manila); and with writers of the newspaper *Malaya.* One memorable evening was spent with Angel Baking and Simeon Rodriguez. And finally I wish to thank the members of the *Free Mila Aguilar Committee* for their generous support, especially to the sisters of St. Joseph's College and to Atty. Rene and Larraine Sarmiento. Together we shall overcome.

E.S.J.

CRISIS IN THE PHILIPPINES

Introduction

The unrelenting avalanche of events in the Philippines has once again confirmed the philosopher Hegel's profound insight that the Owl of Minerva only flies at dusk, when the apocalyptic fury of the carnage has subsided. In this ambiguous twilight zone, I offer the following essays as exploratory and mapping gestures-- prolegomena to the Owl's wide-ranging and depth-probing flight scheduled before the final decisive battle erupts.

Unleashing the unquenchable fury of millions--from the first million who joined the funeral procession to the three million who rallied on 21 August 1984--the summary killing of Senator Benigno Aquino on 21 August 1983 marks a turning point in modern Philippine history, signalling the final phase of the disintegration of the Marcos regime and the breakthrough of the popular-democratic forces into the stage of viable, efficacious and self-directed intervention. An index of the unprecedented height to which years of political organizing and mobilizing by the National Democratic Front (NDF) and other anti-fascist, anti-imperialist groups have reached, may be discerned not only in the all-round participation of the Manila business elite--Butz Aquino's August Twenty-One Movement is one illustration--but in the recent gesture of more critical partisanship shown by Cardinal Jaime Sin, head of an 86 percent Catholic constituency, when he bewailed the "moral dry rot" prevailing in the country.[1] Confronted by the horrendous carnage of 27 September 1984, when heavily-armed police and military, without any provocation, fired pistols and M-16 rifles on 3,000 people, resulting in the killing of at least eleven demonstrators; twelve others with serious gunshot injuries; thirty people hospitalized; and several "disappearances,"[2] Cardinal Jaime Sin lambasted the military's "saturnalia of sadism and violence" and urged business leaders to join the "parliament of the streets" to topple the dictatorship. On 7 October 1984, the Associated Press reported that in response to the Cardinal's call, 30,000 people, from "businessmen in formal wear to workers in rags" demonstrated in Manila and demanded, among other reforms, that foreign governments, chiefly the U.S., cease their support for Marcos without which the dictatorship would not survive.

Ever since Marcos usurped despotic power in 1972, destroyed democratic processes, scrapped civil rights, and took over 100,000 political prisoners (among whom was Senator Aquino), Marcos has received the open support of the U.S. government and the corporate Establishment. He has received a yearly average of 100 million tax-dollars, which accelerated with the Carter administration's payment of $500 million for military base rental between 1979 and 1984. In 1981, Vice-President Bush unabashedly lauded Marcos' "adherence to democracy" in the face of rampant human rights violations reported by the Task Force Detainees of the Association of Major Religious Superiors of the Philipines.[3] In September 1982, Reagan warmly welcomed the tyrant in Washington and boosted aid to Marcos by 80 percent when he agreed to pay $900 million rental for the bases for the next five years (1984-1989). This year Marcos will receive $180 million, next year about $275 million, amounts more than adequate to equip with sophisticated weapons for crowd control and counter-insurgency his repressive military of 300,000 soldiers, including paramilitary "death-squads" or terrorist gangs responsible for the killing of such opposition figures as Dr. Remberto de la Paz and Dr. Juan Escandor, journalist Alexander Orcullo, Mayor Cesar Climaco, and countless others.

According to a series of painstakingly researched and documented studies on the human rights situation in the Philippines--conducted by such prestigious organizations as Amnesty International (1975, 1981), the International Commission of Jurists (1977, 1984) and the New York-based Lawyers' Committee for International Human Rights (December 1983), not to mention the yearly country reports undertaken by the U.S. State Department, United Nations Human Rights Commission, and various church groups--the Marcos regime indisputably ranks as one of the world's worst violators of human rights, surpassing the abysmal records of the Shah of Iran and Somoza of Nicaragua. The 1984 report of the International Commission of Jurists, to cite the most up-to-date, reiterates the ubiquitous theme of all the studies: "Widespread abuses of human rights by military and security forces, including extra-judicial killings ("salvaging"), massacres, burnings, arbitrary arrests," and so on. "Torture is a common practice of Philippine security and intelligence forces." The report stresses the brutal militarization of Philipppine society as a consistent and systematic policy of the Marcos dispensation, enabled by the unlimited decree-making powers of the President (as provided by Amendment No. 6 of the illegal 1973 Marcos constitution), which has for all practical purposes negated the fundamental civil liberties of Filipino citizens--for example, the right of *habeas corpus* and of due process--and denied basic freedoms and human rights (in employment, education, etc.) normally enjoyed by citizens of civilized polities.[4] What has led to this rampant self-righteous barbarism wreaked by a militarized state apparatus subservient to imperialist *diktat*, which Clive Thomas, in his account of this phenomenon *The Rise of the Authoritarian State in Peripheral Societies*, considers a general contemporary trend in Third World formations?[5]

The case of the Philippines in the last two or three decades affords us an uncanny *deja vu*: the Philippine formation and its complex, uneven development and stratification easily recapitulate the genealogy and vicissitudes of backwardness/dependency bedeviling any number of Third World nations today, in Latin America and the Caribbean as well as in Africa and Asia.

One of the key paradigmatic assumptions, the axiological and inaugural premise sustaining the coherent discourse/practice of U.S. intervention (political, economic, military, cultural) is the racist and chauvinist notion that the U.S. brought the redemptive Puritanical enlightenment to a benighted race, the miraculous fiat of "Manifest Destiny" establishing the forever privileged kinship if not "special relationship" between the Philippines and the United States. This is not the place to exhume the archival genealogy of this practice/knowledge. I shall simply note here that the myth of "special relations" has been firmly institutionalized in both journalistic and academic discourses, from W. Cameron Forbes' *The Philippine Islands* (1928) to Joseph Ralston Hayden's *The Philippines: A Study in National Development* (1942). The updated Cold War reformulation of the theory that despite good intentions, the noble and sacred objectives of the civilizing mission of *Pax Americana* were foiled by an entrenched, duplicitous but ultimately pliant Filipino oligarchy, was first enunciated by George Taylor in *The Philippines and the United States: Problems of Partnership* (1964), and subsequently refurbished by "revisionist" historians like Theodore Friend in *Between Two Empires* (1965), Peter Stanley in *A Nation in the Making: The Philippines and the United States 1899-1921* (1974), and their epigones. Central to these latter re-interpretations is the functionalist and normativist sociology of values propounded by Frank Lynch and his associates in *Four*

Readings on Philippine Values (1964) and popularized by the Jesuit Ateneo University's Institute of Philippine Culture.[6]

As propagandistic exempla of the thesis of imperial reformism and "historic ties" now portentously revived to orient impending multifaceted interventions, I cite three versions. In his article "The Question of Democracy in the Philippines: (*Wall Street Journal*, 24 August 1981), Professor Carl Lande vilifies the Filipino Communists for "their persistent effort to undermine the reputation of the U.S. as the early sponsor and long-time friend of democracy in the Philippines," oblivious of the fact that it was precisely the colonial brand of patron-client politics that laid the basis for an authoritarian structure fully sanctioned and assisted by U.S. administrations from Nixon to Reagan. Focusing on the Filipino petty bourgeoisie and intermediate elements likely to use Washington as "a scapegoat for their inability to rouse their countrymen to revolt," Professor Lande then isolates the chief source of the crisis: "the personal misuse of power" by Marcos. Of course, the world is not as simplistic as this, since this distinguished Filipinist has earlier disclosed the breakdown of the mechanism of "checks and balances" whereby one faction of the oligarchy (the traditional elite of landlords, compradors—middlemen for foreign interests—and bureaucrats) can replace another in sharing executive and legislative prerogatives—a system of "musical chairs" which half a century of colonial domination installed in the Philippines. This "experiment in democracy," it seems, habituated the Filipinos to become, in Professor Lande's words, "a people dangerously susceptible to the carrot of corruption and the stick of political intimidation." What a pity!

Not to be outdone, Professor David J. Steinberg, in his testimony to Congress in February 1984, contended that "there is a reciprocity if not similarity of interests" in the military bases because the Philippines, or those who speak for 53 million people, is willing to barter its sovereignty for "$200 million annually (5 percent of GNP)." Why so much alarm then over the political instability and economic decline under Marcos? Professor Steinberg sets forth a pragmatic and somewhat Calvinist explanation: "This was America's one colony, this was the society on which we imposed our will by force. We do not have the luxury of deciding whether or not we want to remain involved with the Philippines. . . . America, seeing itself as the last best hope of mankind, justified its colonialism in the Philipppines by establishing the priceless legacy of democracy. The Filipinos learned, adopted, and came to cherish the Bill of Rights. . . . "[7] Such presumptuous claims, occasioned no doubt by rhetorical exigency, recapitulate the single obsessive goal of mainstream U.S. academic scholarship in regard to the Philippines: to erase from the records the conscious revolutionary initiative and impact of the Filipino people and their status as world-historic actors and agents in the shaping of their destiny; and to reduce them to objects of diplomatic-political machination and of self-serving alienated scholarship.

My last illustration of the monopolist and instrumentalizing textual strategy is the three testimonies presented to Congress by John Monjo, Deputy Assistant Secretary for Asia and Pacific Affairs; Paul Wolfowitz, Assistant Secretary for Asia and Pacific Affairs; and William Sullivan, former Ambassador to the Philippines (1973-1977). All of them converge on one message: the need to rescue Marcos (read: the neo-colonial machinery) so as not to jeopardize U.S. security interests, chiefly the military bases, with Sullivan daring to prophesy that "most Filipinos would welcome an intervention."[8]

Given the recent CIA assessment of the phenomenal growth of the New People's Army--whose roughly 20,000 regular combatants and a mass base of millions now control two-thirds of all provinces--Rep. Stephen Solarz, chairman of the House Foreign Affairs Subcommittee on Asian and Pacific Affairs voiced the real object of U.S. concern: if the nationalists win and affirm Philippine sovereignty, "we would almost inevitably lose our air and naval bases at Clark Field and Subic Bay, which greatly facilitate our ability to preserve the peace and maintain a balance of power in Asia." A less euphemistic and more candid diagnosis is offered by Doan Van Toi and David Chanoff in an article in the *Christian Science Monitor* (29 February 1984): "Our adversaries in the Philippines are antidemocratic forces whose goals are to revolutionize Filipino society along totalitarian lines, sever traditional ties between the U.S. and the Philippines, and eliminate the strategic bases at Subic Bay and Clark Field." Solarz even fears the incredible: Marcos may adopt "a rabidly nationalistic, anti-American stance" in a bid for popularity.[9]

Aside from the ritualistic invocation of "historic ties," the other discursive strategy in the arsenal of U.S. policy-makers is that of portraying Filipino communists and nationalists as enemies of "the democratic tradition," a mode of conceptualizing which Richard Hofstader labels the "paranoid" conspiratorial view of history, in which anyone opposed to capitalist economics and techniques of management is immediately pushed outside the political boundary of those who claim to be the world's only or chief guardian of democracy and freedom.[10] It was this assumed role of guardianship, already conceived of by William Seward and others in mid-nineteenth century debates, that ravaged the Philippines in the Filipino-American War (1898-1902), now dubbed "the first Vietnam," and, by what some scholars call "tutelage," instituted the patronage system: a non-participatory and non-representative arrangement whereby the landed oligarchy, compradors and petty bourgeoisie collaborated with U.S. colonial administrators in shaping a neocolonized society geared to supplying cheap raw materials and labor, a market for investments and industrial commodities, and a site of vital military facilities necessary for protecting and maintaining U.S. strategic interests in Asia. Ex-Senator Jose Diokno aptly summarized the fruit of U.S. annexation of the colony:

> Historically, when the U.S. came to the Philippines they faced the following basic social problems. First, widespread proverty; second, unequal distribution of wealth; and third, social exploitation as the dominant process that maintained the system. When the Americans left 48 years later, they left these same three basic problems behind them and added two more: a totally dependent economy and a military situation so tied to the U.S. that decisions on war and peace, in fact, rest with the U.S. and not with the Filipino people. Today, 34 years after our flag-independence, we are still faced with the same basic social problems. Tremendous poverty, horrendous inequality, social exploitation, economic dependence, military dependence, and two more have been added: widespread corruption in and out of government and we have lost our freedoms to boot.[11]

But the neo-colonial state today cannot just be simply viewed mechanistically, as an epiphenomenon of U.S. designs. Like all socio-political processes, it is a conjunctural historic product. What forced Marcos in 1972 to arrogate autocratic power and centralize state violence, dismantling the consensual rules and compromises institutionalized during almost five decades of U.S. rule, aside from the greed of his clique to perpetuate themselves in power, was the vigorous resurgence of Filipino nationalism in the high tide of worldwide protest against U.S. aggression in Indochina and mounting inter-imperialist rivalry. It was accompanied by a profound and wide-ranging mobilization of various sectors--clergy, workers, students, women, peasants, nationalities, etc.--agitating for a variety of democratic reforms and structural changes. Only authoritarian measures and military force could save the day for U.S. transnationals and U.S. hegemony being challenged by an awakened, militant and outraged people.

Severely undermining the status quo and barely concealed by the electoral rituals performed since 1946 was the sharply growing inequality between the wealthy few and the vast majority of impoverished workers and peasants (at least 75 percent of 53 million Filipinos), slum dwellers, minorities, middle-strata professionals, etc. According to official statistics (1982), 68 percent of all households live below the government's own poverty line. Of the nineteen million in the labor force, about 60 percent live below the poverty level (1984-1985). In MetroManila, 23.3 percent of six million people are barely subsisting in shanties and makeshift dwellings. Given the annual per capita income of $750, 75 percent of rural inhabitants have annual incomes of less than

$200; the poorest 20 percent receive 5.5 percent of total family income, while the highest 20 percent receive 54 percent of total family income. According to World Bank statistics, 70 percent of the people (85 percent of all schoolchildren) suffer from malnourishment, and 40 percent of the population die from it. The Asian Development Bank confirms that the Filipino caloric consumption of 270 calories below the standard minimum daily requirement, is the lowest in all of Asia. The Marcos regime prides itself in having enforced the lowest worker's wage in all of Asia, less than $1 a day. An independent U.S. group, the Center for International Policy, concludes that "there are more desperately poor people in the Philippines today than at any other time in its history."[12]

After nineteen years of Marcos' despotism, it is now clear that the development scheme of industrialization-for-export and reliance on foreign investment and loans from the IMF/World Bank and credit consortiums, administered from above by a technocratic-military bureaucracy centered on a family dynasty and cronies, has only led to the most oppressive plight for the masses and an implacable immiserizing of all classes. With an unconscionably huge debt of $27 billion (87 percent of the Gross National Product), a punishing inflation of 70 percent due to several drastic devaluations of the peso and skyrocketing consumer prices, a tremendously soaring 40 percent unemployment--half a million workers will be laid off before the end of 1984, the bankrupt economy has only been able to carry on production and reproduction because of emergency loans from the U.S. Export-Import Bank, the Asian Development Bank, Japan and Australia totalling $3 billion, while the regime awaits approval of $650 million standby credit from the IMF subject to the implementation of austerity measures such as raising of taxes, cutbacks in social services, a freeze on wage increases, etc. Just to instance the trend of immiseration: workers and salaried employees have suffered a 37 percent decline in real wages between 1970 and 1973. From 1975 to 1979, according to the IMF, real wages declined by 12 percent, and between 1981 and 1984, they dropped by as much as 28 percent.[13]

Despite the much publicized "land reform" program, on the basis of which Marcos tried initially to legitimize martial rule, not a single tenant farmer has received fully a land title. Age-old imbalances in the countryside persist and deepen as corporate techniques in farming displace more and more tenants, and staple food production gives way to the cultivation of primary export crops whose world-price keeps fluctuating and plunging. Clearly, the beneficiary of repressive "constitutional authoritarianism" is not the majority of Filipinos--whose living standards have on all counts severely deteriorated, especially after the Aquino, assassination--but the ruling elite (in particular, the Marcos family's kin and cronies) and the transnationals, whose aim of maximizing profits has inflicted havoc on the people's physical and spiritual welfare, and whose collusion with the dominant class has flagrantly violated the fundamental human rights of millions and sabotaged the sovereignty and independence of the Filipino nation.[14]

Except for the inveterately naive, the unreconstructed flunky, or the happily self-deceived, everyone today perceives behind the routine glorification of infrastructures and Gross National Product the "guiding hand" of U.S. political, economic and military hegemony, besieged since the late Sixties by a people's war in Southeast Asia. With the histrionics of "National Greatness" blasted into smithereens by the First Quarter Storm confrontations of 1970, the Marcos bloc had to invent an ideological machinery to naturalize or normalize the centralization of state power and carry on the extraction of surplus value without disturbance from riotous students, workers, peasants, etc. With glib sophisms and co-opting verbiage, Marcos has tried to project an image of an independent Third World messiah, a parody of a Cesaro-Bonapartist strongman with aborted populist ambitions, whose ideology of "national security" ("We" versus "others") and order discards the customary liberal precepts of pluralism, bargaining/management of interest groups, compromise and clientelism. In his manifesto *The Democratic Revolution in the Philippines* (written by hacks skimming through Machiavelli, Pareto, and Douglas Dillon), Marcos invokes Professor Samuel Huntington, erstwhile architect of Vietnamese modernization through napalm bombing:

> In many modernizing societies, the [Lockean] formula is irrelevant. The primary problem is not liberty but the creation of a legitimate public order. Men may, of course, have order without liberty, but they cannot have liberty without order. Authority has to exist before it can be limited, and it is authority that is in scarce supply in those modernizing countries where the government is at the mercy of alienated intellectuals, rambunctious colonels, and rioting students.[15]

In this text, the formalist code words of "modernizing" (read: transnational investment, IMF/World Bank loans, efficient capital accumulation and circulation), "order" and "authority" establish a putative value-free site of normative values and principles which legitimize the violence of the state and its coercive agencies insofar as they seek to preserve and enhance the Marcos clique's power, guarantee unhampered operations in the U.S. bases, and insure transnational entrepreneurship.

Symptomatic of the acute fragmentation and reification of bourgeois thinking, empiricist and functionalist modes of analysis which posit normative facts as given, divorced from any historical context, and in their metaphysical psychologizing fail to articulate a conception of society as a historical, overdetermined and differentiated totality--these modes of analysis continue to inform the inquiries and researches of Filipino and American experts. One random example is this observation by Claude Buss in his book *The United States and the Philippines* (1977):

> Much of the success that Marcos claimed for his administration under martial law could reasonably be attributed to the values underlying Philippine society. . . It was not difficult to enforce discipline in a society where a family system with deep respect for kinship obligations, a common religion, and confidence in mass education, individual liberty, and social mobility still prevailed. President Marcos fashioned a regime that, while it violated many of the principles upon which recent political experience in the Philippines had been predicated, conformed to the basic Filipino demand for progress within the rule of law.[16]

Despite superficial reservations and demurrers by conscience-stricken liberals, it appears that Marcos and his patrons understand one another perfectly when they conform to "progress within the rule of law." After nineteen years, do we need more time to grasp exactly what such "progress" and "rule of law" signify?

Reflecting a neo-feudal revivalist mood, the discourse of "New Society" apologetics rings variations on the theme enunciated by Huntington and recent Reaganite ideologues like Jeane Kirkpatrick: the bankruptcy of political liberalism. Given the highly fragmented and disarticulated structures of a dependent formation, the state with its legislative-executive power becomes the transcendent symbol of unity, purportedly reconciling contradictory forces of class, gender, ethnicity, race, religion, etc. In the contributions to a government advertisement, *Toward A New Society: Essays on Aspects of Philippine Development* (1974), the regime's brain trust dilated on the priority of community (Hobbes) and its "conscience" over against political liberty (Locke) allowing for conflicts of individual interests obtaining in the free market; the Marcos state incarnates the homogeneous community, the collective will of every member of "civil society." Where the mask of positivist and instrumentalist rationality fails to hide the particularistic class motives which ideology tends to universalize, fascist polemics begin and end in empirical abstraction, where action and thought are sharply demarcated and opposed.

Undeterred by its inconsistencies, tautologies, non-sequiturs and indiscriminate ad hoc allusions to predominantly American authorities, "New Society" discourse vitiates itself with its immanent antinomies whose rhetoric and tropes reproduce and sanction the reified practices of systematic victimization: arbitrary arrests and torture of suspects labelled "subversives"; suppression of workers' right to strike; overt or subtle censorship of the mass media; harassment, terrorism and atrocities inflicted daily on peasants, students, intellectuals; outright killing of priests like Zacharias Agatep, trade union leaders like Alex Boncayao and Ceferino Flores, Jr., doctors like Remberto de la Paz and Juan Escandor, to cite only the well-known cases--practices whose volume and intensity are quite unparalleled in the annals of the Filipino national experience. If the victims are alive, "New Society" textualization has sought to interpellate (that is, ideologically address) individuals in order to constitute them as docile and willing subjects, albeit identities bifurcated in two: a supposedly "free" contemplative consciousness and a body subject to the laws of a deterministic order and therefore a passive instrument of the dictator's will. Try as it might to articulate popular-democratic demands and aspirations, "New Society" ideology--actually a spurious hodge-podge concocted for propagandistic purposes--reveals itself in effect as a demagogic harangue on traditional oligarchs scapegoated for structural iniquities and servile mentality, thus defusing and occluding class contradictions in the grand myth of a "compassionate" New Society or New Republic, its novelty prematurely tarnished by the necessity of violence. We note finally how this ersatz ideology recycles the orthodox notions of bourgeois liberalism, private property, private initiative, even alluding to moralisms about "authentic humanity" and "human perfection," whereby a narrow fraction of the elite's interest is projected as the common interest of all. We detect the characteristic tendency of all authoritarian discourse: on the one hand, to atomize individuals in their formal and abstracted existence, purged of all concrete determinations and therefore exchangeable as commodity or cash; and, on the other hand, to coalesce these privatized monads into a monolithic mass, converting basic class contradications into simple difference; sublimating and condensing the displaced frustrations and anger of the citizens into its messianic gospel of "humanism," the "City of Man," celebrations of *Katotohanan, Kagandahan, Kabaitan* (Truth, Beauty, Goodness). Both tendencies are symptomatic indices of commodity fetishism, aggravated or reinforced by the empiricist/functionalist essentialism pervading not just the ideological state apparatuses (controlled unions, Marcos' party the KBL, schools, mass media), but even the thinking of liberal democrats and bourgeois reformists critical of the status quo.

At this terminal stage of the regime's itinerary, there is perhaps no need to venture an elaborate and detailed deconstruction of "New Society" discourse, especially now that those pre-1983 attempts to resolve the legitimation crisis wither so quickly when juxtaposed with Amnesty International (AI) reports or the regular catalogue of military atrocities and human rights violations published by the Task Force Detainees. Historical circumstance has indeed assumed the responsibility of problematizing Marcos' absolutism, to destabilize the knowledge/power complex he has so far commanded, and finally expose what is relative, discontinuous and alterable within the seemingly unified, autonomous, stable space of the "New Republic." At this conjuncture, when Hobbesian theorizing has yielded to what the Catholic Bishops' Conference calls the naked "rule of the gun," the truth of the permanent crisis of peripheral authoritarianism in the Philippines becomes patent to everyone. The recent findings of the Agrava Commission on the Aquino assassination, particularly the majority report, implicating the entire military cabal surrounding Marcos, only confirms what is common knowledge to millions of Filipinos: the moribund, dehumanized and violent nature of the Marcos dispensation.

Lacking any peaceful or legal channel for the redress of age-old grievances and injustices, with the gains toward a genuine participatory and representative democracy rolled back by a recolonization process which integrates the country more tightly into the crisis-ridden capitalist world-economy, millions of Filipinos have joined the movement in armed self-defense of their ancestral homelands (one million Igorots, six million Moros, etc.) and in the campaigns fighting for a just and equitable share in the fruits of their labor. Thousands of exploited workers, marginalized peasants, displaced nationalities, and politicized middle elements have joined the New People's Army spearheading the broad coalition of forces opposed to the U.S.-Marcos dictatorship. Nowhere else in Asia but in the Philippines has this popular insurgency grown to such proportions—the NDF claims effective control over ten million people in liberated areas or guerrilla zones throughout the islands—and nowhere has the largest number of people been mobilized by events culminating in Aquino's murder, to the point where an interagency task force in Washington has to convene every week to sort out the wreckage of decades of U.S. meddling. Signs of an emerging military solution proposed by the Pentagon over U.S. State Department reformism may be observed in the frequency of joint war games or exercises, the last one of which is the "Balikatan-Tangent Flash '84," an eleven-day mock invasion of Zambales by U.S. Marines on 27 May 1984. From May to July, 1984, U.S. military advisers were seen actively aiding counter-insurgency operations in the Kalinga-Apayao, Ifugao and Mountain provinces.[17]

Because the U.S. government exercises a preponderant influence on Philippine affairs, and is largely responsible for encouraging and abetting the Marcos regime with huge sums of tax dollars for the purchase of weapons like that used in killing Aquino and thousands of innocent civilians struggling for dignity and a decent life, how long will the American people allow this barbarism—the funding and patronizing of torture, deceit and mendacity—to continue with their open or tacit complicity? Cardinal Jaime Sin has anxiously implored the U.S. to halt the supply of weapons to Marcos because they are used only to "slaughter Filipinos." Today, we are faced no longer with an abstruse theoretical conundrum but with an urgent life-and-death question. As a poignant witness of the present and a foreshadowing of what's to come, listen to Father Pedro Salgado, a Dominican priest in Isabela, Northern Luzon: "We have seen that the masses enjoy no hope for a better life within the New Society. Everything in the New Society leads to the enrichment of the foreigners and the local elite, while it impoverishes the masses. A change is necessary, a drastic change, but is revolution the means for this change? Yes. . . . As far as the farmers of Benito Soliven barrio are concerned, I have not yet met a farmer there who believes a drastic change in the structure of the present society is possible by means other than a violent revolution."[18]

What the preceding reflections try to demonstrate above all is the principle or axiom that any searching critical anaysis of sociohistorical phenomena, particularly of the dynamics of social change, cannot be divorced from concrete moral imperatives and conjunctural political demands. Such a fatal divorce characterizes the academic orthodoxy of functionalism and empiricism, even though ultimately they foster bourgeois hegemony and class rule. Our brothers and sisters in the frontline of strikes, boycotts, civil disobedience, and guerrilla war, can tell us that theory and practice, thought and action, are as tightly imbricated or woven together as flesh and bone of the human body--a truth succinctly articulated by Marx in the second and eighth sections of the "Theses on Feuerbach": "The question whether objective truth is an attribute of human thought--is not a theoretical but a *practical* question. . . . All social life is essentially *practical.* All the mysteries which urge theory into mysticism find their rational solution in human pactice and in the comprehension of this practice."[19]

Because the Philippines, conceived as a model of a Third World society, exhibits a state chiefly defined by its political and ideological function and because, given the colonial deformation, classes are either non-existent, inchoate, displaced or articulated with non-class concerns and orientations--gender, ethnicity, religion, race, urban/rural dichotomy, etc.--the ideological-political often becomes primary and mediates the economic. Dialectically put, social relations become productive forces.

Further, in the Philippines not all ideological elements can be assigned a class category. Although based on the labor/ capital contradiction in the level of the mode of production, it is in the sphere of popular-democratic struggles--the ideological and political constituting the social formation--where the more immediate, conjunctural but central people/power bloc contradiction operates. As Ernesto Laclau points out: "The popular-democratic interpellation not only has no precise class content, but is the domain of the ideological class struggle par excellence. Every class struggles at the ideological level *simultaneously* as class and as the people, or rather, tries to give coherence to its ideological discourse by presenting its class objectives as the consummation of popular objectives."[20] My main project is to address the themes and forms of popular-democratic interpellations as part of the collective enterprise of rectifying the vulgar economistic, class reductionist and mechanistic thinking predominant in the movement, concentrating on certain cultural expressions whereby all of civil society--from the family to trade unions and political parties, as Gramsci envisaged--becomes the terrain of a rich, interminable and kaleidoscopic struggle for hegemony.

As Third World analysts like Eqbal Ahmad, A. Sivanandan, and others have perspicaciously commented, the developmental neo-fascist state which had emerged in the sixties and seventies witnessed the displacement of the bloc of Westernized natives (civil servants, military, landlords) and the ascendancy of a faction from it, monopolizing coercive power but more visibly dependent on the imperial center for its economic, political, and military viability. From this perspective, it is understandable that Marcos's praetorian coup further concentrated wealth and power in a fraction of the elite since it was predicated on the existence of an overdeveloped "military bureaucratic superstructure of power" superimposed on "an underdeveloped infrastructure of participation" which has served the function of promoting lopsided economic growth through foreign investment, guaranteeing enormous profit taking by private enterprise, and centralizing administrative power. But it does not follow on those same premises that political power and civil society would sharply collide; that culture and religion would begin to clash with the state apparatus, or that the "national security state" as a whole would remain isolated from the "cultural and political institutions of the people it exploits."[21] On the contrary, the statist, metropolis-oriented policies of modernization (rationalization of the efficiency of the market, army, etc.) exhibits a pronounced consensual dimension, even as it inhabits a necessarily "disorganic" or oscillating locus: the dis-integrated social formation where antithetical modes of production (residual, dominant, emergent) contend.

It is precisely the political and ideological moments, not the purely economic (objective laws of motion), that assume strategic primacy when one grants that the neo-fascist state was precipitated by the Cold War milieu informed by a manichean motivation contraposing "free market stability" to "communist totalitarianism," "national security" to "anarchy," and so forth. In its decadent phase, however, the political survival of such a state depends on the application of systematic, organized violence to depoliticize consciousness and immobilize the polity; to suppress social linkages and fusions in the public sphere and thus prevent the germination of a civic, radically democratic, self-activizing consciousness in the broad masses of people. This is the simplest explanation for Marcos's desperate clinging to his self-ascribed decree-making powers institutionalized by Amendment Six in the regime's constitution.

In the project of destructuring and exposing the internal contradictions of the neo-fascist state, I would emphasize locating them concretely in the specific historical formation, especially in the nodes and interstices of civil society (sexuality, religion, schooling, family, art)--those trenches and fortifications immanent in the praxis of everyday life without whose gradual erosion and eventual overthrow the foundations of a participatory and egalitarian society could not be built.[22] This theoretical move taken here to valorize the political-ideological moments is designed to elucidate the problem of why, after Aquino's death, the Marcos regime did not immediately collapse amidst the profound disenchantment of the majority and the outbreak of widespread and sustained mass actions. It is further designed to answer the more exigent and prefigurative question what it will take--what precise combination of coalition politics, extra-parliamentary militancy, armed struggle, and international pressure is needed to effectively dismantle the Marcos edifice, prevent its recurrence, contain or thwart U.S. intervention, and in the same breath empower the people to initiate a profound, all-encompassing renewal of the whole society.

In the course of this cognitive-pedagogical operation, we need to bear in mind that, with respect to the Philippine formation, the heterotopic and fluid articulations of the peripheral path of capitalist development (as distinguished, for instance, by the regimented extortion of surplus labor-power through extra-economic mechanisms) with the hegemonic U.S. path of monopoly expansion at the historic point of contact (the Spanish-American War of 1898) produced a hybrid result: juridical forms of individual liberty and "self-government" juxtaposed with customary obedience to hierarchies and with ritualized behavior gravitating around public spectacles and the sacred, both phenomena circumscribing patron-client politics. My own exploratory investigations here into the modes of existence (reproduction and transformation) of subjects and signifying practices are meant to illuminate the points of contact, specifically the disarticulations, predicaments, and tensions characterizing the period from 1972 to the present and falling under the rubric "Philippine crisis."

Given the advanced stage of the "war of movement"--the terms "movement" and "position" often coalesce in a dialectical reciprocity--in the countryside, the chapters on the Moro and Igorot resistance and the New People's Army reflect the visible presence of the state in everyday life generating both reformist and jacobinist responses. Little metaphysics of ambiguity or sophisticated decoding is wasted by the present regime when it administers indiscriminate violence on almost everyone. But in the sphere where class struggle hasn't reached that cathartic level of intensity, it would be useful to conceive of the processes of ideological reproduction--a major theme in this book--which constitute individuals as coherent and unequivocal subjects, as in Michel Pecheux's modification of Althusser's thesis, "spaces of *multiform* resistance where the unexpected continually appears."[23] With ideology theorized not as a stronghold defined by "the logic of stable objects" with fixed boundaries but as an indeterminate "paradoxical space," we can now envisage polycentric moves of coalitions--a stage already attained with the public forums on the nature of a post-Marcos coalition government and the shaping of multi-sectoral, legal, extra-parliamentary blocs like the Coalition for the Realization of Democracy (CORD), Nationalist Alliance for Justice, Freedom and Democracy (NAJFD), and the recent, New Patriotic Alliance (BAYAN)--all prefigured by the founding of the National Democratic Front (NDF) in 1973.[24] Complementary to the "labor-versus-capital" frontal assault being waged by the left, these autonomous initiatives may be characterized as "mobile confrontations that do not set in opposition classes, 'interest-groups,' or positions determined *a priori*, but rather bear on the reproduction/transformation of class relations themselves."[25] To map this space of heteroglotic ruptures and displacements where micro-resistances can be mounted in the "war of position," employing the weapon of criticism as a heuristic, ethico-political adjunct to the criticism of weapons, is one of the most urgent and necessary tasks of the struggle to which this work is addressed.

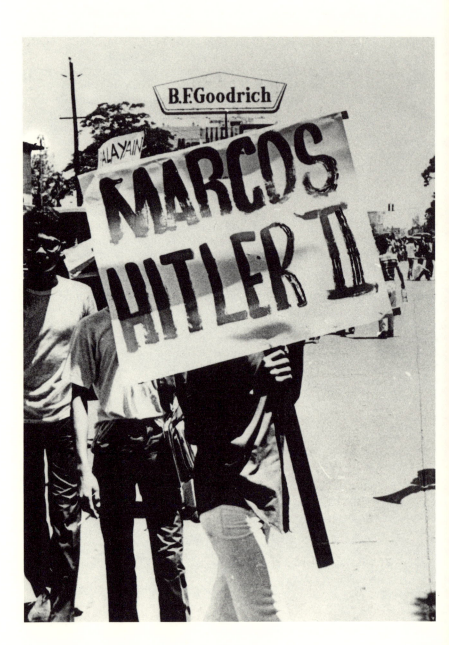

I
Transnationals: The Watchdogs
of Empire

We have pacified some thousands of the islanders and buried them; destroyed their fields; burned their villages, and turned their widows and orphans out-of-doors; furnished heartbreak by exile to some dozens of disagreeable patriots; subjugated the remaining ten millions by Benevolent Assimilation, which is the pious new name of the musket; we have acquired our property in the three hundred concubines and other slaves of our business partner, the Sultan of Sulu, and hoisted our protecting flag over that swag.
And so, by these Providences of God--and the phrase is the government's, not mine--we are a World Power.

> Mark Twain
> on the aftermath of
> the Filipino-American War
> (1898-1902)

The Philippines is one of the Third World countries in which, to quote the United Nations' "Declaration of the Establishment of a New International Economic Order" (1974), "vestiges of alien and colonial domination...neo-colonialism in all its forms continue to be among the greatest obstacles to the full emancipation and progress" of its people.[1] It has nourished a long tradition of revolutionary struggle, now culminating in the broad popular-democratic resistance to the U.S.-Marcos dictatorship, to win and exercise those cardinal rights affirmed by the UN "Declaration": "The right of every country to adopt the economic and social system that it deems the most appropriate for its own development" and "Full permanent sovereignty of every State over its natural resources and all economic activities,. . . .including the right of nationalization."

ADVENT OF U.S. IMPERIALISM

When the U.S. annexed the Philippines in 1898 as its only Asian colony, along with Cuba and Puerto Rico as its Caribbean possessions, its policy-makers expressed unequivocally their world historic intentions. One early proponent of expansionism was William Seward, later Secretary of State, who, a year before Commodore Perry forced the opening of Japan to western commerce, stated that the U.S. "wants the commerce of the world . . . that must be looked for in the Pacific."[2] This logic of nineteenth-century mercantilism, given a Clausewitzian reading by Admiral Mahan's aphorism that "War is not fighting but business," was reinterpreted by Senator Albert Beveridge, whose speech in Boston anticipated by four days the news of Admiral George Dewey's victory over the Spanish fleet in Manila Bay. Senator Beveridge declaimed:

> American soil is producing more than Americans can consume. . . . The trade of the world must and shall be ours. American law, American order, American civilization and the American flag will plant themselves on shores hitherto bloody and benighted but by the agencies of God henceforth to be made beautiful and bright. In the Pacific is the true field of our earliest operations; there Spain has an island empire, the Philippine archipelago. . . . The Philippines is logically our first target.[3]

Beveridge argued that the U.S. was the "trustee" under God of the civilization of the world. . . . Just beyond the Philippines are China's illimitable markets." With far-sighted vision, Senator Henry Cabot Lodge echoed Beveridge's prophecy that "future wars will be conflicts of commerce" and promptly advised then President McKinley that the U.S. "home market is not enough for our teeming industries and the great demand of the day is an outlet for our products. With our protective tariff wall around the Philippine Islands, ... we should have so much additional market for our home manufactures. . . ."[4]

As though enacting a textbook scenario of Marxian over-determination by the superstructure, President McKinley agonized and prayed night after night until U.S. foreign policy doctrine descended as "a gift from God," enlightening him with the evangelical *apercus* that the U.S. "could not give back the Philippines to Spain because it would be cowardly and dishonorable," and that he could not turn the islands over to Germany or France because they were "business rivals." And so there was no alternative but the "white man's burden," the proverbial *mission civilizatrice*: charitable enough not to leave the Filipinos to themselves "because they are unfit for self-government," he "had nothing more to do but take them all, educate them, uplift, civilize and Christianize them." Dutifully, McKinley instructed his emissaries in the Paris Peace Conference in December 1898: "It is just to use every legitimate means for the enlargement of American trade."[5] It was a simple business transaction: the Philippines (300,000 square kilometers and ten million inhabitants) was "ceded" to the U.S. for $20 million--roughly 67¢ per hectare, or $2 per head. Immediately thereafter, the Filipino-American War broke out, lasting officially up to 1902 (although the Moros continued guerrilla fighting until 1916).

To suppress the first Philippine Republic, which had by then effectively vanquished Spain's colonial army, the U.S. sent 126,000 troops, fought 2,800 battles, spent $600 million, and suffered 4,374 dead and at least 3,022 wounded. On the other side, the Filipinos lost about 20,000 soldiers, and a quarter of a million non-combatants in My Lai-type massacres, hamletting and other counter-insurgency tactics. One island, Samar--today a stronghold of anti-imperialist resistance--as well as several provinces, were converted by U.S. generals into a "howling wilderness"--an unforgettable monument of "Manifest Destiny."[6]

A Neo-Colony in the Making

It was in the Philippines where the U.S. first devised and perfected its neo-colonial methods of military counter-insurgency and "civic action" pacification; of cultural desublimation and cooptation; and of economic domination by diplomatic and political machinations. During the colonial period (1898-1946), the Philippines served the classic functions of a peripheral formation: a market for surplus manufactured goods, a field for investment capital; a rich source of cheap raw materials and primary agricultural commodities vital to industrial capitalism; a reservoir of cheap labor. A code of dependent "free trade" was legislated to sanction the unequal political relations, thus fostering underdevelopment by preserving the feudal system of agricultural production geared to yielding a limited number of export crops (sugar, tobacco, hemp). With the help of other legislative schemes, U.S. colonial rule prevented the growth of industry, a viable internal market, and the requisite infrastructure. When the U.S. granted formal independence in 1946, it forced the Philippine government to amend its Constitution so as to give equal or "parity rights" to U.S. monopolies in exploiting local natural resources and in operating public utilities. This scandalous provision, amending the constitutional requirement that 60 percent of corporate shares must be owned by Filipino citizens, was forced on the Philippine Congress as a condition for receiving $620 million in war damage compensation--the Filipinos had fought the Japanese during World War II as colonial subjects.[7]

From the late 1940s to the early 1960s, the Philippine government stimulated economic growth by import-substitution based on control of foreign exchange and discrimination against "non-essential" manufactured goods. To circumvent tariff barriers on such light-manufactured imports, U.S. corporations moved into sectors producing consumer goods which then averaged 12 percent annual growth between 1950 and 1957. Between 1950 and 1963, U.S. investments grew from $23 million to $110 million, faster than any sector of the economy. Before growth stagnated in the sixties due mainly to the limited internal market (depressed wages, the semi-feudal backwardness of the countryside where the majority of the people live, etc.), then President Magsaysay, whose CIA funding and connections have now been thoroughly documented, maneuvered the passage of the Laurel-Langley Agreement in 1955. Whereas the 1946 Bell Trade Act limited parity rights to the exploitation of natural resources, the 1955 Agreement opened the entire spectrum of the economy to encroachment by U.S. transnationals.

By the early seventies, U.S. direct investments, whose value totalled about $4 billion (compared to $200 million in 1935) constituted 80 percent of all foreign investments in the country. In 1978, 324 transnationals represented 52.6 percent of total sales; 66.7 percent of the total income of the top 1,000 corporations. As of 1970, about one-third of all total equity capital of the 900 largest corporations is owned by Americans, representing 60 percent of U.S. investments in all of Southeast Asia.[8] Controlling 46 percent of the net national product, U.S. transnationals dominate strategic sectors: manufacture of motor vehicles (Chrysler, GM); rubber and tires (Goodyear, Goodrich, Firestone); food processing (Del Monte, Carnation, Kraft); soft drinks (Coca-Cola, Pepsi-Cola); oil refining (Caltex, Shell); soap (Procter and Gamble, Colgate-Palmolive); drugs (Bristol-Myers, Mead Johnson); electrical machinery (Singer, GE, GTE); paper products (Scott, Kimberley-Clark); chemicals (Dow, Shell, Bayer), office equipment (IBM, Xerox, Burroughs)--to name only a few.[9] Seven U.S. oil companies enjoy virtual monopoly of the petroleum industry. Ford, GM, Chrysler (and two other foreign firms) enjoyed 86 percent of all automotive sales. In agribusiness, Del Monte and Dole controlled 99 percent of all sales in the fruit and canning industry.

THE POLITICAL ECONOMY OF AUTHORITARIANISM

Together with numerous "bilateral" agreements which allowed the U.S. absolute control over twenty-three military bases and installations, the special privileges enjoyed by U.S. transnationals and their preponderant influence on the state apparatus maintained, modified and reinforced a semi-feudal and semi-colonial formation which, by exacerbating class contradictions, generated the massive nationalist resurgence of the late sixties and early seventies. Confronted by the oppressive rule of a minority elite of landlords, compradors and bureaucrat-capitalists subservient to alien interests and dictates, the progressive classes of rural and urban workers, intelligentsia, peasants, and nationalist businessmen began to unite and demand changes in laws, policies, directives. The Philippine Congress began passing laws limiting foreign ownership of businesses, and the Supreme Court threatened confiscation of U.S.-held lands. With the status quo challenged, Marcos imposed martial law on 21 September 1972, inaugurating the "national security state" which has suppressed all democratic processes and civil liberties, and violated basic human rights. Arbitrary arrests and imprisonment of all dissenters or critics from all walks of life, torture and "salvaging" (kidnapping and murder) have become the *modus operandi*, tacit if not overt, of all the security/police agencies, including terrorist gangs tolerated or financed by the military.[10] With the writ of *habeas corpus* suspended by presidential decrees mandating preventive detention of anyone suspected of being "subversive" or opposed to government tyranny, even though martial law was ostensibly lifted in January 1981, Marcos today still has a monopoly of judicial and legislative powers whose disastrous effects on the economy and the working masses are scrupulously detailed by Edberto M. Villegas in the *Studies in Philippine Political Economy* (1983).

One of the first institutions to proclaim zealous support of the Marcos regime, after the U.S. Chamber of Commerce and the U.S. Ambassador, was the World Bank (WB) which, from 1972 to the Aquino assassination in 1983, provided Marcos with $3.5 billion in aid. The WB-International Monetary Fund formula for reversing the nationalist gains made in the Sixties, "development from above" or authoritarian modernization, became the official policy of Marcos technocrats. The WB-IMF scheme of export-oriented industrialization based on intensified exploitation of labor and periodic devaluation of currency has tightly integrated the Philippines into the capitalist world economy by forcing the country to rely on foreign borrowing (debt dependency), corporate investments, and export markets beyond its control. A thorough inquiry into the WB-IMF's experiment, *Development Debacle: The World Bank in the Philippines* (1982) by Walden Bello, David Kinley and Elaine Elinson, concludes that Marcos' export-oriented industrialization, by gearing production to the markets of advanced industrialized countries and repressing the masses, has led to the severe impoverishment of workers, the massive deficits in the balance of payments ($3.3 billion by 1983) and a phenomenal $27 billion debt (a conservative estimate; up from $2.1 billion in 1970)--

the sixth highest in the world--plus chaos in the industrial, trade and agricultural sectors. Bello uses WB's own statistics in summing up the Marcos regime's achievement:

> Between 1972 and 1978 the wages of skilled workers declined by close to 25% and those of unskilled workers by over 30%. Meanwhile, the productivity of labor rose by 13%. . . . The number of rural families living below the poverty line increased from 48% in 1971 to 55% in 1975. And according to the government itself, the income of rice farmers declined by an astonishing 53% between 1976 and 1979 alone.[11]

One study found that in the category of "manufacturing," the rate of exploitation (that is, surplus paid to the capitalist divided by wages paid to workers) rose by 180 percent within five years, between 1971 and 1975, whereas in the preceding fifteen-year period (1956-1971), the rate of exploitation rose by only 78 percent. In the first two years of martial law (1973-1974), the rate of exploitation increased by 110 percent.[12] Aside from the fact that the sharp decline in wages accompanied by the rise in productivity signified high profits for transnationals, one must take account of Marcos' incentives to foreign firms: privilege of full repatriation of profits and capital (without any time limit), guarantees against expropriation, generous tax reliefs and exemptions, including 100 percent equity in companies engaged in banking, rice and corn production, oil exploration, etc.--a virtual return of parity rights! Of course, the chief attraction is "industrial peace" (outlawing of strikes) and low labor cost, the lowest in Asia: $1 to $1.50 for an eight-hour day.

From banking and finance to consumer goods, the Philippine economy today is still dominated by foreign interests, principally U.S. From the manufacture of vehicles, petroleum products, food, chemicals, tires and machines, etc, U.S. transnationals and their Japanese partners dictate the rules and norms of "laissez-faire" competition. In the first five years of martial law, U.S. banks succeeded in controlling the strategic financial/credit sector: for example, First National City Bank held 10 percent of the country's banking assets and 50 percent of total dollar deposits.[13] Practically all studies have shown that the extraction of surplus value by transnationals in the form of profits, dividends, royalties and other payments has drained the country of capital and resources necessary for independent industrialization and the building of a self-reliant society.

As early as 1967, the Philippine National Economic Council revealed that 85 percent of funds used by U.S. business between 1956 and 1965 was borrowed from local savings. Out of the $79 million invested came a total of $386.22 million net outflow of profits. From 1964 to 1975, the net outflow remitted to the U.S. was a staggering $2.8 billion. Recent figures show that from 1972 to 1975, repatriated income reached $418.3 million compared to capital inflow of $137 million. In 1976 alone, profit remittances of foreign companies amounted to $253.49 million. Between 1971 and 1976, 74 percent of total assets of thirty-one foreign firms came from domestic borrowing (50 percent) and reinvestment of profits. A mere 26 percent of the capital requirement came from foreign loans.[14]

In general, profit for Asia was five times capital input between 1950 and 1965. In Third World countries, U.S. firms receive an average of twice the domestic rate of return on stockholders' equity. In the mid-seventies, U.S. firms in the Philippines earned at least $3.58 for every dollar invested, of which $2.00 is repatriated. Thus, despite unequal terms of trade dooming it to its traditional role of semi-colony sketched above, the Philippines acts as a net exporter of capital, belying incontrovertibly the myth of local capital shortage and of foreign capital as the indispensable catalyst of development. With this obsessive reliance on external forces/agents to stimulate growth and propel modernization, the Marcos regime has become the agency for promoting the interests of the U.S. ruling class at the cost of the incalculable misery and degradation of millions. From 1965, when Marcos became president, to 1975, the Asian Development Bank reported that 65 percent of the population have fallen below the poverty line; in 1981, US AID noted that four million households (about 24 million people) live below the poverty line.

Since my purpose in this book is not to amass figures and statistical tables, suffice it to allude here to one other scandalous project hatched by the U.S.-trained technocrats (I treat the ecological catastrophe inflicted on the nationalities in Chapter II): Westinghouse Electric's construction of the nation's first nuclear plant, costing over $2 billion, on the slope of an active volcano, along a geological fault and tidal wave region, with two hundred safety problems in design.[15] U.S. taxpayers are in large part subsidizing this incredible plant through loans provided by the Export-Import Bank, and $40 million has already been pocketed by a crony of Marcos. This reactor is obviously unsafe, high-profit technology which represents a callous distortion of social priorities because it is intended to provide power for the U.S. military bases and the transnationals in the Bataan Export Processing Zone, one of a number of free trade zones epitomizing the draconian deployment and control of labor.

SPRINGBOARDS FOR INTERVENTION

On the eve of an impending U.S. military invasion in Central America, with the Sandinista leadership of Nicaragua as the target, we might recall that the emergence of U.S. monopoly capitalism at the close of the nineteenth century called for, and was integrated with, a global military thrust. With its debacle in Indochina, Iran and Nicaragua in the last decade and its intensified super-power contention with the Soviet Union, U.S. military-political interest has now supervened as the most fundamental reason for the hitherto unquestioned support of the Marcos dictatorship. All the pronouncements of the White House, State Department and Pentagon expose their overarching concern. No less a figure than former Ambassador Sullivan warned Congress in February 1984 that "one of the consequences of civil and political violence in the Philippines could be the eventual extrusion of the U.S. from Philippine military bases, with broad destabilizing effects upon the entire East Asian region." The codewords of "security interests" and "equilibrium" conceal the hegemonic U.S. offensive to undermine socialist Vietnam and the People's Democratic Republic of Korea under the guise of containing the Soviet "threat."[16]

For US.policy-makers, the Philippines has always surfaced in their consciousness as the Empire's outpost in the Asian frontier. One of the first military governors, General Arthur MacArthur, considered the islands' "strategic position" as "unexcelled by that of any other position in the globe. It affords a means of protecting American interests. . . ."[17] Historically, the bases have been used as staging areas for U.S. interventions in: the Boxer Rebellion in China in 1900; Soviet Siberia in 1918 to counter the Bolsheviks; Shanghai during the insurrection in 1927; Indonesia in 1958; and Indochina from 1965 to 1975. Today, the Pentagon's strategy of fighting a protracted war (nuclear or conventional) on different fronts defines the bases' functions on four levels: first, as logistical center for deployment of nuclear-armed naval units in the Indian Ocean and as a jump-off point and training center for elements of the Rapid Deployment Force (Central Command) designed for war in the Middle East; second, as a means of projecting U.S. military power to the Southeast Asian mainland; third, as provision for crucial back-up support for U.S. forces in South Korea; and fourth, as staging area for deploying naval units and nuclear-equipped bombers to East Africa, and as alternative supply route to Israel by way of the Indian Ocean and the Persian Gulf. In 1983, the State Department reiterated that "the bases are now more important to us than ever."[18]

Perhaps more than the transnationals, the two bases--Clark Air Force Base and Subic Naval Base--are the most visible symbols and proofs of continued U.S. domination of the Philippines. Headquarters of the 13th Air Force, Clark serves as the logistical hub of U.S. military air traffic in the western Pacific. Subic, home to a carrier task force, serves as the main repair facility of the Seventh Fleet and nuclear submarines. Together with seven other installations, these bases are the main storage areas for nuclear weapons in the western Pacific and perform valuable communication and surveillance functions. Garrisoned by about 16,000 military personnel supplemented by 9,000 sailors in port at any given time, the bases' complex (over 192,000 acres) constitute a veritable "state within a state."

Legitimized by the 1947 Military Bases Agreement forced on the Philippines in exchange for formal independence and rehabilitation funds, these bases are not meant to defend the Philippines from any external aggression nor are they designed for deterrence; on the contrary, they are there to maintain a status quo favorable to the U.S. posture of being able to mount a "first strike" against the Soviet Union, participate in a limited or theater nuclear war in the region, and protect/preserve that region for "free enterprise." Aside from the retaliation they invite, these bases have also destroyed the social fabric of the surrounding areas by spawning prostitution, drug traffic, gambling, corruption, etc. and also by repressing political dissenters.[19]

In 1979, the Carter administration, in exchange for $500 million rental for five years, obtained the right to "unhampered use of the bases," so that now the counter-insurgency operations to ostensibly protect the bases can be launched by U.S. troops. Of course, this only legalizes what has been a longstanding practice dating back to the CIA-directed suppression of the Huk rebellion in the fifties, when the U.S. 13th Air Force helped bomb Huk villages and camps. The Joint U.S.-RP Military Advisory Group (JUSMAG) is already in place supervising those operations today, the most recent of which is the military offensive in the Cordillera against the Kalinga and Bontoc Igorots. U.S. base officials have provided the Philippine military with weapons, ammunition and other equipment, intelligence and communication services, staff training and logistical support. One evidence of direct U.S. involvement occurred on 13 April 1973, when three U.S. navy officers were slain by guerrilla forces on the outskirts of Subic. Immediately, U.S. marines participated in a one-month joint operation with the Philippine military, imprisoning numerous suspects, burning the homes of 150 families, and sanitizing the villages of 600 families in the surrounding area.

Proof of the official commitment to a counter-revolutionary role in the context of a broad democratic resistance to the fascist regime is afforded by Lieutenant General George Seignious II, a U.S. Defense Department spokesperson during the 1973 foreign assistance hearings before the Senate Appropriations Committee. Seignious testified that "the danger in the Philippines comes from. . . . insurgencies that are of considerable concern not only to the Filipinos themselves but to the security of our bases. Our concern in the Philippines is the security of our bases. . . . against insurgencies."[20]

In June 1983, the Reagan administration pledged $900 million to Marcos for "unhampered U.S. military operations" in the bases for the next five years—an 80 percent increase of aid for repression. A week before the agreement was finalized, eighteen Congresspersons warned Reagan of the danger of unqualified support for an unpopular, corrupt and brutal regime, pointing out that the aid is "bribe money for continued access to the bases" and is "used largeley for domestic represssion."[21]   A few months earlier, Cardinal Jaime Sin urged the U.S. government to cease aiding Marcos because Filipinos were being "slaughtered and massacred" with American weapons. In talks given at major cities in the U.S. in June 1983, Jose Diokno, head of the Civil Liberties Union of the Philippines, reiterated the position of the Anti-Bases Coalition in the Philippines: that the bases not only infringe on Philippine sovereignty but also provoke nuclear retaliation from the Soviet Union and legalize U.S. complicity with Marcos' violent suppression of his critics.[22]

After the CIA and U.S. Embassy in June 1984 registered panic at the phenomenal growth of the NPA, the U.S. Senate Staff Report of October 1984 prognosticated the imminent demise of the regime, a forecast corroborated by the inter-agency task force in Washington which, confronted by Marcos' failure as expert "crisis manager" to recoup his losses and pacify an infuriated citizenry, recommended urgent action, e.g. increased military aid. In this mood, the Pentagon's Defense Intelligence Agency (DIA) gives the beleaguered Marcos two more months in power, with the Pentagon leasing 18,000 acres on the islands of Tinian and Saipan in case the Philippine bases are lost.

A RETURN TO THE BEGINNING

Ever since the Philippines received its nominal independence in 1946, the progressive and nationalist movement has called for both the withdrawal of U.S. bases and the restriction of the activities of transnationals, because, on the basis of persistent experience and multiplying evidence, instead of supposedly benefitting the people with capital and technology, they only perpetuate and enhance the structure of dependency, underdevelopment and class divisions inherited from centuries of colonial subordination. Thus they not only undermine any attempt at rational, ecologically balanced, and humane social planning of the whole economy so that a program of more equitable distribution of social wealth and utilization of resources can be implemented; but, as with the bases, they also actively participate in suppressing popular struggles for freedom, justice, and genuine independence. They confirm what Senator Fulbright had candidly confessed to be the real motive and purpose of U.S. presence in the Philippines. After hearing military officials explain the imperative of continued military involvement in the Philippines, he commented: "So we will always resist any serious changes in political and social structure in the Philippines which is very likely to be, in the long run, a detriment to the people of the Philippines."[23] On the strength of the historical experience of the Filipino people, both the bases and transnationals stand indicted for unconscionable complicity with the Marcos regime's consistent infringement and violation of those basic human rights affirmed by the UN Charter.

It is disingenuous for anyone to explain away U.S. imperialism by citing evidence disclosing tactical or stylistic differences of administration among officials, businessmen, legislators, etc.--such differences precisely characterize bourgeois competitive politics--and thus obscuring the palpable material effects of such "permissive," "compadre" or "suasive" (these liberal euphemisms are as devalued as the peso under WB-IMF "tutelage") conduct.[24] Once again, the U.S. ruling class is faced, as in 1898, with defining its security interests in terms of political economy: a world safe for capital accumulation by private business and the World Bank.

Professor Richard Falk has recently underscored how the concept of U.S. security is integrally linked with preserving the existing disparity of nations, the capitalist international division of labor, so that we find the moralizing globalist perspective of McKinley, Beveridge and others inflected by the pragmatism of *realpolitik* of U.S. State Department sage George Kennan:

> We have 50 percent of the world's wealth. But only 6.3 percent of its population. This disparity is particularly great between ourselves and the people of Asia. In this situation we cannot fail to be the object of envy and resentment. Our real task is to devise a pattern of relationships which will permit us to maintain this position of disparity without positive detriment to our national security. . . . We will have to dispense with all sentimentality and daydreaming. And our attention will have to be concentrated everywhere on our immediate national objectives. We need not deceive ourselves that we can afford today the luxury of altruism and world benefaction. We should cease to talk about vague, and for the Far East, unreal objectives, such as human rights, the raising of living standards, and democratization. We should recognize that our influence in the Pacific and the Far Eastern World is absolutely vital to our security. And we should concentrate our policy on seeing to it that those areas remain in hands which we can rely on. It is my own guess on the basis of such study as we have given the problem so far that Japan and the Philippines will be found to be the cornerstone of such a Pacific security system. And that if we can contrive to maintain effective control over these areas, there can be no serious threat to our security from the East within our time.[25]

This revealing excerpt from a "top secret" document dated 24 February 1948, proceeds with the unambivalent advice that the U.S. "must preserve the archipelago as a bulwark of U.S. security in the area." With the collapse of the Trilateral Commission's attempts (1972-1978) to contain national revolutions, and with the revival of the "Cold War," the U.S. has shifted primarily to military buildup and confrontations (witness Grenada) to sustain the old disparity frankly endorsed by Kennan, viewing Third World nationalist endeavors as scenarios for superpower interventions. In this context, since U.S. naval supremacy in the Pacific, now being challenged by the Soviet Union, is a desideratum to offset disadvantages in geography and conventional warfare, the Philippine bases have now become pragmatically conceived as of unconditional strategic value. The U.S. will surely hold on to its crumbling outpost, untethering its watchdogs--until the collective, irrepressible might of the Filipino people, in solidarity with the resurgent peoples of Nicaragua, El Salvador, Azania, Palestine, Ireland, and others, seizes the historic initiative and begins to fashion, amid the risks and sacrifices and joys of the struggle, its own autonomous and singular destiny.

II

Strategic Interventions Beyond Class:
The Church, Nationalities, Women

It was then I realized [in military prison]: I prefer fighting for people, for truth. I have only one life, I better make it good.

Sister Mariani Dimaranan

We are all in favor of peace but. . . . my people, the Tinggians, are being evicted from their land by violence. . . .

I am committed to the welfare of my people and the Church has to be revolutionary to represent the interests of the Filipino people.

Father Conrado Balweg

How can we preach the Good News to people who are suffering social and economic injustices? I cannot ask them to strive toward sanctity when their daughters have been raped, their husbands and sons detained without charges, and their properties destroyed or looted.

Unnamed priest in a militarized zone in the Philippines, quoted in Reuben Canoy, *The Counterfeit Revolution* (Manila, 1980), p. 99

In the Philippines today, we are conducting a complex, manifold, protracted struggle against U.S. imperialism and its client regime, the Marcos dictatorship--a struggle which, like similar ones in El Salvador, Azania and elsewhere, offers a crucible to test once more the power of Marxism as a radically transforming praxis, a liberating weapon in the class struggle.

I emphasize Marxism as praxis because, as Lenin said, the richness of revolutionary practice exceeds and defies any attempt at conceptual summation.[1] Recognizing the limits of thought, Lenin (following Marx's example) foregrounded in his dynamic leadership of the Bolshevik revolution the primacy of politics over and against mechanical materialism exemplified in its twin manifestations: economism and class reductionism. After Lenin, it was Gramsci who insistently theorized the imperative of conjunctural analysis. Reformulating the traditional base-superstructure model, Gramsci introduced the conception of political subjects as constituted by a network or totality of social relations, not just economic ones--sex, race, residence, gcneration, nationality, and other voluntary affiliations--which, insofar as they are defined by relations of domination and oppression, become the arenas of political-ideological conflict.[2]

In the Philippines, the arenas of political-ideological struggle encompass the entire social formation: from workers and peasants resisting the grip of transnational corporations to priests and nuns integrating with slum dwellers and urban poor; from students and journalists protesting censorship and reactionary literature to national minorities engaged in violent confrontation with the U.S.-armed military.[3] Unifying all these sectoral, multi-class movements is an evolving coalition called the National Democratic Front (NDF) whose 10-point program (first drafted in 1973 and reaffirmed in June 1980) strives to articulate all the popular democratic themes of 53 million Filipinos around one pivotal center crystallized in its first point: "Unite all anti-imperialist and democratic forces to overthrow the U.S.-Marcos dictatorship and work for the establishment of a coalition government based on a truly democratic system of representation."[4] The NDF comprises an active membership of over a million, in charge of an effective sovereignty (or dual power) over at least 1 million Filipinos. In a dialectically combined "war of position" and "war of movement," the NDF coordinates the actions of various underground organizations, among them: the New People's Army, the *Rebolusyonaryong Kilusan ng Magsasaka* (Revolutionary Movement of Peasants), *Rebolusyonaryong Kilusan ng Mga Manggagawa* (Revolutionary Movement of Workers), *Kabataang Makabayan* (Nationalist Youth), *Katipunan ng mga Gurong Makabayan* (Association of Nationalist Teachers), *Christians for National Liberation,* The Communist Party of the Philippines, and the *Makabayang Samahang Pangkalusugan* (Nationalist Association for Health). The two important sectors that are still awaiting incorporation are the cultural minorities (I prefer the term "nationalities") and women. (The Moro National Liberation Front representing at least six million Muslims, although tactically cooperating with the NPA locally and the NDF internationally, has not yet formally joined the NDF.)[5] Other groups actively opposing the Marcos regime, outside the NDF, are the Civil Liberties Union of the Philippines, composed of lawyers and ex-justices; the Ecumenical Movement for Justice and Peace; and the Task Force Detainees of the Association of Major Religious Superiors in the Philippines.

The program of the NDF addresses the fundamental historic contradiction in a dependent or peripheral formation: between the masses of workers, peasants, middle strata, cultural minorities, etc., and the at present hegemonic bloc of bureaucrats, compradors, and landlords closely tied to U.S. imperialism.[6] This contradiction, overdetermined by concrete historical specificities, dates back to the occupation of the Philippines in 1898 by U.S. forces and the consequent suppression of the First Philippine Republic. It drastically sharpened in 1972, twenty-six years after the nominal independence of 1946. Exacerbated by U.S. defeats in Vietnam and the rise of marginal groups (students, women, etc.) worldwide, Philippine society underwent a tremendous upheaval in which the instruments of bourgeois democracy, originally meant to co-opt and defuse popular demands through patronage/paternalistic mechanisms, were converted into sites or channels of class contestation. With the State apparatuses (Supreme Court, Congress, Constitutional Convention) overwhelmed by the pressures of the resurgent nationalist movement and further disintegrated by intra-elite squabbles, it devolved upon the executive branch then headed by Marcos to abolish bourgeois democratic procedures in order to safeguard the structural-normative functioning of capital.[7]

In essence, the Marcos dispensation today, with its self-described "constitutional authoritarianism" (i.e., palace decrees enforced with the big stick), represents an emergency attempt not only to centralize and concentrate State power in the hands of a pro-imperialist faction of the dominant classes and so stabilize/rationalize the space for undisturbed operations of the transnationals. It also represents an attempt by the bureaucrat-capitalist elements and their military-technocratic associates to harness more effectively the resources of the State by penetrating the interstices of civil society to assert its hegemony there through legalistic, pedagogical and other corporativist devices.

Marcos himself ventured a rationale for his autocratic rule in April 1980: "All that people ask for is some kind of authority that can enforce the simple law of civil society. . . . Only an authoritarian system will be able to carry forth the mass consent and to exercise the authority necessary to implement new values, measures, and sacrifices."[8] Not only have the legislative and judicial branches of government become "transmission-belts" for palace *diktat;* the privileged rituals of representative democracy, referenda and elections, have been thoroughly manipulated under the supervision of the all-encroaching military and security forces.

In 1976, Amnesty International noted the dissolution of the classic separation of powers and checks-and-balances derived from Locke or Montesquieu: "Stripped of its jurisdiction and independence, the judiciary of the Philippines has become totally ineffective in preventing the violations of human rights. . . . The rule of law under martial law is authoritarian presidential-military rule, unchecked by constitutional guarantee or limitation."[9] With popular participation completely cancelled, the military establishment, the model for more regimented hierarchical streamlining of the whole society, has grown in size and function. Together with 112,800 men in the armed forces, double the pre-martial-law total of 60,000, the regime relies on paramilitary forces and local self-defense forces. The total military force of 300,000 men commands 20 percent of the national budget.[10] A deliberate policy to inculcate conformity and passive obedience proceeds, not only in the forced re-structuring of the educational system and mass media, but also through the creation of "barangay brigades" or citizen's armies (analogous to the "Kabataang Barangay," youth organizations directed by Marcos' advisers). By 1979, about 400,000 Filipinos had received basic and advanced military training; the regime's goal is one million. While the Philippines, unlike some Latin-American nations, does not have a tradition of a military caste acquiring wealth or power through its role in government, the Marcos regime has now politicized the army, with provincial and local military officers taking over the civilian functions of governorship and mayorships; they have also assumed highly lucrative managerial positions in state agencies like the National Oil Company, National Electrification Administration, and the huge agro-industrial corporation, PHIVIDEC.

In perspective, the Marcos coup may be viewed as an attempt by the bureaucratic-technocratic faction of the dominant classes-- Marcos had no large private wealth in land or business prior to his election as president--to scrap formal democratic mechanisms of class-mediation (between comprador and landlord elements of the elite), to repair deteriorating hegemony over the masses, and to align the economy more closely with the metropolitan bourgeoisie. Of the latter, evidences are incontestable. Aside from the $4 billion of U.S. investments, the Marcos regime has received an average of $200 million in military assistance annually since 1972--there was a 106 percent increase in military assistance during the first three years of martial law. The largest support came in the form of $500 million rental for the U.S. bases from 1979 to 1984; for 1984 to 1989, the Reagan administration has agreed to give the Marcos regime $900 million in economic and military aid.[11] But with the rapid deterioration of the economy following Aquino's death, characterized by huge capital flight, industry shutdowns, skyrocketing inflation and unemployment culminating in the government's financial bankruptcy and utter loss of credibility, whatever economic gains accumulated during Marcos' incumbency have all been wiped out. Emergency loans of over $2 billion from the U.S., Japan, Australia, and other countries are propping up the mortally-sick regime. The foreign debt of $27 billion is bound to limit the regime's ability to sustain its militarization scheme, its infrastructural projects to open up still untapped resources belonging to the cultural minorities, and its suppression of all dissent.

Before describing briefly three sectors hitherto neglected by orthodox Marxist analysis--the Church, cultural minorities, and women--regarded as marginal to the master-discourse of proletariat and peasantry, allow me to sketch the socio-economic parameters.

THE GOOD NEWS IN BABYLON

Today, we are experiencing an unprecedented crisis resulting from the regime's export-oriented industrialization prescribed by IMF and World Bank: 70 percent inflation, a negative growth rate of 3 to 5 percent, the lowest in 25 years; the peso-purchasing power down to 35 percent (from 1972) and an unemployment rate of at least 40 percent. In 1984, one million workers lost their jobs. Per capita income stands at $450, lower than Taiwan ($1,180) and even lower than Papua, New Guinea ($480).[12] The enormous debt of $27 billion and the expected IMF austerity program are bound to pauperize the majority of Filipinos. On the face of the regime's claim of achieving unequalled progress, two realities cannot be evaded: massive impoverishment, and the widening gap between rich and poor. According to AID and World Bank studies, about 75% of 53 million Filipinos live below the poverty level. While minimum wage is $2.60, the daily cost of food was $4.28 in 1984. Under authoritarian rule, it's not only poverty--hunger, malnutrition, filth, illiteracy, disease, hopelessness--that afflicts workers and peasants; but also the indiscriminate violence of the military in the form of hamletting (Vietnam-style "strategic hamletting"), disappearances, arbitrary arrests (of the 70,000 political prisoners held since 1972, 1,332 remain as of December 1981), tortures, and massacres all documented by Amnesty International, Lawyer's Committee for International Human Rights, and other impartial groups.[13] The September 1984 Mission Report of the International Commission of Jurists confirms the persistence and intensification of widespread human rights abuses despite the "lifting of martial law" in 1981.

It is at this conjunctural stage of economic deterioration and political repression, begun in early 1972, that the Philippine churches, in particular the clergy and nuns of the Roman Catholic Church, underwent a transformation still going on, unprecedented in its over three-hundred years of institutional conservatism. Priests, nuns, and lay workers began integrating with the masses in social action programs launched in the late sixties, parallel to the resurgence of nationalist demonstrations by workers, students, urban slum dwellers, and peasants. One fruit of this convergence was the formation of the Christians for National Liberation (CNL) in February 1972.[14]

Given its historical links with oppressive institutional practices and bureaucratic-authoritarian norms and values, the Church has persisted in its conservative sacramental ministry and its temporizing accommodation/complicity with the secular State. Its astute policy of support for martial law in 1972, modified later to "critical collaboration," can only be judged logical and self-serving since it was intended to protect Church property and investments: land, banks, parochial schools, assorted businesses, etc. In February 1978 Disini (a Marcos crony) attempted to take over the Philippine Trust Company, where the Manila archdiocese had a controlling interest; only then was Cardinal Sin prompted, in October 1979, to begin calling for the end of martial law.[15]

In a country where 86 percent of the population are Roman Catholics (7 percent are Protestants), the thousands of parish priests, nuns, members of religious orders and lay workers came to realize how the government's development policies (which allowed, for example, the encroachment of foreign corporation plantations into peasant farms) were causing extreme suffering and injustice. Applying the method of conscientization--applying the Scriptures to their everyday problems--and employing Marxist tools of class analysis, religious activists became intensely involved with striking workers colliding with police and army. They joined urban squatters fighting the government's demolition squads; they supported the families of political prisoners. All these factors made the clergy, nuns, and lay "conscientizers" part of the regime's three-pronged attack on media, labor, and church.

It was only on 4 November 1976 that some progressive bishops rebuked the Church's general lack of credibility for its "un-Christian" non-involvement, i.e. tacit complicity with, or endorsement of, the "violent status quo." Although between 1974 and 1982, more than 24 priests and lay people had been arrested or tortured, it was only in August 1983 that the Bishops' Conference could unanimously issue a sharp denunciation of the Presidential Commitment Order which had nullified the constitutional system of justice and due process of law. Before this, the most vocal criticism of martial law and human rights violations came from the Association of Major Religious Superiors of the Philippines, which represents 2,500 priests and 7,000 nuns in various orders.[16]

It is true that in 1974 Cardinal Sin denounced the military raid on San Jose Seminary in Novaliches, but subsequently he acquiesced to the regime's summary deportation of two progressive Italian priests working with the Tondo poor. In 1974 the Association established the Task Force Detainees to monitor detentions, cases of torture, "disappearances," and political killings.

For the Protestants, it was the 1974 military raid, arrest and torture of senior officials of the National Council of Churches in the Philippines (NCCP) which agitated eight denominations--the evangelical churches were the most supportive of martial law at the outset--and the Philippine Independent Church into becoming active in social justice and human rights concerns.

The persecution of church workers peaked in 1976 with the expulsion of two American missionaries, and the shutting down of two Catholic publications in Manila and two Catholic radio stations in Mindanao. Over one hundred church workers in Tagum and Mati, Mindanao, were arrested, tortured and detained for several months. In 1980, nine persons involved with the Basic Christian community near Kabankalan, Negros Occidental province, were abducted and killed. In 1981, a pastor of the United Church of Christ was arrested in Agusan del Norte, Mindanao, and tortured; in Nueva Ecija, Luzon, Father Pepito Bernardo, a parish priest working with tribal Filipinos, was arrested by the military. In January and February of 1982, there was another wave of arrests: seven church workers in Tagum, Davao del Norte, Mindanao, were arrested; and three high officials of the NCCP were detained. In the last quarter of 1982, twenty-five church workers were arrested and several Social Action Centers raided and ransacked.[17]

One response to this onslaught was the strike of all parish priests in Samar (where the NPA has the strategic edge over the military). In November 1983, twelve bishops confronted the government and affirmed the Church's pastoral concern for justice and human rights. When Marcos persisted in jailing priests and nuns, the entire hierarchy of 92 bishops castigated the regime in a pastoral letter read in 3,000 churches, accusing the government of "corruption and economic mismanagement." The bishops criticized as the root cause of injustice the regime's development program favoring multinationals and tourism executed through militarization of the country.[18] In February 1983, the bishops withdrew from the Church-Military Liaison Committee established in 1973, the first move in a process of disenchantment climaxing in the November 1983 pastoral letter calling for urgent reforms: restoration of the writ of *habeas corpus*, repeal of repressive presidential decrees, etc. It was only a step away from the Cardinal's somewhat belated imprimatur on urban insurrection. In their 16 February 1983 pastoral letter, the bishops warned that "insurgency, counter-militarization, is the response of segments of Philippine society that despair of any possibility of righting such wrongs. . . . "

Progressive priests and nuns have persistently rejected the regime's argument that the religious should confine themselves to purely "spiritual" tasks, and announced the logic of their participation in current popular struggles:

People are the locus of Christian mission. To render them authentic service is to be with them, as they suffer and even as they struggle. . . . [The church people charged as subversives] are convinced of the justness of the people's cause. It is an inherent right of people to live a decent life where their basic needs are met and freedoms guaranteed. This is the essence of the full and abundant life that Christ speaks of. Where these things are absent it is just and correct for the people to struggle for them. . . . Action in behalf of justice and participation in the transformation of the world is a constitutive dimension of preaching the Gospel.[19]

Polarized in this fashion, the scenario of the Church (more precisely the progressive elements of the Church) confronting the State dramatizes the antagonism of two ideological stances competing in a "war of position": Marcos' ideology of national security and order, which aims to isolate the radicalized religious from the generally conservative or compromising hierarchy, and the prophetic impulse in the Christian evangelical tradition as catalyzed by the CNL's emerging "theology of struggle" and a Filipinized Marxism, whose nationalist-egalitarian ethos coincides with the discourse of Exodus and Christ's frontal assault on the imperial State and the pharisees. Given its established national network of communications and its highly coordinated parishes, the Church is the only hegemonic institution that can withstand and successfully thwart Marcos' autocratic-military rule. In the process of asserting its independence, it has tactically advanced the NDF's call for the restoration of civil liberties. Through the organized efforts to document violations of human rights and critique the causes of such violations, progressive Christians have succeeded in eroding the hegemonic reactionary ideology of the fascist state as it seeks to draw on the historic collusion of the Church as property-owner and the now reconstituted oligarchy of landlords and compradors. A government dossier in 1979 recommended that the State use the conservative mainstream of the hierarchy to curb the radicals.[20] But with the revitalized messianism of the militant clergy, nuns, and lay workers impeding capital accumulation and unmasking State rationalizations, the Church is being pushed to revise its anti-communist policy of neutrality or "critical collaboration" with the regime, lest it suffer a catastrophic loss of credibility and inevitable obsolescence.

SCHISM, EPIPHANY, INCARNATION

The founding of *Christians for National Liberation* (CNL) in 1972 signifies the culmination of a democratic and popular movement in the Church which traces its genealogy to the schismatic nativist and nationalist impulses of the 1896 revolution. It was catalyzed by the Second Vatican Council (1962-1965) and the rise of liberation theology coeval with the formation of "base communities" in the mid-sixties; the 1968 affirmation by Latin-American bishops in Medellin, Colombia, of their "preferential option for the poor"; and the examples of Camilo Torres of Colombia, Archbishop Oscar Romero of El Salvador, and Ernesto Cardenal of Nicaragua. Gustavo Gutierrez's book *Theology of Liberation* (1971), as well as the writings of Paulo Freire (*Pedagogy of the Oppressed*, 1970) and others, were also influential in redefining a "living theology" as situational or contextual, a pilgrim theology of the event which affirms that "salvation is specifically for the poor, the lowly and the helpless."[21] Although a century late behind Leo XIII's encyclical *Rerum Novarum*, the Catholic Bishops' Conference set up in 1966 a National Secretariat for Social Action which attempted conscientization of farmers and workers for organized self-help, trade-union work, etc. This move away from personalism and hierarchical authority to reciprocity, interdependence, and partisanship revealed its limitation when the Church disenfranchised the Mindanao-Sulu Pastoral Council which had engaged in cooperative action with tribal groups endangered by the government's development schemes and also trained lay leaders for the basic Christian communities.

Such a limit to the "prayer-realization of the Christian vocation" had of course already been transcended, if not superseded, by the total commitment to the armed resistance made by priests like Conrado Balweg, Edicio la Torre, Luis Jalandoni, Zacharias Agatep (killed last October 1982), and other martyrs of the faith like Carlos Tayag, Puri Pedro, Alex Garsales, Jerry Aquino, Alfredo Cesar, to name a few. These "bearers" of "Good News" have moved beyond the theoretical moment of reading God's will in the "signs of the times" and individualist ethics to integration with the grassroots poor, the doers of theology, whose empowerment concides with their collective transformation of the iniquitous political, economic and social structures. The target is not development-from-the-top-down but the liberation of the total person-in-community through what Fr. Catalino Arevalo percipiently calls "historico-social praxis": "The liberative praxis of God, mediated in history in and through the liberative praxis of men, is solidarity with the poor and the oppressed in any given society. . . . [which] is the privileged 'space' where the summons of God and his revelation of himself can be met today."[22]

In its 1983 program, the CNL has reaffirmed its allegiance to the principles of the National Democratic Front as a "historical expression of our vocation to help build God's kingdom. It is the political incarnation of our Christian faith at the present stage of Philippine history."[23] Consistently critical of the Church hierarchy's conservative and inherently opportunistic stance of "critical collaboration," recently altered to Cardinal Jaime Sin's populist call for everyone to join "the parliament of the streets," the CNL concentrates on the basic problems of imperialism, feudalism, and bureaucrat-capitalism now embodied in the U.S.-Marcos dictatorship. Emphasizing the people's participation in fulfilling the Christian imperative of revolution, the CNL seeks to promote "revolutionary ecumenism," combat Christian chauvinism, enhance the Filipinizing of Marxism, and change the Church's reactionary political function. On its special strategic task, the CNL elaborates:

> . . . . The CNL must boldly project the participation of Christians in the united front. We must effectively neutralize the anti-communist propaganda against liberation movements, by taking pains to interpret the Christian meaning of the people's struggle and denouncing imperialism's use of Christianity as an ideological justification for counter-revolution.[24]
>
> We declare categorically: The key question facing us is not atheism or theism. It is revolution or counter-revolution!

Based on a reading of CNL documents, one can perceive the matrix of the CNL's praxis in the view of an eschatology in the process of realization--the power of Christ to incarnate a redemptive vision--eloquently addressed by Sister Mariani Dimaranan:

> Christ is the center of our Christian faith. His passion should be seen in the historical perspective of the plight of the Filipino people struggling for truth, justice and freedom. His death is daily re-enacted in the salvaging and murders of the countless Filipinos who have been martyred on the altar of a regime ruled by injustice, violence and oppression. Likewise, his Resurrection should be seen in the ultimate triumph and liberation of the Filipino people and other oppressed peoples as well.[25]

In October 1979, the Catholic Bishops' Conference had condemned as criminally irresponsible "the inciting of the suffering poor to . . . revolutionary violence." To this, in September 1981, 17 bishops, in a "Pastoral of Total Faith-Commitment," responded by arguing that such "non-violent stance is actually a vote for the violent *status quo*." The CNL's influence is gradually being felt even in the higher echelons. Its prophetic vision of achieving a people's church which subsumes the transcendent future, conceiving God as historically active in the concrete struggles of the oppressed, into a strategy for collective renewal and redemption, has perhaps inspired the successful convening of the International Ecumenical Conference on the Philippines (October-November 1983) at Stony Point, New York.

In the light of such cathartic and catalyzing ordeals experienced by practicing Christians, I should like to delineate here the genesis of a Filipino theology of liberation by juxtaposing two contradictory positions, one espoused by Bishop Francisco Claver (in a speech in July 1982 at Gonzaga University, Seattle) and the other adumbrated by random reflections of Father Edicio de la Torre, a CNL stalwart, and by observations of guerrilla priest Conrado Balweg.

Bishop Claver's reputedly "progressive" stance is premised on his assumption of the "total vulnerability" of the Christian who respects "God in all people," presumably also in Marcos and his military cohort.[26] While Claver upholds the Church's mission of *metanoia*, "the transforming quality" intrinsic to the Gospel, unlike praxis-oriented theologians Father Jose P. Dizon and Carlos Abesamis (to cite just two indigenizing thinkers), Claver privileges "the spirituality of the genuine charismatic." But in spite of his prophetic impulse, Claver's sectarian elitism is evinced in his unilateral postulation of a gap between what he conceives as "an all-encompassing faith perspective" and mere "ideological presuppositions," whether capitalist or socialist. While he criticizes Marcos' authoritarianism, he also places the resistance in the same category: all guilty of using violence. This view of being above the battle, above existing secular ideologies locked in combat, directly contradicts the concrete, daily living of the Gospel demonstrated by the armed people and the testimonies (as witnesses and participants in a collective passion) of numerous priests and nuns.

Bishop Claver's easy Olympian lumping of Marcos' fascist repression serving coporate profits and U.S. global hegemony with the NDF's egalitarian vision, plays right into the hands of the very same state apparatus whose troops, after murdering one of his priests (Father Godofredo Alingal), still roam freely today. Not a single day passes in the Philippines without Marcos' military committing atrocities and brutalities on unarmed innocent civilians. No, never mind these; the other side is guilty too, says Claver. This situates such theorizing right in the center of the Constantinian dilemma of the Church as a temporal power dictating an absolute prohibition of violence on what the New Testament calls the "captives" quest to realize the promised Kingdom of God on earth, to realize (by parable) what Karl Barth calls real Christianity in our time: socialism.[27] When the Pope visited Nicaragua in 1983 and then issued a refutation of liberation theology in September 1984, the Vatican was reconfirming its 1700-year legacy of serving as court chaplains to the state, a predicament of captivity to Mammon and Caesar.

If the Filipino people have learned anything instructive in our four hundred years of revolutionary struggle against Spanish monastic absolutism and U.S. imperialism, I think it is the urgency of the need to make clear, historically specific distinctions, as befits the praxis-oriented contextualization of Biblical texts. Who are really our friends, who our enemies? If Claver is speaking only for himself, that should be made unequivocally clear so that we can compare and evaluate his stand with many committed Filipino Christians (in prison, in the battlefront) whose faith is a way of acting (socio-historic praxis) as contra-distinguished from "religion" as a way of contemplative thought. If, however, he is speaking for the institution, then we understand him as the functionary of that ideological-bureaucratic formation which has identified itself historically with the reactionary classes against the dispossessed majority; which helped execute the three militant priests Burgos, Gomez and Zamora; which has always collaborated with the colonial state apparatus from the 1896 revolution, the Sakdal and Huk uprisings, up to the present.

Within this complex dialectical perspective of the relations between organized religion, faith, and the sharpening class antagonisms, and seventeen years after the famous 1967 "Letter from Seventeen Roman Catholic Bishops of the Third World Interpreting *Populorum Progressio*," Claver's formalistic and static notion of the "spirituality of the genuine charismatic" (such as those of *Opus Dei*? or army chaplains and cursillistas?) versus social activism seems blind to the existential or lived experience of the Filipino people today in whose many-sided praxis such a metaphysical dualism has long been surpassed (in the sense of being simultaneously preserved, negated and transformed).

According to Father Ed Saguinsin, the exiled head of the National Federation of Sugar Workers in the Philippines, whose members while engaged in a peaceful strike have been arrested, tortured and killed by the military: "The moment of Gandhi has long been surpassed in the Philippines today."[28] Confronting other socio-cultural traditions, whether the rationalist and logocentric West or the ascetic renunciation of the East, Filipinos today take pride in their 400-year tradition of armed popular revolts against local despots and foreign tyrants.

The central issue is not the use or non-use of violence as a tactical means of struggle--violence, contrary to Claver's opinion, is never "an easy, attractive option" for socialists or Marxist-Leninists; the issue is whether the goal of liberation, equality and collective/communal development can be achieved without pursuing, in total consciousness and responsibility, the project of a national liberation struggle for independence, freedom and justice. This is the problematic articulated by CNL militants, who are forging a Christian praxis, evangelization as "action for justice," by confronting sin as a structural and institutional reality.

Priests, nuns, missionaries and lay activists in the Basic Christian Communities have been pushed by the masses--their flocks--to gradually discover that "eschatological promise of peace and justice for all," not just for the solitary individual, distilled in the prophetic Biblical tradition: a promise of the historical becoming or incarnation of the Kingdom of God in history on which the Church itself is based. This "Good News" has been the theme of iconoclastic or unorthodox discourses by Moltmann, Harvey Cox,

Ernst Bloch, Leonardo Boff, and others. Within this concept of "eschatological hope," we can pose the question of violence from an ecumenical perspective. I would like to submit here the following meditation by the theologian Johannes B. Metz on the decorum of revolution:

> . . . When Christian love becomes active in society as an *unconditional desire for justice and freedom for others*, circumstances can arise in which this love needs to use revolutionary means. Where the social status quo contains as much injustice as may arise by overthrowing it by revolution, then a revolution--for justice and freedom for "the least of the brethren"--may not be prohibited even in the name of Christian love. This makes Merleau-Ponty's accusation all the more pointed, that one has never seen a Church support a revolution simply because it was a just one.[24]

Thus, to confuse the systematic violence monopolized by the neocolonial State in the service of profit with the armed self-defense of the victims who have rejected despair and affirmed hope in fighting for survival with dignity, for liberation of the person-in-community--to confuse these two kinds of historical praxis, and then to implicitly admonish the victims to resign themselves to their fates, to retreat inwardly and thus tolerate daily oppression, is nothing else but to surrender to and justify the domination of the Filipino people by Caesar, the Imperial Legion, and the local Pilates.

In contrast to Claver's temporizing casuistry--Claver is a contributor to the Jesuits' anti-communist book *In the Philippines Today: Christian Faith, Ideologies...Marxism* (1977) incisively anatomized by Exequiel Augustin in the CNL publication *Marxism, Capitalism and the Church* (1982)--Ed de la Torre's testimony as political prisoner and activist uncompromisingly demonstrates the relentless power of a prophetic faith incarnated in the struggle and sufferings of the masses.[30] What distinguishes de la Torre's ideology conceived as lived experience/praxis is, first, his conception of the church's role not as a leader of the mass movement but as "a leaven, the critical element...the creative minority." Stressing the minority position of Christians, de la Torre argues: "When I say Christians will always be a minority, I mean that, regardless of numbers, our position is not based on power but on truth." Contrast this with Claver's claim that "we will also have to have the power" to incarnate the Kingdom--as though that hasn't happened yet, or isn't happening already--and so posits his own anti-Marxist ideology. And second, notice de la Torre's intrinsically dialectical grasp of the tension between the spiritual or interior life ("recollection or gathering of oneself") and the community--not a traditional religious community but "people who are mobile, who can reflect on the run." He urges Filipinos to "develop ourselves as human beings as we work for liberation. Otherwise we're not convincing witnesses."

Unlike Claver, then, de la Torre comprehends the need for the integral wholeness of the person. "Spirituality" for him signifies "a sense of wholeness and direction. That's what liberation is about, I think, a wholeness at every level, from the individual up to the whole society. . . . Wholeness clarifies the basic ideological standpoint: for whom do we struggle, with whom." Since de la Torre believes that spirituality or inwardness is possible only on the basis of participation in a militant community, he possesses a realistic and informed vision of profound social and political change, including "a new and transformed presence of the Church," occurring in his lifetime. Preoccupied more with serving the people than proving his superiority over all flawed ideologies, de la Torre's faith testifies to the always-already-realized promise of *metanoia* in the Gospel:

> There will always be a role for the free, prophetic Christian. Even if the new system is better there will still be problems, and people in charge who don't like criticism. We must be prepared to speak out. We shouldn't place our hopes in any system but be ready to criticize and to expect persecution if we work for the creative transformation of society. It's important to know the uses of power so that we can be effective, but that's not what is important. We must be credible witnesses to all of love, concern and the struggle for justice for ordinary men and women. . . .
>
> In prison I made my decision to be with the poor forever. I took my vows: obedience to a group that is obedient to the call of the people; creative participation, meaning you don't just implement the decision of others, but also make suggestions and act as a subject; and thirdly, perserverance--keep trying, that is.[31]

As the living example of the call for renewal and the continuing realization of the CNL's will to give flesh and blood to faith, Conrado Balweg may still be able to redeem the Church's Constantinian captivity by his constant daily sacrifice in the Communist Party's armed detachment. He asserts: "Christianity is fighting for the things I always believed in. When I joined the NPA it was a logical development of my faith." Asked if he believed in God, Balweg replies: "Which god? The god of the exploiters or the god of the oppressed? I don't see how you can worship both gods at the same time." Balweg believes that Christians must take sides in the class war, on the side of the poor and oppressed; and that Christ never condemned the moral and just resistance (violence) of the people. His total commitment to "deemphasize the sacramental and theologize the local situation, to become co-creator with God" compels Balweg to redefine priesthood and spirituality in an entirely scandalous because nonconformist way:

> I'm not a priest in the traditional institutional sense of priesthood. But if priest means those who totally give themselves in the service of the people, then I'm still a priest. . . . If you're thinking of the traditional spirituality, I don't meet your expectations. But if spirituality means you're selfless, self-giving to people who need your service, even to the point of dying without being afraid, then maybe I am spiritual.[32]

On the question of pacifism or violence as a matter of principle, Balweg responds:

> Before, during the crusades of church expansion, it was in the interests of the church to justify violence. Now, when the authority of the church is challenged it condemns violence. . . . Gandhi or King's nonviolence is a futile endeavor, very temporary. In the end it will not succeed. It's like a baby protesting to its mother, that the mother will have mercy. . . .
> Historically there's always been violence. But in whose interest? If you use violence to exploit, that is not justified. But you have to use violence to destroy exploitation.[33]

Conrado Balweg's disarming candor assures us that whatever the Pope or bishops say, revolution will succeed and the incarnation's promise be fulfilled.

ANNUNCIATION FROM THE MOUNTAINS

Notwithstanding nominal converts, the Church has very little or no influence at all on 7 million Filipinos--16 to 18 percent of the population--comprising the "cultural" or "national minorities," i.e. tribal communities lacking a centralized political structure (except for the Muslims) but undergoing rapid political mobilization and systematically victimized by individual and group discrimination. Today, they face gradual and total dispossession of their ancestral homes--land, water and mineral resources, forests, etc., essential to their lives. The Marcos' technocratic blueprint for modernization requires, for example, the flooding of the ancestral homes of 100,000 Bontocs in Northern Luzon (341,000 hectares of rice lands and fruit-growing trees) to build the Chico River Dam.[34] Another dam in Apayao, funded also by the World Bank and the Asian Development Bank, will destroy 45 villages with 38,000 people, and 9,000 hectares of agricultural land, as well as permanently ruin the ecological balance of the region. In response to this genocidal plan, the Bontocs and Kalingas published in June

1980 an open letter signed by 10,000 people questioning the regime's objective: "In the Philippines, only the few foreign-owned industries and corporations, and only the rich in the rural areas and the cities benefit from electrification. In Benguet, when the Ambuklao and Binga dams were constructed some 20 years ago and there many mountain people were dislocated, the foreign-owned mines are the major users of electricity."[35]

To counteract the militarization of their homeland, in particular the counter-insurgency tactics of the PANAMIN (Presidential Assistance on National Minorities) headed by corporate magnate Elizalde and staffed by military personnel, the Igorots and other groups have mounted resistance in various forms, from legal protest to armed struggle. The most well-known organized rebellion is that of the Moro National Liberation Front and the Bangsa Moro Army which is recognized by the Islamic nations; the MNLF amalgamates Tausugs, Maranaos, Maguindanaos, etc., mostly farmers and workers, into a fighting polity called the Bangsa Moro Republik.[36] (I devote Chapter IV of this book to the Moro people's revolution).

For the Igorots, the pattern of oppositional praxis evolves from custom and tradition based on the communal possession of fields and forests, rivers and lakes, including the spirit of the dead. In the past, the rule of the elders encouraged localism and tendencies to factionalism; but with the incursions of corporate speculators and the military, the Igorots have mobilized and reconstituted the *bodong* or peace-pact. Previously, this traditional institution consolidated geographically adjacent villages for protection against habitual enemies, usually neighboring villages; but now, with the major threat coming from foreign investors (mining and logging companies) represented by the State and the military, the Igorots have re-tooled their pacts to create deeper and wider internal, organized unity. They hope thereby to repel the insidious manipulation of the government to divide and isolate them by terrorism, resettle them in guarded strategic hamlets, assassinate their leaders, and so silence them.

In one peace pact in February last year, the tribes agreed to exclude "any native of the Cordillera. . . . who is a member of the government army" from the protection of the *bodong*, thus establishing a state of war which cuts across kinship and ethnic distinctions.[37] Since the Igorots identify their lives with their physical inhabiting of those lands earmarked for flooding or deforestation, the tribes have vowed to resist any intrusion into the region. A significant leap of consciousness can be discerned in their collective expression of "solidarity with other sectors in Philippine society who are also victims of the exploitation and oppression of the same power structure which have caused the suffering the the Cordillera people"--a powerful disarticulation of the regime's claim of "uplifting of the welfare" of the minorities.

Given the universal, all-embracing character of people's war and the strategic concentration of guerilla forces in the "weak links" of the social formation, the NDF has devoted Point 8 of its program specifically to stressing the right of the national minorities to fight for self-determination. It acknowledges their continuing victimization by "Christian" or "Filipino" chauvinism, "the mentality and practice of discrimination and oppression fostered by Spanish and American rulers, and now exercised by the comprador bourgeoisie and the landlord class." The NDF's articulation of their fundamental interest posits their irreconcilable contradiction with U.S. imperialism and the Marcos dictatorship:

> The national minorities have the right to liberate themselves from such oppression and determine ther own destiny. The right to self-determination includes the right to secede from a state of national oppression or choose autonomy within a state that guarantees the equality of nationalities.
>
> It is our stand that all national minorities, big or small, should enjoy autonomy and be accorded special guarantees for their accelerated progress. Their struggle is not merely for "cultural autonomy" but for all-round progress with due respect to their special characteristics. Where national minorities are mixed with people of other nationalities, they shall be assured of proportionate representation in the political and economic institutions to be set up. We lay stress on the democratic unity of the workers and peasants irrespective of nationality and religion.[38]

While the prophetic and secularizing messianism of the radicalized clergy and lay activists has generated a sizeable body of socio-historical interpretation, with the Basic Christian Communities serving as the paradigm agency for an ambiguous, officially sanctioned disruption of authoritarian hegemony, the complex dynamics of the *bodong* among the Igorots, and the more intricate subversive practices of the Islamic peoples in the southern Philippines, have not yet received commensurate anthropological investigation. Both sectors--religious and cultural minorities--have arrived at a degree of consciousness and organization sufficient for them to offer serious disarticulating challenges to the legitimacy claims of the Marcos state.

It might be instructive to dramatize here a revealing intertextuality of events that would capture precisely the ironic force, the destabilizing impact of Igorot communal awakening on authoritarianism's claim of hegemonic representativeness.

As President Marcos staged his customary exercise in self-apologetics before the ANPA in Honolulu, on the night of 24 April 1980, elements of his 44th Infantry killed Macli-ing Dulag, leader of the Kalinga-Bontoc community of 15,000 families. AFP soldiers also wounded his associate Pedro Dongat. In a peace pact gathering in 1978, Dulag affirmed his people's defiance of Marcos: "Our people are prepared to fight this evil. We will die if we have to protect our land." "This evil" refers to the Marcos regime's World Bank-funded Chico River Basin Development Project: four huge dams to be built in Kalinga-Mountain Province which will submerge 2,753 square kilometers, uprooting 100,000 Bontocs and Kalingas from 16 villages and rice terraces, destroying their whole way of life.

From 1974, the time when the National Power Corporation and Elizalde's PANAMIN cohorts descended on Igorot territory, several hundred Igorots have been harassed and beaten, jailed, tortured, and murdered. Igorot women have been raped by the PC (Philippine Constabulary) and the army (AFP). By late 1976, the Communist-led New People's Army (NPA) started to organize and mobilize the Igorots to repel Marcos' development/relocation schemes. Several encounters between Igorot detachments in the NPA and the Marcos troops have occurred, the latest on 27 February and 5 March 1980. On 27 February Igorot fighters ambushed five members, including one colonel, of the 44th Philippine Military Battalion in Kalinga-Apayao, on their way back from inspection of a dam construction site. In retaliation, the AFP assassinated Dulag--only one of the thousands of victims of Marcos' New Dispensation.

Meanwhile, in Hawaii, Marcos agonized over the complex moral ambiguities of "crisis management"--the actual operation of which is as transparent and one-dimensional as the killing of Dulag.

Marcos' media technicians distributed gratis (thanks to the altruism of the public treasury) his new opus *In Search of Alternatives: The Third World in an Age of Crisis* in which the "fantabulous" achievements of the "New Society" are trumpeted, with the special endorsement of the American Chamber of Commerce of the Philippines, Inc. Need it be said again that like Marcos' first book *The Democratic Revolution*, this one exudes the most banal and hackneyed notions culled from the standard U.S. anti-communist textbooks? However much Marcos' ghost-writers try to disguise the mailed fist with the kidgloves of eclectic liberalism (Solzhenitsyn stuffed together with Fanon and Dependency Theory), Marcos argues *ad nauseam* the rationale for his stale brand of "constitutional authoritarianism."

We can say that this conjuncture, this juxtaposition of Dulag's murder and Marcos' Honolulu antics, once more illustrates the inescapable discrepancy between word and deed, theory and practice, consciousness and action, which the anti-martial law movement here and at home have documented and broadcast throughout the world. There is nothing new in this: it is the classic split of subject and object, of material production and knowledge, of matter-in-motion and thought, that characterizes the social practice of imperialism. If so, then we would be done with it, moralizing that Marcos and his hireling intellectuals are guilty of not recognizing the dialectical truth of reality.

However, I submit that "New Society" political and cultural discourse exhibits a certain unity or coherence itself derived from that discrepancy or split between thought and material production. It exhibits a peculiar transmogrification of bourgeois ideology embedded in the historical specificity of Philippine society in crisis.

STORM OVER THE CORDILLERA

Before the fateful advent of global capitalism in the 1890s and specifically of U.S. military aggression, the lives of the Cordillera people flourished undisturbed in a unique ecosystem or life-world centered on their dynamic integration with the physical environment. For about a million members of the seven ethno-linguistic groups (Ifugao, Bontoc, Kankanai, Ibaloi, Tinggian, Apayao, Isneg) that inhabit the provinces of Kalinga-Apayao, Mountain Province, Ifugao, Abra and Benguet, the ancient rice terraces--universally considered a sophisticated and elaborate feat of engineering--and the adjacent forests and rivers have served not only as sources of livelihood but as the core of the spiritual-cognitive complex that anthropologist Mariflor Parpan-Pagusara calls the Kalinga *ili*: the all-encompassing life-world, the organic and vital harmony of people and their "primary environment and habitat."[39]

During four hundred years of Spanish rule, the Cordillera escaped the penetration of feudal laws and practices instituted in the lowlands; but when the U.S. colonialists arrived to "civilize and Christianise" the natives, they wreaked havoc on the natural communal economy of the people they claimed to help. By enacting numerous land laws dispossessing the tribespeople of their habitat and privatizing land, the U.S. government opened up mining and logging enterprises that quickly reduced the available arable land, destroyed terraces, water reservoirs, and forests, and thus diminished agricultural productivity. Before and after independence in 1946, the U.S. and the native elite applied the then unquestioned capitalist scheme of modernization by colonizing the land for resettlement areas, forest reserves, military installations, parks, and vast agribusiness plantations.

This trend accelerated and worsened under the Marcos regime of martial law with the granting of extensive concessions to foreign capitalists and administration cronies, as witnessed by export processing zones, and the Cellophil Resources Corporation (one of logging companies in the area) with a concession of 200,000 hectares. The fertile land of the Cordillera--for example Tabuk Valley and Trinidad Valley--have been taken over by big landlords, Chinese compradors, bureaucrats and military officials. Part of the high-priority infrastructure to service elite entrepreneurs and foreign investors, the hydroelectric dams have so far inflicted the most irreparable harm and damage. With the construction of such dams as Ambuklaw, Binga and Magat (three of 42 blueprinted by the regime), immense tracts of rice terraces and farmlands have been submerged or dried up, and rendered useless, only to provide power for export-oriented factories and haciendas. Driven to cultivate small farms (one-fifth of a hectare, or 2,000 square meters on the average) with meager yields, the Cordillera peoples are slowly being exterminated; many are forced to leave their homes to work as miners, government employees, farmhands under semi-feudal conditions, and mercenaries in the Marcos military.[40]

First broached in 1973 and chiefly funded by the World Bank and Asian Development Bank, the Chico River Basin Development Project is the single spark that, despite massive but peaceful protests of citizens, has kindled and fanned the Cordillera fire of resistance. As I pointed out earlier, the multilateral *bodong* of 1975, now expanded from intra-tribal to an inter-provincial treaty or united front, marked a turning point in the qualitative evolution of what Joanna Carino calls a "multi-sectoral mass movement of the nationalities" (to be distinguished from "cultural minorities") for exercising the right to self-determination, against neo-colonial genocide.[41] Despite fierce and prolonged opposition which, by 1976, had transformed the dam sites into raging battlegrounds, the regime seems obsessed with pushing through its ethnocidal project, especially Chico Dam 4, the largest, which will submerge six sizeable Kalinga villages, render homeless 4,000 people, and destroy 300 hectares of fertile ricelands (1,200 stonewalled rice terraces).

After the May 1984 elections, more than 3,000 AFP troops invaded the Kalinga-Apayao and Cagayan provinces, ostensibly to drive out about 600 NPA dissidents led by Father Balweg. But, according to local residents and the independent media, the military has committed countless acts of rape, arson, looting, intimidation and harassment of civilians. Airplane bombs and mortar fire have devastated two villages, and 51 inhabitants have been reported killed. Since early June, the military has engaged in a vicious campaign to coerce the people to submit to full-scale military occupation; the techniques of hamletting, mass evacuation, prevention of farmers from cultivating or harvesting their land, destruction of food supplies and rice terraces, etc., are all intended to break their continuing resistance to agro-forestry, mining projects, and construction of the dams for the benefit of transnational corporations. The government's motive of "development" by terror is clear: logging firms (Cellophil) and mining companies (Benguet Consolidated, Batong Buhay, etc.) have declared interest in expanding their operations to the contested, now "free-fire" zones.[42]

Replicating the U.S. "search-and-destroy" operations in Vietnam--after all, U.S. advisers are supervising these military ventures--this massive counter-insurgency campaign represents an enormous escalation of the war against the indigenous peoples of the Cordillera. Sometime in June, Father Balweg disclosed that from April 10 to June 30, the NPA initiated 19 encounters and ambushes, killing 21 soldiers and capturing 11 high-powered rifles.[43] Since the campaign began, at least 44 government soldiers have been killed and 11 wounded by the guerrillas, with two army helicopters shot down. On 5 July 1984, Mario Yag-ao, chairperson of the Kalinga-Bontoc Peacepact Holders Association, denounced "the virtual invasion of our life, liberty, property. . . . We Kalingas and Bontocs are known for being a warrior people. If the AFP pursues its kind of war against the Kalinga-Bontoc people we shall have no other recourse but to fight back in defense of our land, our life, and our well-being."[44]

With the heavy involvement of the U.S. government, IMF/World Bank, Ford Foundation, West German and Japanese firms, the struggle of the nationalities (which includes also the Moros, Tbolis, Mangyans, Aetas, Manobos, Ilongots, etc.) has become truly internationalized, implicating the political economy of the whole nation and elevating their goal from mere cultural autonomy or ethnic self-assertion to survival as distinct peoples with genuine self-determination.

IDENTITY AS DIFFERENCE

Given the uneven and tortuous development of our struggle and the persistent stranglehold of U.S. economic, political and cultural domination of the Philippines through various mediations, the issue of gender and the potential of women as an autonomous force for national-democratic emancipation have been submerged or collapsed into the categories of class or nation by a reductive mode of analysis, allowing capitalist/sexist hegemony to prevail. Except for a conventional reference to feudal sexist culture, the NDF program has ignored the specificity of women's oppression and has subsumed it within the paramount rubric of democratic rights. A recent revision of the program makes the gesture of stressing the goal of promoting the "social equality of men and women," targetting Marcos' tourist industry as an additional technique of degradation. But its formulation remains undialectical: "Cutting across all classes and sectors, Filipino women are raising the issues of their distinct oppression within the common oppression they suffer with Filipino men." In contrast, the proceedings of the 1980 Permanent People's Tribunal in Belgium acknowledges the "double oppression and exploitation" of women by the dominant classes and by "male authority."[45]

It is indeed difficult to ignore the specificity of women's oppression in the Philippines, since they compose one-half of the population--25 million. The majority live in the countryside, performing two-thirds of the work but receiving only a tenth of the usual income earned by peasants and rural workers. In the urban areas, women are subject to substandard wages, limited benefits, sexual abuse and inhumane working conditions. In the decade of the seventies, the unemployment rate for women was 75 percent compared to 10 percent for men. In 1980, 70 percent of women performed unpaid domestic work. Sexist segregation of the labor force has confined women to traditional female jobs with lower wages, longer hours and accelerated pace: domestic service, nursing, sales, clerical work, rank and file workers. Prostitution is the source of livelihood for 300,000 women in the cities, and at least 30,000 (many of them teen-agers) around the U.S. military bases.[46]

The Marcos regime's declared policy of boosting tourism as one major dollar earner and concomitantly legalizing prostitution-- the "hospitality" trade--is only one manifestation of the hegemonic sexist ideology defining woman as an exchangeable commodity, her body and will as conveniently tractable and pliant. This quality has been seized on by advertisements in Europe, New Zealand and Australia, selling Filipinas as submissive housewives.[47] The regime claims that Filipino women are "never degraded nor sexually exploited" by giving statistics of how many women occupy positions in the bureaucracy and local administration, its fetishism of numbers rivalling that of any commercial bank.

Early in 1970, a group of women students founded the first progressive women's organization called MAKIBAKA (acronym for Free Movement of New Women), subsequently driven underground in 1972 and its founder, who had joined the New People's Army, slain in an encounter in 1970. The program of MAKIBAKA, implemented in the establishment of day-care centers, women's consciousness-raising and self-help groups, etc., was the first systematic exposition of a theory of women's liberation in a "semi-feudal and semi-colonial" formation. A similar orientation governs the operation of the Women's Resource Center in Manila, a legal group which disseminates information about women's struggles. Another organization, Concerned Women of the Philippines, consisting mostly of upper-middle class women, has been active in the anti-nuclear movement and the campaign in defense of civil liberties (freedoms of speech, press, etc.). In both the New People's Army and the Bangsa Moro Army, women are integrated as full-time combatants. One can say that women are active in all fronts of the struggle: in human rights groups, mass media, in trade unions, in medical/health care work, in education, etc.[48]

While it must be admitted that such participations do not all target specifically women's issues, their immediate and long-range impact registers in the incessant breakdown of the patriarchal family, the demystification of sexuality, and the dissolution of myths of male superiority and of woman's natural or god-ordained inferiority. Filipina revolutionaries are now recuperating in concrete practice the subjectivity denied to them which, as Luce Irigaray insists, is "the mortgage guaranteeing every irreducible constitution of an object: of representations, of discourse, of desire." Socialist feminism, one can suggest, exists in the Philippines today inscribed in spontaneous practices, unable as yet to fully theorize itself within the precincts of the economistic and class-reductionist inheritance of the traditional left, but yet visible as an insistent lacuna, a hiatus of the thought-process, the necessary key to the decisive undermining of the authoritarian-patriarchal discourse of global capitalism. (I pursue the ramifications of this theme further in Chapter IX.)

CONVERGENCES

One can construe the depth and extent of the economic, political and ideological crisis afflicting the contemporary Philippine formation as a tactical shifting of gears of U.S. imperialism and its dependent allies, but it seems more correct to apprehend it as signifying essentially the oppressor's accelerating loss of hegemony and the substitution of domination by direct coercion--physical violence by the courts, police and military. The shift from a pre-1972 rhetoric/policy of modernization to a rhetoric/policy of order, peace and stability characteristic of praetorian regimes from Chile to South Korea and the Philippines, may be read as a symptom of either the bankruptcy of corporate liberalism, or its flexible re-adjustment in order to contain oppositional practices endangering capital accumulation. The latter seems to be the more likely agenda for the Philippine milieu.

As the National Democratic Front succeeds in forging a broad, firm and vigilant alliance of popular-democratic forces and thus interpellating all the exploited classes, ethnic groups, women, slumdwellers, etc. by connecting their particular alienation and suffering to the structural matrix--the relations of production and reproduction embodied in the dependent totality--it will begin to defatalize reified and fragmented consciousness and unfold possi-bilities for collective efforts toward authentically emancipatory change.

III

U.S. Hegemony and the Ideology
of Neo-Colonial Domination

When the Marcos regime, during the recent drastically concluded negotiations over the tenure of U.S. bases in the Philippines, demurred to labelling the $900 million military-economic aid as "rental," invoking the proverbial U.S.-Philippine "special relations" and American *noblesse oblige*, it unwittingly epitomized its authentic character as a peripheral or, if you like, neo-colonial instrumentality which confesses its total subservience in the same breath that it must perform a necessary gesture of declaring its formal independence.[1] That theater of contractual diplomacy illustrates succinctly the phenomenon of the production or interpellation of the subject--here the present Filipino elite--by U.S. monopoly capital, and the continued reproduction of the dominant social relations.

Recent commentaries by, among others, Professors Stauffer, Wurfel, and Kerkvliet, have acutely noted the "refeudalization of the Philippine polity" since 1972 within the parameter of what Wallerstein calls the "capitalist world-system," more specifically, within the fiefdom of the IMF-World Bank.[2] Such a "refeudalization," however, must be qualified since, as Laclau and other critics of dependency theory have argued, the pressure of the metropolis does not register its impact in a direct way, given the uneven development of the subordinated social formation and the unsynchronic sedimentation of the native sensibility through which U.S. political, economic and cultural domination is exercised.[3]

REPRODUCING THE MYTH OF THE UNCIVILIZED NATIVE

What contemporary analysts of dependency are constantly confronted with, in the Philippine case as distinguished from, say, the classic paradigm of British India or Dutch Indonesia, is the allegedly exceptional nature of the American experiment in "nation building." Conceived during the vicissitudes of the anti-war movement, Peter Stanley's *The Philippines: A Nation in the Making* (1974)[4]--to cite one example--sums up a long, persistent tradition in American historiographical apologetics in attempting to re-vindicate, for the nth time, what he calls an "imperialism of suasion" administered through policies of attraction guaranteed ultimately by force. On his own showing, however, Stanley confesses that "despite its commitment to modernization and prosperity, the insular government achieved relatively little except in the fields of education and health."[5] While the record in health may be conceded pending a more substantive appraisal, the claim for education has been repeatedly belied since the Monroe Survey of 1920 and succeeding reports. A recent study by Glenn May, *Social Engineering in the Philippines* (1980),[6] ably describes the incoherent formulation of U.S. educational policies but fails, because of its empiricist and functionalist reductionism, to specify the structural constraints and efficacy of such tactical programs viewed as a logical extension of U.S. pedagogic practices aimed, first, to train a preponderantly immigrant body of the industrial working class and, second, to pacify and discipline the internal colonies of blacks, American Indians, etc.[7]

It is ironic that contrary to (perhaps really because of) his judgment that the U.S. policy of attraction or co-optation resulted in an elitist, hierarchical and therefore anti-democratic polity, Stanley endorses the "Philippine empire" as an exemplary model for U.S. dealings with the Third World--an inconsistency one finds endemic among American liberal Filipinologists.

It is superfluous to rehearse here the historical process whereby the U.S. succeeded in enforcing its rule by the dual mode of violence and co-optation of the *ilustrado* stratum (the native intelligentsia in the 19th century), a process cogently summarized by Renato Constantino and others; and definitively re-stated by Daniel B. Schirmer in a 1974 paper, "The Conception and Gestation of a Neo-Colony."[8] What I want to point out is a hitherto obscured and neglected area for investigation, namely, the theory and practice of racism (and its corollary, cultural chauvinism) inflected by the social-Darwinist idea of evolution, which may clarify the conditions of possibility for the collective perception (by McKinley, Root, Taft, etc.) that the Filipino race was incapable of self-development or self-government--hence the popularization of the magical/neutral term "tutelage."

Analyzed within the context of the Filipino revolutionary resistance and the intra-class debates within the U.S. government then, "tutelage" denotes a strategic and totalizing scheme of establishing hegemony (defined in the Gramscian sense of "the ability of one class to articulate the interest of other social groups to its own") fully consonant with the needs and imperatives of expansive finance-capitalism and its constitutional juridical/parliamentary machinery.[9] It was marked by such stages as the enunciation of Taft's "Philippines for the Filipinos" slogan, the passage of the Philippine Bill of 1902, the Payne-Aldrich Act of 1909, the Jones Act of 1916, the Harrison administration's Filipinizing measures, etc.[10] If "tutelage" is the code-word for the psychological capture of the non-Western native and its internalized confirmation (a technique fully exposed by Edward Said in *Orientalism*), we can see the subtle and insidious permutation of this overdetermined form of practice in the way the anthropologist David P. Barrows, head of the Bureau of Non-Christian Tribes (1901-1903) and later the Bureau of Education (1903-1907), consigned the Negritos to a realm of "no political significance" but of supreme value as objects of scientific knowledge--a colonial legacy partly informing the rationale of PANAMIN today, as demonstrated by Professor Renato Rosaldo (in his article "Utter Savages of Scientific Value," *Filipinas*, I, 1980, pp. 120-33).[11] So much for the putative ambiguity of "tutelage."

While the formal and informal education system (from the soldier-teacher to the Thomasites, *pensionados*, etc.) effectively advanced the project of "benevolent assimilation" as thus misrecognized, it was not, I think, the most crucial and pivotal factor. It was rather the series of policy decisions and legitimizing tactics which transformed the terrain of ideological struggle: from the formation of the Filipino militia and Philippine Constabulary in 1901, to the appointment of Filipino *ilustrados* to the Commission, to the 1907 elections to the Philippine Assembly. Such institutions (whose latest metamorphosis we find in Marcos "personal satrapy," according to a *New York Times* editorial, 20 May 1983) decisively installed U.S. hegemony and insured its reproduction in everyday life.

And so, even while conducting the "war of maneuver" by defeating Aguinaldo and legislating the Republic's guerrillas into the category of bandits, the U.S. was fully engaged in the simultaneous "war of position" executed chiefly through the *ilustrado* fraction and the new bureaucratic elite (Quezon and Osmena were the most typical)[12] whose political, intellectual and moral leadership yields a peculiar, heterogeneous discourse of aristocratic privilege, laissez-faire individualism and popular democracy--a contradictory unity loosely synthesized by the collective aspiration for "immediate and absolute" independence.

MEDIATIONS/MUTATIONS

It should be emphasized here that while the Enlightenment ideas of liberalism and rationalist values espoused by the 1896/1898 revolution mobilized Filipinos of all classes against foreign rule by articulating the principle of equality between races and nations, its concepts of justice, moral dignity, liberty and progress remained abstract and thus open to factional or class calculation. One can of course allude to exceptional insights: Jacinto once referred to how Filipino peasants are "despoiled of the fruit of their labor" which then sustained the government's tyranny.[13] And Mabini theorized in *The Philippine Revolution:* "If truth is to be found in the synchronization of reason and experience, rectitude lies in the synchronization of theory and practice."[14] Indeed, even Rizal's concept of "civic virtues" can be construed as a potentially powerful weapon for a popular-democratic bloc which did not fully materialize.[15]

In general, however, the constitutive principles and ideals of the Filipino radical intelligentsia derived from 18th-century European bourgeois-democratic philosophy did not adequately orient Aguinaldo and his staff (with the exception of Mabini) to comprehend the logic of U.S. expansionism and the global tendencies of finance capital since the 1870s. Because such abstract notions as "progress" and "individual dignity" operated mainly within the idealist problematic of contestation with the Church's dogmatism and Spanish feudal absolutism, they were easily absorbed into the then-current U.S. discourse of "Manifest Destiny" and articulated within the temporal axis of "tutelage" where liberty and dignity became subsumed under the sovereign rule of property right.[16] It is also in this framework of an unceasing struggle for hegemony that the U.S. authorities could "rewrite or reanimate" the Rizalian texts, making them speak the refusal of violent resistance and the advocacy of passive learning for purely individual success. By incorporating the *ilustrado*, the organic intellectuals of the landlord/comprador classes, into the bureaucratic network, the U.S. colonial administration shifted from claiming mere passive consensus to inducing active consent, in the very same process destroying the effective resistance of intransigent partisans like Sakay, Salvador, Papa Isio, and others.[17]

We would argue then that U.S. colonial domination, while guaranteed by coercion--torture, reconcentration, etc.--should properly be interpreted as a protracted process of conquering hegemony (up to now!) through the daily reproduction of colonial relations of production, based on the then mainly feudal and semi-capitalist mode of production.[18] Such reproduction works through ideology (understood here in Althusser's definition as "a representation of the imaginary relationship of individuals to their real conditions of existence") and the various ideological state apparatuses (ISA), i.e. school, family, etc., whereby individuals are

construed as subjects denominated by gender, race, class, etc.--
decentered agents or bearers of class position, with their concrete
historical specificity.[19]

While for a whole generation of the elite beginning with Roxas
and Romulo,[20] the U.S. educational apparatus served as the most
active and efficient initiating/conditioning force, it is, I submit, the
multi-layered genealogical complex of apparatuses--rituals and
practices tied to school-church-family-profession--which generated
the contradictory subject positions of the Quezon-Osmena group,
the dialectical interaction between psychic drives and social
determinants and their accompanying signifying practices. Within a
neo-Gramscian problematic of the constitution of the subject, in
which hegemony emerges not from a simple confrontation of
antagonistic classes but from the overdetermined complex relations
of forces dispersed in the political, ideological and economic
instances, it might be instructive to consider briefly the case of
Quezon--more precisely, Quezon's subject position inscribed in his
autobiography.

PROBLEMATIZING THE OBVIOUS

Surely one of the most eloquent apologias for U.S. colonialism
and political weapons of the Filipino elite to justify continuing U.S.
intervention, *The Good Fight* (1946)[21] may be read symptomatically
as a myth; that is, an allegory of the ideological formation of the
Filipino bureaucratic elite. Beginning with interpellations posed by
his father, a sergeant in the Spanish infantry, his mother and
various priests and religious advisers-teachers, the first part of
Quezon's narrative concludes with his oath of obedience to his
father (the agent of reconciliation between Quezon's will
circumscribed by kinship status and secular authority) not to join
the Katipunan (p. 21). Later Quezon joins the revolution because
the "U.S. army had broken faith with my people" (p.41). Quezon
then proves that he is a "free subject," acting on his own, as he
shrewdly deals with bandits disguised as revolutionaries (pp. 61ff.);
and as he crosses enemy lines, deciding on his own to celebrate the
Christmas holiday in enemy-occupied Manila. After meeting the
captured Aguinaldo and recording his equivocal testimony, Quezon
(a product of Dominican institutions) launches into his legal career,
still a staunch believer in the Filipino right to self-determination
(p. 86). A series of encounters problematizes his commitment: he
befriends Governor Paras, Colonel Bandholtz, Judge Linebarger
(these two Americans' knowledge of Spanish endeared them to the
non-English-speaking Quezon), Colonel Harbord, and later
MacArthur. Appointed as prosecuting attorney of Mindoro (and
later Tayabas) by Taft, with the recommendation of Doctor Pardo
de Tavera, Quezon finds himself, especially after his victory in the
"Mason case," an independent subject, shorn of nationality or race,
identified as a "free" agent within the formal limits of the

colonial juridical system founded on generalized commodity exchange.

Gradually, interpellated by U.S. officials from President Theodore Roosevelt (p. 110) to Governor and Mrs. Stimson (pp. 146-47), Quezon's nationalist posture becomes precarious. The narrative allows Douglas MacArthur's patronizing voice to occupy a preeminent space (pp. 154-55) where U.S. responsibility for tutoring helpless and undeveloped Filipinos is affirmed. Quezon's "tutelage"--the shaping of his capacity to appropriate (more precisely, expropriate) the corpus of revolutionary experience and its moral vision, to repress its radical popular impulses and transcode them within the locus of reformist discourse--culminates in this revealing passage in the middle of *The Good Fight* where the twin phantoms of Rizal's mother and the captive Aguinaldo are invoked to legitimize the assumption of power by the landlord-comprador bloc and to imply that its corporatist demands need to be restrained (as evidenced, in Quezon's "social justice" slogan) for a national-popular collective will to crystallize. The speaking subject--an effect of representation--unleashes the power of metaphor in the evocation of Rizal's mother (the peasantry/autochtonous tradition) and Aguinaldo (the Law of the Father; emblem of continuity with the 1896 insurrection). These figures serve as nodes of condensation and rupture where the drives are harnessed to a symbolic/libidinal investment of the inaugural moment in which the oligarchy inscribes itself within a historic totality and universalizes its particular class-interest:

From the grandstand, I went through streets crowded with people acclaiming their first President, on to the Palace of Malacanan, the great mansion on the bank of the Pasig River which had been the seat of power of foreign rulers for many decades past. As I stepped out of the presidential car and walked over the marble floor of the entrance hall, and up the wide stairway, I remembered the legend of the mother of Rizal, the great Filipino martyr and hero, who went up those stairs on her knees to seek executive clemency from the cruel Spanish Governor-General Polavieja, that would save her son's life. This story had something to do with my reluctance to believe that capital punishment should ever be carried out. As a matter of fact, during my presidency, no man ever went to the electric chair. At the last moment I always stayed the hand of the executioner.

From the top of the stairs, turning to the right, one saw the very large reception hall, at the end of which on either side of the hall and fronting each other, there were two rooms which reminded me of my first visit to the palace in 1901.

In the room on the right side of the hall, there stood at that time General Arthur MacArthur, then Military Governor of the Philippines, and on the left, there was the room where Aguinaldo was kept as prisoner of war. The first thought which came to me was that I had been right in placing my faith in America, for by cooperating with her my people had won their local autonomy and were on the road to complete independence.

These thoughts were suddenly interrupted by my aide-de-camp who informed me that in the executive office there were waiting for me the general who was Chief of the Constabulary, and the provincial governors of Tayabas and Laguna, whom I had summoned to my first offical conference.

The night of the inauguration there was a reception and ball in Malacanan Palace in honor of the American officials, Secretary Dern, Vice-President Garner, the Speaker of the House of Representatives, and the Senators and Congressmen who constituted the Congressional Delegation. That same night, from every home in the Philippines, whether of the poor or of the rich, a prayer went to heaven for the continued greatness of America and the future safety of the Philippines (from *The Good Fight*, 1946, pp. 161-63).

Note Quezon's first order of business as President and Commander-in-Chief of the military, even as he asserts that rich and poor alike, both the property-owners and the dispossessed, are reconciled in a grand transcendental closure.

What cries out from between the interstices of the signifying chain are the excluded, insurgent voices of the masses--a cataclysmic silence which, by its very absence/presence, hollows and contours the totalizing mandate of the entire text. What rips the seemingly homogeneous, integral, self-sufficient fabric of the text may now be apprehended in such accounts as David Sturtevant's *Popular Uprisings in the Philippines 1840-1940* (1976) which includes the moving testimony of Salud Algabre, one of the leaders of the 1935 Sakdalista uprising (which the Quezon text has marginalized--but not quite).[22]

Quezon the individual thus traversed several stages before arriving at subject positionality: from the primitive economic moment in which he identifies himself as inheritor of his father's land, then to a political moment as lawyer/bureaucratic functionary, and finally to the moment of hegemonic consciousness (from his election as Tayabas governor, p. 104) when political, economic and intellectual objectives coalesce; when the purely corporatist limits of the landlord-comprador classes are transcended and sublimated into a universal, abstract form: independence. With Quezon's progression there also unfolded his extreme alienation from peasants and workers, especially with the growth of militant unions in the twenties, the founding of Abad Santos' Socialist Party in 1929 and the Communist Party in 1930, when antagonistic interpellations began to be addressed to the exploited, propertyless masses.

We can already perceive in Quezon's text the disseminated traces of a self-deconstructing "unconscious": for example, his allusion to "absentee landlordism" (p. 118); or the expedient intrusion of Governor Harrison in the middle of the narrative as a ventriloquist/authorial surrogate assigned to detailing "Executive Problems," chiefly tenancy unrest, the civilizing of the Moros, "banditry", etc.

EXEMPLUM OF THE DIALOGICAL

For the maintenance and reproduction of subject positionality of the Filipino elite, it seems, one needs the ideology of white/West supremacy (especially now when the technocratic ethos of "development" is plotted and coordinated from Washington): an ideology consisting of representations of sex, race, class which are always-already inscribed in the material practices vividly transcribed in the Quezon text. To interrogate further that text and make its silence articulate, we can juxtapose by contrast the first ninety pages of Carlos Bulosan's family chronicle *America Is in the Heart* (1943) which spans the period from 1913 to 1930, in particular Chapter VIII. There the narrator describes the 1931 Tayug uprising from the perspective of a 12-year-old peasant boy harvesting rice with his sister and his nursing mother, after the family was dispossessed of their meager land by usurers and landgrabbers and the father reduced by a mystifying bureaucracy to impotent drunken stupor:

> The land question in Luzon was becoming more acute, and there were rumors of uprisings in the provinces where absentee landordism was crippling the peasant economy. Rice was the main staple and the peasants could not exist without it, but the rich rice lands were owned by men who never saw them. Each year the landlords demanded a larger share, until it became impossible for the peasants to live.
>
> It was at this time that my father's land was taken away from him. A stubborn peasant like his ancestors before him, my father had always believed that life should be rooted in the soil. He sold our animals and came to town, and after a day of secret deliberation with my mother he went to Lingayen to fight in the provincial court for the restoration of our farm.
>
> After three weeks my father returned, defeated and broken in spirit. He has walked to the capital of Pangasinan carrying his sack of provisions and when he arrived there had had great difficulty in locating the proper court in which to present his case. When he found the court he could not locate the right people. He went from one clerk to another and from one room to another, pleading in his dialect and cursing his illiteracy, until he had ransacked the entire provincial capital.
>
> He had no money and the wise men at the court spoke to

him in Spanish and English. What could a poor and ignorant peasant like my father do in an organization such as the provincial government of Pangasinan? He came back and stayed on in town, sitting around in the house until he was driven to drunkenness.

My mother and I went to the town of Tayug, a rich rice land, and helped in the harvest. Tayug and two other neighboring towns belonged to one family. One could see the flowing expanse of gold in the month of October, but in November and far into the month of January there was a continuous procession of carts hauling harvested rice to the granaries of the landlord. There it was threshed and sold to the rice companies in Manila.

Then my mother went to Binalonan and returned with my sisters. Francisca was now nearly four years old, but Marcela was only a baby. They sat in the shade of the umbrella at the end of the long rows, away from the strong sun. My mother stopped now and then to feed Marcela, undoing her rough cotton blouse to her waist and putting her dark, pointed nipple into the baby's hungry mouth. Then she would put her in a makeshift hammock and go back to work.

Francisca was already beginning to be aware of what we were doing. She stayed in the shade watching Marcela, but she came now and then to where we were working to bring us a jar of cool drinking water. Then she would watch over the baby until the day's work was done, singing when Marcela became restless and hungry.

In the middle of the season strange men began coming to the rice fields. They distributed leaflets and talked to us. My mother and I were so deeply absorbed in our work that we were not aware of what was going on. A rugged peasant boy made impassioned speeches to the harvesters, but as he was only a simple peasant like themselves they paid no attention to him.

I remember this fanatical peasant boy because years afterward I met him again in America. His name was Felix Razon. One day he came to the field where we were working with several men wearing black armbands. They told us to leave, but we did not understand.

At night we slept in the field. The stars were so near it seemed we could touch them with our hands. Sometimes when I awakened between the tall rice stalks, I could feel the soft breathing of the earth. The sun came like gold, throwing its first beams downward into the immense plain. It lighted a new day of activity for us, and we cooked our breakfast on an improvised stove.

Working with my mother was pleasant, and it gave me an impetus to strive for a better place. It was actually like working with my father in Mangusmana, with only one difference: I was a little older and more experienced. In the village, life was a simple peasant lullaby; we had our animals and our house. In Tayug the work was harder and harsher, and the people were more varied. And I had two little sisters who interrupted our work with delight.

A few days later Felix and the other men came to the rice fields again to persuade us to sell our shares of rice and to leave. Most of the harvesters sold theirs, but my mother sold only a part of ours. We were some distance from the highway when we saw hundreds of men with black armbands walking excitedly toward the town. They were members of the Colorum Party, a fanatical organization of dispossessed peasants that terrorized Luzon. It professed to be semi-religious, but it was actually a vengeful sect of anarchistic men led by a college-bred peasant who had become embittered in the United States.

As soon as Felix came to our part of the field and told us of the impending revolt, my mother tied our share of rice with a rope and carried some of the rice bundles on her head. I carried some of it, too. But she also carried the baby Marcela. Francisca, however, refused to be carried. When we reached the plaza we saw many of the Colorum at the kiosk, falling in line and preparing their attack. The policemen were running excitedly about the *presidencia*, piling bricks and sandbags outside the windows and doors. They were waiting, ready with their guns.

Then from beyond the *presidencia*, climbing up the river bank like a stream of black beetles, the Colorum came rushing upon the building, dispersing the few guards who were waiting outside with their antiquated pistols. They fired into the air and leaped behind trees when the police challenged them from behind the barricaded windows.

The *caromata* ponies at the station started running away in all directions. The bus that was discharging passengers near the schoolhouse turned around and sped toward Binalonan. The attacking band of the Colorum increased; they appeared from everywhere with their black flag and fired upon the men in the *presidencia*.

My mother grabbed Francisca, and we ran to the tall bushes by the roadside.

"Why are they fighting, Mother?" I asked.

"Why son?" she said, her ignorant face searching for the word to answer me. "Why? I don't know, son."

"Are we not coming back to cut some more rice?" I asked.

"No son," she said.

Francisca started to cry, hanging on my mother's skirt.

"Hush," said my mother.

We looked toward the *presidencia*. A policemen came out bravely, but he had not gone far when he was shot in the back. He fell under a flagpole. Another policeman arrived, then another; but five of the Colorum ran after them, shooting as they emerged in hand-to-hand fighting behind the coffee shop at the station. The Colorum rushed into the *presidencia* and after a while their flag appeared at the window. Then there was a respite; except for the jubilant rebels who were pouring into the town hall, the town was deserted. The dead were scattered on the lawn and in the street.

When it began to get dark my mother told us to follow her. We crept through the bushes, dragging the bundles of rice. We came to a wooded place west of town, away from the rice fields. We stopped and looked back. Then the guns began again, sputtering like a speeding motorcycle. The black flag was no longer atop the *presidencia*.

I saw a mass of men scattering at random, running into the bushes in the plaza and firing. Then the Philippine and American flags appeared on the poles in front of the town hall. The night came on and there was silence.

We walked to Binalonan silently, looking up when a *caromata* came by. I carried Francisca on my shoulders; sometimes my mother gave the baby to me, and she carried Francisca. We met a detachment of the Philippine constabulary rushing toward Tayug.

When we arrived in Binalonan the news of the uprising was already there, and our neighbors assailed us with many questions; but we could not explain the incident. Eagerly we awaited developments: during four days of unrest the local government of Tayug had changed hands several times a day. Finally, the constabulary conquered the rebels and restored law and order.

But the revolt in Tayug made me aware of the circumscribed life of the peasants through my brother Luciano, who explained its significance to me. I was determined to leave that environment and all its crushing forces, and if I were successful in escaping unscathed, I would go back someday to understand what it meant to be born of the peasantry. I would go back because I was a part of it, because I could not really escape from it no matter where I went or what became of me. I would go back to give significance to all that was starved and thwarted in my life.

As against the primacy of the Symbolic Order (the Law of the Father) upheld by the Quezon text, Bulosan counterpoints the semiotic excess of folk ribaldry, the subversive illogic of carnivalesque Otherness: the dream, adventure, utopian hope and desire incarnated in so many mother/virgin figures attending his quest for a primordial and elusive totality disrupted by the defeat of the revolution, that organic wholeness of which he finds himself deprived at birth.[24]

TERRORISM OF THE BUREAUCRATIC CONSENSUS

To seize and map out that totality is the obsessive aim and task of most Filipinologists, but practically the majority are victimized by the naive, uncritical acceptance of the self-serving assumptions and representations of their discipline--assuming that their subjects/objects of study are still Quezon, Osmena, Romulo, their heirs and epigones; and their self-appointed vocation the vindication of McKinley and Taft. But neither Taft nor Quezon is to blame, according to our experts; for our backward, dependent or "transitional" society labors under the pall of a stubborn fact: the bilateral kinship system, the extended family structure.[25] That is the matrix of a particularistic, supposedly fragmented value-system which aborts the wished-for emergence of a full-blown competitive/acquisitive modern society. Allow me to quote from an impeccable source, a pamphlet entitled *Towards the Restructuring of Filipino Values* (1972) published by the Office of Civil Relations, Philippine Army (under Undersecretary of Home Defense Jose Crisol), with the assistance of professors from Ateneo and the University of the Philippines: the Filipino value-system--*hiya*, *pakikisama*, *utang-na-loob*, etc.--begets "family individualism" and an incommensurably "degenerate social life." What the New Society strives to realize is "an expansion of the family to a larger group--the country. Every Filipino should be able to develop a feeling of belonging to one big family--the country where the President is the father and all the citizens his children."[26]

Unintentionally inverting Freud's thesis in *Moses and Monotheism*, the Marcos propagandists would like to bypass the sublimation of the normative work-ethic, latch on to the "spontaneous mechanisms of kinship reciprocity," and finally install a Confucian/Shintoist dispensation! What is demanded is the conversion of the whole nation into one monolithic family managed by one central authority (guess who?), a scenario which does not deviate too far from the prescriptions for a pragmatic, managerial or "preventive" politics of Modernization/Developmentalism theory and its insistent privileging of equilibrium, harmony of interests, order.[27]

It is unfair, of course, to seriously treat this Army pamphlet as a "hegemonic" document on a par with *The Good Fight*. But its scholarly provenance implicates the hegemonic U.S. theorizing premised on Cold War end-of-ideology pluralism, the mystique of civility and consensus, etc. It reflects, to be sure, the prevailing consensus generated by the logic of formalist reification: the existence of the family as an isolated, static institution, not the semi-feudal and dependent relations of production, together with the inequitable stratification of groups with differential access to ownership and control of resources--it's the extended family that explains socio-economic backwardness, accelerating impoverishment of the masses, and concomitant state repression.[28]

Unable to co-opt an always residual and emergent nationalism which would connect the individual to a social totality still accessible to politicians like Quezon because of his organic link with the 1898 revolution, the Marcos regime's attempt to articulate the theme of "One Spirit, One Nation" seeks to do the impossible: to superimpose by fiat the authoritarian family nexus onto the domain of atomized individuals--an aggregation of entrepreneurs calculating means-ends in an irrational market, all somehow beholden to the whims of a charismatic Super-Father! Perhaps such a goal, now relentlessly implemented through the mass media, barangay youth, etc., is bound to founder on the very foundations on which it paradoxically depends: the semi-feudal and dependent political economy.

Especially today when you have an export-led industrialization program dictated by transnational corporations wreaking havoc on people's livelihood and human rights; when you have the IMF/World Bank imposing austerity (devaluation, cutbacks in social services, etc.); when one-half of all families subsist below the poverty line, and the majority are excluded from effective participation in the fundamental decision-making processes, it is a thoroughly "ideological" gesture for any analyst to encapsulate the Filipino "value-system," which in itself incessantly registers and engenders conflicts, in a sphere completely autonomous from the political and economic instances. We don't have to be economic determinists or vulgar reductionists to discern how authoritarian discourse, mediated through the family, school, media, etc., constructs the Filipino into a subject whose main function is to serve the end of capital accumulation for transnational corporations and their local partners by conforming to the hierarchical, unquestioned law of the status quo. To test this, we need only counterpose to any palace decree the oppositional praxis of the Catholic Bishops' recent Pastoral Letter, or that of Senator Diokno in the proscribed 1982 BBC film *To Sing Our Song.*[29]

Nineteen years ago, George Taylor, in his book *The Philippines and the United States* (1964), ventured the opinion that the "overriding problem of Philippine democracy is the tension between the democratic political institutions and the traditional value system" (p.154).[30] Taylor was writing in the milieu inhabited by Modernization theorists like Huntington, Pye, and Almond, whose model and implied agenda (now modified after Vietnam), claiming to be value-free and scientific, occludes the substantive conflict between the direct producers of value (peasants, workers, etc.) and the parasitic minority in Third World formations. These theorists reduce the contradictory space of interdiscourse into a simplified "tradition-versus-modernity" syndrome. Like the Filipino *ilustrados* who collaborated with Taft, Filipino technocrats prove ready consumers of Modernization theory, employing in their practice its archetypal technique of converting class/gender/race contradictions into simple difference.

In *Reproduction in Education, Society and Culture* (1977), Pierre Bourdieu and Jean-Claude Passeron aptly suggest the axiomatic principle in the sociology of knowledge: any dominant class exerts symbolic violence by imposing "meanings" (culturally arbitrary); it imposes "them as legitimate by concealing the power relations which are the basis of its force," and in the process "adds its own specifically symbolic force to those power relations."[31] Ignoring this, Filipino social scientists indulge in what amounts to a pseudo-scientific and banal subjectivism which betrays its hidden if unacknowledged complicity with force and fraud. I note one example: a widely used textbook, *The Filipino Family*, authored by Dr. F. Jocano and Dr. Paz Mendez, after describing current rural practices surrounding conception and pregnancy, slides easily into recommendations on how to effectively implement government programs like "green revolution," "miracle rice production," and "population control" (pp. 87-89).[32]

Any further inquiry into this scarcely explored area of the reproduction of past/present social relations in the Philippines needs to theorize more rigorously those ethical, juridical and political concepts which, articulated within specific historical conjunctures, subsume and exceed speculations on aberrant personal or group motivations, enable a multi-sided dialectical suturing of structural determinations and lived experience (Gramsci's "common sense"). Such an inquiry is, of course, always situated and embedded in a configuration or terrain criss-crossed by struggles of resistance and oppression, subjugation and emancipation.

I conclude with two notations: during the debate over the Hare-Hawes-Cutting Act, Quezon declared that he "strenuously and definitely opposed the retention of military establishments. . . . for it destroyed the very essence of independent existence for the Philippines."[33] When Rizal travelled through the United States in 1888, he witnessed the practice of racism against blacks, Asians, etc. and summed up his impression: "America is the land *par excellence* of freedom but only for the whites.[34] Earlier, when his ship carrying 643 Chinese coolies docked in San Francisco, it was immediately quarantined for alleged health reasons; but contrary to quarantine regulations, Rizal noted in his diary, 700 bales of precious Chinese silk were promptly unloaded without fumigation.

Could it be that, in these instances, both Quezon and Rizal sorely lacked *utang na loob* (psychic debt), *hiya* (shame), and *pakikisama* (smooth interpersonal relations)?[35]

IV

Understanding the Moro People's Struggle: Articulations of Islam, Community, Nation

And we were minded to show favor to those who were brought low in the land, and to make them spiritual chiefs, and to make them heirs.

Qur' an, 28:5

No nation can be free if it oppresses other nations.

Karl Marx

O you poor fellah. You break the heart of the earth in order to draw sustenance from it and support your family. Why do you not break the heart of your oppressor? Why do you not break the heart of those who eat the fruit of your labor?

Jamal al-din al-Afghani

In one of the latest Orientalizing performances by noted Filipinist Professor David Joel Steinberg, *The Philippines: A Singular and A Plural Place* (1983), we encounter a standard formulation of the "Moro problem" which incorporates key rules and procedures for the codification of Philippine realities spanning the range from those treated by Joseph Hayden and Peter Gowing to modernization themes of "New Society" apologists.[1] This passage from Steinberg exemplifies the style of more recent revisionist liberalism which one also finds in historians like Theodore Friend and Peter Stanley:

The U.S. colonial administrators saw the massive and virtually unpopulated island of Mindanao as the Philippine frontier. . . . Offering the carrot of religious protection and respect for Muslim traditions and wielding the stick of U.S. military might, they subjugated the five major Muslim groups. Through legislation, based on U.S. models, they created a homesteading and land policy that was designed to encourage especially the landless peasants of the north to migrate to Mindanao. Since apparently there was an excess of land and since many of the Muslims were hill people practicing slash-and-burn agriculture, this land policy went forward for decades without being aggressively challenged by the Muslims. The establishment of the great Del Monte pineapple plantations in northern Mindanao and the economic investment sparked by prewar Japan in Davao accelerated the changes that occurred in Mindanao. This vast island was integrated into the economic system of the archipelago and was brought forward fairly rapidly (75-76).

Apart from obvious question-begging generalizations and distortions of facts, e.g. "the Muslims were hill people practicing slash-and-burn agriculture," and the alleged lack of protest to the privatization of public land by resettlement,[2] we can observe three major discursive tactics of Western thought in demonstrating its will to dominate: first, it establishes the temporal and hierarchical (logical) priority of Western experience in solving frontier-problems; second, U.S. reformist liberalism asserts a homogeneous, solid but flexible determination which coincides with the march of history; and, third, after marginalizing the natives and reducing them to objects of bureaucratic manipulation, this totalizing project of U.S. rationality culminating in "the great Del Monte plantations" accords with nature, tradition, and human desire. No wonder that in the last chapter of his book, when Steinberg employs his analytic technique to divide the Muslims into hardliners and moderates, the pose of liberal sympathy for the Muslims' plight engenders a binary opposition between the MNLF's (Moro National Liberation Front) "terrorism" and the government's "massive expenditures of money in offering economic incentives to individuals" and "the reallocation of development pesos." None of the MNLF's strategic political claims are cited, whereas the government's Cotabato-Agusan River Basin Development Program is described as appealing to every kind right-thinking person, thus making Marcos into a fabulous development wizard with the good of all the Filipino masses (including the Muslims, of course) at heart.

Practically all the written commentaries on the conflict between the authoritarian regime and the MNLF which I've read are generated from that theoretical matrix and repertoire of Orientalizing discourse embedded in functionalist sociological analyses and its counterpart in journalistic narratives.[3] But not only Anglo-Saxon Filipinists adopt, elaborate and purvey this mode of conceptualizing reality; so do Filipino intellectuals whose Western indoctrination, despite their progressive motives, inevitably victimize them into rejecting the Bangsa Moro people's cry for self-determination and thus legitimizing the dictatorship's draconian policies. For example, anti-Marcos politician Jovito Salonga, in a public lecture (April 1977) during the Tripoli negotiations, denied the Moro people's right to secession because "we cannot agree to the dismemberment of Philippine territory." Who is this "we" Salonga refers to? Afflicted with historical amnesia and chauvinist supererogation, Salonga justifies this denial on the principle that "the common good of the entire country demands the preservation of our entire territory and resources"--a purely economistic/legalist argument. [4]

THE CRISIS OF REPRESENTATION

My aim here is to try to outline the alternative hegemonic articulation (the political intervention) offered by the MNLF to replace the present historic bloc's ascendancy. From a historical materialist perspective, the Moro people's striving to affirm their national identity is basically a broad democratic movement, a recuperation of popular sovereignty as the substance of ethico-political self-determination.

The Moro people's revolution occurs today on two dialectically interacting levels which characterize its concrete historical specificity: first, an anti-fascist democratic resistance of the Muslim community to an authoritarian dependent state based on the hegemony of an unstable bloc (military, comprador, technocratic factions), and its affirmation of the right to repossess the homeland; and second, an anti-imperialist assault on the center, U.S. monopoly capitalism, as represented directly by transnational corporations (since 1919) and indirectly by the U.S. government's military, economic and political assistance to the mediating instrumentality of the Marcos state apparatuses (army, courts, etc.). What is needed is to delineate the field of political and economic practices constituting the site of struggle, not just the actual physical territory in dispute (44,094 square miles and 8 million people) but the identification of productive forces and the social relations--that is, the total social formation--that will define the meaning of the past and the trajectory of the present within a polarized world-system where two paths of Third World development--the capitalist/statist and the socialist--are fiercely competing. Nur Misuari, in a speech to the International Congress on Cultural Imperialism in October 1977, situated the MNLF's challenge within the contemporary "global colonial reality," with "U.S. imperialist hegemony" as the decisive presence, although Marcos' "Filipino colonialism" serves as the immediate target together with its colonial culture, "fundamentally a reflection of

Western Christian civilization--inherited from Spanish and American colonialism."[5]

While I think Misuari hypostasizes unduly the notion of a Filipino culture, a rhetorical move intelligible in its local context, it may be useful to stress that given the alignment of forces and the objective circumstances, the principal contradiction the MNLF focuses on is between the Moro people's freedom and survival as a distinct historic community and the virtually genocidal administrative-military offensive of the neo-colonial state. This contradiction hinges on two inter-related aspects, as enunciated in the MNLF Manifesto (April 1974) establishing the Bangsa Moro Republik: re-appropriation of the alienated territory from the usurpers, and the defense/preservation of the Islamic community (the *umma*). Inscribed in this same document is the mark of an absence, the lack of any allusion to U.S. imperialism--a silence or gap which is, however, immediately corrected by the invocation to the world community of believers (*dar ul-Islam*), thus internationalizing the struggle. On the other hand, the MNLF spokesman at the Permanent People's Tribunal in Oct/Nov. 1980, in presenting its case for self-determination, strikingly omits any reference to Islam and, by foregrounding historic testimonies to the *de facto* existence of a Moro state (the Sulu sultanate, in particular) by the U.S. Government (Bates Treaty, etc.), brings to our attention the "unjust and illegal" invasion and occupation of the homeland by "Philippine colonialism."

Any inquiry attempting to elucidate the complex nexus of practices imbricated in the MNLF's political project will have to confront the fact that this project operates beyond class-reductionism. The self-determination principle subsumes the class into an ideological interpellation fusing the religious and the communal/spatial instances, so that in shifting the locus of antagonism away from the traditional productivist scheme, the present situation requires the need to grasp the dialectics of class, religion, and nation within the conjuncture of a hegemonic versus counter-hegemonic process.

What I would like to propose here is a thesis that may be obvious to everyone. At stake is the answer to the crucial question: who will represent the Moro people? With the crisis of the present hegemonic system of representation felt or experienced not just by the Moros but by the working masses, the Moro as an object constructed by imperialist/capitalist discourse and by the whole range of subordinating practices catalogued by most studies, has dissolved--opening up a space for the MNLF's intervention, whose singular project is precisely the construction of an alternative or counter-hegemonic discourse (complex of practices) that would define the Moro as a historical autonomous subject or revolutionary agency. As noted above, the Moro popular struggle is highly overdetermined so that, contrary to classical Marxism, the subjectivities of the Moro people cannot be reduced simply to class determination--the economistic or essentialist logic of identity--although one may claim that the majority of their interests, in the last analysis, are constituted on the terrain of production relations. If so, then the MNLF should merge with the National Democratic Front and be subsumed in its program. Such a subsumption would simply replicate the very situation the MNLF is endeavoring to contest and displace: the unitary or homogenizing articulation of irreducible differences which converts the Moro and everyone else into juridically free abstract citizens--in daily practice, labor-power for capitalist exploitation. Ultimately, it is not perhaps a question of representation but of the inauguration of a new differential subject-position, the enactment of political struggle to articulate an irreducible Other hitherto denied substantive and effective transforming presence within the existing Philippine polity.[6]

NARRATING WHAT RETURNS

Why is the ideological instance primary in the Moro social formation? A brief historical excursus is warranted here.

From the middle of the 15th century up to the military conquest of Mindanao and Sulu by American forces, the Moro sultanate (Sulu, Maguindanao) evolved as segmentary states, more precisely tributary formations in which lineage or kinship interfaced with more elaborate and partly centralized organizations for production and defense. By "tributary formation" (following Samir Amin) is meant a stage of social development whose mode of production is characterized by extraction of the surplus product by the exploiting class by non-economic means, through the agency of the superstructure (religious ideology); and where the essential organization of production is based on use-value, not exchange-value.[7] With an economy comprised of primitive agriculture using slaves and other servile hands, minimal gathering and hunting/fishing activities, and a flourishing commerce, the *datus* (local chieftains) enforced their rule through the superstructure (kinship, personal attributes, religious ritual) and through violence operating within the parameters of consent.[8] The *datus'* extraction of surplus as tribute/tithes was legitimized by customary law (*adat*) and tradition (*tabiat*) mediated by the *ulama*.[9] It is precisely in this tributary mode where ideology, in this case Islam, assumes the dominant instance, sanctioning obedience and loyalty to the sultan or *datu* as the embodiment of a transcendental authority which unites and consolidates the assembly of the faithful. It may be suggested that the cohesion or solidarity represented by the sultanates really depends on the communal ownership of land in a relatively autarchic economy. Where this state is able to centralize the surplus product in waging a self-defensive war, then the sense of a Moro totality emerges encapsulated within a corporative self-interpretation of Islamic believers.

What the series of persistent Spanish campaigns of conquest (from 1578 to 1876) did, apart from disrupting the Moros' vital commercial transactions with the region, decimating the inhabitants, depleting local resources, etc., was to reinforce the sultanates' exercise of centralized authority. And even though the Spaniards tried to exploit the disputes that existed within the tenuous alliances of *datus*, it was precisely the external threat of *Pax Hispanica* that defused those schisms, suspended whatever internal dissensions simmered or flared up between *datus* and producers, and forged the political-moral unity of the Moro peoples, their proud spirit of independence and self-conscious determination to preserve their collective identity.

By the end of Spanish domination in 1898, the Moro people had reached the tributary stage of state-formation differentiated from others by cultural commonalities, with religious ideology cementing civil and political societies, occupying a continuous and well-defined territory. Its centralized political system exercised a monopoly of the means of coercion in its territory, even though it was uneven and fluctuating. But the self-consciousness of the Bangsa Moro peoples (sublating the ethnic disparities among Tausugs, Maranaos, Maguindanaos, etc.), the MNLF's discourse of self-determination, could not and did not emerge until that state-formation was disrupted by U.S. finance capital and finally nullified by the neo-colonial state.

What the entire period of U.S. occupation of the Moro homeland achieved was to irreversibly erode and quarantine the hegemonic sway of the *datu*/sultanate hierarchy, thereby dispersing the symbolic condensation of Islam in the political institutions. After the abrogation of the deceptive Bates Treaty of 1899 in 1904, the U.S. drastically curtailed the politico-juridical and bureaucratic institutions of the sultanate.[10] Colonial capitalism being indifferent to religious practices provided they didn't interfere with surplus-value extraction, the U.S. objectives of exporting raw materials and opening up markets and investment opportunities were all accomplished without any prior radical re-structuring of the *datu* (or, for the Christianized natives, the *principalia*) system. In the annihilation campaigns at Bud Dajo (1906) and Bud Bagsak (1913), the U.S. used Muslims as part of the infantry. U.S. tactics of bribery, cooptation and force may account for Sultan Kiram's collaboration with the U.S. in the killing of the rebellious Panglima Hassan and Datu Piang's betrayal of Datu Ali's revolt in 1903. Like other *datus* in the Commonwealth and the Republic, Datu Piang welcomed resettlement programs, commercial agriculture, corporate plantations, and military control. Originating from the merchant class, Datu Piang's career, distinguished by shrewd business opportunism, epitomizes the rapid decay of the ancient charisma-laden *datu* system.[11]

With the United States' conquest of the Moro homeland and its integration into a world-system of commodity production and exchange, an unequal division of social labor dictated by the metropolitan power's need for capital accumulation through markets and "free trade," the whole Moroland economy was severely disarticulated. The organization of Moro living-space became oriented to the needs and imperatives of the industrial metropolis, and secondarily to those of the Filipino elite. I need not recount here the long unmitigated experience of land dispossession, discrimination, and exploitation suffered by the Moro people from 1898 to the present, sufferings attributed by the Moros not to the Americans but to the Christian-Filipino as perpetrators. Hence the 1935 Manifesto can be construed as a symptom that thirty-five years (since the termination of Spanish rule) was not enough to erase the historical memory; and that the religious/cultural sphere still functioned as the locus of antagonism. Given the low level of development of productive forces--subsistence farming, petty commodity production, illiteracy, minimal employment in the export-oriented capitalist sector--internal class differentiation was not critical enough to occlude or neutralize Filipino Christian-Moro contradictions. With merchant capital mainly controlled by the Chinese and peasants confined to clan subsistence outside the surplus-generating market, the social relations of an incomplete tributary formation reproduced themselves, buttressed by the pressure of Filipino-Christian distrust and coercion. Whatever internal differences existed within the Moro nation, were displaced by the perception of a greater, more imminent threat: disintegration and extinction as an Islamic community.

RE-INVENTING SOCIETY

In the Western paradigm of nation-state building, the middle class (merchants, entrepreneurs, etc.) is privileged as the revolutionary agency whose self-fulfillment implies systemic political and economic changes, so that the nation-state's emergence coincides with the rise and consolidation of the capitalist mode of production. Such a paradigm is completely useless in understanding the growth of the Bangsa Moro nation whose Islamic and popular (peasants, workers, intelligentsia) foundation supports not a nascent independent captialism but a collective moral vision and will to preserve an ethos of resistance. Bound not by common property interests but by a long deeply-rooted experience of political, moral and military resistance against imperialism, articulated as a dispossessed Islamic community, the Bangsa Moro nation is a product of historic struggles to assert its autonomous identity. Because the political mobilization of the Moro people today in order to reclaim their homeland and restore their sovereignty is motivated not by liberal reformist plans of economic growth but by a revolutionary pur-suit of political independence, economic sufficiency and territorial integrity, it can no longer be led by the *datus*--even though the first public manifestation of its long-germinating independence movement (attributed to Datu Udtog Matalam) was a spontaneous reaction to the March 1968 disclosure of the Jabidah massacre--for, as I've stated earlier, the datu-system has been reified or commodified by its clientelist status and is now an antiquarian curiosity. In the site of this irrevocable rupture, the MNLF is born.

While class and ethnic interpellation of the Moros by U.S. and local capital can be argued as the ultimate or underlying stratum of their exploitation, the self-interpretation of the Moros from the time of the revolts of Datu Ali and Datu Mampurok up to Abdulmajid Panoniongan and Hadji Kamlon in the fifties elicits a subject or positionality defined by what is more than a purely religious/empirical interpellation. In the 1974 Manifesto founding the Bangsa Moro Republic, a month after the destruction of Jolo City, Misuari targetted "Filipino colonialism" which threatened Islam "through wholesale destruction and desecration of its places of worship and its Holy Book"; and reiterated the MNLF's commitment to "the preservation and growth of Islamic culture. . . . "[12] I submit that "Islam" in such discourse operates as an overdetermined signifier, a symbol that connotes more than all its empirical referents and therefore cannot be simply equated with the usual anthropological inventory of folk-Islam customs, etc. What "Islam" performs as a code-word or political signifier in MNLF's project of articulating a hegemonic discourse is the choice and mapping of the terrain of a new society, expressing the ramified grievances of various Muslim classes against the regime (the democratic position) and condensing their multiple impulses into the symbolic unity (the popular position) of the Bangsa Moro nation irreconcilably opposed to the neo-colonial state. "Islam" then coalesces the religious, communal and spatial dimensions of the MNLF project.[13]

In this context, one might add that territory--the Moro homeland never really conquered by Spanish evangelists or American and Filipino invaders--becomes charged with intense symbolic value over and above its function as a factor in production.[14]

In the orthodox Marxist tradition, it has been axiomatic for all revolutionary socialists to unequivocally support the right of all nations to self-determination (which includes the right to secede). Lenin pointed out that the question of self-determination "belongs wholly and exclusively to the sphere of political democracy," of the right of political secession and the establishment of a sovereign nation-state, not just an autonomous federated state.[15] Only if the workers' movement in the oppressor (Filipino/U.S) nation recognizes this right--as the NDF does--can the hostility and suspicion of the oppressed Moros (nourished by decades of discrimination and oppression) be dispelled, creating the conditions for voluntary union.[16] In consonance with the strictly political emphasis of Lenin, the MNLF claims the "sole prerogative of defining and chartering our national destiny in accordance with our own free will," which is being negated by "the terror, oppression and tyranny of Filipino colonialism." Number 4 of the Manifesto commits the MNLF to "a democratic system of government which shall never allow or tolerate any form of exploitation and oppression of any human being or of one nation by another."[17]

Lest I be misinterpreted as equating MNLF discourse with Marxist-Leninist reflections, I hasten to add that as a supplement to Misuari's "culturalist" thesis mentioned earlier (which echoes that of thinkers like Rosa Luxemburg and Otto Bauer, but departs from the rigid and arbitrary definition of the nation promulgated by Stalin), we should locate the subjective element (national self-consciousness) in the concept of the nation within the totality of production-relations which, in the last analysis, circumscribes but does not wholly determine its potential. (I might interject here that the "subjective" element is as materialist as any kind of social practice or work.) Within this framework, one can understand the emergence of the subjective or conscious forces, the MNLF.

DEMYSTIFICATION

It should be clear, at this juncture, that in order to appreciate the unprecedented historic specificity of the Moro revolution--an anti-colonial strategy of overthrowing U.S. imperialism and its peripheral client--we should abandon West-centered paradigms and theorize the concrete historical conditions. However, it might be useful to adapt the insights and innovations reaped from other comparable Third World struggles. In this regard, I think the most seminal source would be Amilcar Cabral's view that in the context of the imperialist disruption of the colonized people's history, what is necessary is to transvaluate our problematic in order to register more accurately the changed historical realities. For Cabral, then, "the level of productive force is the true and permanent driving power of history." Integral to this "productive force" is the "revolutionary vanguard"--a Leninist imperative--that would sum up the historic experience of its people and concentrate/coordinate its spontaneous revolts in the process of organizing popular-democratic institutions at the grassroots, the nascent formation to which it (as the political directive force) provides impetus and orientation. Integrated with the masses, this leadership (drawn from various classes) would articulate "a national consciousness" (but not petty-bourgeois "nationalism", as Fanon reminds us) indivisible from the material practices--political, cultural, military, etc. which, in the case of the Moro people, distinguish and differentiate them from Christian Filipinos.[18] These evolving practices and their dynamics form the counter-hegemonic strategy capable of mobilizing the widest popular bloc, as indicated by Asani's statement in the 1980 Tribunal brief: "Considering the specific condition of our people which is principally composed of rural toiling masses, the Bangsa Moro Revolution and the MNLF adopt the strategy of mass mobilization which gives primacy to the role of the peasants uniting with urban workers, intelligentsia, small merchants and artisans as well as civil servants who have been forced to eke out a living under the colonial bureaucracy."[19]

In a recent paper presented to the Philippine Studies Conference on 3 August 1984 at the University of Michigan, Ann Arbor, Asani summed up decades of MNLF praxis, i.e. the wide-ranging spontaneous and/or organized self-activism of diverse villages, communities, groups condensing the theoretical plottings of MNLF programmatic discourses. I quote him at length:

Already, some factors serving to strengthen the belief in ultimate victory are evident. *Firstly,* an organization institutionalizing the revolutionary structure has been firmly established, vertically from the leadership at the national level down to the rank and file in the village. Today, this structure has, to all intents and purposes, the appearance of a *de facto* government functioning as committee at every level, openly in those areas under effective control of the MNLF while still covertly in the cities and other areas under enemy control. *Secondly,* the mobilization of the masses for support of the Revolution has been more successful than otherwise expected. This is reflected not only in their actual participation in political and military affairs in the field but in the support, albeit secretly, manifested by those even in the service of the regime or claimed by it to "have returned to the fold of the law." *Thirdly,* the creation of the Bangsamoro Army (BMA), military wing of the MNLF. This army of disciplined, well-trained and brave young men have been responsible for liberating vast portions of the homeland, especially the contryside, from enemy occupation. They protect the gains of the Revolution and expand their area of operations. Their resilience is already tested even in the face of adverse conditions. And, *fourthly,* unlike in the past when the struggle has been isolated, today international sympathy and support have been pouring in not only from Muslim countries and organizations but non-Muslim as well the world over. For one thing, the MNLF has been recognized by the Islamic Conference as the sole legitimate representative of the Bangsamoro people and conferred the status of an observer. The prestigious International People's Tribunal which convened at Antwerp (Belgium) on October 29-November 3, 1980, for the trial of the Marcos regime *in absentia,* acknowledged the Bangsamoro people's right to self-determination.[20]

In his 1980 paper, "The Politics of Becoming: The Mindanao Conflict in a World-System Perspective," Robert Stauffer has incisively delineated the linkage-mechanisms between the Marcos development strategy for Mindanao and the U.S. What I would take exception to are: first, Stauffer's largely economistic position which defeatistly predicts the futility of all national-liberation struggles to escape from the capitalist world-economy, thus rejecting the Leninist argument, the MNLF, etc.; and, second, corollary to the first, Stauffer's blindness to the politico-ethical originality of the MNLF project stemming from his dismissal of the Moro people's history and of the rich revolutionary tradition of Islam; from his lack of genuine faith that the Moro people can create new alternative institutions in accord with their needs and aspirations--an ironic stance for a progressive social scientist whose belief in historical becoming should valorize precisely the history-making initiatives and achievements of the MNLF.

Like practically all commentators, Stauffer concurs with the general support for the justness of the MNLF's cause.[21] Whatever the iron-clad laws of commodity circulation the Wallersteinian model might care to enforce, we can suggest that the goal of secession and sovereign control over a definite territory is functionally justified, as the Yugoslavian Marxist Kardelj explains, in order "to enable people to successfully vindicate their claim to an appropriate portion of the social surplus, within an area that is determined by the social division of labor."[22] Of course, what is at stake is precisely a re-arrangement of the unequal division of labor and the unfair sharing of resources. But world-system analysis cannot penetrate and grasp the organic configuration of experiences, norms, habits, sentiments, beliefs, values and hopes crystallized in the Moro national/popular will of which the MNLF is the self-conscious expression. Nor can it really comprehend the possibility of a revolutionary inflection of Islam which an empirical description of the existing Islamic states cannot yield.

ENUNCIATING THE VOCATION

Of the revolutionary tradition in Islam, most commentaries are innocent or deliberately oblivious. While the MNLF is a political-secular movement in philosophy and organization, it would be short-sighted and dogmatic to dismiss the religious moment as epiphenomenal, derivative or even a propaganda concoction of reactionary ideologues.

From the Marxist standpoint, Islam conceived as an expansive worldview (like Christianity, Buddhism, etc.) "is the sigh of the oppressed creature, the heart of a heartless world, just as it is the spirit of a spiritless situation."[23] It is one of those ideal structures humanity has erected to voice its desire for a world where exploitation, physical suffering and injustice prevailing in life have been abolished; where everyone can enjoy a free, equal, prosperous and fulfilled life. When adopted by the ruling classes, these worldviews mutate into state religions, opiates of the people that serve to justify conservative, hierarchical and authoritarian regimes. When inflected by the subalterns, these worldviews generate a democratic-radical interrogation of the status quo, mobilizing the masses for a revolutionary transformation. Especially in the light of liberation theology's ecumenical dialogue with Third World Marxisms today, Marx and Engels' materialist critique and interpretation of religion warn us against any vulgar instrumentalist and mechanical approach: "The religious reflex of the real world can, in any case, only then finally vanish when the practical relations of everyday life offer to man none but intelligible and reasonable relations with regard to his fellow men and to nature."[24]

Of Islam's revolutionary tradition, I will cite the following:[25]

1.) The principle of individual responsibility connected with *ijtihad* (free and rational inquiry), the right of every believer to interpret the Qur'an and *Sunna* for her/himself. This principle rejects blind submission to bureaucratic authority (*ulama*) or any centralized unrepresentative organ of power. Note that Islam has no priestly caste or clergy, though *ijma*, the consensus of the faithful, serves as the chief criterion for the acceptability of any interpretation of Islam. Hence the *umma* is not equivalent to the Islamic state.

2.) The idea of activism: humans make their own history. It is the duty of believers to do right and to strive to create and maintain a just society, by either *jihad* of the sword (revolutionary struggle) or reformist methods (*jihad* of the heart) depending on concrete conditions. With its holistic vision of nature and history, Islam privileges the prophetic summons that mobilizes individuals in a specific historical community oriented toward universal justice. In its stress on the never-ending personal and social struggle, Islam focuses on the total political society, on the solidarity of believers and its historical continuity.

3.) The egalitarian-democratic idea (espoused consistently by the Khawarij) which insists on the equality of all believers irrespective of ethnic origin, lineage, status, sex, etc.; the right of maximum popular participation in the making of decisions at all levels. In contrast to Western hierarchic thinking, Islam embodies a "persistent tendency toward radical egalitarianism" stemming from its goal of "a prophetically integrated civil order."[26] Speculating on the mythic non-teleological character of the Qur'an, Norman Brown concludes that "Islam stays with the dream-life of the masses, the eschatological imagination of the lowly and oppressed."[27]

4.) Austerity, *zuhd*. Simplicity of life and refusal to corrupt or be corrupted.

5.) The idea of universality. The perception of the world split between *dar ul-Islam* and *dar ul-harb* parallels the Marxist categorization of the world divided into socialist and capitalist-imperialist camps.

6.) The idea of history. Revolutionary Muslims look forward to the realization of a just society (regulated by the divinely revealed *Shari'a*) not in heaven but on earth, in historical time. In its Mahdist form, revolutionary Islam shares with Marxism a concept of history as a perpetual conflict between oppressor and oppressed from which, in a situation of profound crisis, a revolutionary movement will surge up to overthrow the prevailing corrupt and oppressive order and inaugurate, with the ultimate victory of the slaves, a just and classless society.

Contradistinguished from the fundamentalist and obscurantist aspects of administered Islam, the above repertoire or themes and practices should unfold the existence in history of an authentic, living and viable revolutionary impulse in Islam which affords a common theoretical ground for dialogue, alliance, and cooperation. While the MNLF, to my knowledge, has not publicized its specific reading of Islam as actually practiced or as it could be practiced, it should be apparent that the political and ideological thrust of the MNLF draws sustenance from the tradition and has in fact graduated to the level of anti-imperialist theory and practice exemplified by such figures as the Iranian militant Jamal al-din al-Afghani, the Muslim Tatar communists Sultan Galiyev and Manafi Muzzafar, and the Idonesian Muslim Tan Malaka. While al-Afghani (regarded as the founder of Pan-Islamism) incarnates the secularizing anti-imperialist trend, Sultan Galiyev provides us the strongest formulation of the socialist kernel in all Third World Muslim struggles:

All the Muslim colonial peoples are proletarian peoples, and, since almost all classes of Muslim society were formerly oppressed by the colonialists, all have the right to the title of proletarian. . . . From an economic point of view there is an enormous difference between, say, the English or French proletariat and the Afghan or Moroccan proletariat. So one can argue that the national movement in Muslim countries has the character of a socialist revolution.[28]

In a similar vein, Galiyev's compatroit Hanafi Muzzafar proposed that it was necessary for Islamic nations to ally with communists without the Muslims compromising their beliefs; for, asserts Muzzafar, "our religion, Islam, is not a class religion, it is a religion which transcends classes, it is universal. It is possible that each class understands the religious domain in its own way, and considers it from its own point of view, but that constitutes precisely a class approach and not an Islamic approach."[29]

Mazzafar's materialist approach finds confirmation in the resolution of the Baku Congress of 1920 to integrate the religious and cultural heritage of the Eastern colonized peoples with Marxism, and by the plea of Tan Malaka (approved by the 4th Congress of the Communist International in 1922) that the

Comintern support Pan-Islamism because, in the global alignment of forces, it corresponds to "the national liberation struggle":

> . . . . For Islam is everything for the Muslim. It is not only his religion, it is his state, his economy, his nourishment and all the rest. Thus Pan-Islamism now means the fraternity of all the Muslim peoples, the liberation struggle not only of the Arab people, but of the Hindu and Javanese peoples, and of all the other oppressed Muslim peoples. This fraternity now means a liberation struggle directed not only against Dutch capitalism, but against English, French, and Italian capitalism, against the capitalism of the whole world. That is what Pan-Islamism means today in the Indies, among the oppressed colonial peoples.[30]

In linking its struggle not only with the Islamic world but also with "the Third World and . . . . oppressed colonized humanity everywhere," the MNLF's totalizing vision and project continues the vigorous if submerged trend represented by al-Afghani, Muzzafar, Sultan Galiyev, Tan Malaka; and the Iranian Mujahedin. Such gestures of self-understanding exhibited by the MNLF, a self-conscious mapping of its place in geography and history, may testify to the presiding spirit of Khidr (alluded to in Sura XVIII of the Qur'an) which, if I may analogize, corresponds to Gramsci's "modern prince," the revolutionary political party which awakens, energizes and impels the masses to blast the continuum of pre-history so as to install themselves as primordial shapers and movers of their destiny on earth. The mythical Khidr can also stand as an emblem or figure for the kind of informed, sensitive and creative materialist praxis needed to clarify, appreciate, and sustain the enormous pathbreaking actions and changes that have been, and are being, accomplished in the world today by the heroic sacrifices of the Bangsa Moro nation.

V

Subverting Authoritarian Discourse

Whoever does not recognize and champion the equality of nations and languages and does not fight against all national oppression or inequality is not a Marxist, he is not even a democrat.

V. I. Lenin

The Philippine landscape is familiarly tropical and East Indian. But the world into which you have stepped is unlike anything of which you have yet had experience in the Orient. It is Spain-- diluted, indeed, distorted, and overlaid with Americanism. . . .

Aldous Huxley

In the official biography of Ernest Hemingway, Carlos Baker recounts what strikes him as the impact of Philippine reality on the fabled inventor of modernist American prose style:

On the 11th [of May 1941] Hemingway attended a "ghastly" dinner given by the Philippine Writers Association where everyone's attempt to be gaily informal bored him so much that he got too drunk to care. . . . In Manila Hemingway made a few more notes and explored some of the Spanish bars of Intramuros. Otherwise his sole gain from the Philippine stopover was a good short summer haircut. [1]

In Hemingway's fiction and journalism, no reference of any importance is made to the Philippines.

In July 1961, the leading Filipino writer in English, Nick
Joaquin, recollected in elaborate quotation-filled scenarios
Hemingway's two visits (February and May 1941), where every
utterance of the author of *For Whom The Bell Tolls* was transcribed
like apocalyptic messages from the guru/avatar of avant-garde
Western modernism.[2] Aside from Hemingway's emphasis on the
necessary political commitment and devotion to truth that writers
must cultivate, and his praise of the Spanish and Chinese people's
resistance to fascism, what struck the small intimate group of
Filipino writers who informally conversed with him was
Hemingway's generous concern for his fellow-practitioners in the
craft, his warm and unpretentious bearing, his simplicity and candor.

What this juxtaposition of past event and "present"
interpretation succinctly captures and foregrounds is precisely the
complex and overdetermined transaction between metropolitan
culture and colonized native sensibilities, between hegemonic
center and de-centered periphery, which has often been construed
in a one-dimensional, positivistic manner. It is of course
indisputable that so long as the Philippines remains a
colony/neo-colony politically, economically and culturally, Filipino
writing in the English language cannot but be a minor, regional or
subordinate extension of the main body of British and American
writing. Within a historical-materialist perspective, however, I
propose here a dialectical interpretation which might elucidate
more adequately the non-synchronic, uneven conjuncture of U.S.
bourgeois ideology and the Philippine formation. The
Baker/Joaquin juxtaposition unfolds two aspects: one, the typical
Orientalizing discourse of Western consciousness (Baker) which
fabricates and marginalizes its alien object for its own prioritizing
ends; the other, the native response (Joaquin) which filters, selects
and organizes the raw material it imports according to its own
local/national imperatives. Despite the deepening controversial
involvement of the U.S. in the Vietnam conflict in 1969, Baker
reflects the primitive, parochial level of U.S. academic
consciousness vis-a-vis Third World revolutionary struggles.
Joaquin, on the other hand, exemplifies a long vigorous tradition of
Filipino literary sensibilities deeply engaged in radical political and
social criticism, a tradition springing from the propagandist
reformers of the 1896 revolution against Spain--exponents of
Enlightenment ideals--taken up, refined and further developed by
the vernacular writers, by the Left-oriented writers of the thirties,
and by the activist generation of the sixties and seventies.

Bearing in mind the subtle and complex distinction between
reception and influence, as explored by comparatists like Ulrich
Weisstein, Guillen and others, we can argue that the Philippine
version of Hemingway is not only historically valid by itself but
probably more true than the biographer's resume--although it may

be granted that each one reflects polar ends of a dialectical totality--in that it reveals the symptomatic lacunae and silence of the purportedly veridical and authoritative biography.[3]

MAPPING THE CRACKS AND FISSURES

In analyzing the problem of influence, reception and exchange between the imperialist capital and the peripheral dependencies of the Third World, it is imperative to emphasize the concrete specificity of the social relations of production and reproduction, together with their reciprocal dynamics, which characterize the colonial/neo-colonial formation. Here I contend that this is the correct and adequate methodology to map out the vicissitudes of Philippines-U.S. literary exchange from its inception and demarcate its prospects. For texts to speak, their contextualization in a global space of contradictory practices is needed. Whose language is being played in the game? Writing for whom? Who is speaking? Is anyone listening or reading?

FROM SYNCHRONIC TO DIACHRONIC

In my recently published book *Toward A People's Literature: Essays in the Dialectics of Praxis and Contradiction in Philippine Writing* (1984), as well as the the earlier treatises *Balagtas: Art and Revolution* (1967) and *The Radical Tradition in Philippine Literature* (1970), I mapped out in elaborate detail what Gilles Deleuze refers to as the three discernible lines constituting any sociocultural phenomenon: the nomadic, the migrant, and the sedentary lines (see his "Politics" in Gilles Deleuze and Felix Guattari, *On the Line,* New York, 1983). Suffice it here to sum up the thrust of the native popular discourses marginalized by U.S. cultural hegemony, for it is the hegemonizing process which I chiefly address in this essay.

Disrupting the sedentary line of medieval Christian evangelism introduced by the Spanish colonizers (1635-1898) which segmented into the molar codes of religious ritual and patriarchal familialism were the agitrop writings of revolutionary, decolonizing democrats like Jose Rizal, Marcelo Del Pilar, Emilio Jacinto, and later Apolinario Mabini. Targetting specific mobilized audiences (in either Spanish or Tagalog), their praxis integrated aesthetics and politics and generated the migrant or molecular line which effectively subverted the transcendental organizations maintained by the Church and the colonial bureaucratic machinery. Their writings were proscribed, their bodies incarcerated or destroyed. But it was principally the nomadic line of vernacular writing which displaced the molecular politics of Rizal and his contemporaries. One can cite here the productions of "seditious" playwrights like Aurelio Tolentino and the founders of the native *zarzuela*, Severino Reyes, Patricio Mariano and Hermogenes Ilagan; novelists like Lope

K. Santos and Inigo Ed. Regalado; poets like Jose Corazon de Jesus and Pedro Gatmaitan. A popular-nationalist discourse emerged using the vernacular languages and exposing the impossibility of an illusionist, homogenizing bourgeois representation through a consistent allegorical-didactic figuration of political and social questions. This contestation characterizes the period from the U.S. invasion to the consolidation of English as a viable literary medium in the early thirties. Instead of indigenizing the notions of Faustian virtu and Puritan individualism propagandized ' by Europeanized intellectuals like Rizal and Isabelo de los Reyes, exponent of a modified Proudhonian anarcho-syndicalism, vernacular discourse articulated a process of dissolving the interiority of the centered subject (now being interpellated by U.S. republican ideas in the abstract) in plays, novels, and poems which presented the breakdown of familial codes, the collapse of binary structures (male/female; urban/rural, etc.) and the release of a "rhizomatic" Desire mistakenly condemned as sentimentalism or pathos by formalist critics inventing Philippine literary history. An analogy to the temper of pre-romantic "sensibility" in the late eighteenth-century can be argued provided the native context and specific life-experiences are not ignored.

I would suggest that vernacular writing, with the cooptation of the migrant line by U.S. entrepreneurial discourse and the emasculation of the sedentary line, became temporarily hegemonic, dramatizing flows of intensities, quanta of affects immune from the overcoding machine of bourgeois Kantian aesthetics. This is the autochtonous tradition suppressed, marginalized, and subordinated by the encroaching U.S. colonial-ideological apparatus whose operations and effects I attempt to outline here.

ARCHEOLOGY OF SUBORDINATION

Like other colonized formations, the Philippine pre-capitalist or tributary mode of production engendered in 300 years of Spanish rule was disarticulated and reworked by U.S. political-military power when it suppressed the Filipino revolutionary forces in the Filipino-American War of 1899-1903. This event subsumed the natural and human resources of the archipelago within the domination of finance capital. But while the U.S. altered the economic-juridical mechanisms and adapted the feudal institutions to serve the paramount goal of capital/profit accumulation, the Philippines did not evolve into a full-fledged industrial state since, following Hamza Alavi's formulation, the circuit of commodity circulation needed the metropolis to complete it, and the surplus generated in the colony was not reinvested there to develop generalized commodity production and an independent, expanding internal market, but instead accumulated in the metropolis.[4] Given these two salient characteristics of peripheral capitalism which entailed definite consequences in the ideological or cultural spheres, we can understand how Philippine writing in English is constrained to find its self-confirmation and continuity in the larger circumscribing context of official Anglo-Saxon literature.

When the United States annexed the Philippines, it encountered an already highly stratified formation with a considerable landlord class, differentiated peasantry, emergent working class and an educated stratum of intellectuals called *ilustrados*. To attain its imperialist objective, the U.S. employed a dual policy of force and persuasion, violently crushing the revolutionary partisans and co-opting/bribing the *ilustrados*, who were then subsequently installed in the lower echelons of the bureaucracy, provincial and municipal administrations, and other state apparatuses of the colonial government. The institution of the public schools and the town administrations, the chief ideological state apparatuses in the first two decades of pacification, helped establish the groundwork for the incessant reproduction of capitalist social relations centered on the market (the contractual exchanges of juridically free and equal individuals) and the striving for rational efficiency within petty-commodity and comprador enterprises.

Within this schematic formulation of the base, the Philippines "received" U.S. 19th-century culture which was dominated by the themes and style of a resurgent racism (documented by historians like Gabriel Kolko, Christopher Lasch and others), popularized "social Darwinism", and the unifying ethos of "Manifest Destiny"-- all these gradually rationalized during the post-Civil War reconstruction, the suppression of the populists, Indians and socialists; and applied in the mass-media propaganda of the Spanish-American War at which time the Philippines entered the consciousness of the U.S. ruling bloc. Couched in McKinley's rhetoric of "benevolent assimilation"--the U.S. version of its *mission civilizatrice* --U.S. bourgeois ideology was transmitted to the younger generation of Filipinos through the imposition of English as the official language, and through various educational and administrative policies geared to a reformist neo-colonial strategy. Somewhat anachronistically (but a proof of uneven development), the literary culture introduced by the American teacher-volunteers, however, reflected the "genteel" and elitist milieu of a pre-industrial era (Irving, Longfellow, Bryant, etc.), devoid of any social criticism. In her pioneering study of American literary influence in the first three decades, Lucila Hosillos notes some exclusions from the curricula, among others: George Washington Cable, Joel Chandler Harris' folktales of American and Indian origins, Mary Wilkins Freeman's fiction, etc.[5] Such exclusions were not conspiratorial but indicative and symptomatic. Since U.S. policy makers adjudged the Filipinos quite uncivilized and at best children requiring "tutelage"--the codeword of imperialist apologetics from McKinley's Proclamation of December 1898 to the latest U.S. State Department pronouncement supporting the Marcos dictatorship--it was the available texts embodying the conservative didacticism of New England patriarchs that were used to illustrate English grammar and idiom, and convey an image of idealized U.S. social harmony to the natives.

For a whole generation of Filipino intellectuals who participated in the 1896 revolution, reared on or exposed to the writings of Balzac, Zola, Galdos, Tolstoy, Chekhov, Flaubert and Maupassant, the moralizing of Longfellow, Holmes and Lowell seemed a useless curiosity, distracting Filipinos from the urgent challenge of a drastically changed environment. Not even the British humanist-liberal trend of Macaulay, Arnold and George Eliot, standard textbook fare, could deflect the Tagalog novelists and dramatists, or the poets using Spanish, from invoking the Enlightenment ideals of republican liberties, equality and social justice absorbed from Spanish anarchist and French socialist publications.[6]

It was not until the maturation of intellectuals born at the turn of the century and during the first two decades--already distanced from the radicalizing impact of the Filipino-American War, ignorant of the suppressed culture of dissidence, canalized into reformist diversions, and allocated niches in the bureaucracy and other state apparatuses (schools, mass media, etc.)--that the American naturalist/realist revolt against the "genteel tradition" and the provincial conformity of the twenties would evoke a sympathetic and emulative response from Jose Garcia Villa and his coterie, alienated from the vulgar commercialism of Manila and the "nationalist" polemics of the oligarchy. By the late twenties, the Filipinos who chose to write in English had acquired a sense of caste since they conceived themselves privileged in speaking the master's language; to this corresponds a cult of aesthetic form, the metaphysics of the sovereign Word.

While one can still argue, as the orthodox literary historians do, that the obsession of Villa's generation with form and technique,--which supposedly accounts for their interest in O. Henry, Ring Lardner, Poe, Wilbur Daniel Steele, and later with Gertrude Stein, E.E. Cummings, and even Saroyan--stemmed from their sensitivity to criticism from teachers and editors (like A.V. Hartendorp of *Philippine Magazine*) of the grammatical and stylistic defects of their works, the emergence of aestheticism in a colonial society has to be explained by the convergence of multiple factors. The most decisive of these are the function of the writer/intellectual, the level of class struggle, and the constellation of cultural modes in conflict, which constitute the historical specificity of any cultural practice.[7] For indeed, how can one explain adequately that instead of the more profound critical questionings of rapacious capitalism and racism by Melville, Thoreau or Twain, it was Sherwood Anderson's vision of discontinuity, fragmentation and grotesque psychodrama (in *Winesburg, Ohio*, 1919, and *A Story Teller's Story*, 1924) and its corresponding plotless syntax that would exercise such a catalyzing spell on Villa, Arcellana, and their clique? Whatever democratic or populist impulse may inhere in the inaugural productions of American modernism was transmogrified into elitist renunciation or anarchist individualism when imported into the U.S's only Asian colony.

SHADOWING THE MISRECOGNITIONS

What I would argue here is that the essentialism or formalism which served as the keystone for the dominant aesthetic ideology in the years from 1946 when the Philippines gained formal independence, up to the late sixties (with the rediscovery and renascence of Marxist critical theory and its underground flourishing after 1972), springs from the peculiar function and location of the Filipino intellectual in the sphere of the reproduction of social relations. Writers like Villa, Romulo, A.E. Litiatco, Arcellana and others, whether employed in the universities or in private business, understood themselves as privileged, superior intellects who would assimilate "the best that has been thought and said" in Western civilization and thereby purge the stigma of their Otherness. They patterned their careers after the Anglo-Saxon model. Not to question or undermine the hierarchical order of authority and property-relations but to affirm and reinforce them on the level of spiritual discriminations—such was the role defined for them, whether they were conscious of it or not, in the historically determinate colonial structure.[8] To transcend their alienation and uprooting, they invoked a cosmopolitan and eclectic humanism inferred from archetypal myths or extrapolated from the Cold War liberalism of Lionel Trilling, *Partisan Review*, etc.

Removed from the sufferings and struggles of the laboring masses and subsidized by the state or living off rentals and inheritances, the "English" (short for "English-using") writers may be categorized as products of U.S. tutelage and the "Filipinization" movement promoted by William Howard Taft, the first American civil governor, and particularly by Francis Burton Harrison, whose administration (1913-1921) provided the seductive simulacra of neo-colonial self-determination. In the late thirties, the aestheticist faction opposed the short-lived Philippine Writers' League (1939-1941) and its cogent advocacy of a committed art by foregrounding the primacy of the artist's subjective inwardness at the time of fascist aggression in Europe and the advance of Japanese militarism in Asia.

Consonant with intensifying class contradictions, the Philippine Commonwealth era (1935-1942) witnessed the ideological polarization of the "English" writers, a conjunctural phenomenon illustrating my thesis that the Philippine cultural formation should be construed as an articulation-process of several modes of practices/discourses in various stages of conservation and

dissolution.   What   is   being   conserved   is   a   personalistic   or
metaphysical outlook (coeval with feudal familism) which inflects
public predicaments into personal dilemmas. While one strand of
this quite banal attitude may be traced to the medieval Christian
deformation of our culture, its immediate provenance includes,
among others, the romantic transcendentalism of American
literature mediated by editors like A.V. Hartendorp, Edward J.
O'Brien, etc., and reinforced by the instrumentalized craft-specific
dicta of Flaubert, Chekhov, and other modernists.[10] What is being
dissolved or neutralized is the organic and dynamic fusion of the
public and the private which has so far materialized in three
moments: the 1896 revolution and the resistance against U.S.
pacification in the first two decades of this century; the eve of
World War II with the merger of the Communist and Socialist
parties in 1938; and the explosion of the national-democratic
movement in the early seventies.

No longer linked to subaltern resistance like the guerrilla
insurgency of the first decade which precipitated the rise of the
Tagalog novel and seditious drama, the "English" writers could not
harness the subtle idiomatic nuances of dialogical representation
(Bakhtin) nor exploit the rich generic potential of allegory and
ritual available to the vernacular artists. So then, rather than
being a direct mechanical reflection or transposition of U.S.
bourgeois ideology, Philippine writing in English before World War II
manifests   the   ambiguous   positioning   of   the   middle-level
(non-oligarchic) intelligentsia between the rebellious masses and
the colonial state. Whether our indigenous revolutionary tradition
or the *ilustrado* opportunism and vacillation parasitic on it will
materialize at a certain conjuncture, depends crucially on the level
or intensity of the masses' opposition to exploitation--as in the
Colorum and Sakdalista insurrections of the twenties and the
thirties, enabling the emergence of Marxist-oriented thought and
expression--and the crystallization of the national-popular will in a
vast array of oppositional discourses and practices.

With the onset of the Cold War and the McCarthy-inspired
climate   of   total   suppression   of   dissent   accompanying   the
CIA-directed counter-insurgency campaigns against the Huks in the
late forties and early fifties, the groundwork was laid for the rapid
and thorough dissemination of American New Criticism dogmas
together with variants like neo-Aristotelianism, myth criticism, and
structural functionalism. While the surviving left-wing critics of
the thirties had been either co-opted by the bureaucracy and
private business or silenced, imprisoned and killed, the aestheticists
continued to espouse the primacy of aristocratic taste, combined
with   imports   of   amateur   existentialism   and   consumer
avant-gardism. Meanwhile, during the traumatic postwar recovery,
in the classrooms of Paul Engle and Robert Lowell at the University
of Iowa; from sessions at Breadloaf, Stanford, Kenyon and
elsewhere, a generation of New Critical evangelists was being bred

who would later reign in their classrooms (in the University of the Philippines, Silliman University, Ateneo), or pontificate in the columns of Manila weekly supplements.

How can we explain the appeal of New Criticism when the problem and focus, according to consensus, was no longer the imitation of models but the alignment of language with experience? In the context of the U.S. academy, Terry Eagleton ventures an explanation:

> . . . . New Criticism's view of the poem as a delicate equipoise of contending attitudes, a disinterested reconciliation of opposing impulses, proved deeply attractive to sceptical liberal intellectuals disoriented by the clashing dogmas of the Cold War. Reading poetry in the New Critical way meant committing yourself to nothing. It drove you less to oppose McCarthyism or further civil rights than to experience such pressures as merely partial, no doubt harmoniously balanced somewhere else in the world by their complementary opposites. It was, in other words, a recipe for political inertia, and thus for submission to the political status quo. [11]

In the Philippine context, there was really no credible danger or temptation that the majority of intellectuals suffering from unemployment, poverty and paralysis of the will would incite students or agitate peasants and workers to overthrow the neo-colonial establishment. Years of their mendacity to U.S. charity and habitual subservience to the oligarchy enabled the uninterrupted reproduction of elitist arrogance, narcissistic withdrawal, and cynical temporizing. Having internalized the logic of dependent rationality, the Americanized writer generally defended and justified his marginality or irrelevance by the cliche of universalism, by technocratic specialization or by an obscurantist mania initially meant to counteract the commodifying stranglehold of programmed corporate modernization.

In 1951, with the Huk rebellion curtailed, the critic Manuel Viray attempted to summarize the transitional curve of the writer's odyssey, from the quest to discover the technical secrets of Sinclair Lewis's *Main Street* and Carl Sandburg's *vers libre* to the act of exploring thematic-cultural issues, as in Steinbeck's *In Dubious Battle*, Dos Passos's *USA* and in the novels of Theodore Dreiser and Thomas Wolfe. It appears from hindsight that the writer's appropriation of method or technique gravitates to the moment of inquiring: method for whom? technique to accomplish what purpose? Given the global crisis of monopoly capitalism in the thirties and the internalization of modernist revolt ("the Lost Generation"), Filipino intellectuals seemed to apprehend that neither formalist reductionism nor mythical determinism could yield satisfactory answers to those urgent questions. They felt a need to contextualize and indigenize. From a distance of twenty years, Viray reflects that his generation failed to metamorphose into integral artists capable of synthesizing moral vision with intelligible form, victimized (as he puts it) by the "dehumanizing influence on culture which started with the machine age and which has, with World Wars I and II, forced almost every man of sensibility to retreat into his inner self and write about his private experience."[12]

This predicted withdrawal into a supposedly pristine and liberated interior space that Viray alludes to no longer coalesced, in the fifties, with the anarchist stance of *pour epater les bourgeoisie* (such as that displayed by Villa and his numerous epigones) but instead brought with it a pseudo-objectivist attitudinizing and a narrow craft-oriented moralism which might be considered the local analogue of the Weberian end-of-ideology trend. One obvious example of the utilization of New Critical machinery to interpret and evaluate Philippine writing is the two introductions by Edith Tiempo and Edilberto Tiempo to the 1953 anthology *Philippine Writing* edited by T. D. Agcaoili. With their methodology and criteria of judgment derived from the founding texts of Cleanth Brooks, Robert Penn Warren, John Crowe Ransom and Allen Tate, the Tiempos fetishized "the organic evolution of a universal truth or experience which represents the story's theme", and apotheosized the ideal of "internal consistency" and "artistic congruence of denotative and associational elements."[13] In a recent article, Edith Tiempo reiterates her adherence to a metaphysical notion of the artist ("in thrall only to his art and to his deeply personal commitments") that still informs the thinking of a few diehard reactionaries. Amid the massive brutality of a terrorist authoritarian regime, she conceives of the artist maturing "beyond any chauvinistic-nationalist framework" in order to "continue to celebrate the profoundly human, the exultantly and tragically persisting themes in the heart of man."[14]

SYMPTOMS OF REIFICATION

Probably the most rigid and thoroughly Americanized proponent of New Critical dogmatism is Prof. Ricaredo Demetillo whose arsenal of ideas dates back to his stint in a Baptist seminary and in the University of Iowa. Demetillo's essentialism lacks the pedestrian pedantry of Edilberto Tiempo and the pop sociology of the American Filipinist Leonard Casper (of whom more later), but it makes up for the lack by an indiscriminate trumpeting of slogans glorifying Western humanism that would eventually be standard fare for Imelda Marcos' unconscionable publicity stunts: "All these men [Joyce, Gide, Faulkner, etc.] project the human condition of their time in all its manifold aspects, not merely the political. . . . This capacity to illuminate the human condition is the reason, too, why we think Dostoevsky and Tolstoy, along with Cervantes, the greatest novelists. No theory of class conflict or social change can do justice to the works of these geniuses."[15] This fetishism of an abstract "human condition" has been canonized and codified by the Marcos regime's speechwriters (most of whom use "English") to the point where, with the opportunistic permutation of Third World themes which render Western democracy antithetical to the native "despotic" heritage, the paradoxes and ironies of a moribund "New Society" are more flagrantly revealed.

Compatible with, and in fact complementary to, New Critical universalism is the minor theological/scholastic school of criticism centered in Ateneo de Manila University and the journal *Philippine Studies*. The conservative function of this group may be discerned in one Jesuit critic's insistence on "Christian humanism as second nature to the Filipino mind" and his exhortation that writers "must seek cultural unity with Shakespeare and his cultural heritage," a tautology which betokens a pathetic last-ditch stand or rearguard action to delay the inevitable collapse of the hegemonic culture sustained by English. One contributor to the anthology *Philippine Fiction* (1972) exhibits the group's typical casuistry, when, in a retrogressive gesture, he denounces Nick Joaquin's fictional mimesis of lust as "the literary counterpart of a current Hollywood heresy" which purveys "filth" rendered attractive by charming stars. So much for the bankruptcy of this reactionary trend.[16]

The subsequent inflection of New Critical formalism into archetypal and anthropological commentary may be grasped as an adaptive modification of the function of academic criticism, a response to the crisis of U.S. global ascendancy beginning with the Korean stalemate, the victories of the Cuban and African revolutions, and the technological breakthroughs of Europe and Japan. Besieged by historical-materialist interrogation and other radical interventions, writing in English became contested terrain so that the linguistic space could no longer be so openly used as a neutral, value-free medium to extol Madison Avenue consumerism and sophistication. With autotelic form deconstructed by its internal inconsistencies and untenability, there occurred a gradual and uneven shift to a relativist permutation of its concerns, thus rendering more plausible its inherent ahistorical, cosmic universalism.

We can perceive this mutation clearly exemplified in the novelist N.V.M. Gonzalez's series of speculations on the limits and possibilities of the Filipino imagination. In a lecture of May 1952, Gonzalez observes that Filipino writers experience difficulty achieving "integrity of personality," much less nationalistic conviction, because of the temptations of the "materialistic spirit." Although he tries to sketch in the historical coordinates within which the practice of writing has been performed, and given the presence of Anglo-Saxon literature as the cultural capital of "English" writers unmatched by the impoverished vernaculars, Gonzalez refuses the lesson to be learned. He cites the local awareness of the "raw and unrelieved realism of Erskine Caldwell and Steinbeck," "the hard-boiled Hemingway prose," the stockpile of techniques afforded by Henry James, Faulkner and Henry Green, only to exorcise history and validate the ego: "art ceases to be art if impelled by historical self-consciousness, ... its fullness of growth is attained only through some independent artistic experience."[17] Gonzalez's assertion that the only useful literary theory is that of literature as an "act of discovery" attests more to a stark impoverishment of thought than to originality of insight. In pursuing the ordeals of the "English" artist, Gonzalez (in a USIS symposium of March 1964) portrays him as a heroic protagonist of the Ibong Adarna myth--the only one of three sons who succeeds in redeeming his ailing father through his self-laceration and self-sacrifice. But again, instead of the central cognitive thrust of the myth and its collective, decentered subject, it is the individualist *agon* that for Gonzalez symbolizes the Filipino writer's irresoluble tragic predicament. A sudden tremendous upsurge of mass demonstrations, strikes and widespread peasant revolts against the neo-colonial exploitative system pervade the period from 1964 to 1968; but this rich condensation of texts or experiences Gonzalez fails to apprehend when, in an essay "The Filipino and the Novel" published in 1968, he repeats platitudes drawn from the depleted treasury of the the New Critics, e.g. the view that the manifold density of social experience is only "an aspect of self-consciousness." Unlike his academic colleagues, Gonzalez spices his makeshift metaphysics with a sprinkling of assorted guidebook statistics to produce an eclectic commentary which, however, fails to disguise its fundamental essentialist presuppositions.

INTERDICTING THE HETEROGENEOUS

This essentialist kernel of the hegemonic ideological formation in the first twenty years of the Philippine Republic (1946-1966) has, as I've noted earlier, evolved from the social division of intellectual labor, with the "English" practitioners allowed to invest linguistic capital not from the autochthonous popular tradition but from a narrow safe region of Anglo-Saxon culture. Such a privilege of drawing rights, however, entailed the penalty of conformism. A highly effective agency in the inculcation of this conformity was the Fulbright exchange professorships sponsored by the U.S. government and various foundations. One exchange professor in the fifties, perhaps the most fanatical missionary of New Critical orthodoxy, was Leonard Casper, whose model and standard of judgment for Philippine writing is explicitly derived from "southern agrarian ideals and rural actualities" realized in the works of Robert Penn Warren, Faulkner, and others. His opinions and judgments, summed up in New *Writing from the Philippines* (1966), employs hackneyed social science functionalism to lend scientific credence to "Christian-agrarian humanism," with the customary underscoring of irony, autonomous form, and symbolic revelations occluding what is disruptive, heterogeneous and discontinuous in the national experience. This last category of "experience" is defined as intrinsically conservative, "essentially defensive, self-conserving"[18] so that, in effect, what is claimed to be universal or transcendent turns out to be a grossly empiricistic and naively parochial reading of the complex dialectics of Philippine reality in accordance with plantation aristocracy norms. To this quite logical regress, the corresponding response by militants in the late sixties was the popularization of Black expression by Malcolm X, George Jackson, Aime Cesaire, Amilcar Cabral, and Frantz Fanon.

In his contribution on "Philippine Poetry" to the *Encyclopedia of Poetry and Poetics* (1965), Casper demonstrates a refurbished strategy (New Critical orthodoxy by this time has been assimilated, qualified and supplemented by phenomenology, Northrop Frye, and assorted structuralisms) employing an arbitrary chronological grid to deliver scarcely concealed political judgments. One finds not only factual distortions--e.g., "English served to help unify an archipelagic nation divided among nine major dialects"--but also highly prejudiced and presumptuous claims such as the following:

> . . . . Zulueta da Costa's *Like the Molave* is in the declamatory tradition of Whitman, badly imitated--the pseudo-epic style so attractive to chauvinistic writers substituting enthusiasm for art. . . . More recent poets in English, often trained and published in the United States, have achieved coalescence of native traditions . . . , New Critical formalism . . . , and personal vision. . . . Even if Tagalog succeeds in becoming the language of literature as well as of elementary communication, American emphasis on the dramatic and concrete has at least hastened the decline of romantic abstract and essays-in-rhyme in Philippine poetry.[19]

When one can so easily assert that Tagalog is not "the language of literature"--whose literature?--it is not difficult to realize whose chauvinism is on trial.

Virtually colonizing (in the passage quoted) the ideals of Western modernism under the aegis of an exposed and decadent *pax Americana*, Casper seeks to re-validate the apriorist outlook implanted in the twenties, first, by ascribing solely to U.S. domination the effect of homogenizing disparities and unifying the schizoid native sensibility; second, by inventing its own version or, more precisely, caricature of the vernacular achievement purged of its radical, communitarian historicity and thus marginalizing it as a negative force; and, third, by authorizing the hegemonic if precarious supremacy of English with its putative monopoly of the "dramatic and concrete," an honorific rubric for the pragmatic empiricism which today governs the programmatic memoranda of the IMF/World Bank and their corporate accomplices. Ironically, this formalist sacralization of art legitimizes both capitalist reification (the conversion of all social relations into exchange-value) and that administered mode of "repressive de-sublimation" imputed by Marcuse, Adorno and others to "affirmative" bourgeois culture.[20]

Rather than engage in an anecdotal diagnosis of how the mainstream Filipino critics were spawned in the breeding-grounds of the Iowa Writing School, Breadloaf, Stanford, and assorted foundation subsidiaries of the U.S. Empire, I would like to call attention to what could be an excellent sourcebook, a veritable museum of imperialist platitudes and prejudices: namely, Casper's "The Critic of Philippine Literature as Provocateur," a paper read at the Association for Asian Studies 1974 meeting in Chicago and published by the Center for Southeast Asian Studies, Northern Illinois University. I advert to this document, a representative performance which synthesizes all of Casper's opinions on Philippine writing contained in his other publications, not only because I was personally vilified in it, but because it unfolds in a fortuitously revealing manner the constellation of concepts and value-judgments which, through various mediations, informs "New Society" discourse.

True to his background, Casper defends the New Criticism--a crude and frankly reactionary formalist movement launched in the thirties to consciously counter-attack the nascent proletarian culture, until it gained ascendancy in the universities during the early fifties as part of the triumph of the anti-communist Cold War campaign. Casper unblushingly describes New Criticism as an "objective scientific methodology" with a "humanist orientation." Embodying "the whole agrarian tradition" (that is, the aristocratic ethos of the owners of slave plantations), the New Critics "have decried finance capitalism," as well as "over-collectivized socialist institutions." Casper is correct: the New Critics want to restore the ante-bellum Southern mode of production and social relations. These worthy humanists, like their Filipino epigones, reject "Marx and his [to them] one-answer system."

Casper is disingenuous: if the New Critics are really scientific and objective, how can they ignore the historic contradictions between capitalism and slave society? (Or between slave-society and socialism? Of course, they don't. Not wanting to appear utterly contemptuous of historical reality, Casper assumes the role of a transcendent, harmonizing sensibility trying to reconcile the "participating detail" of experience and "New Critical form-searching," "doctrinaire reduction" and "self-sufficiency of form." He insists on the "New Critical method's non-impressionistic, non-prejudicial objectivity," although he himself is prejudiced against Marxist theory and ignorantly repudiates it as "group think" or "party line."

Try as he might, Casper cannot but betray his chauvinist and obscurantist stripe. Casper's literary practice is founded on an orthodox metaphysical world-outlook, a type of philosophical idealism, which manifests itself unevenly in various ways.

First, there is a pretense at objectivity as "healthy ambivalence," objectivity being merely a mental attitude or verbal stance, a perpetual dilettantism of consciousness. But whenever proletarian or revolutionary art is mentioned, Casper runs amuck. He denounces Marxist insights as "proscription," "rhetoric of evasion," "distortion, abstraction, stereotype, name-calling, overgeneralization," etc. He deplores committed or partisan literature in such bluntly pejorative terms as "social tractarianism" and "literature-to-specification, " versus honorific terms for pro-status-quo literature. Consider Casper's exemplary writers, the familiar Establishment stars already memorialized in the "New Society" pantheon: National Artist Villa, Gonzales, Kerima Polotan, Demetillo, etc. Thus the hollow claim to objectivity evaporates swiftly.

Second, Casper's patently formalist bias inheres in reducing literature to language, the "verbal icon": it's the medium that "humanizes." The true alternative to proletarian writing, for him, is "whatever mode of language, whatever technical improvisation, whatever intuited apperception can be used to become not a way out of reality but a way in." (More on Casper's notion of reality later.) Consequently, as an antidote to the concrete analysis of the overdetermined structure of literary art and a way of abolishing ideology from the lexicon of the critical enterprise, Casper recommends tracing socio-linguistic patterns based on the pragmatic or instrumentalist method of John Dewey, a philosopher *par excellence* of commodity production and profit.

But the pragmatic view that whether objective reality exists or not, it's the methodology that counts, presents its obverse side in a gross empiricism and mechanical positivism ostensibly abhorred by the New Critics themselves, yet integral to their world-view. The contemplative dualism of subject and object leads to a total mystification that denies the reality of class conflict: "Most writers seem to be lovers of people. . . . Their own motive-- to describe what is, out of respect for its *being there*. . . . " Such description of course implies selection, assumption of a stance or judgment, a moral vision which Casper attributes to the "true literature of protest" which is, for him, the "literature of faith-becoming-hope-again." In other words, from description we graduate to faith and hope. What is there, the real world, actually exists only in the writer's monadic and self-nihilating consciousness.

New Criticism which repudiates Marxist writing and dismisses outright all revolutionary/proletarian art, according to Casper, offers insights "more descriptive than prescriptive, providing flesh-and-blood evidence of quality in persons worth salvaging. . . ." We know what "salvaging" means in the "New Society," for both Marcos and Casper are "humanists."

It will be apparent to anyone that throughout the essay,

Casper, who doesn't profess to be a pluralist or an eclectic, prescribes his own definite set of standards, his own specific and determinate criteria. And together with it he insinuates a mechanical-formalist frame of mind which discloses itself, in the final analysis, as a ruse to legitimize his advocacy of the status quo, the harmony of exploited and exploiting classes, under the banner of humanism. Isn't all this seemingly sophisticated discourse a not-too-subtle defense of bourgeois social relations prevailing in the "Free World"?

What finally situates Casper's reactionary metaphysics which dissolves class struggle into the mystification of atomized and inscrutable selves in a space called the "New Society," is his self-confessed bondage in the prison of individualism sustained by vestiges of artisanal or petty commodity production. The elitist critic complains of class divisions but rejects the only unsurpassable philosophy (Sartre) and guide to action of our time--Marxism, the scientific critique and historic resolution of class society. Casper complains: "In an open society, in any earnest search for the whole truth, the presumption that man is exclusively a political animal or encapsulated in caste or class (or, indeed, devoid of significant differentiation) is dangerously deprivative" (p. 86).

This statement illustrates the classic bourgeois conception of the individual as the "free" atomized competitive entity whose essence can be grasped in isolation, detached from all social determinations. In contrast, Marx pointed out that individuality is only the totality of social relations; that a human being is "not only a social animal but an animal that can be individuated only within society." Further, human freedom arises from a practical understanding of necessary laws which express social forces at work, the real contradictions in society and their motion. In *praxis*, in the revolutionary project of changing society, humans collectively act, thus unleashing the power of each individual to actually play a meaningful role. Individuals act in the last analysis as representatives of classes; it is the masses who make history.

From a radical perspective, in capitalism and in dependent societies subjected to imperialism, all social relations are reified as exchange relations of commodities in the market, so that the true position of individuals vis-a-vis social production is dissimulated or inverted. That is why individuals, in class society, cannot be grasped without the ensemble of concrete determinations, whether Casper likes it or not. So long as private ownership of the means of production prevails, and so long as the fetishism of commodities (including human labor power) whereby people and their activities metamorphose into things, is not overthrown by the consciously organized working masses, any protest of Casper's that the human potential is being suppressed by inequalities and class divisions, will only be pathetic self-indulgence. In fact, this "humanistic" complaint is being rendered by the U.S.-Marcos dispensation, as a cheap, sanctimonious slogan to hide the ruthless oppression of real, living people in a commodity/profit-centered world.

What connects Casper's apology and defense of imperialist ideology as crystallized in the New Criticism are a few premises that should by now be platitudes to most of us: for example, great literary art transcends social classes and their mundane conflicts. It possesses eternal import, unlike any social or political action. In this light, literature should be studied on "its own terms," as an autonomous and private creation independent of the milieu, the social and political contexts which attended its genesis. Because great literature deals with a permanent and unchanging human nature—this is Casper's reality—it is timeless and universal. Whatever social, political or moral effects the literary work may incidentally generate, they do not affect its geniune aesthetic worth. Besides, the only group that can fully appreciate authentically great works are a few privileged minds, an elite which understands and appreciates the New Critical exaltation of qualities like ambivalence, irony, symbolism, tragic vision, and "the total human condition." All these premises are subsumed within a metaphysical or essentialist world-outlook.

INTERFACE: UNKNOTTING, SUTURING

To what conditions and factors then can we attribute the insidious and preemptive influence of New Critical doctrines before the First Quarter Storm of 1970 which marks its long anticipated demise? We can suggest here the outline of a diagnostic analysis in three interconnected levels. Socially, in a milieu of political repression and economic harassment, the "English" writers strove hard to maintain their role as defenders/apologists of the status quo for the sake of jobs, scholarships, amenities and perquisites. Recall that at this stage the educational institutions and publishing networks still privileged English as the prestigious medium of communication. With exacerbated class conflict threatening their middling status, they repudiated commercialized and degraded "mass culture" identified with the unlettered underclass. Psychologically, they retreated to a frozen, abstract realm of the intellect—a monadic private space. They denied class struggle and refused history for myth, conjuring in fantasy a permanent equilibrium or synaesthesia (I.A. Richards) of the passions. Their plight may also be described as an abortion of Fanon's paradigm of the evolution of the Third World intellectual toward emancipation. Aesthetically, they exalted the virtues of symbolic form, the space for hypostatizing images and impulses into a unified autonomous structure. With progressive critical thought suppressed, neutralized, or incorporated in the secular resistance then mounting against religious/sectarian propaganda (e.g., the controversy over legislating Rizal's novels into the curriculum), New Criticism preempted and monopolized the field of hermeneutics and judgment by maximizing its Orientalizing scope, intensity, and persistence.[21]

Having charted the inter-animating forces, actors, and parameters in this field and triangulated the political, ideological and economic instances to define the concrete phenomenon "Philippine writing in English," it might be instructive, before concluding, to articulate the postwar literary situation with U.S. perceptions. Long before the Philippines surfaced in the horizon of Hemingway's consciousness, the U.S. occupation of the islands and its barbaric pacification campaign (1899-1913)--its military commanders fresh from exterminating the Indians in the Western frontier--had aroused the consciences of luminaries like William James, Mark Twain, George Santayana, William Dean Howells and others whose anti-imperialist critiques demystified the missionary rationale, a rationale which vitiates U.S. scholarship on the Phillipines up to now.[22]

The distinguished novelist Wallace Stegner, professor at Stanford University, visited the Philippines at the peak of Huk insurgency in 1951 and assessed the outcome of half-a-century of American tutelage. Stegner accurately depicts the country's "economic and cultural dependency " and the Filipino "cultural inferiority complex" arising from what he believes to be the lack of any literary tradition--Stegner's complacent ignorance does not deviate from the stereotype. He notes the absence of any political consciousness among the "English" writers--"a disturbing evasion of the hard realities" such as landlord exploitation, usury, poverty, etc., by writers whose vocation strikes him as that of "chroniclers of the nostalgic barrios of their childhood." Literature ignores "the shadow of violence and fear (that) hangs over even well-policed Manila." Whether "living in a dream or a hole," the "English" writers are thus defeated by "the sense of being an extra, unwanted, unregarded fringe on their national life, an irrelevancy." While Stegner is entirely correct in ascribing the irrelevancy to the adoption of an alien language, he is completely mistaken in alleging that the vernaculars have no "tradition."[23] His implicit view that Philippine writing is only a minor emerging "branch of English literature" is reasserted in 1962 by Professor Donald Keene of Columbia University.

Our last intertextual exhibit comes from John Leonard, reviewer for the *New York Times,* who visited in 1977. This testimony of an East Coast liberal bemused by the sociocultural enigma he encounters in the Philippines may remind us of Stegner's patronizing expertise and, before him, the skeptical wonder of nineteenth-century European travellers like Jagor and Goncharov:

And the American visitor is sick of his own lazy generalizations on American culture. His "imperial self" is missing the point. . . . Why--in a nation where English, after 50 years of

American rule, is an "official language"--do they want to convert Tagalog into the dominant vernacular? Why, in a nation--7,000 islands, really, and 87 languages, and 300 dialects--where students have enough trouble understanding a sonnet of Skakespeare or a chapter of Dickens, or distinguishing in English between a subject and predicate, are the faculty all trained in American New Criticism? R. P. Blackmur? John Crowe Ransom? Yvor Winters? In the country of Leyte and Corregidor? What has Percy Lubbock or Cleanth Brooks or Rene Wellek to do with little bananas and active volcanoes and nipa huts and caribou?[24]

What these rhetorical questions betray, aside from their tone of chic worldliness, is the fatal deficiency or flaw in all American Filipinology: the failure to comprehend the Filipino people's history as a process of national liberation and self-affirmation. Underlying this is the prior incapacity to perceive the difference and understand the Filipino's Otherness as the intransigent negation of U.S. racism/imperialism.

PLURALIZING THE MONOLITHIC

The resurgence of progressive art and criticism in the period between 1967 and 1972 exposed the fragility of U.S. ideological supremacy and in turn disclosed the subterranean vitality of the radical democratic impulses of the Enlightenment program broached in 1896 and its distinctly socialist inflection in the thirties and forties. However, the residual attachment of activist intellectuals to notions of "organic form" and mechanical, class-reductionist formulas prevented organizations like PAKSA (*Literature for the People*) from forging and consolidating what Gramsci calls "a national-popular bloc" of discourses and practices. Consequently, one will still find U.S.-trained professors preaching the tenets of idealism and pragmatism together with the technocrats, while the regime's ideological state apparatuses (for example, the Cultural Center, Philippine Writers' Union, National Media Center, and assorted journals) attempt to contrive nativist revivals couched in the spurious lexicon of development and "Third World liberation." A peculiar innovation may be the slogan "Humanism: The Ideology," with the dictator himself proclaiming that his vision "is mankind as the purpose, the heart and the center of development," a move to preempt or muffle whatever cries of protest about human rights violations may be launched by the United Nations, PEN International, or Amnesty International.[25] This invocation of a "humanist ideology", meant to assuage the conscience of bureaucrats and Western diplomats, sounds like an unintentional parody of Wallerstein's paradigm of the capitalist world-system and the ubiquitous dependency *problematique*; but its affinity with, and descent from, the colonial apologetics of Taft or William Cameron Forbes and New Critical agrarian humanism, seems fairly evident.

Authoritarian *diktat* has not completely succeeded in turning the tide of revolutionary cultural practice--nationalist militants operate above and underground, in the folds and interstices of civil society--chiefly because it does not have a coherent, tested, all-encompassing theory (such as Marxism-Leninism) which can totalize the complex, diverse relations and interpellate individuals toward collective action. What it has done is to provide official channels for the already obsolete or anachronistic aestheticism and its updated variants in the controlled media. One example (chosen at random) is the article by Cirilo Bautista, "Conversations with Jose Garcia Villa" in the government publication *Archipelago* where Villa performs as the exemplary logocentric guru: "Form is art; art is form. . . . It is not the idea that is important but the form."[26] After recording Villa's acknowledged indebtedness to E. E. Cummings, Bautista then endorses Villa as the paragon of "New Society" artists:

> In the late 1960s, Villa's poetry provided an alternative to the blood-and-bullets rhetorics of the Proletarian writers. . . . While theirs spoke of physical transformation, to restore civil order, his spoke of spiritual transformation, to restore sanity to a dehumanized world; while theirs raged in street parlance about economic statistics, social deprivation and fascist tactics, his enlightened in a noble language about the innate dignity of man, moral liberty, and the uses of religion.[27]

The obvious discursive strategy here is to split the unity of theory and practice achieved by Filipino writers--like Carlos Bulosan, a worker-exile in the U.S. during the Philippine Commonwealth--at those precipitating conjunctures triangulated earlier. Because his sensibility was deeply embedded and rooted in the proletarian struggles of his time, Bulosan was able to register the latent subversive impulses and their accompanying utopian vision in what V. L. Parrington calls the liberal, realist or populist tradition in U.S. literature: from Whitman to Twain, Dreiser, and Richard Wright.[28] Challenged by the Philippine counterpart of that tradition, Villa and his disciples can only gesture toward, or even parody, U.S. neo-conservative styles ranging from the compromised liberalism of the Welfare State to religious fundamentalism, *laissez-faire* pragmatism, and packaged counter-cultural fads.

One last development in U.S.-influenced theorizing I would like to cite here is a brand of specious historicism intended to supplement or rectify New Critical tendentiousness. One example is Nick Joaquin's widely quoted lecture "The Filipino as English Fictionist" where McLuhan's ghost hovers somewhere in the background. Joaquin argues that in contrast to vernacular writers-- not really writers but "oral fictionists" devoid of a historical sense--the "English" writers participate in a visual (that is, literate and historically-minded) culture, proving themselves the authentic heirs of Western (Spanish, Anglo-Saxon) civiliation. Like the autocrat in Malacanang Palace, Joaquin is not averse to issuing arbitrary decrees sanctioned only by the coercive force of prejudice or ignorance: "For good or ill, our literature in English is that standard against which our literature in the vernacular will have to measure itself. . . . "[29] But Joaquin's apologetics, self-deconstructed by its unwitting aporias and non-sequiturs, can be more significantly deciphered as a cathartic figure, a therapeutic emblem for the passing of an epoch in which U.S. cultural ascendancy (neo-colonial norms, sentiments, values masquerading as universal and absolute) was taken for granted, was in fact deemed normal, right and natural.

Contrary to what Joaquin and his coterie claim about the "English" writers' cultivation of the Western patrimony, it was actually the vernacular writers of the first two decades--the *agitprop* theater of Abad and Tolentino, the Horatian poetics of Lope K. Santos, Jose Corazon de Jesus, and others--and, in the thirties, the Marxist principles and precepts of the Philippine Writers' League--that preserved and revitalized the Enlightenment project of *prodesse-delectare* initiated by Rizal's novels (*Noli Me Tangere* and *El Filibusterismo*); the polemics of Isabelo de los Reyes, Claro Recto, etc.; and the encyclopedic scholarship of Jaime de Veyra and Epifanio de los Santos, among others. In general, I would contend that the "English" writers have as a group never represented the nation, much less the people; and that the authentic organic intellectuals who sought to organize the spontaneous collective/popular impulses and infuse them with ethical-scientific coherence are the vernacular writers like Amado V. Hernandez, Magdalena Jalandoni, the anonymous artificers of the Moro epics (*parangsabil*), the great Cebuano novelists and dramatists; the collaborators of *Hulagpos* (1980) and *Mga Tula ng Rebolusyong Philipino* (1982).

INAUGURATING THE DISCOURSE OF THE OTHER

The unprecedented debacle of U.S. imperialism in Indochina in the mid-seventies, the summing-up of the lessons of the Cultural Revolution in China, the upsurge of worldwide rebellions against capital involving new historic agents such as women, youth, nationalities, etc.--all these signalled the acceleration of the process of collapse of U.S. cultural suzerainty in the Philippines.[30] The once celebrated image of the United States championing freedom, democracy and equality--the originary and obsessive premise of its interventionist policy--had been shattered by its counter-insurgency barbarism in Vietnam, Cambodia, and Laos; by the U.S.-instigated military coup in Chile; the systematic violence inflicted on the domestic opposition (Black Panthers, anti-war dissenters) and outright cynical brutalization of ordinary citizens by the U.S.-subsidized Marcos clique.

Once lauded as an antidote against the generally recognized capitalist perversion of humanist values, New Criticism exposed its partisanship by its consistent obliviousness to corruption and military terrorism grown rampant since the imposition of martial law in 1972, and its reflex rehashing of anti-communist slogans to deflect attention from the systemic causes of poverty, injustice and oppression. In business, media and schools, U.S. social science methodologies (positivist empiricism, functionalism, etc.) harmonized neatly with formalist aesthetics in their ahistorical valorization of feudal familism, patronage or "reciprocity" patterns (*hiya, pakikisama*), and the newly-hatched authoritarian scheme (made academically respectable by invoking Weber, Pareto, Hobbes and Samuel Huntington) of development which now implements the new U.S. post-Vietnam strategy of more tightly integrating the periphery to monopoly industrial needs and IMF/World Bank imperatives by replacing parliamentary institutions with the militarized corporatist state.[31]

With the precipitous obsolescence of English as medium of instruction and communication, the growth of nationalist forces in all sectors, and the rapid disintegration of the new oligarchic ruling bloc as we approach the terminal decades of this century, the rupture of U.S. hegemony in the seventies and its supersession by a resurgent national-popular consensus will become finally irreversible--if that has not already happened. Hypothetically fulfilling Bakhtin's aphorism that "the sign becomes an arena of class struggle," the ensemble of signifying practices (which includes writing) is now envisaged as heavily contested terrain.[32] While imperialist values and the "colonial mentality" syndrome (whose contemporary tropes are the Free Trade Zones, warm body exports, prostitution-tourist industry, etc.) continue to be fostered by the controlled mass media, an oppositional trend (in underground newspapers, teach-ins, music, poster art, Brechtian theater, films, etc.) recuperating the vitality of the submerged if immanent revolutionary genealogy of our culture, is evolving throughout the islands. This trend seeks to fuse the mimetic-cognitive function of art (where, by nuanced sublimations, "the imaginary resolution of real-life contradictions" is inscribed) with its ethical-educative power in order to invent new subject-positions, contest dominated terrains hitherto pacified, mobilize mass energies, and incite emancipatory subversions in all areas of life.[33]

At this pivotal juncture, our paramount decolonizing project--an integral component of the ongoing national democratic struggle--is the construction of a national-popular canon of discourses and practices that would release energies and catalyze wills, ushering the stage for a dialectical transaction between past and future, between folklore/common sense and scientific socialism, between tradition and the creation of "the new person."[34] It may not be premature or anti-climactic to announce here that we have long passed the stage when the rhetorical juxtaposition of texts by Jefferson and Schlesinger with those by Jose Maria Sison and Father Conrado Balweg can be a useful ecumenical game; such intertextuality would neither entertain nor deceive anyone. And proposing for the *n*th time that we re-read T.S. Eliot, Faulkner, Henry James, Ezra Pound, and the classics only serves to lend moral credence to World Bank/IMF directives for the more intense exploitation of Filipino peasants, women, Moros and Igorots, students, workers, etc., and in the long run to legitimize U.S. political, military and economic aid for developmentalist terrorism and repression. Given this unremitting complicity of the U.S. administrations with the daily brutalization of the Filipino people by its well-tutored client, perhaps Hemingway himself would, if he could revisit now, be painfully surprised and even outraged.

Today, the praxis or science of writing in the Philippines manifests itself in its unrelenting and experimentally versatile drive to Filipinize dialectical materialism so that by purging it of Orientalizing elements and productivist constraints, and applying the method of materialistic dialectics to the analysis of multilayered conjunctures, we can liberate our people's trans-formative genius in a profound popular-democratic renaissance--a permanent recovery and affirmation of our national identity in the process of being/becoming--that would be our singular contribution to the advance of socialist revolution on our planet.

VI
Unleashing Dreams, Mapping the Space of Desire

Space is political and ideological. It is a product literally filled with ideologies. . . . There is an ideology of space. Why? Because space, which seems homogeneous, which seems to be completely objective in its pure form, such as we ascertain it, is a social product. . . . Today, more than ever, there are no ideas without a utopia. . . .

Henri Lefebvre

The terrible irony has been that the real processes of absolute urban and industrial priority, and of the related priority of the advanced and civilized nations, worked through not only to damage the "rural idiots" and the colonial "barbarians and semi-barbarians," but to damage, at the heart, the urban proletarians themselves, and the advanced and civilized societies over which, in their turn, the priorities exercised their domination, in a strange dialectical twist. . . . Thus the "rural idiots" and the "barbarians and semi-barbarians" have been, for the last forty years, the main revolutionary force in the world.

Raymond Williams

Is the city in modern Western discourse an archetypal idea or an originary, totalizing metaphor crying for deconstruction, as critical post-structuralist theory suggests? Or is it a unique "spatial-distributive pattern," as technocrats of the multicentered urban fields propose, susceptible to empirical and quantifying market analysis?

But which city are we speaking about? Where? When? Whose and for whom?

LOCUS OF THE EXORBITANT

If the Philippines as part of the developing Third World occupies that fated peripheral space, the last hinterland of global capitalism now being irreparably mechanized via export-industrialization schemes (as my previous chapters have shown), it is then not to Frederick Engel's reading of the classic industrial city Manchester, in *The Condition of the Working Class in England* (1844), that we should turn to as Baedeker and cicerone, but to the periodic, voluminous World Bank Country Reports. The major source of development funds for the Philippines, the World Bank, through its president, Robert McNamara, unequivocally enunciated the Bank's rationale for its containment and urban counter-insurgency program: "Historically, violence and civil upheaval are more common in cities than in the countryside. Frustrations that fester among the urban poor are readily exploited by political extremists."[1] For the administrators of the corporate empire, a Third World city like Manila (population: eight million, with annual growth rate of 3.5%) is legible, nonplural, a volatile and "naked" city but still utterly comprehensible to them.

Neither quite the Enlightenment city of Virtue nor the Victorian city of Vice, Manila as the locus of class conflict and overdetermined displacements/condensations may be apprehended as already "beyond good and evil." Possessed and walled-in by Spanish conquistadors, it was seized by U.S. imperialists, then ravished by Japanese hordes, and then flung open to the highest transnational bidders. Its process of transvaluation may be said to reverse the trajectory of its Western archetypes like London, Paris, New York: from the Babylon of the Spanish adventurers, it evolved by the end of the 19th century into an inchoate Babel, the delirious city of Baudelaire's *vie moderne*--a pale imitation, to be sure--which celebrated the permanently transitory and the artificial.

From the rubble of World War II, Manila loomed as the "unreal" hallucinatory mirage--the depraved, gutted, infernal city of Dante, distinguished by a concentration of heterogeneous uprooted rural folk and war survivors, and a sharp division of labor--an ecology and morphology exacerbated by class divisions and historical sedimentation. It replicated the dynamics of the 19th-century European city whose market economy and elaborate bureaucracy generated that peculiar, amorphous urban sensibility theorized by Max Weber, George Simmel, Oswald Spengler, and others.[12] The advent of a military authoritarian regime in 1972 sought by fiat to transform Manila and its environs into a New Jerusalem ("the city of Man," according to its governor, Imelda Marcos) symbolizing the perfectibility of the species; but so far it has turned out to be a tawdry simulacrum concealing, like those whitewashed fences thrown up to hide shanty towns lining the streets to the city's international airport, an egregiously plastic, perilous but besieged Sodom.

A Third World metropolis like MetroManila and mirror-counterparts like Cebu, Davao City, etc., cannot be read and deciphered by positing the "total intellectual and imaginative structure" of urban experience posited by Weber, Mumford, and Kevin Lynch. It can only be comprehended, as Bryan Roberts points out, within the uneven and combined development of world capitalism, within the parameters of underdevelopment.[3]. Roberts refutes the hitherto unquestioned axioms of Wirth and Simmel's urban sociology by demonstrating that in Third World cities, primary relationships such as kinship, ethnicity, and religion, not secondary ties, organize and give meaning to the lives of their inhabitants. However, it would be grossly mechanical and reductive to associate the city's spatial and ideological configuration with the all-determining mode of production and technological instrument--the organized process of capital production, reproduction, circulation, accumulation, etc. That is the reflex of dogmatic or vulgar Marxism. I would suggest that given the direction of Manila's development toward a more "polycentric ecological field," to use a current formulation, a decentered urban field crystallizing as Malacanang Palace (the local White House) loses its pivotal leverage at the onslaught of the new oppositional strategy of dispersal and deterritorializing tactics (Deleuze and Guattari). Manuel Castell's consistently dialectical approach seems more heuristic and cogent: "The urban system is not external to the social structure; it specifies the social structure, it forms part of it. But in every concrete practice, account must be taken of its articulation with other levels than those specified in the system."[4] This articulation of the urban "subject," Manila, as refracted in literary symbolism, character and imagery, is what I shall now sketch in the following exploratory notes.

A DREAM OF THE INFRASTRUCTURE

Unlike the western industrialized metropolis sprung from the eleventh-twelfth century *burg* (bourg, borough) of the nascent merchant class built in a circular pattern outside the walls of the medieval monastery or ecclesiastical enclave, the city of Manila (now MetroManila, embracing Quezon City, the official capital, and adjacent suburbs and sub-cities) was "founded" by the Spanish conquistador Miguel Lopez de Legaspi on 19 May 1571 on the ruins of an Islamic settlement, the fortified hamlet of "May-Nila" ruled by two native Rajahs.

I want to emphasize this initial and initiating fact as the constitutive element of difference between the western conception of the city and the Philippine (in a sense peculiarly Third World) approach. For the truth is that it was not through the clearing of wilderness to establish guilds and market-fairs, but through organized violence and the forcible imposition of feudal Christianity and theocratic authority that the scaffolding of the Philippine cities—not just Manila—was erected. In retrospect, this twofold motion of negation and gestation—a dialectical unity of opposites—significantly parallels the artistic process itself as a double movement of exclusion and synthesis, and subsumes the linguistic phases of metaphor and metonymy.[5]

Suffice it for the limited scope of this inquiry to extrapolate the nature of three centuries of Spanish subjugation of the Philippines, beginning from Legaspi's ritual act of concluding a peace treaty with the vanquished Muslim chiefs whose town was reduced to ashes, with the artillery of twenty-odd vessels presiding over this reconciliation. The treaty demonstrated to all the collusion of the Cross and Sword, church and state. But the narrative of the chronicles suggests an inverted anachronism, or more precisely a kind of conflation of two socio-economic formations: the tribal-communal and the mercantile-capitalist. We are told that to symbolize taking possession of the land, the Spaniards ceremonially lopped off the branches of a tree; but the Filipino chiefs, instead of enacting the performance of a traditional blood pact to signify their vassalage to the Spanish monarch, chose to have a public notary attest to their irreversible conversion.[6]

I submit that we have, in this tell-tale foregrounding of the written contract in the native consciousness, a seminal conjuncture whose archeology has not yet been fully explored, the elements of an interpretive model of the city, its integrity and protean manifestations, in literature.

This model would derive from the proposition that a city whose genealogy is inscribed in a contract forged from conquest and expropriation can reproduce itself in literary form in two ways: first, as a metaphor of the primordial unity and sacred origin of social life, celebrating the victor and its numinous or mystical aura; or second, as a metonymy/synecdoche, a differential or displacing technique correlating action and thought, the document or theory animating practice and the future projects we contemplate. Conversely, the projects evolving will dictate in the process the narrative of the making of contracts, coalitions, parties, etc. In Philippine literature, if I may anticipate what follows, the city of history, as the raw material worked into ideology and thus overdetermined in its meanings and implications, contains within itself a dialectical mode of resolving historic contradictions—not just in the mechanics of literary form but in the logic of their content—only insofar as the writer abandons the mythic potential of the city and pursues its metonymic thrust and direction.

This meditation on the city, on "Manila" as one term of the opposition of which the other could be virgin islands/the countryside, aims to describe in somewhat schematic fashion the ambivalent and polarizing attitudes Filipino writers have assumed toward the city. Adopting a chronological mapping-out of the terrain, we begin before Manila's founding, from the eighth century to Magellan's arrival in 1521, when commerce and trade with China, India, and desultory European merchants flourished. The growth of coastal towns into trading centers testifies to a rupture analogous to the transformation of Manila not as a Muslim citadel but as terminal of the galleon trade linking Mexico and Europe to Asia.

A novel (now in progress) that may propose a symptomatic reading of Manila's genesis is being completed by Ninotchka Rosca, a Filipina fictionist now in self-exile in Hawaii, entitled *Soliman of Manila: A Historical Novel.* Her outline uses the fortified village of the Muslim rajahs less as picturesque setting than a conflict-ridden milieu where the material crystallization of "racial and historical memory" (as artifacts) persist, becoming the prize-object of contestation. Predictably, in her version, Soliman succumbs because his understanding operated within a limited organic framework, within a personalistic ethos based on a communal mode of production, whereas the Spanish invaders had bargained time for space, winning allies by force or propaganda among inland tribes surrounding Manila. The Spaniards eventually encircled Soliman's palisades by insuring their control of supply lines, finally conquering by a strategy of detour and displacement.[7] A footnote to this novelistic drama can be cited here: on the wreckage of Soliman's village, the Spaniards built Fort Santiago, the nucleus for what later became in 1571 a Walled City called "Intramuros." This Asian outpost of the Spanish empire, a springboard for trade with China and not, as originally conceived, for raiding the spices of the Moluccas, was awarded a royal coat of arms by King Philip II and christened "the Noble and Ever-Loyal City."[8]

An existentialist reading of Manila as the site of a moral dilemma, the vicissitudes of a metaphysical doubt, has been rendered in the story "I, Suliman" by Adrian Cristobal, a leading technocrat of the Marcos dictatorship. For Cristobal, Manila is only a copy of the absurd universe of Kafka or Camus which occasions Soliman's stoic quest for self-fulfillment. In a sustained interior monologue, Soliman mechanically orders the burning of Manila as a solitary decision, to prevent the "seat of our happiness" from being "the cursed prison of our race." The city serves only as a pawn in the game of competing wills or monads. Cristobal establishes an ironic equivalence between the city and subjective freedom, identifying the city's destruction with a personal heroism based on the will to risk one's life in a struggle predestined to defeat. This is less a diagnosis of the inadequacy of the tribal formation than of the uprooted Manila intellectual's resentful

dream of power evaporating in mock-heroic impotence. Charac-
teristically, Cristobal is trapped within solipsistic idealism as he
attributes the Spaniards' conquest to their single-minded devotion
to faith, an irrationalism which an ostensibly religious writer like
Nick Joaquin would not be found guilty.[9]

TERRESTRIAL DECENTERING

From the sixteenth to the eighteenth century, Manila failed to
emerge from the cocoon of Intramuros, the "Walled City" environed
by numerous churches, with its suburbs functioning as country seats
for the aristocratic Peninsulars (Spaniards in the Philippines but
born in Spain) and as quarantined sectors for certain aliens like the
Chinese. For two years, 1762-1764, the British occupied
Intramuros, revealing thus the internal contradictions of Spanish
hegemony over the archipelago. But the literature produced by the
friars, as well as the reproduction of medieval romances, saints'
lives, sermons and commentaries on the Gospels, etc., in an
atmosphere of censorship and inquisition, failed to articulate or
even hint at the long-smoldering contradictions in the city, as
witnessed by the innumerable deadly skirmishes and feuds between
the secular office of the Governor-General and the religious orders.

One incident, the central exhibit of this fatal cleavage in the
power bloc defining the city's primal unity, is the assassination of
Governor Fernando Bustamante y Bustillo (1717-1719). His honesty
and fidelity to the King impelled him to challenge the undisputed
hegemony of the friars, provoking the latter to murder him in his
palace within the Walled City. An extremely multi-faceted,
self-conscious narrative, formerly ascribed to Father Jose Burgos
(1860-1872), the first nationalist martyr, of the Bustamante affair
is found in *La Loba Negra* (The Black She-Wolf). This work spans
the period 1717-1726 and revolves around Bustamante's attempt to
purge the city of corruption, specifically the friars' manipulation of
the galleon trade and their tampering with the public treasury. It
appears that the city officials then were extorting bribes from
wealthy citizens, as evinced by the testimony of a Dutch observer
describing Manila circa 1717, which is incorporated into the text of
the narrative:[10]

It's a big city protected by a strong wall surrounding it. The
houses are large and beautiful. . . . The inhabitants, mostly
Spaniards, live a life of ostentation and leisure with nothing to
worry about. Most of their foodstuffs and general merchandise
are brought over by the Sangleys [Chinese merchants] who
come from China and who own attractive and well-stocked
stores displaying a lot of clothing brought over by their ships
and some caravels from New Spain. Gold and silver coins are
in abundance and foreign exchange is a thriving business.

A seaport which the natives call May-Nilad is washed by a swift and treacherous river, the Mapagsic, somewhat big and navigable.

The writer thus disrupts the myth of the city's original unity with the intrusion of a Protestant (Dutch) conscience, emptying the plenitude of the city as symbol of harmony between Church and State.

In the fable's analysis of the ordeal and killing of the King's representative, the city assumes the form of a labyrinth of masked, frocked or hooded conspirators staging a *putsch,* with the churchyards, streets and plazas serving as the theater for an inquisitorial pogrom. The syntax of intrigue cancels any transparency of motivation. With the city depicted as a microcosmic altar for the sacrifice of the King's surrogate, the widow and children of the murdered Governor proceed to carry out their vow of revenge by retreating to the countryside. Their strategy recapitulates Legaspi's outflanking and centrifugal move to isolate Soliman. A year after her pilgrimage away from the city, the widow (or her daughter) metamorphoses into the legendary outlaw, the "Black She-Wolf," displacing the city's control of the countryside and doubling the friars' rule of terror by her own incarnation of what has been repressed: the real historic contradiction between the Filipino masses and the exploitative institutions of the Church, agents of Spanish colonialism. The Black She-Wolf's reprisals assume the magnitude of a natural force, a figure of nemesis resolving social contradictions in practice and giving substance to the law of mercantilist competition deprived of pietistic rationalizations. The method of quasi-chronicling events is meant to demystify the notion of divine intervention in history: calamities—assault by pirates and pestilence—devastate Manila and its suburbs between 1720 and 1725, "years of dark terror and criminality stained by persecutions between Spanish civilians and religious."

Since Manila up to 1870 served primarily to support the lucrative Mexico-Philippines galleon trade for the benefit of the church and a tiny stratum of bureaucrats, it virtually existed as an island unto itself—a trope suggesting the profound discrepancy between the ideology of Christian salvation and the practice of the friars throughout the islands. The concurrence of thriving commercial activity and disintegrating civic unity, the crisis between secular administrators and religious orders, and later between Spanish and native priests, intimating sharpening class antagonisms underlying the crisis, powerfully registered by the landscape drawn at the end of *La Loba Negra* amid the irrepressible terror inflicted on the Church by the female victim-avenger—the concrete vehicle also of the mute, aggrieved millions tilling the soil and supplying food and other necessities to the city:

Manila . . . . was in the zenith of her commercial life. In her bay were anchored many ships flying the flags of different Europeans and Asian countries. There were large and commodious homes on her principal streets, and business was brisk. The citizens as well as the religious were secretly carrying deadly weapons on their belts under their capes. There were bloody encounters among them, often resulting in death, while Manila sparkled on the horizon as one of the most prosperous cities of the Orient. The documents we have before us, however, show that two-thirds of the islands were completely neglected so that Manila authorities were not aware of events in these places until after a year. In many places, the little rulers kept administering their respective territories and *sitios*, practising their own laws and their ancient religion which was partly Muslim and partly Hindu from India, where it was propagated to the last confines of the islands of Malaysia and Polynesia.[11]

The situation described above persisted, explaining in part the British capture of Manila in 1762-1764, until the mercantile system which artificially isolated Manila from international contacts was phased out by the reforms of Governor Basco y Vargas (1778-1787).

The year 1834 saw the opening of Manila to world trade, exposing the "walled-fortress" sensibility to the dynamic pressures of expanded commodity production. From 1809 to 1846, with thirty-nine merchant firms owned by English, American and French entrepreneurs operating in Manila, the city burst out from the cloistered atomosphere of Intramuros and pursued the adventure of commodities through the arcades and bazaars of adjoining districts like Binondo, Quiapo, Paco, etc. In parallel course, the Filipino imagination unshackled itself from the bonds of medieval romanticism and adopted the liberal and democratizing outlook of realism prevailing in nineteenth-century Europe.

A little less than fifty years after the fall of the Bastille and the rise of the European bourgeoisie as the ruling class of industrialized and urbanized nations, an epic romance by Francisco Balagtas entitled *Florante at Laura* (1838) was published. Using an elaborate allegorical plot (to escape official censorship), Balagtas dramatized the duplicitous stratagems of an individualist usurper who seizes control of a feudal city, Albania, from its rightful heir. The heir Florante is offered as a prey to ferocious beasts in a nightmarish jungle, the absolute antithesis to the city as the fountainhead of love, beauty, wisdom, joy. Ironically, Balagtas is supposed to be attacking the city, Manila, and what it stood for; but his adherence to the Greek idea of the city-state and its ideals of decorum, virtue, and civility, seems to undercut his intention--until we realize, on deeper probing, that the city he seemingly acclaims is the space of treachery; the space of predatory competitiveness, avarice and greed for power; it is the space where individuals can conceal private selfish motives through stylized manners, conventional gestures, formulas of speech and thoughts. In the city, the inhabitants are easily duped by charlatans and demagogues, coaxed to act as a rebellious mob (see stanzas 378-379). Not that Balagtas is trying to render Le Bon's psychology of the crowd into metrical romance. Himself victimized by the landlord-elite, Balagtas targetted not the fact of a hierarchic, sacramental order but rather its degeneration, its subversion by putative or nominal guardians. Disintegration of this civic, hierarchical system--the source of peace, love, harmony, creative self-fulfillment--will yield only the reign of the brute, the reign of *lex talionis.*[12]

SUBTERRANEAN CARTOGRAPHY

It is not surprising at this point to observe our interpretive model of two possible modes of representing the city, the metaphoric and the metonymic, grounding itself in the historical transition of Manila from the "Walled City" resembling Balagtas' "Albania" to the dispersed commercial/trading center adumbrated in *La Loba Negra*. In the same breath, we perceive the emergence of the semiotic disparity implicit in those modes between the classical conception of the city which informs Balagtas' allegory, and the romantic critique saturating the text of *La Loba Negra*. In the latter we may recall the tendency to valorize the primitive as a "return of the repressed" and the nihilistic repudiation of the degenerate ethos of the city. (Balagtas succeeds in thwarting this possibility by the ruse of inventing the character of Aladin, the chivalric Moor, who rescues Florante from the beasts and helps him recapture the city, thus validating the hierarchical order and legitimizing absolute monarchy.) We encounter at this point a vast amount of didactic writing--the ubiquitous example from the anthologies is the collection of moralizing letters by Father Modesto de Castro entitled *Urbana at Felisa* (1864)--with the all too familiar motif of the city as the diabolic snare or trap for innocent, virtuous maidens venturing from pastoral retreats. In this context, the world (read: *Manila*) abounds with sinful temptations, so that transactions with the Other must be performed in strict obedience to Church-sanctioned rules of conduct and propriety. In other words, without a patriarch-oriented hermeneutics and code, the city is a many-layered text of puzzling insinuations and ambiguities to be deciphered at one's own risk. We are now at the threshold of the modernist interpretation of city experience.

By the middle of the nineteenth century, the paradigmatic and centralizing role of Manila, its dream of becoming the womb and matrix of Renaissance *virtu* and Roman piety, has been severely undermined by the emergence of petty commodity production, competition between import-export middlemen or *compradors*, and the concentration of the *principalia* (the native elite) on cultivating export-crops. For the elite, the city now becomes a constricting playground good only as a jumping-off point for travel to and study in Europe. While it was the city-born-and-bred worker Andres Bonifacio who would rally the masses at the city outskirts, inspired by such books as Hugo's *Les Miserables* and Sue's *The Wandering Jew* (Sue's forte was the Parisian underworld milieu), it was the *principalia's* offspring, Jose Rizal, born and raised in the province of Laguna but educated in Madrid, Paris and Berlin, who would privilege the city as the historic social text, the veritable palimpsest, of class contradictions.

In his first novel *Noli Me Tangere* (1886), Rizal charted the trials of a Creole *ilustrado* as he falls victim to the repressive maneuvers of the religious orders in the bucolic setting of his home town in San Diego. The novel begins with the protagonist Ibarra's arrival in Manila from Europe, discovering "the phenomenon of an unchanging city in a country of uncertainties."[13] Immediately Ibarra learns the tragic fate of his father who, accused as a heretic/freethinker, had his body condemned to lie outside the Catholic cemetery. Before shifting the narrative to San Diego, Rizal (in Chapter 8) unfolds the city's signifiers as indices and symbols of class conflict. However, unlike the dilettante *flaneur* of Baudelaire's time apprehending the decay of the *interieur* in the department store's labyrinth of merchandise (as Walter Benjamin has acutely noted),[14] Rizal's embattled hero surveys the panorama of crowds. He anticipates the coming of a chain-gang of native prisoners based on childhood memories:

> . . . The prisoners were usually tall men with stern faces, whom Ibarra had never seen smile but whose eyes flashed when the whip fell whistling across their shoulders. . . . Once in his boyhood Ibarra had witnessed a scene that had struck his imagination. It had been high noon; the sun's rays fell mercilessly. Under the poor shade of a wooden cart lay one of those unfortunates, unconscious, his eyes staring wide. Two of his fellows were silently putting together a bamboo litter, without anger, without sorrow, without impatience--that, it was said, was what the natives were like. You today, our turn tomorrow, they seemed to be telling themselves. People hurried by without a glance; women passed, looked and went on their way; the sight was common enough, so common that hearts had grown calloused. The carriages rolled by, their varnished bodies gleaming in the rays of a brilliant sun in a cloudless sky. He alone, a boy of eleven, newly arrived in the city, had been touched; he alone, he felt sure, had slept badly because of it.[15]

It is thus that the narrative reflects from the surface of the city landscape the agonies and resistance of the populace, splitting the character's sensibility into discordant fragments, allowing the submerged historicity of the city to problematize his stance of detachment. The doubling of the protagonist's consciousness allows him to glimpse the materiality of dreams, hopes, memory itself in the presence of human labor:

> To his left, from the cigar factory at Arroceros, came the rattle and clatter of the women cigar-makers beating tobacco leaves. . . . He imagined the women's lively chatter, the broad jokes, so reminiscent of the district of Lavaples in Madrid, where other cigar-women rioted and put the despised policemen to rout with ribald laughter.
>
> The Botanical Garden dispelled these pleasant recollections; an odious comparison put before his eyes the botanical gardens in Europe, in countries where it cost much money and determination to make a leaf grow or a bud flower. . . . Ibarra turned his eyes away and saw to his right the old city of Manila, surrounded still by its walls and moats like an undernourished adolescent wrapped in her grandmother's finery.[16]

In Rizal's second novel, *El Filibusterismo* (1891), the city becomes the testing ground for realizing Simoun's (Ibarra in disguise) plan for revenge. The city becomes thick, equivocally plural and dense with dissonant character-types, ramifying into diverse and multiple locations. But Simoun's scheme to rescue his former sweetheart Maria Clara from a convent collapses with her death, resulting in amplifying the general atmosphere of chagrin and bitter disillusionment of many Filipinos, illustrated vividly in the youth Isagani's "bitterness for his unrequited love" so that

> . . . even the interminable port works [outside the Walled City], to which in other times he had dedicated no less than three odes, appeared to him absurd, ridiculous, puerile.
>
> The port, ah, the port of Manila, a bastard that from the moment of conception had brought only humiliation and shame to all! If, at least, after so much sacrifice, it were not to turn out a disgusting abortion![17]

Rizal's imagery and comparisons in the preceding two quotations convey an explicit devaluation of the city from its mythical stature. Just as the *Noli* introduced the hierarchical structure of society at a dinner party in the city, the *Fili's* climactic episode occurs during a wedding feast in the same house where the city's high secular and religious officials would be assembled.

I would argue that Rizal could envision the conspiratorial and *putschist* scheme of Simoun, the masquerading ironist fabricating revelations behind the scene, only in the city because by offering infinite possibilities of chance encounters, coincidences, fortuitous and accidental happenings, Manila generates the conditions for the individual subject disappearing and merging with the interplay of collective forces, social classes, in order to trace the path of his/her personal destiny. This also explains why the city is the principal arena where games, performances, tricks and illusionary inventions of all kinds--I emphasize the episode of the talking mummy in Chapter 18--can thrive naturally, so to speak, though all are contrived, with their impact transgressing normal routine and exposing the truth of social domination. Although Rizal concludes Simoun's quest with his suicide, with the organic life of Nature in the background naturalizing his death, it is the city of Manila which we sense seething underneath and convulsed with all the unresolved conflicts temporarily pacified by nostalgic utopian longings. For Rizal, imprisoned in Fort Santiago and executed just outside the Walled City, it is the political struggle for control of the city that will elucidate the truth of ideas vis-a-vis objective reality, and the power of will. For whoever commands the city, determines the destiny of the whole nation.

Despite massive popular support for the 1896 revolution against Spain, it failed to seize the city chiefly because the vacillating *ilustrado* leadership of the revolutionary forces temporized and trusted the invading U.S. army to liberate it for the Philippine Republic. It took the intellectual-critical energies of a whole generation to recuperate Rizal's insight that Manila determines the fate of the nation, insofar as it extracts the wealth of the laboring masses in the countryside. The cardinal lesson gained in the period before the seizure of Manila in 1898 by the American invaders and the Sakdalista revolt of 1935, apart from the fact that the city cannot survive without its parasitism on the peasantry, is the need to analyze the concrete forces germinating within the city--trade unions had been organized, the petty bourgeois intellectuals had grown in alliance with the proletariat. These developments rendered obsolete the artist's quest for an ideal synthesis of the European city in an Asian setting, given the formation of a comprador merchant class and with it the seeds of national and class solidarity between the workers in the city and the peasants in the rural hinterlands. But for a few years, especially the first two decades of American domination, Filipino writers ignored the peasants as potential revolutionary allies and concentrated on the plight of the city worker.

Except for the untypical aestheticist cataloguing of local color in such works as *Ninay* (1885) of Padro Paterno, we can sum up by saying that the city for the Filipino writer in the nineteenth century signified the locus of power, the unifying metaphor that short-circuits the infinite substitutions of instinct and desire. When the United States supplanted Spain as the metropolitan power in 1898, the city--or what was left of it after General Aguinaldo, the Republic's President, surrendered--ceased to be the goal of the revolutionary forces and was converted into the arena of working class struggles as they coincided with the ideological resistance of seditious playwrights like Aurelio Tolentino, Severino Reyes, etc. But it was in the novels of Faustino Aguilar (*Pinaglahuan*, 1907) and Lope K. Santos (*Banaag at Sikat*, 1906) that the city recovers its metonymic potential; that is, its function of establishing those intricate mediations between private or psychic obsessions and the imperatives of class struggle.

From the twenties to the forties, when Filipino writers strove to wield English as an expressive medium, the city loomed as a felt absence, an unknown integer whose plural significations coexisted with all the empty longings, disillusionments, resignations of peasants and young people in love trapped in villages and farms. Examples of this genre include Jose Garcia Villa's *Footnote to Youth*, Paz Marquez Benitez's "Dead Stars," Delfin Fresnosa's "Tragedy at Lumba's Bend," and Juan Laya's novel *His Native Soil*. The trend is broken by Narciso Reyes' "Tinubuang Lupa" ("Native Land", 1943) where the retreat from the city occupied by Japanese invaders brings about a rediscovery of authentic national identity through contact with the soil, folk customs, and organic impulse.[18]

Only in three writers--Arturo Rotor, Hernando Ocampo, Manuel Arguilla--do we find the realistic transcript of city experience treated as a means of projecting the totality of social life which has been hidden, occluded, or suppressed in the immediacy of pure feelings or abstract notions. Rotor remains the only Filipino writer in English who has seriously described the lives of prisoners (see, for example, "Convict's Twilight") as a critical mirror of the whole society, an antithetical image to the predatory individualism of the city.[19] In contrast, the elegiac celebration of urban pathos--the pathos of workers' lives circumscribed by physical need, scarcity, and exploitation--found expression in the stories of Hernando Ocampo (for example, "We or They"), and continued in the postwar stories of Serafin Guinigundo, Andres Cristobal Cruz, D. Paulo Dizon, Teodoro Agoncillo, and the generation associated with Kadipan, an organization of Tagalog writers in the universities.[20] For his part, Arguilla attempted to explode the profit-centered milieu of the city by a relentless diagnosis of the panicked sensibilities of petty bourgeois characters fighting to survive and maintain their dignity (see his "Caps and Lower Case").[21] Arguilla's 1940 collection of stories *How My Brother Leon Brought Home a Wife and Other Stories* signalled the exhaustion of the pastoralizing trend in Philippine writing, and heralded the advent of a cosmopolitan openness on the eve of the Japanese occupation of Manila. Such a decisive event, like the British capture of Manila in the eighteenth century, released energies directed to the revival of Tagalog as the viable medium of expression and communication. On the other hand, the destruction of Manila by Japanese dynamite and United States bombs precipitated its crystallization into myth precisely because of its loss.

GEOGRAPHIC FETISHISM

The single Filipino author who has elevated the city of Manila into archetypal stature is Nick Joaquin. In his famous essay "La Naval de Manila" (1943), Joaquin asserted that "the basic form, the temper, the physiognomy" of the Filipino nation was created by Spanish colonial tyranny, not by the people's struggle for liberation. And it is Christianity, its doctrine of free will, that freed us from pagan custom and taboo, "the tight fixed web of tribal obedience." The Spanish legacy is embodied in Manila, whose patron saint, the Holy Virgin of the Rosary, is responsible for miraculously saving the city in 1646 from the clutches of Dutch Protestant heresy. The city preserves "the prime work of Christianity," namely, "the awakening of the self, this release and expansion of the consciousness."[22] The city then symbolizes Christian freedom emblematized by the annual celebration of "La Naval de Manila," a religious procession in honor of the Virgin. Without this devotion to the Virgin, Joaquin alleges, Filipinos will not possess "a sense of infinity," of "being at home in history."

Together with the feast for the Virgin, Intramuros or the Walled City represents, for Joaquin, a standard to measure and judge the quality of modern progress. The choral narrator of Joaquin's play *A Portrait of the Artist as Filipino* apostrophizes Manila as the antediluvian, paradisal origin before the Fall:

Intramuros! The old Manila, the original Manila. The Noble and Ever Loyal City. . . . To the early conquistadores she was a New Rome. Within these walls was gathered the wealth of the Orient--silk from China; spices from Java; gold and ivory and precious stones from India. And within these walls the Champions of Christ assembled to conquer the Orient for the Cross. Through these old streets once crowded a marvelous multitude--viceroys and archbishops; mystics and merchants; pagan sorcerers and Christian martyrs; nuns and harlots and elegant marquesas; English pirates, Chinese mandarins, Portuguese traitors, Dutch spies, Moro sultans, and Yankee clipper captains. For three centuries this medieval town was a Babylon in its commerce and a New Jerusalem in its faith. . . . This is the Calle Real--the main street of the city, the main street of the land, the main street of our history. Through this street the viceroys made their formal entry into the city. And on this street the principal families had their town houses--splendid ancient structures with red-tile roofs and wrought-iron balconies and fountains playing in the interior patios. . . .[23]

The house of Don Lorenzo Marasigan (and it is the house which defines time and space, interpellating subjects to take up their positions in society) where survivors of the 1896 revolution gathered every year to watch the Naval procession, functions as "the conscience" of the city, upholding traditional civic virtues against commodity-fetishism and the reified exchanges of the market. World War II destroys the house so that, with the influx of displaced rural folk into the city, it is left to the artist (personified by Bitoy) to preserve the city now only as a trope of the imagination:

> It is gone now--that house . . . . It finally took a global war to destroy this house and the three people who fought for it. . . . They died with their house and they died with their city--and maybe it's just as well they did. They could never have survived the death of the old Manila. And yet--listen!--it is not dead; it has not perished! . . . . Your city--my city--the city of our fathers--still lives! Something of it is left; something of it survives, and will survive, as long as I live and remember--I who have known and loved and cherished these things! (He stoops down on one knee and makes a gesture of scooping earth).
>
> Oh Paula, Candida--listen to me! By your dust and by the dust of all the generations, I promise to continue, I promise to preserve! The jungle may advance, the bombs may fall again--but while 1 live, you live--and this dear city of our affections shall rise again--if only in my song![24]

With allusive eloquence, Joaquin is endeavoring to recapitulate in his art the Platonic evocation of the ancient city, implicitly invoking Legaspi's founding act of fusing the King's secular power and the priest's divine-magical wisdom, the military machine and religious mythology. Lewis Mumford reminds us of this utopian function of the city in history:

> . . . . As Fustel de Coulanges and Bachofen pointed out a century ago, the city was primarily a religious phenomenon; it was the home of a God, and even the city wall points to this super-human origin; for Mircea Eliade is probably correct in inferring that its primary function was to hold chaos at bay and ward off inimical spirits. This cosmic orientation, these mythic-religious claims, this royal preemption of the powers and functions of the community are what transformed the mere village or town into a city: something "out of this world," the home of a god. . . . The city itself was transmogrified into an ideal form--a glimpse of eternal order, a visible heaven on earth, a seat of the life abundant--in other words, utopia.[25]

What I suggested earlier as a binary opposition between the

city and the countryside may serve to organize my comment here on Joaquin's novella *The Woman Who Had Two Navels.* The chief protagonist, Paco Texeira, born and bred in Macao and Hong Kong, where East and West interpenetrate, succumbs to the spell of postwar Manila residents Dona Concha Vidal and her daughter. Manila serves the twin function of metaphoric vehicle for reconciling contradictions, or alternatively, a synchronic device to advance Paco's quest for self-fulfillment. I quote the beginning of a long passage to illustrate this point:

> By the time he met the Senora de Vidal he had become deeply interested in Manila and was ready to be interested in any woman who most piquantly suggested that combination of primitive mysticism and slick modernity which he felt to be the special temper of the city and its people: pert girls dancing with abandon all night long in the cabarets and fleeing in black veils to hear the first Mass at dawn, boys in the latest loudest Hollywood styles, with American slang in their mouths and the crucifix on their breasts; streets ornate with movie palaces and jammed with traffic through which leaf-crowned and barefooted penitents carried a Black Christ in procession--and always, up there above the crowds and hot dust and skeleton ruins and gay cabarets: the mountains, and the woman sleeping in a silence mighty with myth and mystery--for she was the ancient goddess of the land (said the people) sleeping out the thousand years of bondage; but when at last she awoke, it would be a Golden Age again for the land: no more suffering; no more toil; no rich and no poor.[26]

In Joaquin's later stories, like "Candido's Apocalypse" in which the pressures of urban middle-class upmanship are registered in the main character's adolescent revolt against adult norms, and particularly "The Order of Melkizedek," Joaquin's prophetic or utopian impulse drives him to incorporate the primal, mythical impulses of the countryside into his totalizing vision of a resurrected Manila.

In stories like "Guardia de Honor," "May Day Eve," and "Summer Solstice," the city occupies the foreground as an actor or protagonist in a drama of cross-purposes and epiphanic reversals. Manila seems to approximate Henri Lefebvre's notion of the rediscovery of the Festival, though in another context.[27] Custom and tradition channel erotic drives into ritual and ceremony inseparable from the city's corporative life: "In October, a breath of the north stirs Manila, blowing summer's dust and doves from the tile roofs, freshening the moss of old walls, as the city festoons itself with arches and paper lanterns for its great votive feast to the Virgin."[28] While the city, in "May Day Eve," presents family tradition and memory as agencies resolving the characters' moral predicaments, in "Summer Solstice" Joaquin contraposes to the patriarchal order of the Walled City the feminine aspect of the countryside, in this case the Paco suburb of 1850 where the primitive rite of the Tadtarin centered on a fertility cult of a Mother Goddess restores in a dramatic moment the pre-Spanish ascendancy of women in society. At this point, one may note how this centrifugal movement to the outskirts of the Walled City symptomatically betrays the cracks and fissures in Joaquin's myth.

Both the allusion to the female profile of the mountains in *The Woman Who Had Two Navels* and the resuscitation of the fertility goddess in "Summer Solstice" can be interpreted as Joaquin's unconscious attempt to exorcise the negative, the contradictory force opposing the patriarchal city, instead of being read as an indictment of the myth and an affirmation of the primitive. We can see Joaquin confronting the historical contradictions already grasped by the author of *La Loba Negra*, by Balagtas and Rizal; but his way of resolving such contradictions proceeds by an effort to absorb and institutionalize the irrational, the repressed. In "The Order of Melkizedek," the sectarian movement trying to revive a pre-Christian cult of a fertility god uses as headquarters an old nunnery in the Walled City. Joaquin's point of view is represented by Sid Estiva, absent from Manila for ten years, who sketches the decline of the city, the loss of homogeneity and cohesion:

> This was, thought Sid, jolting through downtown, a Manila his backside did not recall. If I closed my eyes, this could be the dirt road to a childhood summer in the provinces. But how shut eyes as agape now as then at the primitive? Rizal's image of the city as a frail girl wearing her grandmother's finery no longer fitted; this was a dirty old broad got up all wrong in a ye-ye girls' clothes. The old city walls that came into view across the soiled air and a bridgeful of chaos astonished with their look of calm and dignity.[29]

This montage or juxtaposition of temporal layers, a metaphoric substitution as static as Ezra Pound's ideogrammic style, informs the thematic layout of Joaquin's other stories--"A Pilgrim Yankee's Progress," "The Mass of St. Sylvester," "Three Generations," etc. and though the city unfolds a thick, multi-layered grid of contradictions, the glory of its past affords a mystifying and transcendental mechanism to obscure and cancel those real-life conflicts, tensions, antagonisms. The War constitutes a turning-point when the city as a metaphor for Jerusalem disappears, buried by the acute sense of time as a process of cyclic unfolding or a quasi-allegorical spiral where periodic climaxes of self-discovery serve merely to reinforce familial and clan pieties. It might not be altogether premature to conclude here that Joaquin conceives of the Filipino experience as so many varied permutations on the historic predicaments and moral crises that transpired in the Walled City of Intramuros; but this time, spatially, the stage has moved to the plush, gentrified suburbia of MetroManila once inhabited by farmers with carabaos and wooden plows. For all his subtle skill in deploying time-shifts and loops in his narrative sequence, Joaquin could not insert in his text the reality of what today Intramuros contains: the monumental headquarters of United States transnational corporations--the totality of global monopoly capitalism.

Myth and metaphor could not survive the literal annihilation of its support; reduced to ruins, Manila becomes dispersed in a constellation of gratuitous images signifying alienation. Manuel Viray's poem "Elegies," for example, fashions a montage of impressions laid out in metonymic sequence. "The past is a scar," descants the poet (in an unwitting riposte to Joaquin); "Here in the hard city block summer/Brings rank smell of estero and your smile . . . ."[30] Another postwar poet, Amado Unite, engages in a similar rendering of the city as an epitome of what Lukacs termed "reification," the reduction of human relationships to the mechanical connection between things:

Manhood in a House in Cabildo

Not one window now may mend
My manhood my house by the street
Of slow and rapid transit and
No door define or divide me
A secret and definite geography.
Yet they hand a blue anomaly between
My waking and the oblique day.
I can not fly them, house or manhood,
In the dead and desiccated city.[31]

Occupied by the Japanese military forces on 2 January 1942 and relinquished by them reluctantly in February 1945, not without fierce hand-to-hand combat, Manila was wiped out by both the enemy's incendiary and the liberator's bombs. Next to Warsaw, it was the most gutted and devastated city of the war. Millions suffered atrocities, tens of thousands were killed in Intramuros. Under the stress of utter privations during the war years, there sprang a solidarity hitherto absent in the Darwinian milieu depicted by Arguilla and Ocampo in the thirties, a communal unity vividly captured by Amado V. Hernandez in his article "Pasko ng 1944 at iba pang Mga Araw" ("Christmas of 1944 and Other Days"). I translate his original Tagalog:

More than at any other time, the old walls that divided the citizens, walls of three levels and classes obtaining in pre-war Manila, collapsed under the force of circumstance. In the ordeals of misery suffered by the majority, and amid hovering perils, the owners of property were forced to step down on bare earth and mix with the ordinary people. In those days, quite unexpectedly, the power which money and material possessions commanded faded away. . . .[32]

This levelling of status, however, concealed within it the sharpening of class dissensions, as shown in Hernandez's epic chronicle of the war *Bayang Malay (Liberated Country,* 1969), where villages under guerrilla control displaced Manila as the organized reservoir of energies, wills, dreams. In his earthy notations of city life, exuberant market scenes and comic-farcical festivities particularly in slum areas like Tondo (a radical shift in spatial and aesthetic orientation in contrast to Joaquin), Hernandez reaffirms the self-renewing folk energies and dynamic futurism of the plebeian and proletarian majority which, in Mikhail Bakhtin's cogent commentary, informs the fantastic urban allegories of Rabelais.[33]

Hernandez's militant empathy for the under-privileged, the outcasts and victims of class exploitation, defined the aesthetic and moral sensibility of a whole generation of writers in the sixties and seventies. Manila, in the performative texts of committed writers, displayed itself as the microcosm of the class-divided social totality in which personal compulsions coalesced into collective responses; but in the same breath these committed writers located within it those recalcitrant and disruptive forces that challenged the hegemony of the dominant elite who owned the material structures in the city, who controlled not just the physical artifacts but also the psychic patterns of life. In Hernandez's novel *Mga Ibong Mandaragit (Birds of Prey,* 1969), and stories like "Langaw Sa Isang Basong Gatas" ("A Fly on a Glass of Milk") and "Ipinanganak ang Isang Kaaway ng Sosyedad" ("An Enemy of Society is Born"), and his prison poems in *Isang Dipang Langit (A Breastful of Sky,* 1962), the decentering of the city as the goal and object of the struggle unfolds, culminating in the dispossession of squatters from their ancestral land as private urban housing encroaches. This topographical fusion of individual predicaments with the hidden mechanisms of capital investment and extraction of surplus-value in Hernandez's art eclipses the banality of petty bourgeois opportunism recorded in the superficially urbane fiction of Kerima Polotan-Tuvera and Gilda Cordero-Fernando, proving once more that the significance of the city in literature inheres in its metonymic, temporary dimension.

FROM THE MIGRANT TO THE NOMADIC

Before concluding, I would like at this point to explain why Manila is the only Philippine city that has preoccupied Filipino writers, in addition to what I have already said. The empirical evidence insists on the following: the Manila urban complex is today the country's most populous and most industrialized region. As the prime market and manufacturing center of an archipelago of

7,000 islands, it has experienced far greater growth in the last three decades than the whole nation, in terms of population and purchasing power. Two-fifths of more than 11,000 large-scale manufacturing establishments are found in the Manila area; they employ more than half of the total work force, and about two-thirds of all women workers.[34]   As distribution center, Manila's foreign trade surpasses in value that of all the other ports of entry combined. With the huge amount and variety of managerial talents, the abundant supply of diverse skilled labor; with the terminus of transportation lines located there, Manila as a conurbation of over eight million (compare the 1939 population of 623,493) easily functions as the administrative, educational, financial, cultural and commercial center of the nation. Formed not by the industrial revolution but by colonization and imperialist annexation, Manila as the prime city--the most westernized in monsoon Asia, according to one geographer--has preempted other sites in the Filipino imagination in its dual role of centralizing paradigmatic authority and as interlinking, syntagmatic influence.

In the seventies up to January 1981, the crisis of Western hegemony over the Third World reached a critical stage, with the victory of the Indochinese people in their war aginst U.S. imperialist aggression and in the upsurge of popular resistance from Iran to Zimbabwe and Nicaragua. In most of these underdeveloped regions, the theory and practice of protracted people's war, first formulated and applied by Mao Zedong in China, spelled the doom of the neocolonial cities by the revenge of the countryside, and by analogy the overthrow of the metropolitan power preying on these cities. For the Philippines, the strategy was proposed by Amado Guerrero in his epochal work *Philippine Society and Revolution* (1971):

> Chairman Mao's strategic principle of encircling the cities from the countryside should be assiduously implemented. It is in the countryside where the enemy can be compelled to spread his forces thinly and lured into areas where the initiative is completely in our hands. In the countryside, we can develop several fighting fronts, ranging in quality from guerilla zones to base areas. We can turn the most backward areas in the countryside into the most advanced political, military, economic, and cultural bastions of the revolution. We can create the armed independent regime in the countryside even before defeating the enemy in the cities.[35]

What underlies this perspective is the key principle of uneven development of the social structure whose articulation in literature oscillates between metaphoric and metonymic tracks.

In the late sixties and early seventies, the idea of the city as an immense prison (a mutation of the image of the besieged Intramuros, and later of Fort Santiago, where the national hero

Rizal was held before his execution and where thousands of guerrillas were tortured and murdered by the Japanese) informed the writings of political prisoners like Edgar Maranan, Jose Maria Sison, Father Ed de la Torre, Satur Ocampo, and others. Before martial law was imposed in 1972 and converted Manila into a militarized bunker, the city's atmosphere as an anarchic jungle where each pedestrian resembles a rabid wolf stalking the streets pervaded the works of Rogelio Mangahas, Ave Perez Jacob, Jose Lacaba, Ricardo Lee, Lualhati Bautista, and their comfreres. This mood and motif attained melodramatic scenario in Edgardo Reyes' novel *Sa Mga Kuko ng Liwanag (In the Claws of Light,* 1966), replicating the recurrent romantic theme of chaste women from the villages lured and raped in the city and the naive, trusting youth from the province driven to roam the alleys like a beast with fangs bared.[36] We thus recapitulate here the moment in *La Loba Negra* where, metonymically, the contagion of violence and corruption in Intramuros engenders the fierce black She-Wolf, the precursor of Joaquin's iconoclastic heroines, encircling the city from the countryside.

In the late seventies, Manila continued to suck in the uprooted and dislocated masses, totaling forty-nine million. This entailed a tremendous acceleration of density (particularly in slums where over two million people live and two thousand persons occupy a hectare, or 2.47 acres), as well as an exhaustion of resources. According to 1977 World Bank statistics, 39 percent of families (90 percent of slum dwellers) in Manila subsist below the poverty threshold of $250 per person.[37] Under the Marcos dictatorship, where profits from export-industries determine priorities, the policy of maintaining a steady supply of cheap labor by uprooting and dislocating millions of peasants guarantees the perpetuation of the vast slum areas. One can speculate that this invasion of the city may be deemed a mock-rehearsal of the encirclement strategy. But there is more than a rhetorical nuance to this socio-historical upheaval, for historically the authoritarian regime of the ancient city based on its military machine was limited and "passively challenged by the archaic, democratic, life-conserving village culture that has always embraced the larger part of mankind".[38]

Should we then abolish the city, as Blake, Thoreau, William Morris and others have argued? Or should we capture it?

ECOLOGY OF THE RHIZOME

Filipino partisans of the progressive imagination reply as follows. When the producers and creators of social wealth have begun to mobilize their transforming powers, even as the writers are remolding their consciousness and linguistic practice, the city will finally lose its privileged position as a machine wielded and directed by a parasitic minority, an oligarchic elite subservient to transnational corporate interests, and eventually become a hospitable and fertile milieu for human reason and desire. By then, the city as the primordial symbol of a lost metaphysical plenitude will disappear, having yielded to the city as the metonymy or narrative of a self-renewing praxis in which the objective, dynamic and sensuous world--the raw material and product of collective action--will provide the conditions for abolishing the historic demarcation between city and countryside, the outcome of social development from feudalism to capitalism. This revolutionary *praxis* will resolve the contradiction between intellectual and manual labor, allowing the imagination its playful transcendence over nature in a process by which the city metamorphoses into its Other, the garden of worldly pleasures. One poetic evocation of this dialectical promise is this lyric by Mila Aguilar, the title poem of a collection printed by Fishy Afoot Press, San Francisco, in 1984, with prefatory note by Jack Hirschman (also included in *A Comrade Is As Precious As A Rice Seedling* published by Kitchen Table Press):

Pall Hanging Over Manila

As the boat glides slowly
Portward
Carrying still the fresh winds
From sea and countryside
One can see the pall hanging over Manila,
City of one's birth,
One's most fevered child.
The dissonance of cars bustling to and fro
Greets ears used now to the silence of cicadas
Chirping warmly from cool treetops--
And later the gray smirking faces lined up
In jeeps reeking of sweat
And soot-laden collars.

Oh the pall that hangs over Manila,
City of my birth to violence,
My most fevered child!
On a hilltop at night
Far from the smokestacks belching
The daily black of exploitation
I watch her, bejeweled now
With varicolored gems of light
Moving seeming slow from a distance.
She lies,
Hard black stone inlaid
With clusters of gold and diamonds and rubies,
Hiding the many sins lurking behind
Esteros and seedy bars,
Knowing yet unthinking

Of the unfathomable grief she causes,
Grief causing lonely acts
Lonely acts pushing onward
A hungry desperate people.

Manila: metropolis mushrooming
Not out of any dream
But the sweat of millions
On steel-hot machines
And the toil of millions more
On placid-fertile greens.

With her arrest by the military on 6 August 1984, together with Professor Cynthia Nolasco, directress of the Extension Services, St. Joseph's College, and her subsequent solitary confinement in Camp Crame, Mila Aguilar has dramatized without any premeditation the immensely creative and versatile roles of the Filipina woman intellectual (she has been a journalist, poet, professor of English, educational administrator, and militant activist)--roles thousands more could play if the progressive movement could expand its theoretical latitude and modify its monolithic formula of "surrounding the city by the countryside." For the concepts "city" and "countryside" are less geographical terms than political.[39] A vast multi-sectoral protest campaign has sprung up to free Mila Aguilar, Cynthia Nolasco, Willy Tolentino and other political prisoners, mobilizing not only local organizations but also solidarity and libertarian forces in the cities of the U.S., Europe and other continents--the cities that now surround the countryside.

It is true that with the unprecedented and not quite anticipated mammoth demonstrations from Aquino's assassination in August 1983 to the 21 September 1984 demonstrations, a critical awareness of the crucial importance of urban struggles has recently surfaced. An article in *Ang Bayan* (November 1983), for example, emphasizes how cities--sixty of them comprising 38 percent of the entire population play a role in the formation of the united front, allowing the middle forces to make use of bourgeois democratic forms, channels, mass media, etc. However, this non-armed, peaceful and legal struggle is conceived simply as a subordinate instrument to provide direct material support to the "Red fighters" in the countryside, a programmatic *leitmotif* repeated endlessly. Notwithstanding demographic trends and, more important, the rapidly changing levels of political consciousness and organization which, I think, allow us again to rediscover Lenin's "polychronic" urban-oriented strategy--hitherto eclipsed by Mao's "monochronic" "Yenan way"--the static and essentially conservative view of people's war as chiefly a peasant/agrarian struggle still prevails.[40]

Space (the earth's face, landscapes) is inescapably political, the French Marxist philosopher Lefebvre insists, because it is a social and historical product: the city as bureaucratic headquarters, "sink," ethnic enclaves, etc.[41] The city as a form of social organization of space, the physical basis for the social division of labor, sensitively registers the tempo and intensity of the class struggle in any society. If the modern city in general serves as the principal locus for the production, realization, and regulation of labor power and for consumption, exchange, and accumulation of capital, then we can surely track down and chart the subtle movements of the Filipino spirit in the periodic outbursts of anger and wrath in the streets of Manila, the carnivalesque orgasms of desperation and joy intent on redeeming fallen time, the Babel of history, with an ever-differing, forever deferring space of communal solidarity in combat: the festival of the oppressed.

"City of Dreams, City of Nightmares," intones a writer in *Rolling Stone*: "Manila, city of my dreams. Our dreams. Our Weimar, our Havana, St. Petersburg, Teheran. . . . Part Camelot, part Calcutta. Manila, city of my dreams".[42]

VII
On the Praxis of People's War

No uprising fails. Each one is a step in the right direction.
Salud Algabre, leader of the
1935 Sakdalista rebellion

When a U.S. Establishment magazine like *Newsweek* (27 July 1981) could venture to publish a not too distorted report of how the New People's Army (NPA) in the Philippines has grown into a formidable force of about 10,000 fighters with millions of staunch supporters, it indicated a crucially new world-historical turn of events. What are the implications? First, the U.S. ruling class is alarmed at the precarious fragility of its client state and seeks to drum up public opinion for increased military aid to the beleaguered Marcos dictatorship, especially after the 1983 economic-political catastrophe. Second, it denotes the fact that (to quote the article) "in all of Asia, only the Philippines confronts an armed communist insurgency that is gaining ground". And third, the world's corporate media are trying desperately to manipulate the facts before the U.S. and world public begin to lend substantial amounts of material support to the revolutionary forces.

What is the NPA? For *Newsweek*, it is a ragtag band of "poor, young and uneducated" Filipinos, an outlawed group "shadowy" and "deadly". For the regime's Defense Minister, the NPA "does not pose a serious threat, merely an annoyance", estimating the NPA to consist of merely 2,500 scattered fighters with 50,000 supporters.

129

In June of 1984, the Commander-in-Chief of the U.S. Pacific Command, Admiral William Crow, the U.S. Embassy and the CIA drew up a country report on the Philippines, advising caution as to the mounting threat posed by the NPA to the crisis-stricken government, accompanied by the immediate prospect of profound destabilization and social upheaval. The latest U.S. inquiry estimates the number of NPA combatants at 12,000 to 15,000, and the villages under NPA influence or control at 17 percent of the nationwide total.[1]   Compounded with the serious split in the Marcos power bloc, the open disaffection and intransigent defiance of large sections of the urban middle classes (from corporate executives to clerks, professionals, state employees, merchants, etc.) which had previously supported the regime, this "rapidly expanding strength of the Communist-dominated NPA, as Representative Stephen Solarz puts it in an Op-Ed page of the *New York Times*, should be viewed as a warning not to tamper with proposal appropriations lest the U.S. " jeopardize its access to the bases."[2] On 26 June 1984, Marcos expressed shock at how the NPA has proliferated, indicating not too subtly that the U.S. should give urgent priority to granting more military assistance lest U.S. security and economic interests be irretrievably jeopardized.[3]

PRIVILEGING THE CONTRADICTIONS

With the class contradictions in the Phillipines exacerbated by the global capitalist crisis whose early symptom was the U.S. defeat in Indochina, a crisis registered locally by the emergence of the authoritarian state, we find in the beginning of the seventies an experienced and deeply-rooted mass resistance against the imperialist-sponsored bloc of landlords, compradors (middlemen for foreign interests) and bureaucrat-capitalists like Marcos. This resistance is presently led by the broad coalition of forces called the National Democratic Front (NDF) to which the NPA belongs. The NPA is today the chief military-political organization of the Filipino people consistently fighting for national independence against foreign domination, and for socialist democracy against fascist terrorism. Overall, it is the largest people's mass organization of the majority sectors (peasants and workers) comprising 90 percent of the population, including students, professionals, nationalities, priests, and others who are not communist party members (only one out of five belongs to the party). In the southern Philippines, the NPA coordinates with the Moro National Liberation Front and its Bangsa Moro Army in their common resistance to the U.S.-Marcos dictatorship.

From the time of the 1896 revolution against Spain, the Filipino people have realized that without their own army they cannot permanently liberate themselves from oppressors who employ state violence to maintain/reinforce their hegemony. This is the bitter lesson learned after the defeat of two hundred uprisings prior to 1896, and a dozen revolts ruthlessly suppressed by the American colonial government before 1946.

When the Communist Party of the Philippines (CPP) was founded in 1930, its leadership did not recognize the paramount role of the peasantry in a semi-feudal and semi-colonial country. After its merger with the Socialist Party and the exigencies imposed by World War II, the CPP founded the peasant-based HUKBALAHAP (People's Forces Against the Japanese) and established organs of popular power in central Luzon. After the war, however, the opportunist-revisionist Lava-Taruc leadership betrayed the revolution and compromised with U.S. imperialism. It contended that since guerilla war could not succeed lacking a single main base or headquarters immune to enemy encirclement, therefore only the "parliamentary road to socialism" was viable. This now appears a fatal misunderstanding, a fetishistic reduction, of the Chinese People's Liberation Army experience. Moreover, it demonstrates a gross falsification, if not a conscious rejection, of Lenin's insights into the political problematic of guerrilla warfare and insurrection, as I will show in a moment. The Lava-Taruc leadership decided to liquidate its armed detachments, opting for parliamentary reform as its dominant and sole strategy. This capitulationist tendency led to the disintegration of the Huks into bandit elements and gangster clans, with the remnants of the leadership degenerating into surrender to Marcos in 1974 and open collaboration with U.S. imperialism. Many of the basic errors in the ideological, political and organizational spheres in the party's thirty-five years of existence have been analyzed, summed up and corrected (see the document "Rectify Errors and Rebuild the Party," 1968) with the party's re-establishment in December 1968. The re-established party affirmed the fundamental political line of people's war: "Only through revolutionary armed struggle could the decadent semi-colonial and semi-feudal system be overthrown and an independent and democratic society be established."[4] The NPA was born from that founding principle.

Founded on 19 March 1969, the NPA started with only sixty men and thirty-five rifles, confined to a single district of Tarlac, one town in Pampanga and another in Zambales. In 1972, contrary to Marcos' claim that the NPA had 100,000 regulars, the NPA counted only 350 guerrillas (versus 100,000 AFP regular personnel; ratio 1:285) confined to a few provinces in northern and central Luzon. Subequently the NPA experienced a rapid if tortuous growth. In 1977, NPA rifles reached 1,500 (versus 150,000 AFP personnel; ratio 1:100) deployed in all nine territorial regions, in more than forty provinces with guerrilla zones and fronts. By 1982, the NPA rifle strength reached the critical mass of 10,000 (as against 164,000 AFP personnel; ratio 1:16), with thirty-six fronts in more than sixty provinces, capable of launching wide and frequent tactical offensives. There are now more riflemen in the NPA than in the regular corps of the MNLF; counting the NPA's supplement of armed propaganda teams and armed city partisans, with a militia (the local revolutionary police force and trained reserve force of the NPA), there are several times more.[5]

In 1983, the NPA controlled forty guerilla fronts (up from (twenty-eight in 1980) covering over 530 municipalities with a population of at least ten million--equal to the total number of farmers and agricultural workers in the whole country--in fifty-three (up from forty-three in 1980) out of seventy-three provinces. About ten million people in the fronts render active support to the NPA. From 8,000 in 1980, the fulltime and parttime guerrillas have grown to 20,000 in 1983. The CPP estimates its membership at 30,000 in 1983, up from 10,000 in 1980.

Meanwhile, in September 1980, the NDF announced that it had 40,000 full-time organizers operating in two-thirds of the country's provinces, with a total mass base of 4.5 million. NDF propaganda reached an estimated ten million. By the end of 1981, 10,000 more organizers had been added, with the mass base reaching to ten million, four million in the urban areas and the rest in the countryside.[6]

In 1984, the struggle evolved to the advanced sub-stage of the strategic defensive phase. The NPA can now launch tactical offensives in 30 to 40 percent of 1,500 municipalities or 400 towns. Guerrilla units up to company size (sixty to a hundred men) are found in all the major islands. In 1983, NPA tactical offensives averaged over one a day, yielding the biggest harvest of high-powered weapons; in the first six months alone, the NPA netted 1000 firearms, compared to 1000 for the entire year of 1982.[7] This growth in quantity and quality can be further appraised by the fact that whereas in the beginning, NPA fighters originated from the ranks of students and intellectuals, with poor weapons, now the bulk (over three-fourths) of the NPA comes from the peasantry and the working class (up by 100 percent in the last five years) equipped with many more high-powered rifles (up by 200 percent in 1981) mostly captured from the enemy. Also a significant index of growth is that for every NPA member, there are roughly five to eight members of the people's militia providing support.

Not that these achievements were won easily. The party frankly admits that in the early period (1972-74), the NPA underwent setbacks and sustained heavy casualties owing to serious limitations in skill, organization, equipment and mass support. Propaganda units assigned to areas where the peasant movement was quiescent or dormant were annihilated. Nonetheless, during that same period, the NPA vigorously regrouped, surmounted losses, and geometrically expanded to virgin territory: some islands in the Visayas, and in the second largest island of the archipelago, Mindanao.

In 1972, the Marcos regime used 7,000 troops with air support and a dozen U.S. advisers to suppress the NPA in Isabela. Suffering over 400 casualties, the almost total annihilation of the 5th Infantry Battalion, it failed to destroy the guerrillas' main forces. However, it succeeded in driving 50,000 people from their homes and relocating them in "strategic hamlets" in order to deny the NPA its mass base. Nonetheless, the NPA and NDF organs of power in Cagayan Valley survived intact the suppression campaigns from December 1977 to March 1978, in which thousands of peasants were tortured, evicted from their homes and arrested.

Two months after Marcos pronounced the demise of the NPA in September 1979, with the capture of NPA Commander Dante and NPA training officer Victor Corpuz, 150 heavily armed NPA guerrillas skillfully staged an extensive, ninety minute raid on five villages on the edge of the huge Clark Air Force Base sixty miles north of Manila. They seized forty-three firearms from the surprised paramilitary Civilian Home Defense Force (CHDF) and escaped unharmed. It was the first major NPA action in central Luzon since 1972. A few days before this action, NPA fighters in Davao Oriental province in Mindanao had ambushed a company of Philippine Constabulary (PC) soldiers, killing eight and wounding three others. In May 1977 the NPA capped its resurgence by seizing and holding for a few days the towns of Arteche and San Policarpio in Samar. When Sison was captured in November 1977, Marcos again pronounced the NPA's obituary; but the next year the controlled media reported fierce clashes in Bataan, Davao del Norte, Eastern Samar, Tarlac and Palawan (a new front). Most of the ambushes of AFP soldiers were carried out in broad daylight.

Only in 1979 was the NPA completely successful in foiling AFP "encirclement and suppression" campaigns without great losses or serious disruptions. Bold NPA offensives multiplied. Unleashing intense organizational energies, the guerrillas escalated selective, tactical challenges to the regime, designed mainly to forage for weapons and protect the village dwellers from military repression. Throughout June and July 1979, encounters occurred in the provinces of Quezon, Nueva Ecija, Cagayan, Tarlac, Basilan, Sulu, Agusan del Sur, Lanao del Norte, Bataan, Eastern Davao, and Samar. One NPA action which reflects the value of a proportionately advanced level of organizing and politicizing is the successful ambush of seven AFP troopers in Tagkawayan, Quezon, on 24 June 1979. The guerrillas escaped without a single casualty, after confiscating eight M-16 rifles, 1000 rounds of ammunition, and various materiel. Taking the initiative and concentrating their small force, steps made feasible by the active, conscious support of the peasants, the NPA succeeded in punishing three notorious criminals and ambushing the Philippine Constabulary patrol sent to retaliate. "Seeded" in 1970 by NPA propaganda units, northern Luzon now has ten guerrilla fronts, each covering about twenty to thirty towns, with numerous consolidated zones where people's power prevails uncontested, and also many expansion districts where NPA influence is strong and political work critical. In both areas, the party is organized down to the barrio, with a militia unit in every barrio.

A glance at some tactical offensives conducted in the period 1975-1979 by the NPA reveals that most are swift small-scale ambushes, raids or quick-decision battles. They have invariably capitalized on the element of surprise, focusing heavy fire on small enemy formations with the purpose of destroying as many troops as possible and gathering weapons and ammunition. In the island of Samar, for example, where the Marcos regime has amassed an unprecedented total of 10,502 troops and police, the NPA applies the technique of evading decisive frontal battles with the numerically and logistically superior enemy, constantly shifting to seek out small detachments and wipe them out. Using this strategic maneuver, the NPA also seeks to disperse the enemy forces throughout the archipelago, converting a geographical constraint into a political asset.

TACTICS OF RENEWAL, STRATEGY OF INNOVATIONS

The NPA learning and tempering process recounted above coincides with the strategy of protracted people's war that the NPA is resolutely waging in the context of the besieged U.S.-Marcos fascist hegemony and the ferocious contention of the superpowers in Southeast Asia and all over the world. In the first stage of its long march, the NPA may have followed too mechanically the examples of its predecessors at home and abroad, but now it has accumulated invaluable lessons, some of which have been formulated in Amado Guerrero's *Specific Characteristics of Our People's War* (1974). It appears also that the CPP guidelines enunciated in *Our Urgent Tasks* (1976) have been astutely implemented. This signifies that the conscientious rectification of dogmatist tendencies such as "left adventurist errors" for which some comrades have paid with their lives, has been assiduously carried out. Where adequate political work had been achieved, the NPA could execute operations without unnecessary sacrifices, and was able to withstand the enemy's counter-attack because the people were willing to provide information and logistics, stable sanctuaries and other material support.

What I would like to underscore here, partly in reponse to those who accuse the NPA of being pallid imitators of the Chinese model, is the principle of self-reliance which the NPA type of guerrilla warfare is meant to articulate and institutionalize. Self-reliance, party documents insist, is the key to armed struggle in an archipelago without any friendly country as rear base and source of arms. Self-reliance serves as the motivating principle whereby the NPA endeavors to develop fighting skills, mastery of the terrain, popular support and, of course, creative assimilation of practices engendered by local and foreign struggles.

In the last few years, the NPA has concentrated on intensifying military operations in established guerrilla zones throughout the islands. With NDF's mobilizing reach encompassing larger areas every year, people's war by the end of 1980 is said to have attained the advanced sub-stage of the strategic defensive phase: over 4,000 rifles were being used by the NPA in twenty-eight guerrilla fronts covering 4,000 barrios in 376 towns of forty-three provinces.

One sign of the NPA's accelerated and improved striking power can be seen in its ability to concentrate a company, or two or three dispersed companies with a regional operational command, in most of the forty-five fronts today where the guerrillas enjoy a considerably enlarged scope and frequency of planning and coordination. With the regularizing of the NPA into a full-time fighting force, the NPA has been able to conduct raids into towns and to seize vast quantities of weapons, as demonstrated in the raids on Mabini and Maco towns, Davao del Norte, on 12 January 1984. In Mabini, forty-five high-powered rifles were captured from the police force without firing a single shot. One spectacular ambush on AFP troops occurred on 29 September 1983 in Zamboanga del Sur, where thirty-nine enemy soldiers--the largest casualty total in one attack--died.[8]

With more party cadres in the NPA and Red fighters concentrating on military operations while NDF militants assume the tasks of political mass mobilization, the NPA hopes to efficiently bolster its full-time fighting units, as well as to expand and consolidate the guerrilla zones for eventual positional warfare. A guerrilla zone or front obtains where popular power coexists with the government--an instance of dual power. A guerrilla base area is characterized by the dominance of people's power, though the enemy may still be able to penetrate it depending on the concrete political conjuncture. A party cadre explains the prospect for the next decade when 25,000 rifles will have been acquired by the NPA:

Having 25,000 rifles is no longer just a dream. It is within reach. At this prospective strength, the majority of the 1,500 towns and provincial capitals in the country would already be within the scope of NPA offensive capability. Certainly, with this rifle strength, the NPA shall have reached the stage of the strategic stalemate.

The strategic stalemate shall be characterized by a seesaw of battles for control of towns and provincial capitals until the strength of the enemy is exhausted in the process. The essential objective of the people's army shall not be to hold territory but to seize large numbers of arms repeatedly over wide areas. In the end, reactionary power shall collapse in these areas and the strategic offensive shall be launched against the last holdouts of the enemy that shall already be on the strategic defensive, such as Metro Manila and a few other strategic points.[9]

What is absent in this reflection is obviously the likelihood of massive U.S. military intervention to save its bases.

AGENDA: PEOPLE'S SELF-ACTIVITIES

One cannot properly appreciate the nature and function of the NPA without the historical perspective delineated earlier, but especially not without the prior act of inscribing the NPA in the site of ongoing mass struggles against the U.S.-Marcos dictatorship. As the CPP's statement on the NPA's 12th anniversary pointed out, "the armed struggle is not separate from the revolutionary mass movement. In fact, as the main mass organization under the Party leadership carrying out the main form of struggle--armed struggle--the NPA is an indispensable part of this movement." The armed struggle "supports the underground and open mass movement in the rural and urban areas, while these in turn help to advance the armed struggle. . . . One draws strength from the other." Indeed, a dialectical reciprocity transpires: as the NPA intensifies its offensives, more people in the countryside and cities are mobilized to assert their democratic rights in heightening mass actions, encouraging more advanced elements to join the NPA and participate directly in combat.

It must be emphasized that contrary to popular and academic mythologizing, the NPA is not simply or only a military formation. That is a militarist fallacy, a species of elitist determinism. The NPA cannot be just a war machine, a behemoth similar in form and substance to its enemy, the mercenary AFP precisely because it strives to overthrow the hierarchical and authoritarian system generated by the class contradictions in a peripheral polity. In striving to radically transform this setup, the NPA is therefore striving to embody participatory democratic principles and practices designed to arouse mass involvement in a conscious and creative manner. While each NPA unit has leaders, these leaders are elected or chosen by the fighters for their political experience and organizational capabilities. Grass-roots democracy operates through discussion, criticism/self-criticism, and summing-up sessions which include everyone, party member or not. For its survival, growth and success, the NPA must needs depend on intimate organic ties with peasants, village folk and town dwellers--the sea in which the guerrillas swim like fish.

Like fish in the water, the NPA as the armed political agency of the people is fully immersed in the popular resistance against feudal and fascist oppression. It rejects the technocratic and instrumentalist fallacy that a revolution is nothing but a coup or anarchist insurrection where the quantity of weapons, technological expertise, immense vanity and infinite capacity for martyrdom decide the issue. This conception of revolution as a mere change of administrative personnel is a version of the fashionable mechanistic or narrow empiricist thinking which considers technology/technocrats as the key determinant in social change. While weapons are important and necessary, the radical transformation of people's lives inheres in pursuing the organized deepening of people's political consciousness the development of which is not totally dependent on arms supply *per se.* With the correct political and ideological line sensitively and resourcefully applied in consonance with the uneven level of people's understanding and the specific conjuncture of multiple factors, the problem of arms and logistics is unrelentingly tackled and solved everyday. Proof of this is supplied by a party cadre whom John Witeck, an American trade union militant, interviewed in mid-April 1984:

> We used to put serving the people foremost, but now we see that these economic, co-op, self-help projects are not good to initiate until the people are politicized. Otherwise they will see us like a civic action team, and become dependent on us as "economic saviors." But political unity is the foremost objective. The economic problems of this region or the country cannot be solved within the system; they will be solved primarily through revolutionary means. We must emphasize military struggle now to gain the needed changes.[10]

Given the uneven process of development throughout the country, however, the "military moment" must still be synchronized with the three interconnected tasks the NPA attempts to fulfill simultaneously: armed struggle, agrarian revolution, and base-building, in order to promote autonomous, decentralized people's power.

A report in the *Wall Street Journal* (21 June 1980) describes the NPA's integration with the Igorot masses in northern Luzon. Ka Dexter, the leader of the NPA unit, noted that "most of the time when we take military action, it is at the demand of the people. It isn't to be separated from our political work and propaganda. . . . We helped with irrigation, farm work, any kind of labor, even house building." He asserts that the NPA is "the primary form of organization waging armed struggle, the primary form of struggle."

In Cagayan province, adjacent to the Igorot homeland threatened by the World Bank-funded Chico dam, the NPA has entrenched itself by persistently implementing its "Revolutionary Land Reform Program": rent reduction by as much as 50 percent or more, elimination of usury, increases of farm laborers' wages, confiscation of abusive landlords' property, etc. It has also promoted "exchange of labor, mutual aid, and cooperatives" with fair prices arranged between peasants and merchants. Since 1969, the NPA has wiped out thousands of the dictatorship's officers and soldiers, policemen, para-military personnel, enemy spies and informers, despotic landlords and their armed goons, bandits, and assorted bad elements engaged in land grabbing, tenant harassment, embezzlement, cattle rustling and grain stealing, and rape. According to a recent article in the underground paper *Liberation*: "In its areas of operation, the NPA builds, and strengthens the organs of democratic power (committees of self-government), working committees in various fields (organization, education, defense, health, arbitration, etc.) and mass organizations for workers, peasants, woman, youth, children, and cultural activities in order to bring into full play the people's support for the armed revolution."[11]

A California journalist, Reese Erlich, who toured the Philippine countryside where 60 percent of the people live, interviewed Rene Bonifacio, a sixty-year old peasant in a central Luzon province:

> We are poor people, but we never stopped fighting. . . . Back in the early 1970s this barrio wasn't organized, because irrigation is poor. We can't grow enough rice. We can grow no vegetables at all. Back then we paid 50 percent of our crop to the landlord, more when he cheated us. My cousin from another barrio came one day and told me about the NPA. First it helped us set up a peasant association. We organized every peasant in the barrio to demand lower rent. When we first met with the landlord, he just laughed. But then he heard the NPA were in the area. At first he sent his overseer to bribe them with a few M-16 rifles. But the NPA turned him down and backed our demands for lower rents. After about a year he saw that all the barrio was united and the PC couldn't wipe out the NPA. He lowered the rent. Today he even pays taxes to the NPA.[12]

As the organized peasant masses gain material benefits and acquire both realistic and visionary perspectives from agrarian revolution, the most conscious of them will perceive the correctness of the NDF program as a whole and enlist in the NPA, while others offer support in manifold ways: providing food and shelter, keeping surveillance on the enemy, safeguarding communication lines, harassing and demoralizing the enemy, etc. In effect, the NPA fights to systematically organize the masses in the countryside, defend their gains, improve their livelihood, and destroy the coercive apparatus of the exploitative classes. In 1979, Lawrence Johnson, a correspondent for *Mother Jones* magazine, visited the NPA zones and witnessed the extensive guerrilla network in place throughout the islands.[13] In the same year, the Indian journalist Ajit Roy of the *Economic and Political Weekly* interviewed NPA cadres and formed his judgement that the NPA is "slowly but steadily bringing about changes in the life of the rural poor. . . . raising the social consciousness and literacy levels as well as imparting education about sanitation and health."[14]

Practically all the printed accounts of the NPA's vicissitudes, their setbacks and triumphs, testify to the highly successful integration of the guerrillas with their mass base, and the impact of the NPA's victories on the urban mass movement (both legal and underground) which is essential for the anticipated insurrection in the cities when the reactionary forces have been paralyzed, neutralized or demolished in the surrounding countryside. While the traditional precept of "encircling the cities from the countryside" still informs party pedagogy, it seems that a mechanical or dogmatic interpretation of the theory is eschewed for an authentically dialectical grasp of the relation between city and countryside, so that in the ultimate reckoning the NPA's role cannot be appraised separate from the fate of the whole multi-sectoral struggle against fascist-imperialist hegemony. Thus, while there is a need to increase automatic rifles to 25,000 to realize the strategic stalemate in the next five to seven years, enabling the NPA to launch tactical offensives in all regions and wipe out entire AFP companies, this is qualified by a political calculation, as one cadre puts it: "We only have about half as many party members and organizers as there are barrios (64,000) in the country. So we only have half of our minimum needs. We consider about one-fifth of the fifty two million Filipinos as our mass base that we now influence, and about four million are organized. It is not insignificant, but we still have a good way to go."[15]

IN QUEST OF PREFIGURATIVE POLITICS

What then, one might ask, is the key factor to the almost miraculous burgeoning and flourishing of the NPA? I submit that it lies in the rigorous and creative application by the vanguard party of materialist dialectics in the articulation of concrete tactics within the strategic totality of people's war, in the context of the objective conditions of unmitigated repression, ravaging poverty, and spontaneous mass protests. In particular, it stems from the comprehensive theoretical summing-up of the rich complex experiences of cadres and Red fighters found in Guerrero's *Specific Characteristics* which, together with *Philippine Society and Revolution* (1970) and *Our Urgent Tasks*, provide the theoretical self-interpretive framework for correctly defining the historical context, structure and direction of people's war in the post-Vietnam era.

Historical experience points to Mao Zedong as the first Marxist-Leninist who formulated with lucidity and precision the cardinal principles of people's war in his writings, specifically "Problems of Strategy in China's Revolutionary War" (1936), "On Protracted War" (1938), and assorted pieces. The concept of "strategic defensive" used to define the present conjuncture is a theoretical construct from Mao's problematic. Without further argument I suggest that it is the totality of the profound political lessons, not the single notion of a "fixed liberated area," that makes the experience of the Chinese revolution a useful but not exclusive paradigm for understanding protracted people's war in a semi-feudal and semi-colonial society like the Philippines.

The fundamental principle of Mao's dialectics is expressed succinctly in what might strike Western pundits as a simplistic, even vulgar formula: "The enemy advances, we retreat; the enemy camps, we harass; the enemy tires, we attack; the enemy retreats, we pursue." This code of maneuvering is now embodied in the "Basic Rules of the NPA." The corollary insights associated with it may be exemplified by other aphoristic instructions, such as that of "concentrating a superior force to destroy the enemy forces one by one," and the theses: "Destruction of the enemy is the primary object of war and self-preservation the secondary," in which self-preservation depends reciprocally on the enemy's destruction; and "The pivotal strategy must be mobile warfare." I hasten to advise skeptics that this is not a matter of indulging in a game of quotations from the "sacred" Red Book, nor a mere exercise in citatology. Based on the actual combat experiences of the NPA, these generalizations reveal their heuristic force and efficacy in the corpses of fascist troops and wreckage of U.S.-made helicopters and tanks littering the countryside.[16]

All observers agree that before 1979 the NPA, logistically and numerically overshadowed by the AFP, could only engage the enemy in sporadic clashes where it has an unquestioned tactical superiority. This first phase of a whole process known as the "strategic defensive," which comprises the serious problem of conserving the NPA's meager size while seizing every chance of destroying the enemy, pivots around the project of arms procurement through selective ambushes on dispersed and therefore weaker enemy forces. The enemy is lured deeply into the hinterland and spread thinly so as to be vulnerable to the guerrillas' concentrated firepower. With its up-to-date intelligence of enemy movements supplied by the peasants and its superior vantage point, the NPA exploits the element of surprise in annihilating the enemy.

For Mao, the strategic defensive phase is "the most complicated and most important problem" for the revolutionary forces, and as a solution he propounds the principle of active defense, which means, in practice, "defense for the purpose of counterattacking and taking the offensive."[17] This insight epitomizes Mao's dialectical genius in apprehending any conjuncture of events as "overdetermined"; i.e., overlaid with multi-layered contradictions, decentered by dynamic oppositions which are then analyzed, differentiated, and temporarily resolved in a dynamic and flexible way.

Situated in this problematic, we can now try to elucidate the controversial theme of the archipelagic nature of the Philippines which some commentators have postulated as the central inhibition or obstacle in waging protracted guerrilla war. It is argued by these geographical determinists that since the Philippines consists of 7,000 islands, such physical reality imposes "severe limitations on mobility."[18] Further, the country is surrounded on all sides by sea, lacking common borders with friendly states. These mechanical materialists also contend that the "Chinese concept" of a liberated base area, as they define it, is not applicable to the Philippines because, for one, Marcos' intelligence network is almost omniscient. Consequently the NPA's strategy of scattered units fanning all over the islands, dividing and dispersing enemy troops, is based on the archipelagic nature of the country, which exerts a "narrowing effect" on fighting fronts. These fatalists also argue that whereas the Chinese Red Army "established an 'open presence' in liberated areas to pave the way for economic reforms and popular mobilization," the NPA "chiefly concentrates on a silent, 'invisible' process of politicization and organization of poor peasants." A review of the infinitely rich heterogeneous praxis of people's war in the Philippines will easily refute such allegations.

In an interview with *Liberation* in 1974, a political officer of the NPA in Pampanga, in central Luzon, defined the principal role of the NPA:

Revolution is mainly capturing and defending political power, and this connot be done without armed struggle. The NPA is the arm with which the people and the Party wield the gun. This does not mean, however, that all we do is fight in the battlefield. Besides being a fighting force, each NPA unit also engages in propaganda and production work. The NPA helps the people, particularly the peasants in the countryside, build their own democratically chosen local governments.[19]

From its inception, the NPA applied the guerrilla tactic of maximum mobility and flexibility in its operations. The normal NPA formations ranged from squads of regular full-time guerrillas (or of part-time guerrillas with people's militia units) to platoon and company units (in 1974 four companies existed in Cagayan Valley), but a battalion-size formation can be assembled by combining smaller units from adjacent provinces. Each guerrilla front is expected to be relatively self-sufficient materially and fairly autonomous politically. As John Witeck observes: "Quick decisions and major initiatives often have to be made locally and cannot wait for national or regional confirmation. Party education classes teach this need and skill to be self reliant, to show initiative, to think for one's self and be creative."[20]

Adapting Mao's instruction on the choice of border areas (mountain boundaries of several provinces) as administrative centers, the NPA sought whenever and wherever possible to consolidate guerrilla bases established in earlier time, by expanding later into the Ilocos-Montanosa-Pangasinan region west of the Cagayan Valley. It also began to develop the east coast regions of Aurora and Quezon, a crucial linkage between the Cagayan Valley in the north and the southern Tagalog and Bicol regions. This phenomenon, however, is limited so far. Based on the experience in Luzon, one can hypothesize that the decision to concentrate on border areas is explicable not just by the presence of favorable geographical conditions (thick forests, mountains, etc.) and population density--significant factors in themselves--but, from a Marxist-Leninist point of view, more importantly by the ripeness of the political developments inhering in them. I shall allude simply to the intensifying Igorot resistance against the Chico Dam project discussed in Chapter II, the advanced political consciousness of key allies in Bicol, the availability of experienced cadres in central Luzon and Cagayan, the regime's "weak link" in Samar, and the phenomenal explosion of resistance in Mindanao. This pattern cannot be interpreted simply as a mechanical reflex or dogmatic mimicry of the Chinese revolution.

Governed by the uneven development of subjective and objective forces, by the oscillating and overdetermined balance of classes locked in conflict, by the decentered agenda of the revolutionary process throughout the country, the growth of the NPA pursues a direction which registers the mode and pace in which people's power--their consciousness, organizing experience, resources--begins to exercise initiative, acting to transform the historically constrained circumstances of their lives.

One cannot emphasize too much the essential point that the NPA is not a military *foco* but primarily a political-organizational instrument aimed at arousing and mobilizing the peasantry, 75 percent of fifty-three million Filipinos. The CPP, the NPA's guiding force, articulates proletarian ideology according to the national-popular will. While the NPA seeks to destroy the reactionary classes and their military force, it simultaneously engages in political education and organizing farmers, rural workers, etc. To illustrate: when an NPA armed propaganda unit arrives in a village, it first undertakes the required "social investigation." With the help of liaison contacts or recruited cadres from the village, the unit performs a thorough class analysis of the population, identifying types of allies and possible or actual enemies. The next step is the organizing of inhabitants into mass associations of poor peasants, women and youth, after which a village organizing committee--the first phase in the process of forming the village revolutionary committee--is established.

In a 1974 article, the journalist Bernard Wideman compressed the whole program in two sentences: "The NPA works by approaching farmers and offering instructions on better farming methods, improving irrigation and giving medical aid. Later, discussions are held on the rising cost of living and the growing inequities in Philippine society."[21] But the two aspects--serving the people and political education--are fused indivisibly. For organizing the peasants serves primarily the objective of implementing the CPP revolutionary land reform program which seeks to solve the basic problems of land distribution, high rent, chronic debt and poverty, landlord abuses, military and government repression that have traditionally plagued the peasantry, rural workers, artisans, etc. Depending on the strength of the NPA and the NDF's mass organizations, reforms ranging from reduction of exorbitant rent and hiking of rural wages to the confiscation, division and free distribution of big landlord estates, are undertaken. Thus, by step-by-step painstaking mass work in which the NPA concretely addresses specific immediate problems (linked to the basic, long-range problems of the whole nation), the people's consciousness awakens. And the whole village realizes its latent powers when it actually proceeds to set up the village council, political education classes, cooperatives and work teams for mutual labor exchange and mutual aid projects. In addition, the village folk organizes self-defense militias to guard the equitable justice system whose embryo they are nurturing, as well as to preserve their other gains.

In sum, the NPA acts as an initiating, participatory agent and a catalyzing force to assist the peasants in analyzing their experiences within a historical materialist perspective, demonstrating in theory and practice how their plight arises from class exploitation. By sustained practice, the peasants gradually acquire confidence from their unity, resourcefulness, wisdom and strength. Exercising self-reliance, the peasants and the NPA work together to increase production by improving irrigation and planting methods. They cooperate to resist coercive manipulations by landlords, usurers and foreign agribusiness (e.g., Dole, Del Monte, etc.). They also devise ways to improve the low market prices for crops and the starvation wages of the agricultural workers, defying at the same time the unjust exactions of government agencies masquerading as "development" or "modernization" reforms. Cattle rustlers and other anti-social elements or criminals are tried by people's courts and punished. Aside fom literacy campaigns, the NPA also attends to the people's health needs by establishing clinics in guerrila zones, teaching elementary hygiene and pre-ventive care, dispensing Western and herbal medicine, and so forth.

Assuming elaborate forms, those mass actions coalesced with the daily lives of the people afford the space, the arena, in which the peasants begin to exercise their democratic rights and erect local governments. Through the formation of worker teams, the seeds for the socialization of agriculture in the future are being implanted in thought and deed. Integrating the defense of everyday interests with the overall struggle for a radical transformation of the entire system, the NPA has firmly rooted itself in the homes of millions of peasants and workers throughout the country and thus fixed the irreversible course of the national democratic revolution.

Linking the underground mass movement in the cities with insurrection in the countryside, the NPA unfolds its mandated historic role not just as the politico-military expression of the CPP but in real practice as the effective agency or apparatus of the people's bloc, the united front. Its initial composition reflected diverse class backgrounds: workers, students, women, peasants, clergy, professionals, nationalities, even ex-politicians, etc. However, with the re-deployment of some urban cadres in the cities and the refinement of study methods and work-styles, etc., workers, poor farmers, displaced tenants, small settlers, and landless laborers increasingly predominate in the ranks.

What has driven more volunteers into the NPA, aside from its demonstrated genuine concern for the daily needs of the masses, is the relentless atrocities of the regime's counter-insurgency moves, such as hamletting and base-denial operations which create the standard Vietnam-style "free-fire zones" aimed at deterring or containing the spread of the NPA. Ironically, that has generated the antithetical effect. In the latter half of 1977, for example, while the regime's Task Force Isarog conducted a three-month "encirclement and suppression" campaign together with civic actions to disguise arrests, harassments and killings--the familiar dual tactics of U.S. imperialism--the CPP regional branch in Bicol reported a 25 percent increase in membership. Moreover, the bases in Camarines Sur and in the border areas of Albay and Sorsogon, all in the Bicol region, remained intact.

TERRAIN OF COUNTER-HEGEMONIC VISIONS

By virtue of the total domination of the whole country by the military and security apparatus of the U.S.-Marcos state, the national democratic revolution cannot but embrace all regions and provinces where the people suffer fascist-imperialist oppression in one degree or another. Uneven development exists, but the whole socio-economic formation suffers from a serious multifaceted crisis (as outlined in the Introduction and the first two chapters). Therefore a people's army cannot help but be national in scale and presence--not immediately but as a historic project now gradually being accomplished--to effectively challenge the still entrenched but rapidly eroding authoritarian hegemony. To disperse the huge government army (now nearly 300,000 men) and prevent its focusing on any single place, it is necessary to open fighting fronts in as many islands where the objective and subjective conditions are conjuncturally feasible.

We can conclude then that the protracted nature of the struggle (protracted is of relative duration in revolutionary diachronics) is not dictated by the splitting-up of the NPA nor by the archipelagic nature of the country. Rather, it is overdetermined by the plural mediating factors crystallized in the shifting alignment of class forces, the ideological level of various sectors, the international situation: for example, the capacity or willingness of U.S. imperialism to maintain or maximize its level of intervention in propping up Marcos or other factions of the oligarchy; the Islamic nations' attitude to the Moro people's resistance, etc.

People's war is in essence protracted because, first, its strategy of encircling the cities from the countryside requires slow and careful political-organizational interplay with people; second, the guerrilla army's accumulation of strength depends not just on recruiting of peasants or gathering of arms but also on the decimation and demoralization of the enemy's effective forces; and, third, the relatively long process of struggle in the countryside influences and impacts on the struggle in the cities, precipitating urban insurrections bound to catalyze the pace or rhythm of the struggle on all levels nationwide. The manifold tendencies subsumed in the historic conjuncture called "people's war" has been anticipated by Lenin in his remarks on "Guerrilla Warfare": "Guerrilla warfare is an inevitable form of struggle at a time when the mass movement has actually reached the point of an uprising and when fairly large intervals occur between the 'big engagements' in the civil war. . . . It is engendered by powerful economic and political causes. . . . In certain periods of acute economic and political crisis the class struggle ripens into a direct civil war, i.e., into an armed struggle between two sections of the people."[22] With the rapid isolation of the Marcos clique vis-a-vis a popular democratic front involving bishops and fractions of the elite, the CPP is calling for more centralized, tighter coordination of urban underground activity in MetroManila (an urban complex where 30 percent of fifty-three million Filipinos live) with NPA actions. This reflects a dialectical "law of motion": urban agitation catalyzes guerrilla organizing, and vice versa. In 1977, the upsurge in united front work in MetroManila marked a higher development in the overall struggle, with demonstrations and rallies mobilizing over 100,000 (culminating in millions after Aquino's death), synthesizing spontaneous economic or single-issue demands with anti-imperialist objectives.

On 24 May 1984, the Alex Boncayao Brigade of the NPA initiated its first politically decisive act of urban warfare: the well-planned partisan operation that executed Brigadier General Tomas Karingal, Superintendent of the Northern Police District of MetroManila, responsible for massacres of workers and violent suppression of peaceful assemblies, among other crimes against the people.

Utmost flexibility and total self-reliance, both qualities embodying the dialectical materialist orientation of people's war, distinguish the NPA's tactics and strategy. It has been observed that one persistent problem is the lack of modern sophisticated weapons. But we should remember that the NPA is a political instrument of the CPP, and that two other weapons needed to achieve national democracy and freedom are the party itself and the united front. To ignore those two other components and refuse to coalesce them dialectically in the unfolding of people's war is to succumb to a one-sided militarist or technicist prejudice.

Lenin repeatedly emphasized that insurrection, from a Marxist perspective, must rely on "the revolutionary upsurge of the people," upon the most daring actions of the advanced class in the crisis of the old exploitative system. Consequently, the ultimate defeat of the reactionary army can also come about not simply through physical annihilation (Mao advised that the revolution should first annihilate "the enemy's *effective* strength," not hold or seize a place permanently), but through its demoralization and disintegration--that is, the dissolution of its hegemony--because of the loss of support from the broad masses, as exemplified by the unanticipated collapse of the much more powerfully entrenched dictatorships of recent memory in Iran and Nicaragua.

My analysis here in effect privileges the priority and desideratum of people's war, whose general political line has been forcefully expressed by Amado Guerrero on various occasions: the task of the revolution "can be accomplished only by waging armed struggle as the main form of revolutionary struggle and developing the broadest possible united front among the motive forces to isolate and destroy the target or enemy." It has become axiomatic in this context to define revolutionary war, following Mao, as "a war of the masses; it can be waged only by mobilizing the masses and relying on them." With the main content of the Philippine revolution as the peasantry's demand for land and democratic rights, the peasantry serves as the main force, the principal ally of the proletariat whose leadership is the evolving project of cadres deeply embedded in the mass movements. The basic alliance of the peasantry and working class serves as the firm foundation for the united front incorporating the urban petty bourgeoisie, women, the middle strata of intelligentsia, the nationalities, the religious elements, etc., forming the people's bloc competing for hegemony.

VANGUARD OF TRANSFORMATIONS

Before concluding, I would like to focus on the exemplary and decisive confrontations between the NPA and the Marcos regime occurring today in the island of Samar.

One of the most cogent and dramatic confirmations of Guerrero's thesis that "the most powerful weapon" of the people's army is not an inexhaustible depot of M-16 rifles but the people's committed support, the fruit of careful political organizing, is the resistance in Samar. The third largest island after Luzon and Mindanao, Samar is the poorest in the whole country, with the lowest per capita income. Two-thirds of the farmers (84 percent of the total inhabitants) are landless tenants who must pay 70 percent of their crop as rent; 15 percent earn their livelihood as fishermen, while .05 percent are landlords.

In 1974 the NPA struck at the AFP in southwestern Samar, but subsequently suffered setbacks because of inadequate support from the people. For the next five years, the NPA concentrated on organizing the peasantry to demand reduction of land rent and control of usurers and merchants. They helped farmers apply advanced techniques, draw up work teams and production cooperatives. Health teams were formed to popularize ideas on hygiene, nutrition, acupuncture and use of herbal medicines. An educational program was set up: from literacy training (only 66 percent are literate) to political discussion on the systemic roots of exploitation. The result: 10,000 people, one third of the entire population, are now organized into people's militias. The NPA today commands a broad base of popular support; and NDF cadres live in about 800 villages in the guerrilla zones and in over 300 villages in the "white" or contested areas of the province.

In July 1978, the NPA opened a third fighting front in western Samar when it ambushed a five-man Philippine Constabulary (PC) patrol in the town of San Jose de Buan, killing two on the spot. After the others had been divested of their firearms, the wounded survivors were set free in line with the NPA policy of sparing the lives of enemy soldiers. The political program of the NDF was explained to them in the hope that they would begin to reflect critically on their situation. Twelve hours later, the same NPA unit ambushed an eleven-men PC team sent to recover the bodies of the earlier ambush; nine soldiers were wiped out.

In April 1979 the NPA raided the towns of Mapanao and Gamay in northern Samar, disarmed the police and military, and after conducting a day-long discussion with the people concerning their needs and problems, departed safely with abundant weapons, typewriters, and radio communications equipment. After a month, two other towns in the same region were simultaneously occupied, with the NPA following the same procedure. Because of these unprecedented victories, the dictatorship has militarized the whole island: three battalions were sent to supplement the two battalions already stationed there. Over 10,000 troops, which includes the 60th PC "butcher" battalion, notorious for its atrocities against the Igorots in northern Luzon, rampage and terrorize the inhabitants. Consider the harvest of this systematic brutality: 400 unarmed civilians have been killed, thousands tortured, women consistently raped. Soldiers practice the barbaric habit of beheading and mutilating their victims. Between 42,000 and 50,000 refugees have been forcibly evacuated from the interior areas where they lived, now converted into free-fire zones, and confined to centers kept under surveillance amid the most horrendous squalor and privation. These "base-denial operations" have resulted in clearing up lands rich in uranium, bauxite and timber that are now targetted by the Australian government and the World Bank for $75 million infrastructure projects needed before transnational corporations move in.

With the northern region saturated with mercenary troops, the

NPA carried out a tactical shift, exchanging space for time. In August, with the island under heavy siege NPA regulars swept on a PC outpost in Taft municipality, central-eastern Samar, killed nine soldiers and captured nineteen automatic weapons, including two 60mm. machine guns. Even more astonishing, the NPA has begun to field its ensemble of acrobats, jugglers, and other "artists" to entertain village folk amid the barbarous depredations of the Marcos juggernaut. The *Far Eastern Economic Review* (August 1979) reported that NPA women performers also function as medical teams involved in health care and education. Together with cultural-political endeavors, the NPA continues to assist in public trial and punishment of anti-people elements like rapists, informers, thieves, cattle rustlers, etc.[23]

So deep was the revolutionary commitment of the people of Samar and so fierce their hatred of the dictatorship that on 23 September 1979, 5,000 people converged in Catbalogan, the island's largest town, after defying 600 troops, and held a rally to demand an end to martial law, freedom for all political prisoners, a halt to pacification campaigns in Samar and all over the country, and the safe return of all evacuees.

As I remarked earlier, although 10,000 Red fighters compose the village militias, very few can be incorporated into regular units because of insufficient arms, although recent developments may have already remedied this deficiency. Today the NPA continues to engage the enemy in Samar, using their expert knowledge of the terrain and the cooperation of the people to acquire more weapons, implement the revolutionary land reform program, literacy campaigns, health training, etc. The peasants are also being trained in active defense, ways to enhance productivity and revitalize their culture. Even though the NPA regulars withdrew temporarily from the north, cadres of the party and NDF activists remained with the refugees and experienced the same hardships and brutalities, enabling them to continue providing leadership in the refugee camps, prisons and other sites of underground resistance. Thus, after several years of sustained political mobilization under conditions of severe fascist repression, no less than one-half of Samar's total population of 1.2 million actively support the NPA and NDF.

Fifteen years after its formation, the NPA as the genuine people's tribune finds itself at the pivotal threshold of a new, qualitatively higher stage of class war in the Philippines. Based on numerous firsthand accounts and testimonies which I have used here, the NPA's capacity to multiply its size and its political strength inheres in its all-round systematic integration with the mass struggles in both cities and countryside.

Tempered by over a decade of victories and setbacks, the NPA derives its staying power and capacity for growth from the creative application of Marxist-Leninist principles adapted to the concrete conditions and the specificities of the struggle. Filipino revolutionaries constantly analyze, deconstruct and sum up the class alignments and their fluid mutations, charting the dialectic of political, economic and ideological forces which constitute the overdetermined, dynamic process in which the Filipino people, with their unremitting sacrifices, courage and scientific wisdom, strive to affirm their historic subjectivity. The NPA thus incarnates the realistic/utopian hope of the people immanent in its transforming quotidian presence, its play of schematizing rupture and desire, its demystifying alterity. What Amilcar Cabral posits as imperative criteria for a people's army--"the principles of unceasing initiative, boldness, courage, heroism, and the principles of mobility, speed and swiftness"--improvising according to the nomadic dictates of necessity, making the impossible possible: all yield the groundwork for new, open-ended, authentically liberating relationships.[24] That is ultimately the NPA's project of permanent subversion.

Because it is the integral expression of the Filipino people's steeled resistance to U.S. imperialism and the Marcos dictatorship; because it is coeval with the people's daily lives, their ordeals and raptures, the NPA cannot be defeated; its only future dawns in the inexorable conquest of the power and initiative that will usher the Philippines from the prehistoric dark ages to the history of the heroic tillers of the soil and the dispossessed workers--the defiant and rebellious "wretched of the earth."

VIII
Toward Socialist Feminism

In the decades before and after the 1896 revolution against Spanish colonial domination, Filipino women performed a vital and necessary role in destroying the shackles of feudal oppression which sustained patriarchal tyranny against women, together with a clerical and authoritarian culture whose ideological kernel was male chauvinism.[1]

One can cite here the resourceful and intransigent participation of women revolutionaries in the historic confrontations between the Filipino people and the tyrannical Spanish colonizers. One of the earliest freedom fighters was Gabriela Silang (1731-1763). In the 1896 revolution against Spain, we can invoke the heroic sacrifices selflessly rendered to the cause of independence and democratic freedoms by Teresa Magbanua (1871-1947), Teodora Alonso (1826-1911); and Gregoria de Jesus (1875-1943), wife of Andres Bonifacio, the proletarian leader of the revolutionary organization *Katipunan*, who counselled the younger generation in her autobiography: "Fear history, for no secret can be hidden from it." Foremost among the partisans of the *Katipunan* was the inimitable Melchora Aquino, better known as "Tandang Sora" (1812-1919), who joined the rebels at the age of 84 and spent six years of exile in Guam. To the deportation order imposed on her, she responded: "I have no regrets and if I've nine lives I would gladly give them up for my beloved country."

In the fight against U.S. colonialism, which invaded the country in 1899, Filipino women also stand in the frontline of the armed struggle.   In   the   Sakdalista   revolt   against   U.S.   imperialist domination in May 1935, which involved over 65,000 armed peasants, thousands of women like Salud Algabre and others played leadership roles. And prior to the September 1972 imposition of martial law and a fascist dictatorship, Filipino women workers, peasants, students, etc. in all sectors of society through their own organizations fought pitched battles against the U.S.-trained and U.S.-equipped police and army in the streets of Manila and elsewhere.

One of the martyrs of the May 1, 1971 mass demonstration against U.S. imperialism and its lackeys is a militant woman worker, Liza Balando, killed in cold blood by police armed and advised by the Public Safety Office of the U.S. Agency for International Development (AID).

Amado   Guerrero,   Chairman   of   the   Central   Committee, Communist Party of the Philippines, states in his book *Philippine Society and Revolution*:

> The women compose about one-half of the Phillipine population and they cut through classes. The vast majority of Filipino women, therefore, belong to the oppressed and exploited classes. But in addition to class oppression, they suffer male oppression. The revolutionaries of the opposite sex should exert extra efforts to make possible the widest participation of women in the people's democratic revolution. They should not take the attitude that it is enough for the men in the family to be in the revolutionary movement. This attitude is actually feudal and it would be to aggravate the old clerical influence on women if they were to be kept out of the revolutionary movement. Women can perform general as well as special tasks in the revolution. This is an effective method for liberating them from the clutches of feudal conservatism and also from the decadent bourgeois misrepresentation of women as mere objects of pleasure.[2]

Guerrero's observation has served for many years now as the most influential theoretical orientation for determining the historical roots of female oppression. For example, a recent article in *Philippine Resistance* (1982) summarizes the impact of 300 years of Spanish rule and over five decades of U.S. hegemony: Spanish rule propagated the European notion of the superiority of men primarily through the Church, exhorting women to be meek and passive wives/mothers. "Later, U.S imperialism, bringing with it the culture of business, further propagated the decadent concept of women as mere objects of pleasure. Since males were considered the prime movers of production, labor power became entirely male-oriented. Most women were relegated to the task of reproducing and rearing future sources of fresh labor power. . . . In general, women were reduced to mere chattels--private property of men." However, Guerrero's economistic bias betrays a strong paternalistic note of charity: instead of women initiating their own autonomous strategy and organization for self-determination, they are conceived as objects who will benefit from enlightened concessions from male revolutionaries. Thus, we need a more thoroughgoing self-critique and transvaluation of the orthodox Marxist perspective on women's position in a semi-colonial and semi-feudal society such as the Philippines.

REGROUNDING THE "PROCESS WITHOUT A SUBJECT"

We can summarize the socio-economic position of women in the Philippines today by citing a few salient statistics: of the more than twenty-five million, who constitute one-third of the nation's labor force, the majority live in the rural areas, underpaid and overworked. From 1970 to 1980, the total unemployment rate for women was 75 percent compared to 10 percent for men. Sexist segregation of the labor force can be illustrated by the concentration of women in lower-paid jobs in domestic services, nursing, sales, clerical work, tourism and prostitution, while males monopolize jobs in transportation, construction, mining, management, and other administrative functions. Thus we find 94 percent of school teachers are women, and only 1 percent occupy administrative roles. Eighty-one percent of women are condemned to performing unpaid household chores, while 86 percent of domestic help are women receiving wages below the legal minimum and forced to work any time of the day. Of the professional stratum, 9 percent are women, and less than 1 percent hold positions as managers and supervisors[3]

In the two notorious cities of Olongapo and Angeles surrounding the U.S. bases, the majority of the 30,000 prostitutes are minors or teen-agers who are viciously exploited by the owners of bars and nightclubs. They enjoy none of the benefits accorded to ordinary business employees. Meanwhile, the Marcos government extracts tax revenues from them averaging 14.5 million pesos annually. A bill to legalize prostitution and brothels has been presented to the Marcos-controlled parliament recently.

A shocking and cruel proof of the present regime's sexist policy toward women can be seen in the recent exposure of the "Olongapo Twelve": twelve young girls, aged nine to fourteen, afflicted with syphilis, gonorrhea, and herpes; victimized by a prostitution ring in Olongapo (next to Subic Naval Base) which includes an American navy man as ringleader. This culprit has been allowed to escape the clutches of Philippine law; after all, Marcos needs the rental for the U.S. bases ($900 million U.S. tax dollars) to finance his corrupt and repressive apparatus.

Of the alternatives to prostitution and the dream of marrying a U.S. serviceman to escape poverty, the most blatantly exploitative is the "warm body" export advertised by travel agencies. These firms promise employment in Hong Kong, Italy, Spain, Canada, and elsewhere. In at least one case, twenty-one Filipino women were arrested in Belgium for not having work permits, victims of these agencies. In Norway and New Zealand, "friendship clubs" announce the availability of Filipino women as wives, emphasizing their ability "to please a man." A feature article in Belgium explains its growth potential: "The business marriage bureau flourishes. In the Philippines there are about fifty million inhabitants. Of this number, two million women are extra. You see, we are not yet out of stock." Talk about consumerism and commodification in the West! This traffic in women's bodies, which tries to arouse racist impulses in European men fearful of assertive wives, receives the full support of the Marcos regime, since the compulsory remittance of earnings from women provides the regime with over a billion dollars worth of foreign exchange every year. It also conveniently relieves the country of a segment of the population that would otherwise be clamoring for jobs.

Concluding a path-breaking assessment of the contemporary women's struggle in the Philippines, Delia D. Aguilar situates their struggle in a global context:

> It ought to be clear that the brutality of an inherently unjust society knows no bounds. Filipino women and men, who experience exploitation in their blood and bones, cannot but come to the understanding that all those with common interests must work together to radically alter their society. In doing so, they are simultaneously chipping away at the system that, in different ways, suppresses women's potential in the West. If many feminists do not yet see that this is the case--in a women's conference in the U.S. recently, someone proposed to a panel of Third World speakers that perhaps they could hoist "Support ERA" placards alongside their own while picketing at U.S. embassies in their respective countries--seizing the opportunity for solidarity work opened up by a global assembly line, as suggested by Ehrenreich and Fuentes, could prove very instructive. From such unity in practice will eventually emerge a much broader vision that will inform feminist theory and practice.[4]

This call for solidarity may have been the impetus for the bomb attack on the Philippine embassy in Bonn, West Germany, by a group known as Rote Zora (Red Zora) to mark International Women's Day 1983. An open letter in the *Berlin Tage Zeitung* claimed that the attack was a denunciation of the "degrading trafficking of women" promoted by the Marcos regime (*Solidaridad* II, 7, 1983, p. 9).

MOBILIZING THE FURIES: TO EMANCIPATE,
PARTICIPATE

Today, in a semi-feudal and semi-colonial society, the broad masses of the Filipino people--men, women, children--are conducting a national democratic revolution against U.S. imperialism and its local allies, the Marcos clique of bureaucrat capitalists, compradors and feudal landlords. Because the "New Society" of the Marcos dictatorship promotes male supremacy and male chauvinism in a blatant fashion with the blessings of the Church hierarchy, the bastion of feudal culture, the women in the united front against the fascist regime have intensified ideological struggle in particular against sexist ideas. While the dictator's wife indulges Christina Ford and her jet set with fashion parades and beauty contests--the Miss Universe pageant held a few years ago in Manila cost millions of dollars of people's money used to advertise the neo-colony as a tourist haven and international brothel for monopoly corporations' capital--revolutionary and progressive women are politicizing the masses in legal as well as underground actions, combining theory and practice, to get rid of sexism in actual struggle.

The extremely reactionary ideology of male supremacy enforced today by the Marcos martial-law regime and guaranteed by the instruments of State violence sanctions the continued exploitation and degradation of Filipino women. While the government acclaims the dictator's wife as the paragon of liberated women, the fascist military continue to arrest, torture and kill patriotic women like Maria Lorena Barros, Mila Astorga-Garcia, Nelia Sancho, Julie DeLima-Sison, Liliosa Hilao, Purificacion Pedro, and hundreds more who languish in prison or fall in combat. One recent victim is Trinidad Herrera, the intrepid popular leader of millions of poor slum dwellers in Manila. Apologists for this outrageous degradation and barbarity, like Kerima Polotan Tuvera, Carmen Guerrero Nakpil, and assorted prima donnas of the "New Society" dish out hackneyed myths or echo the bourgeois feminism rampant in capitalist Europe and America. They propagate bourgeois hypocrisy, feudal decadence, and the mendacious servility of women to the order of the "New Society."

But the implacable reality of the protracted revolutionary struggle for women's genuine emancipation, which can only be realized in the concrete process of the socialist transformation of society as a whole, has been irresistibly advancing by leaps and bounds, through twists and turns, throughout the Philippines. The vicissitudes, setbacks and triumphs of this epoch-making endeavor can be gleaned from two volumes: *No Time for Crying,* edited by Alison Wynne (Hong Kong, 1979); and *The Women's Struggle in the Philippines,* soon to be published by the Philippines Research Center.

Of the thousands of women who have committed their bodies and spirits to the raging underground resistance to the ruthless forces of the U.S.-Marcos dictatorship, we can cite two exemplary figures: Maria Lorena Barros (briefly alluded to in Chapter II), and Nelia Sancho.

An anthropology graduate student at the University of the Philippines in the late sixties and early seventies, Barros took the initiative in forming the first all-female revolutionary organization, MAKIBAKA, because the development of female activists was being impeded by traditional habits and mores: "If there were things to be done late in the evening," Barros points out, "the boys would be left behind to do the job because the girls had to be home early. In our system of values, a woman who uses her brains is regarded as an anomaly. The women in our society are encouraged to be passive creatures good only for bearing and rearing children." Contrast this viewpoint with the glorification of motherhood implied in a statement by a Marcos appointee, Ambassador Leticia Ramos-Shahani: "I wish men could bear children so they would know the aches and pains of motherhood. Perhaps then they would father fewer children; perhaps they would stop waging war because they would then know how it feels to have children killed in wars."

Confronting the rampant injustice and oppression of millions of Filipinos around her, Barros gave up her studies and immersed herself in the anti-imperialist struggle. She was interviewed before the declaration of martial law in 1972. Now a martyr-heroine of the revolution, Barros's words yield a prophetic resonance: "Considering the quality of the young people today, the country has a good future. . . . The interest of the ruling class and of the exploited masses are diametrically opposed; the former will never allow the latter to wrest power without a struggle. . . . The revolution is inevitable, it is dictated by necessity. The Philippines might become another Vietnam. If we don't endure and do something about it now, the succeeding generations will suffer even more. . . . If an armed conflict does arise, we will fight alongside the men. We should take up arms, if necessary. We are working for a better society for men and women alike, so why should the men always bear the brunt of the struggle?"

In line with Barros' urgent advocacy of women's total participation in politics, MAKIBAKA did not just stress the unity of women with men as oppressed subjects; it also targetted the conservative sexist practices of the whole society. MAKIBAKA sought to unleash "the vigor, intelligence and creativity of Filipino women" and unite them "into a potent and cohesive force for the struggle." The influence of this thinking can be discerned in the actual practices of women members of the New People's Army as described by Tom Morton, "LNS Interviews Women of the Philippine Underground" (LNS, 28 April 1978), and also in *Ang Bayan* (31 March 1977), pp. 12-13.

Reflecting on the vicissitudes of MAKIBAKA after 1972 when

Barros was driven underground and then, after a series of arrests and escapes, subsequently killed in an encounter, Professor Dolores Feria of the University of the Philippines comments on what she considers the failure of that organization to mobilize the energies of Filipino women: "MAKIBAKA went down the drain because our culture was not yet ready for anything other than the standard conception of a woman in a supportive role: as feminine, attractive, and always keeping her voice down. . . . I hope the Left would wake up one day to the fact that, with the Right, they think exactly within the same framework of reasoning to downplay women's lib. Their conservative sense would say: no, never mind, I don't want my wife to behave like that. For me this kind of thinking is incredible, and does not belong to the twentieth century. Another reason I made a comment about the Left is that the Left could have successfully spearheaded such a movement. But for 'tactical considerations' (whatever that is), they decided not to do so right now" (*Diliman Review*, March–April 1983, p. 27).

One of the most distinguished women activists, Nelia Sancho, may not fully agree with Professor Feria's somewhat premature judgment of earlier feminist ventures. Born into a middle-class family descended from peasant sharecroppers, Sancho was exposed (like Barros) to the reality of the intensifying class contradictions of society while a student at the same university in 1971. She helped set up barricades in the campus to block military troops suppressing protest marches against price-hikes of commodities allowed by the government. In that same year, she was chosen Queen of the Pacific in a beauty competition in Melbourne, Australia.

"The personal is political"--the truth of this axiom is poignantly registered by Sancho's experience immediately before and after the crisis of 1972. When she joined the Movement for a Democratic Philippines in 1972 in its relief work and educational program among the flood-stricken peasants of central Luzon, she witnessed the extreme fascist brutality of the Marcos military: volunteers--students, doctors, nurses, etc.--were summarily arrested, their relief goods confiscated. Sancho saw the exploitation of rural women whose poverty and feudal family traditions continue to stifle their humanity, allowing only 25 percent to complete elementary education. Not only do rural women share field work with men, they also perform necessary household tasks which are unpaid and socially discounted. Working with peasants and learning from them, Sancho saw how her own personal roots in the peasantry coalesced with her evolving political principles and commitment.

When martial law was declared, Sancho was one of those wanted for empathizing and identifying with the downtrodden peasants and workers. When she was captured in October 1973, two of her comrades were killed: one a chemistry instructor at the University who was shot dead through the heart; and a student,

Fred Malikay, who was wounded and then strangled with a rope by the barbaric military. This experience burned itself in her heart as she endured a painful month-long detention. After her release, she worked for an American firm in Davao City, but her profound devotion to the cause of freedom and justice compelled her to quit her job, and all the seductions of money and elite glamour, to resume the sharing of the struggle with the masses. As a result of that decision, her whole family was interrogated by the military, and her younger sister Agnes severely tortured by electric shock and "water cure." She was also sexually molested for 26 days in a safehouse until pressure from the religious community of Davao secured her release.

On 5 February 1976, Sancho was arrested in Cagayan de Oro City. Her subsequent trial before a military tribunal was used by the fascist dispensation to mock the image of the "liberated woman" solely interested in "mayhem and adventure," an utterly "misguided girl." This trial in Manila occurred while thousands of women were being degraded every day as "hospitality girls" or prostitutes, victims of unemployment and the Marcos-promoted tourist industry. In Manila's tourist belt alone, there are over 120 flesh shops; twenty-one are accredited by the Ministry of Tourism and licensed by City Hall. Each shop has eighty to one hundred "hospitality girls" employed by accredited tourist agencies (*Bulletin Today*, 21 August 1980).

Thousands of Filipino women like Nelia Sancho are today becoming aware that the people's struggle for social justice and national emancipation from the Marcos dictatorship and U.S. imperialism cannot be a genuinely collective effort without the unqualified support and participation of women. Sancho's cause is not just a solitary private one, for the liberation of women is a fundamental imperative, a *sine qua non*, for a successful radical transformation of a neo-colony. Sancho is also part of an emerging autonomous women's movement targetting what the Permanent People's Tribunal witness called "the exploitation and domination of women by male authority" inscribed in a Third World historical formation.

BE REALISTIC, DEMAND THE IMPOSSIBLE

Of immense significance is the direct participation of women in the armed struggle currently raging in the countryside, with the formation of a Red Women's Detachment as an integral part of the New People's Army, a member of the National Democratic Front. Red women fighters have distinguished themselves in ambushes, raids, organizing work, etc., on all fronts. They have also worked side by side with male guerrillas in consolidating the liberated base areas and supervising the creation of Barrio Revolutionary Committees, the chief administrative body for initiating revolutionary land reform, building up the people's army, and strengthening the united front.

In January 1974, a woman cadre of the New People's Army (NPA) spearheading the armed struggle against the U.S.-Marcos dictatorship was interviewed by a correspondent of the Manchester *Guardian* (January 30). Solita Esternon, a 24-year-old university student, was captured by the reactionary army in December when she was four months pregnant, supposedly armed with a .32 caliber pistol and bound for Sorsogon City, Sorsogon province, southeast of Luzon, to establish a revolutionary base.

Solita had refused to disclose the whereabouts of guerrilla comrades in exchange for milder prison treatment. She recalls the attempt of a mercenary government officer: "He told me, 'You'll be inside for thirty years and then you'll be an old woman and you won't be able to get married.' I was shocked that he thought that such a threat would frighten me. I told him, all right, I said, I've been married once already, and that was enough to last until I die." Solita had been married to an NPA regular who was killed five months after, in an encounter with neo-colonial troops. The wedding, as she described it, was a simple promise made over a Filipino translation of *Quotations from Mao Tsetung*, with NPA comrades as witnesses.

While a student in Manila before martial law was imposed in September 1972, Solita had been exposed to the fierce mass demonstrations and discussions about U.S. imperialism, to which she responded positively. "One thing though: I was not converted," Solita asserts. "I object to the religious, forcible connotation of the word. I was clear about what I was doing."

Since its re-establishment in 1968, the Communist Party of the Philippines has gained tremendous victories in the countryside, winning the allegiance of peasants (which comprise over seventy-five percent of fifty-three million Filipinos) by genuine land reform: reduction of rent, elimination of usury, and confiscation of land owned by oppressive landlords and its free redistribution to the tillers. All these depend on the heightened level of political consciousness of the rural masses and the intensity of organized struggle in different areas. Solita found that "the people in the villages wanted to know all about communism. We tell them that under communism there will be no landlords, that the land will really be theirs, and their families', we teach them the problem of bringing about Communism in a feudal society like the Philippines; that the first stage of the struggle would be to industrialize the Philippines, but that this cannot be done as long as we are a semi-colony of U.S. imperialism."

To organize the peasants, the party sets up barrio organizing committees of six or seven persons. In Solita's group there were two student cadres and four peasants. They were warmly protected by the villagers, cooperating with them and learning from them.

"Serve the people!" was the fundamental principle they applied in actual practice, integrating closely with the masses. Because of this policy of pursuing the mass line faithfully and developing with all available resources the theory and practice of people's war, the NPA time and again has defeated Marcos' encirclement and suppression campaigns (over twenty-five U.S. military personnel have been killed so far) and has expanded its bases many times since its founding in 1969. Asked about the "New Society" of the dictatorship, Solita says: "There is no difference between the 'New Society' and the old, except that in the old one political power was shared by several politicians and now it is concentrated in one man. It is not just Marcos that has to go, but the whole system." Solita adds: "Marcos' social and economic 'reforms' are doomed to failure. . . . If the peasants were really liberated there would be no basis for revolution."

What is the situation of the revolutionary forces now? Solita says: "We're right at the beginning. We have to build up our mass base in the villages. We have not yet even reached the Yenan stage." As to her own personal future, Solita alludes to Ho Chi Minh, who was "imprisoned twice but lived on to lead the revolution." The future promises the victory of the Filipino national liberation struggle as part of the world socialist revolution. Solita Esternon, imprisoned NPA cadre and symbol of militant Filipina womanhood, wanted to name the child in her womb (if a girl) Nadina--"That means [she tells the reporter] *hope* in Russian, doesn't it?"

NEGATING PHALLOCENTRISM

The unifying theme of the multi-faceted and dynamic thrust of the contemporary (pre-1983) women's movement, both in the sphere of ideology and daily practice, is that class struggle is the key link to the "woman question," that women in any class-divided society cannot be free until the people and the class to which she belongs have been freed from national oppresion and class exploitation. Of course, that is only a precondition for continuing the struggle against patriarchy and sexism in all forms. This is what Engels pointed out in his classic study *Origin of the Family*, which demonstrated the material basis of the inequality of the sexes in private property of the means of production, inheritance, and wage labor. Faced by the "idealist", ultimately bourgeois distortions of Engels' argument and the insidious petty-bourgeois notion of "free love," etc., Lenin in his time insisted on a principled dialectical materialist analysis of man-woman relationships. From a consistent class perspective, Lenin attacked the liberal, narrowly subjectivist and essentially bourgeois trend of "sexual freedom":

The revolution demands concentration, increase of forces. From the masses, from individuals. It cannot tolerate orgiastic conditions, such as are normal for the decadent heroes and heroines of D'Annunzio. Dissoluteness in sexual life is bourgeois, is a phenomenon of decay. The proletariat is a rising class. It doesn't need intoxication as a narcotic or a stimulus. Intoxication as little by sexual exaggeration as by alcohol. It must not and shall not forget, forget the shame, the filth, the savagery of capitalism. It receives the strongest urge to fight from a class situation, from the Communist ideal.[5]

It is this militant, uncompromising stand of Lenin, sustained and enriched by the living practice of revolution in Russia, China, Cuba, Vietnam, and elsewhere, that has inspired since the sixties the theoreticians and practitioners of Marxist feminism in the Philippines today.

It would not be quite faithful to the historical record at this point if I omit the observation that even now (1985) compared to the substantial theoretical advances that Western Marxist-feminists have made in the last two decades in applying historical materialism to the analysis of patriarchy and its transhistorical persistence through various modes of production, the mainstream of Filipino radical thinking on this classic question still labors from a crude, dogmatic materialism which mechanically subordinates the woman's struggle to the peremptory needs and imperatives of the anti-imperialist struggle. Perhaps this infantile phenomenon is an inevitable part of the vicissitudes of any socialist movement proceeding through uneven, zigzag stages. One can see this level of consciousness in articles from the underground paper *Liberation* or form earlier formulations by writers like Astorga-Garcia, Sison, Fortaleza, etc.

Usually, the refusal to think through the intricate complexity of women's oppression manifests itself in righteous usurpation of the privilege of urgent engagement in the battlefield. More specifically, it manifests itself as a symptom of fear that male leadership roles and chauvinist attitudes are being challenged, and thus supposedly males are distracted from fighting the immediate enemy, the U.S.-Marcos dictatorship. The characteristic gesture of anti-feminism is to dismiss any critical thinking with the vulgar formula of the anti-imperialist effort as "primary," and the struggle for equality of the sexes as "secondary". Such a defensive tactic, if not a strategic ploy to escape self-criticism or necessary "house-cleaning", vitiates the appeal for a united front, suppresses the initiative from both genders, paralyzes energies and thought on all sides, and perpetuates the very problems it seeks to solve. Naturally, resort is made to quotations from the classics. Engels indeed is partly to blame for the anthropological error of postulating a non-existent matriarchal stage, and an economistic determinism which complements the metaphysical image of bourgeois feminism it seeks to exorcise.

However, I believe the actual experiments and elaborations in practice being carried out in the battlefront, as well as in clandestine legal/illegal work, may be pre-empting the space left vacant by conscious theoretical reflection. The latest Althusserian/Lacanian analysis displayed in such books as *Feminism and Materialism* (1978), ed. Annette Kuhn and Ann-Marie Wolfe, Michele Barrett's *Women's Oppression Today* (1980) and Rosalind Coward's *Patriarchal Precedents* (1983), may not yet have registered its impact on the Philippine scene. But as Althusser himself noted, the Chinese cultural revolution preceded his own interventions, in fact was its *sine qua non*: Minerva's owl takes flight only after the smoke of historical crisis and transformations have lifted.

Within the gaps, fissures, *lacunae* in the thickness of the struggle, one can already see inscribed, as "traces" or the site of marginal articulations, the emergent theory of Filipino materialist feminism coeval with the class struggle, interrogating it and insistently renewing its internal dynamism with what is seemingly the irreconcilable and yet somehow essentially dialectical contradiction of the sexes we are living through anywhere, any time.

The advent of this materialist feminism may be clearly perceived in the following selections by Filipina activist Delia D. Aguilar. Written on various occasions, they constitute the initial premises for an ongoing project of a thorough and all-sided analysis of the position of women in the Philippines today. They reflect the most advanced and uncompromising critique of the vulgar "Marxist" position on women noted earlier and still officially espoused by some elements and sectors of the revolutionary movement. In a way, what I have quoted and summarized, juxtaposed with Aguilar's commentaries, exhibits the dialectical unity of the traditional view of women's emancipation as conditional on a prior class emancipation, and its emerging critique.

As an illustration of the traditional or orthodox view, it might be instructive to cite a well-known speech by Mila Astorga-Garcia. a former member of the Women's Bureau of *Kabataang Makabayan* (Nationalist Youth), entitled "The Filipina's Role In the National Democratic Struggle" (published in *Kalayaan International* Nov.-Dec. 1973). Astorga-Garcia emphasizes the theme that the filipino women's liberation "from the bonds of a feudal and colonial culture" can be attained only in a national-democratic society. At the same time, she notes that bearing and rearing children "is a very noble task and a very important responsibility which we the Filipino women should never shun," a duty women must fulfill together with other tasks. Moreover, "our male brothers are not the ones responsible for our [female] status," rather it is "U.S. imperialism. . . . " She concludes: " . . . Let it be stressed that whatever role [the Filipino woman] assumes, so long as she is significantly participating in the national democratic struggle, and so long as she has freed herself from both feudal and bourgeois values, she may be considered liberated or emancipated."

While Astorga-Garcia--only one among numerous exponents of the role of women as childbearers and "desexed" activists in the struggle--merely articulated the most accepted "radical" opinion in the sixties and early seventies, an article from the same group (now operating underground) written in the eighties ("When the Filipina Holds a Rifle," published in *Philippine Resistance*, 1982, pp. 13-15) replicates the standard dogma that "the exploitation of women is but part of class contradiction," which is Astorga-Garcia's point of departure and ideological/political destination. Oblivious to the specificity of the socio-political construction of gender as irreducible to economics, the article, after attacking "feudal conservatism" and "the decadent bourgeois misrepresentation of women as mere objects of pleasure," proceeds to a familiar, short-circuited conclusion: "Therefore, the only road to the emancipation of Filipino women from their bondage is by uniting with the workers and peasants in the rapidly advancing national democratic revolution aimed at overthrowing the vicious triad plaguing Philippine society--imperialism, feudalism, and bureau-crat-captialism on the one hand, and its perpetrators, U.S. imperialism and its partner, the ruling elites, on the other." Thus in one stroke, women and their problems are dissolved.

With the following commentaries Delia Aguilar seeks to recover the submerged, occluded but irrepressible presence of the Other (Woman as "negation of the negation"), without which the space of freedom and desire cannot be mapped in our everyday pursuits.

DELIA AGUILAR: FOUR INTERVENTIONS

Some Thoughts on the Oppression of Women (1981)

In the U.S. and other Western countries, the superstructural aspects of women's oppression have been subjected to close scrut-iny. Indeed, the bulk of bourgeois social science research, impelled by the force of the movement, has been on gender roles and the nature of female-male relations within the family. This is to be expected in a "liberal democracy" where the real source of the problem, the capitalist system of production, cannot be exposed. Instead, attention is directed toward the socialization process and the preparation for adulthood in which the boy is groomed for his worker/breadwinner role, and the girl as wife/mother/emotional tension-manager in a world in which the public sphere (the world of work in which the man strives for success) is separated from the private one (the household where the woman's domesticity and nurturance are given full play). Emphasis is laid on attendant values and psychological malformations that, in typical liberal fashion, are presumed to equally debilitate women and men. The contribution of various institutions, all placed on the same continuum--educational institutions, government, church, industry, etc.--to the resulting inequality of women is not ignored; but to no one's surprise, bourgeois analysis falls far short of putting the finger on the real culprit.

Because of this failure, an anti-male tendency is bound to arise, culminating in radical feminism whose ideas are largely hostile to Marxism. For instance, radical feminists denounce socialist countries for what they see as their "betrayal" of women.

Now why did Marxist feminism come about at all? Marxist feminists have disagreed with Engels' position that the entry of women into production could of itself spell the end of male dominance, and have taken issue with the concept that the family as the center of women's oppression is simply a relic of the pre-capitalist period. They argue that the oppression of women and the sexual division of labor are entrenched in capitalist relations of production and must be analyzed in this light, stressing that Marxism must take into account women's domestic labor, their role as poorly paid workers in the labor force, and the familial ideology that heightens their oppression.

As a result, formulations of various sorts have sprung up to correct this mechanical or vulgar Marxism which adheres to a rigid economism and which has marginalized gender relations and the question of male dominance. Thus the explorations of patriarchy, its relation to capitalism, etc. Suffice it to say that in much of this there is a tendency to postulate ideology as autonomous or relatively autonomous from the mode of production, a characteristic pitfall when theory is not closely linked with practice.

Fortunately for us, because our struggle is carried on within a revolutionary context, we don't have the problem of attempting to find solutions on a merely theoretical plane. However, I think that some of the charges that Marxist feminists have levelled against Marxism hold true for our movement. We cannot dispute the fact that Filipino women can be liberated only in the struggle for national liberation. But just as some Marxist feminists err in giving primacy to ideology in order to call attention to the oppression of women, we have in the main paid little heed to the ideological constructs that both reflect and intensify the concrete conditions of women's subjugation.

To say that activists in the Philippines do not find sexism a problem is to deny the existence of women's oppression in a semi-feudal, semi-colonial society. On the contrary, sexism in our society is virulent--bourgeois sexual objectification tacked on to the belief in women's inferiority (their "superiority" springing only from their sexual chastity and devotion to wifely and motherly duties) combines to cement women's exploitation in production where they are singled out for stultifying work and measly wages.

More likely what is meant by "sexism is not a problem" is precisely that the cultural forms through which male dominance is manifested have not been given the kind of attention they have received in the West. As we have seen, in the U.S. the more innocuous thrusts of the women's movement serve as safety valves, a nice way of slaying the dragon by striking mercilessly at its tail. Since we want a thoroughgoing change and since we are not vulgar Marxists, we must tackle both material conditions *and* ideology. The fact that there exists an underlying fear that considerations of ideology pertaining to women might be divisive or that these could result in elevating women's oppression to priority status, testify to the insidiousness of sexism. We must help one another become aware of the ways in which our ideas, attitudes, and behavior reflect and perpetuate the subordination of women. It is not always easy to do so because, unless our feelings have been totally blocked out, female-male relationships, especially intimate ones, are enveloped in emotion. We should bear in mind that gender divisions at work and at home have created a female object who has been taught to delight in servitude while modestly claiming the "power behind the throne," and a male subject whose self-image derives from a certain degree of authority at home (often exacerbated by its denial at work) over a wife whose function is, among other things, to assure him of his worth. Concepts of femininity and masculinity are so deeply ingrained in all of us that it soon becomes simply natural to assign a biological basis to these distinctions. Thus, we can expect such discussions to be in many ways unsettling.

These are very important considerations for the revolution because we want maximum participation from everyone and because we went to create a society in which both material and psychological forms of subjugation can be eliminated. Moreover, it is men, particularly those who are otherwise politically developed, who should take responsibility for correcting their sexist behavior once they have become aware of it. In such an atmosphere, conscious and deliberate measures can be taken to encourage women to participate more fully in a more equal manner, and we can then begin to give substance to the slogan, "Women hold up half the sky."

Comments on "Ang Kilusan Para Lumaya Ang Kababaihan" ("Movement to Emancipate Women")

The document "Ang Kilusan Para Lumaya ang Kababaihan" is to be commended for legitimizing the struggle of women. However, it has some shortcomings which stand out sharply in the light of developments in Marxist theory and practice in different socialist countries, and even in current Marxist formulations in the West.

The assumption that serves as underpinning for this *Maikling Kurso* is the notion that the liberation of women will automatically result from the society's transformation into a national democracy. This flies in the face of the experience of all existing socialist oountries where, despite the very real gains won by women, their subordination persists. That is, the change in the mode of production simply lays the foundation on which women's equality is made possible, but other facets of their oppression (as embodied in reproduction of labor power, gender role formation, male/female relations. etc.), if not fully recognized and dealt with, will impede women's wholehearted participation in the building of a new order. The forms this oppression takes necessarily vary in different societies, but it would be a real disservice to Filipino women if the revolutionary movement simply continues to lump the struggle of women along with that of peasants, workers, etc., without paying careful attention to their *specific* oppression as women.

The tendency to gloss over the "woman question" is, to be sure, not peculiar to our movement alone. In the U.S., Marxist-Leninist (M-L) groups are noted for doing exactly this as proof, almost, of their adherence to a "correct" political line that would meet the M-L seal of approval, any deviations being judged symptomatic of "bourgeois feminism." Quite understandably, reasonable people hesitate to take up a "divisive" issue. But there is an objective difference in the material conditions of women and men in general, vis-a-vis the mode of production but also in ideological constructions of gender. One is bound to suspect that for men this is merely an excuse not to have to rectify their own individual (read: oppressive) practice with women. The other factor is that Marxism needs to be developed more to adequately address the needs of women; indeed, some revolutionary societies have already begun to do so (Guinea-Bissau and Cuba, for example).

In the *Kurso* are a couple of passages (pp. 10, 18) citing women's unequal status within home and family; however, proposals for changing this are too general and, at best, ambiguous, and they are to be undertaken not so much for women's sake as to provide an environment for the development of politically conscious children. The exhortation for women to participate actively outside the home is laudable in itself even if the tasks are for the most part extensions of "women's work." Yet the emphasis is always laid on some other purpose extraneous to women themselves, never on the liberation of women as women, effectively cementing the martyrdom and self-effacement that has been painstakingly cultivated by feudalism and capitalism, and that continues to be so endearing to men. Thus, women are to be active in production and political work, but who is to do the housework? Are we simply imposing on them a double shift? Why is there no mention of men's responsibilities in the home regarding this and care of the children?

To reiterate, I think there is a dire need to focus on specific forms of Filipino women's oppression. How about problems associated with reproduction (birth control, abortion, etc.)? What practices are there--within the family (gender role socialization, courtship, marriage, etc.) and in insitutions outside the home--that apply to women alone, and how do these affect women? Do these need to be changed so that women can achieve their potential? Because there are no clear examples of how women are exploited differently from men, it seems as though the only distinction is when they become *putas*, whores (p. 7); furthermore, their exploitation is viewed as a purely economic one. In effect, their liberation as women is important only insofar as they can be mobilized for the national democratic revolution and that, in themselves, women remain insignificant. Would the movement similarly treat tribal minorities?

The example of other countries (e.g., China) suggests the necessity for women to have their own independent organization, working within the general guidelines of the broader movement, and empowered to make policy on women. There must also be serious efforts toward having equal representation of women in all decision-making bodies at all levels. The struggle of women clearly requires structural changes and a continuing battle against deep-seated ideological reflexes during the revolution and after.

Women are oppressed in the workplace as women; they are also subordinated through psychological/sociological mechanisms which, along with the former, comprise the material conditions leading to their secondary status. Unless these issues are urgently addressed and practical solutions immediately applied, our vision and ideals for a truly egalitarian, non-exploitative society will not be realized.

Two Letters

July 7, 1982

Dear Comrades:

Those of us in the U.S. who support the revolutionary movement are always inspired by the resolute courage of comrades in the thick of the struggle that we see mirrored in the documents we receive from home. Your commitment forces us to reflect on the limitations of our own situation here, at the same time that it encourages us to seek ways in which we might be of help. It is in this spirit that I write this criticism.

I have carefully read a number of papers on the woman question produced by the movement, and one thing clearly stands out. The liberation of women is viewed as an integral component of the struggle for national democracy. This is as it should be, for no Marxist would argue for the removal of such a struggle from its societal context. The latter is a position, of course, that the bourgeoisie would like women to take; to be sure, there are such groups in the U.S. However, since the advent of the women's liberation movement in the late 60s, a great deal of refinement in theory as well as in political action has taken place. Hence, the insistence by

Filipino revolutionaries on caricaturing and summarily dismissing the Western women's struggle as a "burn-the-bra movement" is, unfortunately, more a symptom of our own appalling ignorance on women's issues than it is an accurate description of what progressive women are doing in the United States.

I call attention to two *Liberation* articles in particular ("Not Merely a Socio-Cultural Question," March 1981; Leon Fortaleza, "Daughter of the People," March 1982). As I mentioned earlier, implicit in both is the conviction that Filipino women can be liberated only when Philippine society is transformed. This is not a point of contention. However, also implicit in this (especially when female/male relations are denigrated as "merely socio-cultural") is the notion that women's liberation will automatically result from a change in the mode of production. This class reductionist, vulgar form of Marxism is being called into question by the experience of women in existing socialist countries, and if revolutionaries in the Philippines are serious about the role of women, they must pay heed to this development in Marxist theory and practice.

In none of the writings on women is there a concern for women's oppression resulting from the sexual division of labor, particularly within the domestic sphere, and women's roles associated with reproduction of the species, of labor power, of social relations, etc. We cannot at this point in history persist in resorting to the old, worn-out, and highly suspect charge of "divisiveness" hurled at those who raise these questions. Indeed, the theoretical backwardness evident in the presumably humorous play of "hysterical materialism" (see Fortaleza article) is a shameful disclosure of the movement's inability to grapple with the pernicious sexism in a semi-feudal, semi-colonial society.

This is a serious plea for the movement to study the woman question. I need not stress that the issue of priorities (nothing must distract us from the main struggle, that of national liberation, et cetera) is a false one. National liberation cannot occur without the participation of women, and their full involvement can be assured only if they see a stake in it.

I am pleased that you reviewed the work of Stephanie Urdang on women in Guinea-Bissau. What makes their approach different from ours is their recognition of the significance of the liberation of women *qua* women, not simply as instruments to bear arms, raise politically aware children, and so on. In short, their struggle shows a genuine respect for women that our movement thus far has been unable to muster. It will be an embarrassment before the international progressive movement if we do not work toward a theoretical reconsideration of our position. We must not allow the weight of feudal traditions governing gender relations to drag us down, for there, too, we need courage to face the real issues.

20 Nov. 1984

Dear Editors of BAI:

Congratulations on Kalayaan's new publication! A forum such as this is absolutely essential in the formulation of a theory that would articulate the emancipation of women as an integral, not a subordinate component of national liberation.

I do want to make some comments on the editorial. [According to the editorial, "it is indeed absurd that the entire issue [of feminism] should revolve around the question of who shall wash the dishes, who shall do the laundry and marketing, etc.] I think we ought not shun the topic of gender division of labor, especially in the domestic realm, for fear we will be perceived as petty or trivial. To do so is to grossly underestimate the significance of the mother and housewife roles in defining the Filipino woman's social identity. While household work may well be less a burden to her than to Western women where the nuclear family is shriveled in size and where hired domestic help is available only to the affluent, the Filipino woman's primary identification remains firmly tied to the family and household even when she engages in paid work.

Given this, we need to look at what Marxist economist Lourdes Beneria refers to as women's "reproductive work," that is to say, the sum total of the work performed in the home setting in which the gender division of labor is often distinctly elaborated. What does the woman do in the home? She not only reproduces children, but also reproduces the social relations and the existential basis of daily life; and produces and reproduces the working capacity of the wage earner (increasingly, the category of wage earner includes herself). Household work involves meeting the needs of the wage worker in tangible (e.g., feeding and clothing him) and in less tangible ways (servicing the husband's emotional needs, managing psychological tensions, creating a "good family environment," etc.). The woman is responsible for socializing the children congruent with society's requirements, her own enactment of what the culture defines as "feminine" and her husband's playing his "masculine" role serving as models for them to imitate. In doing so, she also reproduces the social relations necessary to maintain the hierarchical, gender-biased structures of our semi-colonial and semi-feudal society.

It is as much in this more innocent, "natural" set of gender relations within the family that woman's subordination is fortified as it is in the more public economic sphere where the profit motive and sex-typed occupations can be easily linked. In fact, what we must recognize is the near impossibility of neatly separating economic from social/psychological aspects of male domination, particularly in the home where intimate, personal ties tend to conceal the economic character of the household unit; after all, a woman conducts her reproductive work--which includes biological and social dimensions and the entire spectrum of daily living--as a labor of love, not in exchange for a wage.

If we agree with the above, then we need to pay close attention precisely to the material conditions of Filipino women's everyday life at home. We need to analyze the relation between the daily maintenance of the labor force that transpires in privatized form in the domestic sphere and the socialized labor of public production. Finally, we need to begin to study the intersection of class and gender in Philippine society in order to discover what specific changes must be made simultaneously with the struggle for national independence so that the liberation of women can become a reality.

Aguilar's call for a renewal of historical materialist thinking on gender in the Philippines is wholly unprecedented, timely, and overdue. In a second-world country like Canada, for example, Mary O'Brien has recently proposed that "the critique of male supremacy which can uncover the revolutionary structure of women's history and create a living feminist practice must be conducted from within Marxism."[7] The advent and long-range significance of a specifically Filipino socialist feminism may be appraised more accurately in the context of the phenomenal resurgence of black/Third World feminism in North America and Europe, particularly in Britain where two powerful critiques of white chauvinist/racist feminism have been launched: Jenny Bourne, "Towards an Anti-Racist Feminism," *Race and Class* (Summer 1983), pp. 1-22; and Valerie Amos and Pratibha Parmar, "Challenging Imperial Feminism," *Feminist Review* (Autumn 1984), pp. 3-20.

BEYOND A ROOM OF ONE'S OWN

The post-August 1983 explosions reverberated and unleashed polymorphous energies and desires hitherto dammed-up or sublimated in legitimate activism and dissipated in seething boredom and chagrin. Boundaries are being crossed, frontiers opened up once again.

In the November 1983 issue of *Ang Bayan* (the official organ of the underground Communist Party), one "Ka Lucia" confesses that "until now I am bothered by the lack of studies on the woman question, which will serve as the source of a political program of the women's movement in the current (national-democratic) stage of the revolution." The reference to a widely-circulated 1972-1973 document "On the Relationship Between the Sexes" by the Women's Bureau, which sought to elevate a monogamous "proletarian" relationship as a monolithic ideal or norm, simply underscores the paleolithic level of consciousness then prevalent which no amount of administered bureaucratic measures can renovate and redeem.

And so it comes as an almost miraculous achievement that about fifteen women's groups—among them KALAYAAN (Association of Women for Freedom), SAMAKANA (Organization of United Nationalist Women), PILIPINA, WOMEN (Women in Media Now), NOWRP (National Organization of Women Religious in the Philippines) and others—spearheaded a multi-sectoral establishment of a broad coalition called GABRIELA (General Assembly Binding Women for Reform, Integrity, Equality, Leadership and Action) whose principal aim is "the total emancipation of women." It seeks chiefly "to develop a broad and comprehensive women's movement in the Philippines to actualize the demands of the Filipino women for a just, egalitarian and humane society."

After an all-women assembly and forum held in March 1984, GABRIELA was formally organized on 28 April 1984, with forty-two affiliated organizations. (GABRIELA is named after the Filipina heroine Gabriela Silang who fought the Spaniards in the eighteenth century, thus becoming the symbol of the capacity of women to transcend the traditional supportive role ordained by the culture and assume leadership of the national-liberation struggle.) I quote the objectives and basic principles of GABRIELA from its brochure:

The organizations affiliated to GABRIELA are bonded together by four major principles, namely:

One, the women of GABRIELA are united and determined to restore democracy. They join forces with the men in opposing, at whatever cost, the dictatorial rule imposed upon the entire Filipino people.

Two, as part of the nation's productive force, the women of GABRIELA adhere to actively and decisively work for the attainment of a genuine sovereign and independent Philippines where women will be true and equal partners of men in developing and preserving national patrimony.

Three, recognizing the strength of the majority of the Filipino people, the women of GABRIELA believe that it is their primary responsibility to enhance the development of women in the grassroots and oppose any move that dehumanizes our less privileged sisters. We resolve to support the struggles of the women workers, peasants, and urban poor settlers to attain their economic well-being.

Four, national liberation is incomplete without women's

liberation. The women of GABRIELA are determined to advance the women's movement that seeks to eliminate all forms that oppress women, particularly the feudal-patriarchal structures which relegate women to an inferior and lower-status position and restrict women from fully and actively participating in all spheres of endeavor.

With the four major principles as bases, GABRIELA aims to educate, organize and mobilize women towards:

1. Equipping each woman with the consciousness, motivation, and skills to institute socio-cultural transformation;

2. Actualizing each woman's potential for political leadership; and

3. Tapping and consolidation of the organized strength of women for political action.

In the March assembly, the focus of concern was the suffering of women caused by "unjust and discriminatory labor, civil and other laws and practices as well as socio-economic conditions that not only reduce them to lower-status citizens but limit their productivity and their capacity for socio-political action." In general, GABRIELA's platform is not different from the productivist position paper on women read at the International Ecumenical Conference on the Philippines held at Stony Point, New York, September-October 1983.

While the Assembly endeavored to identify "women's issues that are truly Filipino" contradistinguished from those imposed by western thought, the three major lectures given at the gathering tried to breach and escape the problematic of orthodox materialism which shortcircuits the four spheres Juliet Mitchell has defined as crucial arenas of struggle: production, reproduction, socialization and sexuality.[8] In her paper "The Woman Problem: Gender, Class and State of Oppression," Cynthia Nolasco (arrested last August 6 and now a political prisoner of the regime) outlines the classic tripartite conceptualization of women's subordination in the Third World: sex, class, neo-colonized society. But while she correctly delineates female oppression by the feudal patriarchy--women treated as commodities (prostitutes, erotic models, mail-order brides, domestic slaves)--she clearly stresses women's exploitation as a class; e.g., wage discrimination (only 35 percent of every peso goes to a woman worker), assignment to jobs with high health or safety risks, warm-body export as domestics, etc. And also as nationals victimized by a militarized dictatorship supported by U.S. imperialism. The key to solving these afflictions? Nolasco answers: "None else but the struggle for nationalism and democracy. Nationalism would bring an end to the violations of human and sovereign rights of the Filipino people. Democracy paves the way to the full participation of women in the total life of the Filipino nation."[9] On the whole, however, Nolasco's perspective enlarges the standard Marxist formulation of women's role in the national-democratic struggle, as found in the program of the National Democratic Front or in the writings of Amado Guerrero, by preventing the complete subsumption of sexuality into socialization and the conflation of reproductive with productive activities.

Luzviminda Tancangco's paper "The Historical Roots of Women's Oppression: A Perspective," on the other hand, provides a necessary re-orientation by pointing out "one of the earliest and most persistent sources of male supremacy and misogyny," namely, the identification of women/family with nature as opposed to culture, and the subsequent hierarchical demarcation of private female, and public (male) spheres with their corresponding asymmetrical codes. By a historical reading of the development of the bourgeois (nuclear, conjugal) family, Tancangco shifts us a little nearer to unfolding the reified institutions and practices that have not only mystified but truly occluded the realm of women's sexuality and reproductive function. It was left to Aida F. Maranan, a member of KALAYAAN (founded in July 1983), to repudiate the vulgar, mechanical and reductive thesis of class liberation as a prerequisite of/prior to women's liberation, an argument which reduces women's urgent and basic concerns to "mere appendages to the broad economic and political demands" espoused by national-democratic groups. Maranan's resume of the women's struggle in the country from the late nineteenth century to the present patently demonstrates the constant reinscription of women into a male-dominated discourse despite the rhetoric of inequality or democracy. Noting the failure of MAKIBAKA to systematically incorporate within its analysis the feudal-patriarchal system "which has been effectively and efficiently maintained by the mechanisms and values of a capitalist-dominated world," Maranan points out that the sexist ravages of tourism, child prostitution, brides-for-sale, exploitation in the export-processing zones, sex crimes, and the degradation and abuse of women by the militarization of society cannot be grasped simply as class phenomena. Ultimately, she affirms the cardinal feminist imperative: "to develop alternative consciousness and structures for women that shall make us realize our own potentials, individual and collective."[10]

A proof that KALAYAAN's evolving feminism has to some degree transcended the economistic and class-reductionist legacy of the Philippine left is Maranan's observation that sexist practices persist in "actually existing socialism," as in People's China, Cuba and Nicaragua. This could not have been said publicly, without censure or ostracism from the male left, before 1983.

A recent survey of women's thinking on the feminism/nationalism duality, or more precisely interface, published in *Diliman Review*, July-August 1984, confirms my initial insight into the tendency of uneven and combined development characterizing this moment. A salutary appeal for a truly dialectical approach was sounded by an official of the Center for Women's Resources who critiqued the fatal but inveterate "tendency to dichotomize women's problems as secondary and national problems as principal," an error perhaps traceable to a dogmatic reading of the classics such as Mao's "On Contradiction" and "On Practice."

A group like Concerned Women of the Philippines (CWP) composed of upper-class, aristocratic women can be tolerated for outright espousal of backward essentialist views--rectification is in order!--but an experienced activist like Maita Gomez, representing WOMB (Women for the Ouster of Marcos and Boycott), finds herself in a defensive quandary when responding to a question about her material responsibility to her children: "My being politically active is the most adequate expression of the priority I attribute to my children."[12] Meanwhile, Flor Caagusan of KALAYAAN perceives the need to develop and sharpen a Filipina feminist theorizing, a process consonant with an emphasis on the subjective: "conscious, resolute, collective choice to assume a feminist role in the struggle."[13] This stance is expressed also by Remedios I. Rikken, Irene Santiago and Teresita Quintos-Deles of PILIPINA: "We accept the support and encouragement of men. But we believe that women themselves must organize and be the prime movers of their own liberation."[14] Of the 120 women's groups in MetroManila, PILIPINA and SAMAKANA seem to be the most sensitive to issues involving reproduction and sexuality.

On 28 July 1984, the Concerned Artists of the Philippines created a Woman's Desk in their association which resolved to mobilize "women for committed and concrete actions toward gender inequality and national liberation." Together with artists like Julie Dalena, Lualhati Bautista, Fe Mangahas and others, Marra Lanot insists on the primacy of the revolutionary feminist axioms that "the family cannot be divorced from sociopolitical and economic life," that "the qualitative productivity of women" cannot be measured by the mode of production, that "the personal is political," etc.[15]

COMBATTING PATRIARCHY/IMPERIALISM

So there's no doubt about it: a quantum leap has occurred, even though it is just the germinal or incipient stage of a thoroughgoing and profound reversal of the terms of discourse, of the univocal and deductive logic of identity invested by male Reason which underlies the profit-centered status quo. No longer do Filipina activists accept unquestioningly the hegemonic representation of women, a mode and strategy of representation based on biology ("anatomy is destiny") and on assorted cultural determinisms (nature/woman vs. culture/man). No longer is the dominant phallogocentrism--the logocentric discourse of male supremacy--left unchallenged in the Philippines to hierarchize gender and affirm the male as the transcendental subject of order, reason, progress. We are at present witnessing an irreversible displacement and transvaluation not just of concepts, rhetoric, vocabulary, figures in our language--but in effect of the whole frame of mind, the theoretical problematic with which the themes and inflections of the "woman question" are broached to our modern consciousness.

Indeed, what appears to be the unifying principle of the various emerging feminisms in the Philippines may seem to exhibit in its project a more substantive than formalist thrust and intention. On the surface (unlike French feminists, for example, whose psychoanalytic and deconstructive orientation privileges the feminine unconscious, the unrepresentable female drives, over masculine consciousness, and at the same time asserts the subversive priority of female *jouissance*), Filipina feminists seem preoccupied with sexism in practice: at home, in the workplace, in business, etc. Their arguments against gender inequality, articulated in the categories of sex, class and nation (race), may be said to operate within the same parameter ruled by the rationalistic and hierarchical discourse of the enemy. However, when Dolores Feria, for instance, performs a tactical revision of the slogan "Political power grows out of the uterus," we discern the profoundly disruptive impetus of the feminist agenda: the destruction of that symbolic order that has negated the specificity of feminine sexuality: the plurality, otherness and difference of the feminine subject and her right to self-determination. [16]

If indeed today, whether in capitalist or socialist dispensations, woman can only forever be constituted as the unrepresentable Other--the contradiction-filled unconscious, the non-identical body, *jouissance*--this essay renounces any claim to capture, much less represent, the complex dynamic and inexhaustible potential of its putative subject: the Filipina woman's fight for autonomy, for socialist emancipation. This movement and project--the discursive and materialist practice that brings into play the interdicted and forbidden, the unspeakable and multiple--exceeds the notion of the feminine imaginary or "specular economy" posited by Irigaray and the cultural feminism proposed by North American discourse, because it endeavors ultimately to settle accounts with psychoanalysis, racism, *ecriture*, Western supremacy and imperialism in its historic task of overthrowing their necessary material supports and, in the process, transforming itself by creating a new subjectivity that has not yet been thought of or invented anywhere on earth.

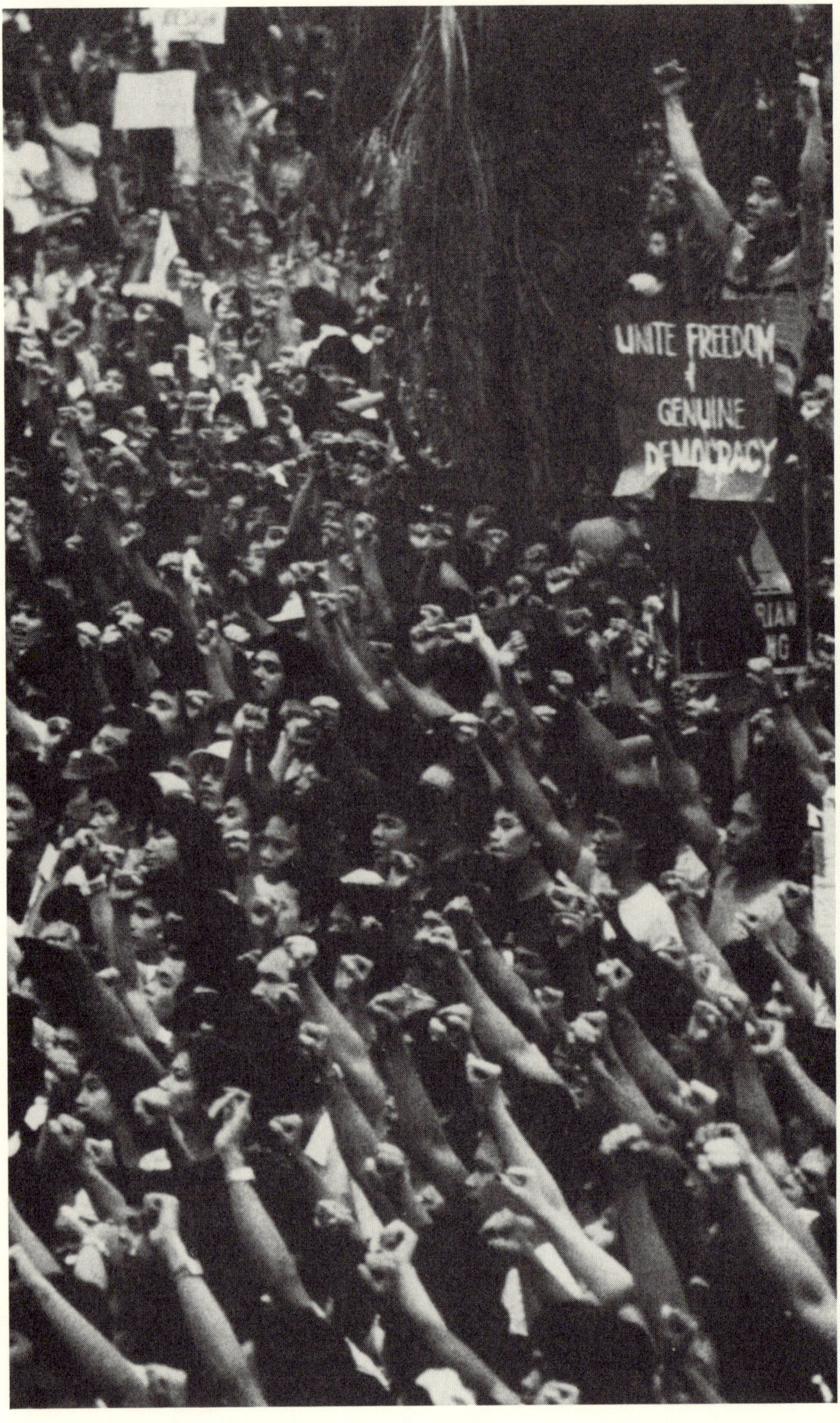
UNITE FREEDOM
GENUINE
DEMOCRACY

IX

Epilogue: Tunnelling Out of
the Belly of the Beast

On the Asiatic coast, washed by the waves of the ocean, lie the smiling Philippines. Six years ago we saw the benevolent Yankees, we saw the Washington Senate at work there. Not fire-spewing mountains--there, American rifles mowed down human lives in heaps; the sugar cartel Senate which today sends golden dollars to Martinique, thousands upon thousands to coax life back from the ruins, sent cannon upon cannon, warship upon warship, golden dollars millions upon millions to Cuba, to sow death and devastation.

Rosa Luxemburg

Every power relationship implies, at least *in potentia*, a strategy of struggle, in which the two forces are not superimposed, do not lose their specific nature, or do not finally become confused. Each constitutes for the other a kind of permanent limit, a point of possible reversal.

Michel Foucault

In what may be a fortuitous and dramatically heuristic turn of events, the central thematic burden of the preceding chapters--the Philippine revolutionary cataclysm as U.S. imperialism's most dangerous post-Vietnam crisis, surpassing in immediate and long-term consequences the local conflagrations in Central America--

177

seems to have been rendered less speculative and more urgently plausible by the flurry of anxious debate and lobbying that surrounded the recent passage of the 1984 Foreign Appropriations Act, specifically with reference to the Philippines.

Frightened by the huge and increasingly militant mass demonstrations against the U.S.-Marcos dictatorship in the weeks and months after Benigno Aquino's murder, U.S. evangelists of IMF/transnational corporate "laissez-faire" ideology are now frantically maneuvering to phase out the corrupt and hated Marcos clique, to split and isolate the nationalist and radical forces, and to manipulate a "peaceful" transfer of power to another pro-U.S. faction of the comprador-bureaucratic-military elite. But it is too late in the day, I believe, for the technocrats and apologists of U.S. hegemonism to reverse the tide of national-popular resistance in the Philippines.

In the writings of his life's last decade (1875-1883), such as the *Ethnological Notebooks*, letters, and prefaces, Marx extended his empirical probing and discovered new revolutionary subjects, e.g. the peasantry, and new forces and possibilities in non-capitalist Europe (Russia, Algeria, etc.), displacing a unilinear evolutionist determinism usually imputed to his previous works with a genuinely dialectical mode of understanding. In his preface to the 1882 Russian edition of the *Communist Manifesto* Marx suggested that the Russian village commune need not succumb to the process of decomposition that overtook similar communities in Europe if the Russian revolution sparks structural changes in the developed West "so that each complements the other," each change in one region catalyzing upheavals and mutations in the other. Marx observes further in another letter: "The intellectual movement now taking place in Russia testifies to the fact that fermentation is going on deep below the surface. Minds are always connected by invisible threads with the body of a people."[1]

Those hidden but profoundly organic connections which Marx so acutely sensed may be instanced in the ramified transactions and interdependency between the rapid changes occurring in the Philippines and the collective sensibility of the dispersed Filipino nationality in the U.S. I would now like to explore this hitherto neglected aspect of the Philippine crisis--if only as a challenge to the chauvinist, ethnocentric and backward U.S. and European Left, whose infantile fixation on the superiority of bourgeois democracy, technology and their "Marxist" brand of academic theorizing cannot but perpetually scandalize resurgent Third World peoples, including those trapped "in the belly of the beasts," and unmitigatedly give immense comfort to the enemy that they can only mimic. Could the presence of over a million Filipino immigrants in the U.S. today, polarized by intensifying class struggles in the islands, generate an oppositional and critical praxis in the multinational U.S. working class? Could this phenomenal "warm body export" be a new historic agent of demystification and liberation, or at least a transmitter of utopian energies and impulses unleashed in the homeland?

EXILE DEGREE ZERO

Although Filipinos have lived and worked in this continent--in California (New Spain) in the sixteenth century; in Louisiana in the eighteenth century--several hundred years before Benigno Aquino ended his exile last August, it was not until his assassination that Filipinos became suddenly visible in the U.S. mass media. But this visibility was less a reflection of the historical conjuncture than a mirage, a fiction invented by the hegemonic essentializing culture: Filipinos as violent people, the Filipino as amuck.

When the revolutionary forces of the first Philippine Republic were defeated in the Filipino-American War of 1898-1902 by U.S. troops, and their oppositional voices silenced for the next five decades, the Filipino disappeared. This antedates the "disappearance" of thousands in the last ten years, "salvaged" by the Marcos regime. What appeared later, displacing the bodies of the insurgent masses, was the image of the uncouth, "uncivilized" and "treacherous" native: the object/recipient of U.S. political, cultural, and economic manipulation (also known as "American tutelage," in the scholars' euphemism).

Unlike the Japanese, Chinese or other Asian immigrants to the U.S., whose first experience of victimization was administered by the immigration authorities, the Filipino is exceptional among Asians precisely because of his origin as the object of colonial subjugation and the product of what Althusser calls the mechanism of "interpellation" in which individuals, addressed by the interacting codes of race, class, and gender, become subjects who can appear or disappear as bearers of specific functions within the framework of an overdetermined social process marked by class violence. As Frantz Fanon and Malcolm X have reminded a whole generation of Third World activists, violence ineluctably characterizes the birth pangs of an emerging new consciousness and the destruction of the old system.

There are now over 1.3 million Filipinos in the U.S. One of them wrote recently to the *Hartford Courant* (12 September 1983) a personal confession which symptomatically registers the spontaneous and subtle mutations occurring in the collective psyche. The killing of Aquino was just a media event for the majority, our immigrant compatriot testifies; but for her the violence "hit home in more ways than one." A crisis of the subject dislocates/decenters the speaker:

I was born a Filipino. That may seem like an easy statement to make, but, even as I write it, I am amazed at the embarrassment I used to feel. Ever since my parents brought me to the United States, I had been ashamed of who I am, and ashamed of my nation. . . .

I was ashamed [as my brother was] of being different. When friends at school said it was disgusting to see my mother serve fish with the head still intact, or for my father to eat rice with his hands, or to learn that stewed dogs and goats were some examples of Filipino delicacies, I took their side. I accused my own of being unsanitary in their eating habits. . . . When Marcos flaunted his tyranny and declared martial law in 1972, and my aunt said that it was the best thing that ever happened to the Philippines, as long as you kept your mouth shut, I accused Filipinos of lacking the guts to fight for themselves. . . . But everything changed for me when that man [Aquino] I had laughed at landed in my homeland and died on the airport tarmac.

For the first time, I accused myself of not having enough faith in, and hope for, my own people.

In the past, I felt that I had no right to be proud of my people. Now, with the cruel Marcos regime tottering, I have finally awakened. Filipinos all over the world need the strength that comes with pride, now more than ever. . . .

A familiar combination of suicidal naivete, anger, traumatizing shame, and resentment pervade the mentality, the psychic economy, of every colonized subject atomized in the world of commodity-exchange, a milieu where human relations are reified, labor-power and the products of labor alienated, and hierarchy absolutized. Our letter-writer of course, had not heard of Carlos Bulosan's epic chronicle of rebellious Filipino workers, *America Is In the Heart* (1943). She had not heard of the April 1924 strike of 31,000 Filipinos in Hawaii, which lasted seven months, cost them sixteen lives and numerous casualties. Nor of the great Salinas strike of August 1934 where 3,000 Filipinos resisted white vigilantes hired by the farm owners to terrorize them. Nor of the militant Delano grape strike of September 1965 initiated and spearheaded by Filipinos--the convulsive birth pang of the United Farm Workers Union.

Without a historical imagination, without the collective organized projects of the working people to counter-interpellate and introduce the power of the negative and its differential transvaluations, the individual is condemned to recapitulate what every Filipino undergoes: the painful vicissitudes of colonial servility and bourgeois demoralization. That imagination was born only during the thirties with the union-organizing drives of the Congress of Industrial Organizations (CIO), amid the flagrant racist violence of the Depression when Filipinos were ostracized, gunned down, and lynched throughout the West Coast.

Space constraint does not allow a thorough documentation of this conjuncture. Instead I offer here two statements that capture in microcosm the process of demystification catalyzed by the sharp class/radical contradictions of that period, the first by Manuel Buaken (*New Republic,* 23 September 1940), and the other by Carlos Bulosan (from a letter of April 1941):

> Where is the heart of America? I am one of the many thousands of young men born under the American flag, raised as loyal, idealistic Americans under your promises of equality for all, and enticed by glorious tales of educational opportunities. Once here we are met by exploiters, shunted into slums, greeted by gamblers, and prostitutes, taught only the worst in your civilization. America came to us with bright-winged promises of liberty, equality, and fraternity--what has become of them?
>
> . . . I came to know afterward that in many ways it was a crime to be a Filipino in California. I came to know that public streets were not free to my people. We were stopped each time those vigilant patrolmen saw us driving with a car. We were suspect each time we were with a white woman. . . . It was now the year of the great hatred; the lives of Filipinos were cheaper than those of dogs.[2]

Considered neither citizens nor aliens, Filipino "nationals" in the thirties (about 150,000, mostly single males) suffered class, gender and racial oppression imposed directly by the coercive agencies of agribusiness, or mediated by the categorizing techniques of the State apparatuses: legislature, courts, police, etc. It was the collective resistance to such oppression, an oppositional strategy of "positional" war (as theorized by Gramsci), that Bulosan described in his writings, specifically *America Is In the Heart.*

Bulosan's obsessive theme is the Filipino's project of attempting to deconstruct his anonymity and deracination as a colonized race and uprooted class. To help perform a cognitive mapping of the future as the space of desire and emancipated labor, Bulosan's texts mobilize dreams and memory to reconstitute the inchoate or aborted 1896 Philippine revolution as orienting coordinates for resistance. He memorializes the figure of the courageous, persevering mother associated with planting/harvest rituals; he celebrates the beauty and fertility of the homeland which, amid his panicked flight from racist lynchers, becomes symbolic of a permanent inner harmony, an emblem of a smoldering hope. When his partiarchal family disintegrates and the promise of independence, family and heirs vanishes, the Filipino worker discovers multiple links with his compatriots and recuperates the submerged impulse of national solidarity in gambling houses, labor barracks, union halls, brothels--the marginal sites which circumscribe his illusion of vertical mobility, the Hollywood "dream of success." He finds also allies and collaborators among the white workers and middle-class women in particular, harnessed to picket frontlines and strikes.

In Bulosan's story "Be American," for example, the wanderings of a migrant worker chart his identity on the predictable rhythm of seasonal harvests, an uprootedness which in turn undermines the concept and fact of private ownership of land and private possession of the collective fruits of labor.[3] The protagonist fails in his ambition of obtaining a formal education and thus citizenship; he ends up publishing a newspaper "defending the workers and upholding the rights and liberties of all Americans, native or foreign born." He "had to go to jail a few times for his ideas about freedom and peace." Concluding his friend's unfinished odyssey, the narrator utters an elegiac hymn to the land, "a great mother . . . rolling like a beautiful woman with an overflowing abundance of fecundity and murmurous with her eternal mystery." Bulosan's strategy of metonymic displacements anticipates Gilles Deleuze's provocative insight that "A society or any collective arrangement is defined first by its points or flows of deter-ritorialization."

MASKS OF THE OTHER

While Bulosan's texts interpellate the Filipino as exploited worker, colonized rebel, and desexed subversive able to pursue his existential quest only through collective struggle in which theoretical or reflective moments crystallize, the fiction of another Filipino exile, Bienvenido Santos, renders with more self-conscious irony and defeatism the peculiar predicament of the second (1941-1959) and third (1960-1972) waves of Filipino immigrants, mostly dependents of the "old timers" and veterans; and later, of professionals. Their predicament is worse than the ordeals of isolation and brutality suffered by Bulosan's comrades, for it focuses on a more fatal loss of the historical imagination aggravated by a much more insidious metaphysical displacement of the material contradictions in society during World War II and the subsequent McCarthy/Cold War era.

Santos' texts embody the pathos of an obsolescent liberal humanism still endemic among Third World intellectuals. In a famous story "Scent of Apples" (1949), the narrator, a petty bourgeois intellectual, visits a poor Filipino farmer in Kalamazoo and notices his "fat blonde" wife who "was willing to work like a slave. . . . "[4] The text neutralizes their poverty by an appeal to a putative Chekhovian aura of dignified simplicity and mute resignation; but overall, there is no hope, no vision of an evolving totality in which the meaning of their individual lives is inscribed. In a later story "The Day the Dancers Came" (1960, revised 1967), the limitation of humanistic ideology exposes itself in the protagonist's helpless dependence on profit-oriented technology, instanced here by his attempt to record the music and talk of visiting Filipino dancers. The chief character, "an old timer," strives to affirm his continuity with his homeland and youth by freezing the commodified sounds of touristic spectacle on tape, forcing himself to cut off communication with his dying friend. He then moralizes the betrayal of his faith by the breakdown of capitalist technology thus: "I guess we can't complain. We had it good here all the time. Most of the time, ahyway. . . ."[5]

With the resurgence of the revolutionary mass movement in the Philippines in the late sixties and early seventies, a new generation of Filipinos born here (children of migrant workers, veterans, professionals) re-discovered Bulosan by a circuitous route, through a detour mapped by the examples of Fanon, Mao Zedong, George Jackson, and others.

What radicalized this generation of Filipino-Americans was not so much the myth of "identity crisis" privileged by sociology textbooks, as the deepening civil rights struggles begun in the fifties, Che Guevara and the Cuban revolution, the heroic resistance of the Indochinese peoples against U.S. aggression, and above all by the fiery street battles in Manila between the U.S.-backed fascist state and the progressive students, workers and peasants. Appearances were problematized. Here is the oppressor nation, more precisely the monopoly elite and their political representatives, to which they have, from grade school on, pledged allegiance, committing bloody crimes and genocide against relatives, people of the same color and blood as their fathers and mothers--it may even be against brothers and sisters still in the Philippines, fighting in prison or in the underground resistance. The Pinoys here, simmering and seething at the bottom of the mythical "melting pot," have renounced their status as "little brown Americans" propagated by Carlos P. Romulo and any number of Filipino clubs and associations. Consider the poignant testimony of demystification in Serafin Malay Syquia's writings. In his poem "Pinoys in America," he speaks of "the silent minority" of "assimilating Filipinos" lost in the restricted quota for Orientals; "and our parents came/to share the American dream/yes they made good workers. . . ." He traces how Pinoys, interpellated by the hegemonic culture to hate "the pagan Indians," succumbs to the temptation of the great "American Dream" only to recognize later that the "dream/was their dream/and not ours." Syquia reflects on his vocation from a dialectical perspective:

The commonalty that bridges white and third world poets in politics. . . . To face the reality of politics as *the* factor that governs our lives is a necessary step in the development of a consciousness that transcends an elitist concept of poetry.[6]

END OF THE ALIEN'S ADVENTURE

With the accelerating passage of Filipinos (over 20,000 a year) from a neo-colonial outpost beleaguered by a raging people's war into the continent, we shall witness a sharpening of the critical interrogation of the "free enterprise" notions of "assimilation," "integration," "ethnic pluralism," and their variants. Precipitated by the global crisis of monopoly capital, this questioning of the rhetoric of equality and the freedom to buy-and-sell is also a process of disarticulating the conventional paradigms of ethnicity and marginality. What the agenda calls for is a new politics of spatial discontinuities registering those "movements of deterritorialization and the processes of reterritorialization" that constitute the social/political text we are challenged to read.

Together with the autonomous efforts of Afro-Americans, Chicanos, Native Americans and other Asians, the history of the Filipino struggle for self-determination marks what Foucault conceptualizes (in the epigraph) as a "permanent limit, a point of possible reversal" of a racist and imperialist hegemony now revealed to be profoundly historical, not a truth of nature--desperately and futilely lashing out with Marines, slogans of peace and freedom, and Pershing missiles.

Our endeavor to distill a coherent historical sensibility from the immediate lived experience of Filipinos in the U.S. and to invent a narrative of the artistic and cultural projects meant to organize in intelligible forms those impulses, feelings, practices, evanescent hopes and dreams never fulfilled in the colony and forever repressed in the metropolis, now compels us to return to our original point of departure.

For it is ultimately in the Philippines, the concrete physical and spiritual site of warring interpellations and contradictory inscriptions, that the "weak link" (Lenin) may still be found. As Gramsci noted in another context, "the line of development is to-wards internationalism, but the point of departure is national. . . ." That vulnerable spot, that chance opening through which the specter of technological and consumerist plenitude forever escapes, refers not just to the rural zones liberated by the New People's Army and the Bangsa Moro Army, but also to the space of the imagination--whose bodily vessels are often circumscribed by military prison walls--where the collective body of desire germinates and blossoms.

In this space we find the agenda of socialist construction in the Philippines crystallizing: the creation and articulation of a national-popular canon of discourses/practices replacing the imperialist-feudal hegemonic culture and opening up new liberating subject-positions by a rigorous, sustained deconstruction of all exploitative institutions, habits, values, paradigms, etc. In this arena of contestation, we find one of the leading Filipino revolutionary intellectuals and political prisoners, Jose Maria Sison, fully engaged in a risky process of aesthetic production, unfolding in a convulsive process the dynamics of the political unconscious of the whole nation whose ludic somersaults and flights cannot but prefigure the complicit, prophetic destiny of both slave and slave-master, colonizer and colonized, capital and labor.

THE PARTISAN IMAGINATION:
WHAT IS IMPOSSIBLE IS REAL

What distinguishes the worst architect from the best of bees is this, that the architect raises his structure in imagination before he erects it in reality. At the end of every labor process, we get a result that already existed in the imagination of the laborer at its commencement.

—Karl Marx, *Capital*

When I visited London in the summer of 1981 on my way back from Yugoslavia, where I chaired a postgraduate seminar in Third World poetics, I had the fortuitous occasion to talk to the Asian editor of *Index*, a European journal devoted to exposing and indicting press censorship and assisting persecuted writers anywhere in the world. I then conceived myself the bearer of messages from home. Despite my impassioned effort to convince the editor to publicize the brutal, inhuman punishment being inflicted on Sison by the Marcos regime, the simple and naive retort was: "Sison is in prison not as a writer but as a revolutionary partisan, an organizer of armed struggle."

From the Westernized perception of an Asian exile, Sison's writings are incidental, even accidental, to his revolutionary calling. Whereas *Index*, given its aristocratic bias, privileges the full-time artisan of the Word whose craft happens, by circumstance or sheer bad luck, to have incurred the ire of the authorities. Thus, Sison the radical exponent of the national democratic cause would not qualify. I dared a riposte: "But surely Byron, Malraux, Ho Chi Minh, Neruda. . . ." But in that milieu of a fragmented and commodified metropolis, the fortress of a moribund empire where the centuries-old ideology of reification and orientalizing essentialism still reign supreme, my plea for upholding the old bourgeois illusion of the total integrated person--of Sison as an artist *and* revolutionary--evaporated in the pollution and cacophony of London traffic.

It is now the close of 1985, marking thirteen years of martial law and also thirteen years of popular resistance. This all-embracing dialectical unity of opposites informing our national development finds its poignant emblem in Sison's latest poem "The Forest Is Still Enchanted."[7] While the disintegrating feudal cosmos of superstition and natural abundance (an ironic figure given the rabid transnational plunder of our resources) inevitably yields to the World Bank-funded infrastructures and to the electronic counter-insurgency apparatus, still the element of awe and the new, now displaced as a trope of the people's will to resist alienating and exploitative forces, persists:

But the forest is still enchanted.
There is a new hymn in the wind;
There is a new magic in the dark green,
So the peasant folks say to friends.
A single fighting spirit has taken over
To lure in and astonish the intruders.

The understated allusion, of course, is to the peasantry's allegiance to the New People's Army and the prairie-fire resurgence of people's war. But what is striking here is the coalescence of myth and history--already prefigured in "The Guerrilla Is Like a Poet," "From a Burning Bush," etc.--which, I submit, defines the fundamentally prophetic thrust and vocation of Sison's linguistic practice, a praxis whose visionary mission is to simultaneously demystify the alienated world and project images of apocalyptic rebirth.

From the viewpoint of traditional hermeneutics, this prophetic impulse which transforms linear time to kaleidoscopic space, memory into action, and in the process enacts a creative dialogue between spirit and matter, can be explained by Sison's confinement and the claustrophic syndrome coinciding with it, as evinced, for instance, in Gramsci's motto: "pessimism of the mind, optimism of the will." Pursuing this trend, one can plausibly analogize the theme of such poems as "In the Dark Depths," "I Have Walked Mazes of Pain," "A Furnace," and others, with Sison's litany of suffering and anguished privations distilled, for example, in his May 1982 Statement (*Political Detainees Update*): "Our prolonged solitary confinement has cumulatively increased the intensity of our imprisonment so much so that we have in effect suffered by so many times the bare number of five and six years that we have already spent in prison". . . . and so on.

It might be more appropriate, however, to reflect on the idea that subsuming the personal or biographical context, the raw materials worked on by a rigorously dialectical mode of literary production, is precisely that *sine qua non,* the constellation of first principles, which at once incorporates critical realism, supersedes it, and elevates it to the level of prophetic allegory: proletarian ideology, dialectical materialism.

For this occasion, I will not elaborate on those first principles and will limit myself to emphasizing the crucial determining function of a Marxist theoretical perspective in elucidating Sison's poetics. Contrary to the mistaken academic notion, this perspective is not a specialized "workerist" bias, or reductive economistic presumption. It is fundamentally a totalizing historical outlook without which (as Lukacs points out in *History and Class Consciousness*) one falls into the dualistic chasms of abstract formalist idealism and of mechanical materialism. Sison himself, in his recent *Message to the U.P. Writers Club* (its intertextuality with his previous messages to PAKSA, LEADS, and also to the relevant chapters of *Struggle for National Democracy* needs to be explored) reformulates that proposition and urges progressive writers to leap beyond neo-colonial liberalism and position themselves in the pregnant and fertile space occupied by the working class. Why? Because, to quote Sison, "It is not only the productive vanguard for industrialization and modernization but it is also the basis for the most progressive world outlook and methodology for comprehending all social forces and their development in the current national democratic revolution as well as in the subsequent socialist revolution."

Also synthesized by implication in Sison's message is the basic materialist principle of analyzing overdetermined contradictions: literary production as an instance of ideological practice cannot be divorced from the socio-economic formation, the entire oscillating totality within which it interacts with other regions as a relatively autonomous force. Hence, like Lenin's strategic reminder in his critiques of Tolstoy, Sison also posits literary specificity (distinguished from the political or programmatic) as a tension between spontaneity and discipline, the private realm of feelings vis-a-vis the socializing effect of linguistic practice and the task of art to systematically humanize reality.

Such a distinction, however, reinforced by the arguments of Althusser and Gramsci, should not obscure the truth that all art springs from and is nourished by human needs and passions that transpire in history. And its fabled transcendence of empirical contingency, the so-called universality of art, exists only because we, humans, resurrect, reincarnate and renew those once fluid energies now petrified in museum fetishes and gallery commodities; those living energies which, once unleashed in the "festival of the oppressed," begin to crystallize our hope and desire to change life (as Rimbaud and Rilke vowed to do) and thereby transform the world. Conceived then as the living science of praxis, i.e., the consciousness and sensuous activity of the human species, poetry cannot but be politically/historically engaged.

To further underscore the primacy of the materialist framework, I quote Sison's concluding words in the *Who Magazine* interview (12 December 1981): "In sum I would say that my books are linked to the great tradition of the Philippine revolution and the mass movements of workers, peasants, urban petty bourgeoisie and other patriotic forces." Whether in 1896 (Rizal and the propagandists), in the 1950s (Baking, Hernandez, Lansang), or today, the Filipino intellectual finds himself always already embedded, knowingly or unknowingly, in the compromising, recalcitrant "thickness" of class struggle; and to such a situation he can only respond in two mutually incompatible ways: by full commitment to the side of the progressive forces, or by temporizing ruses—the mirror-image of blatant collaboration with the fascist agents of U.S. imperialism.

Isn't our history replete with the lessons of Biak-na-Bato, with the ordeals of making a choice at those peaks of crises: the Filipino-American War, the Sakdalista uprising, the Huk rebellion, and now?

Given our historical predicament, the Filipino writer then finds himself "compromised" in both the pejorative and honorific senses, only because his practice of language, his processing of signs, occurs within a concrete, specific site of conflict which necessarily stakes his body and the bodies of his affections--a site within which is inscribed as in a constantly deciphered palimpsest the incandescent dynamics of hope evolving into will, of personal desire unfolding in the matrix of a collective dream.

There is in Sison's corpus of poems no more eloquently moving and intransigently perspicuous testament to this materialist aesthetics I have sketched above than "The Bladed Poem." Here we perceive the two phases of the social process: workers objectively defined as functions within a commodity-oriented system, and workers emerging as the collective subject organized and cohering around a project of self-knowledge and self-activity achieved only in revolution. We have then the workers depicted as the artificers of the social totality in motion in which labor metamorphoses into play, the play of struggle, in which they experience the pleasurable release and fulfillment of needs, phantasies, desires. Art is then grasped as both a pedagogical instrument (a learning tool, Brecht would say) or a weapon for collective organizing, and the play of Eros in our psyches.

So far we have moved from the romanticized equation of the earlier "The Guerrilla Is Like a Poet" to the imaginative fusion of theory and practice, consciousness and action, in the prison poems where the symbols and archetypes of freedom are glimpsed, presaging its eventual conquest in real life. Sison's poems are thus incomplete, denied organic closure, because the materialist textualization of struggle escapes from the prison-house of language in order to eventually and definitively emancipate itself in the discourse of physical combat.

SCHIZOID PLEASURE: ONE DIVIDES INTO THREE, SEVEN, THIRTEEN. . . .

In an essay written for an UGNAYAN pamphlet (1979) designed to publicize Sison's case to an international audience, I tried to articulate the nature of the prophetic or utopian motivation in Sison's poetics, in these terms: "Life is not a natural phenomenon governed by implacable laws; it is, for Sison and other Third World militants, a project shaped by, and shaping, history. The solidarity of human wills, the fusion of participating subjects in organized action, intervenes in the world to create the groundwork for the future: a new society and culture that is genuinely popular, democratic, libertarian." I use the word "utopian" in the sense of Ernst Bloch's "hope principle": an apocalyptic gesture of precipitating the resolution of crisis (here, Sison's unspeakable brutalization) by evoking a hidden significance prefigured in it, an evocation both retrospective and anticipatory in effect, and in so doing memorializing an eroticized, Orphic harmony of nature and man (note the recurrent image of rain, wind, tropes of the spirit) and summoning in vision the lineaments of a long expected reunion many times postponed, many times presaged, a communal celebration suggested in microcosm by Sison's communication to his children: "Across Blue Waters" and "To Jasm, My Captive Child." This prophetic impulse both preserves the anguish of a repressive order (class domination, fascist instrumentalization of life) and supersedes it, in much the same way as the Promethean refusal of taboos and prohibitions--its text of negations and annulments--contains within it an affirmation of a liberated realm of incessantly gratified desires. This impulse we encounter every day as an inherent quality of the labor process itself whose end, for humans, is already anticipated in thought, consciousness, above all in the imagination.

Intrinsically dialectical in operation and materialist in grounding, this prophetic/utopian tendency in Sison's poems--a trait one discovers as an obsessive rhythm in *Florante at Laura,* Rizal's novels, Bulosan's and Amado Hernandez's writings--explains the choice of allegory as a formal device to transmute the individualized flux of experience into the differential system of rhetorical figuration. This allegorical drive manifests itself most vividly in "Against the Monster on the Land," "The Woman and the Strange Eagle," and "Defy the Reptile" which, rehearsing a historical moment of demystification, converts the narrative sequence into the illusion-breaking stasis of parable.

What happens in allegory is this: instead of inducing an easy reconciliation of antinomies, an existential leap into faith where all class antagonisms vanish and rebellious desire is pacified, allegory heightens the tension between signifier and signified, between object and subject, thereby foiling empathy and establishing the temporary distance required for generating critical judgment and ultimately cathartic action. Nowhere is this allegorical method of structuring more intensely sustained than in "Fragments of a Nightmare," Sison's "inferno" stage to a quite undivine comedy.

It is possible that a reading of "Fragments," I hazard to suggest, will not add to one's conceptual understanding of Sison's suffering and the political-ideological issues at stake. Such an effort can more heuristically be advanced by grasping the evidence and import of all his published essays and testimonies. What this mode of oblique staging unfolds is precisely the primordial incongruity between what exists and what can be, the disparity between fact and possibility, the unassimilable dissonance between the reality-principle and the pleasure-principle which may be how Sison aims to register the fact of repression, the dominance of commodity-fetishism, in our neo-colonized society with its host of sharpening internal contradictions.

Allegory, then, as a process of misaligning opposites, focuses on the crux of the contradictions and discharges a call, a polemical challenge. It images the transitional movement of difference from passive contemplation to active involvement, converting objects into process: the process of social production rupturing social relations. Note the desynchronizing of perceived and perceiver: "As I struggle and scream for air,/American rock music screens my screams/Outside the torture chamber" (#16).

CARNIVAL OF THE ARMED SPIRIT

I imagine Sison's aesthetic project as an invitation for us to accompany him in his abortive Virgilian pilgrimage. For in this ironic, inverted realm of the anti-romance, the legendary paradise longed for, the classless society which is the object of humanity's compulsive quest, is displaced by a double estrangement: imprisonment as fact and as metaphor. In those epiphanic moments of the past's desublimating self-reflection, the duplicity of imprisonment reveals itself as a temporary unity of opposites, a momentary paralysis but also a phase of gradual but inexorable becoming. By employing the imperative and subjunctive mood, a dialogic and carnivalesque technique (Bakhtin), Sison seeks to preempt any idea of organic plenitude or mimetic equivalence between language and reality which would thereby make art a self-sufficient, autotelic object, the hypostasis of psychic drives in some Lacanian prison of the imaginary.

What Sison's poems consistently undermine is the aura of a language of self-presence (whose libidinal investment one finds in the exuberance of Villa or Joaquin), a language of ritualized sublimation which is incessantly decentered by the heterogeneity of imagery and tone in "Fragments." The logic of this somewhat convulsed style and the theoretical rationale for revolutionary art in general (Sison's included) are succinctly expressed by Walter Benjamin and Christopher Caudwell:[8]

> The utilization of dream-elements in waking is the textbook example of dialectical thought. Hence dialectical thought is the organ of historical awakening. Every epoch not only dreams the next, but while dreaming impels it towards wakefulness. It bears its end within itself, and reveals it--as Hegel already recognized--by a ruse. With the upheaval of the market economy, we begin to recognize the monuments of the bourgeoisie as ruins even before they have crumbled.
> --Benjamin, "Paris, Capital of the 19th Century"

> Of the future one can only dream--with greater or less success. . . . Even dream is determined, and a movement in

dream reflects perhaps a real movement into daylight of material phenomena at present unrecognized. That is why it is possible to dream with accuracy of the future--in other words, to predict scientifically. This is the prophetic and world-creating power of dream. It drives its world-creating power, not by virtue of being dream, . . . but because it reflects in the sphere of thought a movement which, with the help of dream, can be fully realized in practice. It draws its creative power, like the poetry of the harvest festival, from its value as a guide and spur to action. It is dream already passed out of the sphere of dream into that of social revolution. It is the dream, not of an individual, but of a man reflecting in his individual consciousness the creative role of a whole class, whose movement is given in the material conditions of society.

--Caudwell, Illusion and Reality

Long before I encountered the *Index* editor in London in 1981, one of my periodic interventions in the cultural front in the Philippines took the form of a booklet, *The Radical Tradition in Philippine Literature* (1971), where I pointed out in one chapter how Sison's 1961 collection *Brothers* succeeded "in projecting the democratic tendencies of the Filipino bourgeoisie" in the period of Recto's nationalist crusade. Subsequently, a qualitative leap occurred in the mid-1960s. In hindsight I should now qualify that it is rather the progressive national-democratic ideology of our intelligentsia aligned with class-conscious workers and peasants that ultimately constitute the enabling condition of possibility for *Brothers*. Contrary to idealist aprioritizing, such a condition--a description of which, for the Marxist critic, replaces any mere formalist explication of texts--is the intensifying class confrontations in city and countryside to which we are all witnesses, in which the whole society (as the political prisoners testify in *Pintig* and *Pumipiglas*) is unveiled as a huge, tumultuous but crumbling prison replicating the State apparatus and thus allowing the victims to recover in the same breath their oneness and integrity with those outside who are poised to blast their chains and bars in one last decisive, apocalyptic act of liberation.

THE TIME IS FULFILLED

What is the prospect before us then?

As millions of Filipinos relentlessly storm the ramparts of transnational Capital in the closing years of the twentieth century, the emerging shape of a collective and global enterprise--the transitional mutation from dependency to relative autonomy, the forging of a distinctly Filipino path to socialism--may be perceived in the seemingly haphazard ruptures of language, codes, styles; the unpredictable discontinuities of thought and action that I have cited, interpreted and analyzed in this book.

One may demur that my investigations have centered largely on aesthetic theory and literary practice, relegating the economic base or infrastructure to the background. Rejecting the now generally condemned misleading metaphor of base-superstructure, I would contend that the most crucial questions of the social-political transformation of the Philippines, the burning issues coeval with the destruction of one mode of production and the building of its antithesis, do not present themselves positivistically as purely economic or political questions. Rather they are lived and felt as questions and issues of everyday life. They surface most vividly as ethical/moral questions, and acquire sensuous immediacy as cultural forms or practices. In short, the theme of change and metamorphosis inheres in a complex phenomenon which we can designate here as cultural revolution. It is this complex conjuncture of heterogeneous trends and tendencies, the alignment of diverse forces and agents, that I have attempted here to describe and conceptualize through specific texts, discourses, exempla, allusions and references.

On the eve of the French revolution, Schiller meditated in *Letters on the Aesthetic Education of Humankind* that the resolution of political questions can be achieved by grappling with the aesthetic predicament, that "it is through beauty that we arrive at freedom." No wonder that from Rizal and our Propagandist activists of 1896 to Marxist intellectuals like Hernandez and Sison, Filipino revolutionaries have articulated their permanent project as the profoundly radical criticism of Philippine culture--the deconstruction of traditional norms and values, the disruption of reified schemes. My readings of selected key texts of the historical process known as the Philippine formation should thus be conceived as an integral part of a collective project--not just a formulaic deciphering but a new reinscription, an innovative recoding of signifiers--where literary or artistic expression functions as the emblem or figure for that otherwise ineffable and ungraspable experience of historical change that can only be thought or comprehended as intelligible after its fateful occurrence.

And so we return to our inaugural symbol, the Owl of Minerva, whose differentiating and totalizing vision penetrates through the shroud of smoke and turbulence of the battlefield, apprehending the dying convulsions of the old order mixed with the shrill birthpangs of the new, targetted on those protagonists committed to blasting open the continuum of history. Commenting on Hegel's pregnant aphorism, "Seek for food and clothing first, then the Kingdom of God shall be added unto you" (1807), Walter Benjamin writes in his "Theses on the Philosophy of History":

> The class struggle, which is always present to a historian influenced by Marx, is a fight for the crude and material things without which no refined and spiritual things could exist. Nevertheless, it is not in the form of the spoils which fall to

the victor that the latter make their presence felt in the class struggle. They manifest themselves in this struggle as courage, humor, cunning, and fortitude. They have retroactive force and will constantly call in question every victory, past and present, of the rulers. As flowers turn toward the sun, by dint of a secret heliotropism the past strives to turn toward that sun which is rising in the sky of history. A historical materialist must be aware of this most inconspicuous of all transformations.[9]

To seize and elucidate such "inconspicuous transformations," immanent or incarnate in culture defined in its broadest sense as the ensemble of collective practices and discourses operative in a specific conjuncture of Philippine history, has been the primary aim of this work. An alternative formulation of its obsessive and urgent thrust may be grasped in Mao's permanently timely advice: "Never forget class struggle."

Notes

Introduction

[1] Boston Globe (3 October 1984). For recent assessments of the situation, see: Solidaridad II (October 1984); NDF Update (October 1984); "Interview with Agapito Aquino," Ka Huliau (Oct.-Nov., 1984), p. 11; Katarungan (July-August 1984); Peacemaker (September 1984); P. B. Daroy, "The National Assembly and the Parliament of the Streets," The New Philippine Review, I (August-October 1984), pp. 15-17, 42; Philippine Report (October 1984).

[2] Philadelphia Inquirer (28 September 1984); Hartford Courant (22 August, 8 October 1984).

[3] See the fortnightly publication of the Task Force Detainees, Political Detainees Update. Bush is quoted in The Lawyers Committee for International Human Rights, The Philippines: A Country in Crisis (New York, 1983), p. 4; P. N. Abinales, Militarization: Philippines (Manila: Nationalist Resource Center, 1982). In June 1984, one thousand "secret marshals" or "death squads" were unleashed in Manila and killed "at least twenty-five suspected criminals" in the first week; see Church Coalition for Human Rights in the Philippines, Philippines Update (July 1984), pp. 1, 8.

[4] The International Commission of Jurists, The Philippines: Human Rights After Martial Law (Geneva, 1984); Richard Falk, "Views from Manila and Washington," World Policy Journal (Winter 1984), pp. 419-432; "The Philippines After Aquino, After Marcos," Southeast Asia Chronicle (December 1983); Nur Misuari, Political Turmoil in Manila and the Need for Caution (Tehran, 1983); Francisco Nemenzo, "The Current Philippine Crisis and the Immediate Post-Marcos Future," paper delivered at the Research School of Pacific Studies, Australian National University (20 October 1983); Belinda Aquino, "The Philippines Under Marcos: Political Decay," paper presented at the American Political Association (Washington, D.C., August-September 1984).

5 Thomas' book is published by Monthly Review Press (New York, 1984). Cf. Alexander Magno, Developmentalism and the 'New Society': The Repressive Ideology of Underdevelopment (University of the Philippines, Third World Studies Center, 1983).

6 The Lynch school has been challenged by various critics, among them Virgilio Enriquez, Filipino Psychology in the Third World (Quezon City, 1977); and "Decolonizing the Filipino Psyche: Philippine Psychology in the Seventies," Philippine Social Sciences and Humanities Review (January-December 1981), pp. 191-216. Of great relevance are the studies in Anthropology and the Colonial Encounter, ed. Talal Asad (London, 1975), pp. 21-118.

7 Philippine News (7-13 March 1984), p. 13. A thoroughgoing expose of U.S. academic personnel working for the CIA has just been published: Erik Guyot, "CIA Cultivates Academia on Philippines," Resist Newsletter # 173 (February 1985), pp. 6-7. Focusing on the activities of Professor David Rosenberg of Middlebury College, Vermont, the account documents the complicitous roles of Professor David Joel Steinberg (vice-president of Brandeis University and history professor) and Professor Justin Green of Villanova University. In defense of such CIA involvement, Professor Carl Lande of the University of Kansas has begun a campaign in the academy to exonerate his colleagues. Several years earlier, the work of Professor Frank Lynch, S.J., of the Institute of Philippine Culture, Ateneo University, has been linked to counter-insurgency activities; see Walden Bello, "Cultural and Social Distortions in the Philippines," Philippine Times (1-15 July 1975), pp. 21-23; and reply by Mary Racelis Hollnsteiner, Philippine Times (1-15 Nov. 1975), pp. 4, 6. It is no secret that U.S.-trained local experts connected with the Institute of Mass Communications and Department of Psychology, University of the Philippines; and with the Department of Psychology, Ateneo University, have collaborated with the Armed Forces of the Philippines to put out the propaganda booklet Towards the Restructuring of Filipino Values, Office of Civil Relations, Philippine Army, Manila, 1972.

8 Philippine News (7-13 March 1984), p. 13. Also Philippine News (3-9 October 1984), p. 5.

9 New York Times (8 August 1984), p. A23.

10 The Paranoid Style in American Politics (New York, 1965), passim. See Eqbal Ahmad, Political Culture and Foreign Policy: Notes on American Interventions in the Third World (Washington, D.C.; Institute for Policy Studies, 1982).

11 "US Policy and Presence in East Asia: An Insider's View,"

address to a conference sponsored by the Coalition for a New Foreign and Military Policy (Washington D.C., 1 May 1980); see also Jose Diokno, "On the Struggle for Democracy," World Policy Journal (Winter 1984), pp. 433-445.

[12] CIP Report (October 1979), p. 1. Other souces of statistics are: Jim Morrell, "Aid to the Philipiines: Who Benefits," Center for International Policy Report, V (October 1979); Filippinengroep, Makibaka Join Us in Struggle (London, 1980); Permanent People's Tribunal, Philippines Repression and Resistance (London, 1981); KSP/Filipino People's Committee, In the Face of Adversity (Utrecht, 1982); and Health--the Fruits of Struggle (1983).

[13] International Finance Statistics (May 1979); Philippine Labor Monitor (June 1984), p. 4.

[14] On land reform, see Benedict Kerkvliet, "Land Reform: Emancipation or Counterinsurgency?" in Marcos and Martial Law in the Philippines (Ithaca, 1979), pp. 113-44; Vicki Ross, Land and Hunger Philippines (Bread for the World Background Paper #55, July 1981); Filipino People's Committee for the Permanent People's Tribunal, The Filipino People Versus the US-Marcos Dictatorship (Background Dossier, October 1980); Fred Poole and Max Vanzi, Revolution in the Philippines (New York, 1984), esp. pp. 245-68.

[15] Quoted in Ferdinand Marcos, The Democratic Revolution in the Philippines (1971), pp. 263-64. On Huntington, see Colin Leys, "Samuel Huntington and the End of Classical Modernization Theory," in Introduction to the Sociology of "Developing Societies," ed. H. Alavi and Teodor Shanin (New York, 1982), pp. 332-49.

[16] Buss, p. 82. On the colonizer's paradigm, see Roger Bresnahan, "Our Little Proteges: Models of American Colonial Rule," Philippine Social Sciences and Humanities Review, 43 (January-December 1979), pp. 162-171.

[17] "Gearing for Direct Intervention," Katarungan (July-August 1984), pp. 12-13; Roland Simbulan, "Counter-Insurgency and the US Bases," Katarungan (August-October 1983), pp. 12-13, 17-19; E. San Juan, Jr., "Philippines: The Bases for US Intervention," Changes (October 1983), pp. 4, 23; on the militarization of the Cordillera, see Philippine Trends (July-August 1984), p. 3.
News of the sudden massive influx of U.S. military advisers has surfaced: "U.S. Advisers in RP," Philippine News (13-19 February 1985), pp. 1-8. The information is attributed to Paul Wolfowitz, Assistant Secretary for East Asia Affairs, State Department; and Richard Armitage, Assistant Defense Secretary for International Security Affairs. The report follows the marked

shift of U.S. policy from democratic reforms to more military and "civic action" programs, as documented in "U.S. Provides More Aid," Philippine News (16-22 January 1985), pp. 1-2. See also the analyses by Walden Bello, "Showdown in the Philippines," The Progressive (December 1984), pp. 16-17; and "The Pentagon and the Philippine Crisis," Southeast Asia Chronicle, No. 95 (November 1984), pp. 20-24; the latter article cites studies prepared by the Center for Strategic and International Studies, and the National Defense University, Washington, D.C.

18 KSP, Signs of the Times: The Church in the Philippines (Utrecht, 1984), p. 20.

19 Karl Marx and Friedrich Engels, The German Ideology (New York, 1947), pp. 198-99.

20 Politics and Ideology in Marxist Theory (London, 1977), pp. 108-109. For a survey of recent discussion, see Stephen Katz, Marxism, Africa and Social Class: A Critique of Relevant Theories (Montreal, 1980), pp. 73-102. On the interplay between nationalism and internationalism which should qualify the excesses of dependency theory, Antonio Gramsci reminds us that "the internal relations of any nation are the result of a combination which is original and unique: these relations must be understood and conceived in their originality and uniqueness if one wishes to dominate them and direct them. To be sure, the line of development is towards internationalism, but the point of departure is 'national'. . . . The leading class is in fact only such if it accurately interprets this combination--of which it is itself a component and precisely as such is able to give the movement a certain direction, within certain perspectives"; Selections from the Prison Notebooks, edited and translated by Q. Hoare and G. F. Smith (New York, 1971), p. 240.

21 Eqbal Ahmad, "The Neo-fascist State: Notes on the Pathology of Power in the Third World," Philippine Collegian (15 September 1983) p. 4. Reprinted from Third World Studies Dependency Papers Series No. 30, October 1980, University of the Philippines. See A. Sivanandan "Imperialism and Disorganic Development in the Silicon Age," A Different Hunger (London, 1982), pp. 143-161.

22 For a lucid exposition of Gramsci's revolutionary politics, see Carl Boggs, The Two Revolutions: Gramsci and the Dilemmas of Western Marxism (Boston, MA, 1984).

23 Michel Pecheux, "Ideology: Stronghold or Paradoxical Space?" Minnesota Review (Fall 1984), p. 161. See also Ernesto Laclau, "Transformations of Advanced Industrial Societies and the

Theory of the Subject," Rethinking Ideology: A Marxist Debate, ed. Sakari Hanninen and Leena Paldan (Berlin, 1983), pp. 39-44.

24 On the revised 12-point program of the NDF, see Central Committee, Communist Party of the Philippines, Ang Bayan (March 1985), pp. 15-16; Solidaridad II (January-March 1985), pp. 6-7; and International Office, NDF, "The Major Economic Policies of the NDF," NDF Update (December 1984), pp. 5-8. For an excellent analysis of counter-hegemonic trends in this transitional period, I recommend Temario Rivera, "Political Opposition in the Philippines: Contestation and Cooperation," Wisconsin Papers on Southeast Asia (Center for Southeast Asian Studies, University of Wisconsin-Madison, March 1985). See also David Wurfel, "The May Elections," Philippine Research Bulletin (Fall/Spring 1984-85), pp. 2-4, "Toward A Coalition Government," IDOC International Bulletin, 10 (1984), pp. 20-23.

25 Pecheux, op cit.

Chapter I

1 Resolution adopted by the General Assembly, UN Sixth Special Session, May 1974, reprinted by American Friends Service Committee in The New International Economic Order, Nov. 1976. See also Michael Barrett Brown, The Anatomy of Underdevelopment (Nottingham, 1974) for earlier documents on economic policy in the Third World.

2 Qouted in R. W. Van Alstyne, The Rising American Empire (Oxford, 1960), p. 146.

3 Quoted in Claude Bowers, Beveridge and the Progressive Era (New York, 1932), pp. 69-70.

4 Cited by D. B. Schirmer, "The Philippine-American War of 1899-1902," lecture given in Chicago, Illinois (3 February 1974).

5 Quoted in William J. Pomeroy, American Neo-Colonialism: Its Emergence in the Philippines and Asia (New York, 1970), p. 51.

6 The tabulation of war casualties are in Scott Nearing and Joseph Freeman, Dollar Diplomacy (New York, 1966), p. 199. On U.S. atrocities, see the compilation of Congressional Records by Henry Graff, ed., American Imperialism and the Philippine Insurrection (Boston, 1969). An excellent resume of the Filipino-American War is Luzviminda Francisco, "The First Vietnam," in The Philippines: End of an Illusion (London, 1973), pp. 18-49; see also James H. Blount, The American Occupation of the Philippines, 1898-1912 (Quezon City, 1968, first printed 1913);

Leon Wolf, Little Brown Brother (London, 1960); Stuart Creighton Miller, "Benevolent Assimilation": The American Conquest of the Philippines 1899-1903 (New Haven, 1982).

7 On the colonial period and the war years, see: Teodoro Agoncillo and Milagros Guerrero, History of the Filipino People (Quezon City, 1970), pp. 280-488. On the parity controversy, see Renato Constantino and Letizia Constantino, The Philippines: The Continuing Past (Quezon City, 1978), pp. 198-205; Labor Research Association, US and the Philippines (New York, 1958); Stephen Shalom, The United States and the Philippines: A Study of Neocolonialism (Philadelphia, 1981). On the shaping of a neo-colonial formation, cf. Jonathan Fast, "Imperialism and the Ruling Class," in The Philippines: End of an Illusion, pp. 1-17; D.B. Schirmer, "The Philippine War and U.S. Neo-Colonialism," Perspectives on Development and Social Change (Cambridge, Mass., 1974), pp. 1-12.

8 All figures are derived from: Corporate Information Center (NCC-USA), The Philippines: American Corporations, Martial Law, and Underdevelopment, IDOC, No. 57 (November 1973); Guy Whitehead, "Philippine-American Economic Relations," Pacific Research (January-February, 1973). On the nature of transnationals, see: John Cavanagh and Frederick Clairmonte, The Transnational Economy (Washington DC, 1982) and Hugo Radice, ed., International Firms and Modern Imperialism (New York, 1975).

9 See Mamoru Tsuda, Rigoberto Tiglao and Edith Atienza, "The Impact of TNCs in the Philippines: A Study of Major Foreign and Foreign-Affiliated Corporations in the Philippines," University of the Philippines Law Center, June 1978; and Third World Studies Program, Political Economy of Philippine Commodities (Quezon City, 1983). On the cases of Dole and Del Monte in the Philippines, see Lorenzo Tanada, Nationalism: A Summons to Greatness (Quezon City, 1965), pp. 53-67; and Jovito Salonga, "Role of Multi-National Corporations in Development," lecture delivered at Loyola Retreat House, Rizal, Philippines, 8 May 1974.

10 On the circumstances before and after martial law, see the following analyses: Samuel P. Bayani, What's Happening in the Philippines? (New York, 1976); Robert B. Stauffer, "The Political Economy of Refeudalization," Marcos and Martial Law in the Philippines (Ithaca, 1975), pp. 180-218; Felix Razon, Powder Keg in the Pacific Time Bomb in the U.S. Empire (New York, 1981). For militarism and repression, aside from the reports by AI, Task Force Detainees, and International Commission of Jurists, see Resource Center for Philippine Concerns, Christian Responsibility and Asian Solidarity (Hong Kong, 1980); Jim Zwick, Militarism and Repression

in the Philippines (Montreal, 1982). For the Filipino perspective, see: Civil Liberties Union of the Philippines, Three Years of Martial Law (San Francisco, 1975); Diosdado Macapagal, Democracy in the Philippines (Ontario, 1976); Reuben Canoy, The Counterfeit Revolution (Manila, 1980).

[11] "The World Bank and Economic Crisis in the Philippines," Science for the People (September-October, 1984), p. 26. See also Ma. Theresa Dioko, The IMF and How It Affects the Filipino People (University of the Philippines, 1983).

[12] Philippine Liberation Courier (15 December 1978), and the calculations of surplus value by Edberto Villegas, Studies in Philippine Political Economy (Manila, 1983), pp. 152-155. See also data published by the monthly IBON (Quezon City, Philippines); Enrico Paglaban, "Philippine Workers in the Export Industry," Pacific Research (March-June,1978).

[13] People Toiling Under Pharoah (1976), quoted in NARMIC, The Philippines (Country Profile Series #1, Philadelphia, 1978), p. 5. For recent assessments on TNCs and the Philippine situation, see: Robert Stauffer, "The Manila-Washington Connection: Continuities in the Transnational Political Economy of Philippine Development," paper presented at the Association for Asian Studies, San Francisco, 25-27 March 1983; Gerald Sussman, David O'Connor and Charles Lindsey, "Philippines, 1984: The Political Economy of a Dying Dictatorship," Philippines Research Bulletin (Summer 1984); Robin Broad, "The Transformation of the Philippine Economy," Monthly Review (May, 1984), pp. 11-21.

[14] Figures cited in Villegas, Studies, pp. 11-14; Renato Constantino, The Nationalist Alternative (Manila, 1979), p. 38; Alejandro Lichauco, The Lichauco Paper (New York, 1973), pp. 26-28. For data on poverty and income distribution, see The Economist (13 October 1979), p. 58; and Far Eastern Economic Review (2 October 1981), pp. 33-34.

[15] E. San Juan, Jr., "Blueprint for Disaster: Westinghouse Brings Nukes to the Philippines," Science for the People (January-February, 1980), pp. 23-26; Walden Bello, John Harris and Lyuba Zarsky, Nuclear Power in the Philippines (Quezon City, 1983).

[16] Philippine News (7-13 March 1984), p. 13. On the rationale of U.S. interventions, see Richard Barnet, Intervention and Revolution (New York, 1972); and Noam Chomsky, Towards A New Cold War (New York, 1982).

[17] Campaign Against Military Intervention in the Philippines (CAMIP), U.S. Bases in the Philippines (New York, 1983), p. 2.

18 Quoted in Walden Bello, "Springboards for Intervention, Instruments for Nuclear War," Southeast Asian Chronicle, No. 89 (April 1983), p. 3.

19 The best documentation on the function of the bases and their contextual implications is Komite ng Sambayanang Pilipino (KSP), Seeds of Intervention (Volume II of Kilusan), Utrecht, 1983. See also Walden Bello and Severina Rivera, eds., The Logistics of Repression and Other Essays (Washington, D.C., 1977).

20 Liberation (March 1983), p. 4. For documentation on U.S. direct counter-insurgency involvement, see Roland Simbulan, The Bases of Our Insecurity (MetroManila, 1983), esp. pp. 169-190; cf. David Wise and Thomas Ross, The Invisible Government (New York, 1964), p. 138; Victor Marchetti and John Marks, The CIA and the Cult of Intelligence (New York, 1974), pp. 50-51, 129.

21 Philippine News (1-7 June 1983), p. 4.

22 E. San Juan, Jr., "Philippines: The Bases for U.S. Intervention," Changes (October 1983), p. 4. On the reports of the CIA and the Pentagon, see International Herald Tribune (1 October 1984), and Newsweek (22 October 1984), cited in Philippine Trends, No. 11 (September-October, 1984), p. 7.

23 Quoted in Jose Diokno, "U.S. Policy and Presence in East Asia: An Insider's View," published by the Friends of the Filipino People, Washington, D.C., 1980.

24 See Norman Owen, "Philippine-American Economic Interactions: A Matter of Magnitude," in The Philippine Economy and the United States (Ann Arbor, 1983), pp. 177-198; Glenn Anthony May, Social Engineering in the Philippines (Westport, Conn., 1980); Norman Owen, ed., Compadre Colonialism: Studies on the Philippines Under American Rule (Ann Arbor, 1971). Typical of diehard apologetics is that of Frank Golay (see his article "Taming the American Multinationals" in Owen's 1983 volume) whose highly selective manipulation of statistics--shades of the "dismal science"!--supposedly gives him the right to chide independent-minded Filipinos for their "anthropomorphic escapism." Golay's sad performance is emulated by numerous Filipino collaborators, e.g. Gerardo Sicat et al., Economics and Development (Quezon City, 1965), and Gerardo Sicat and John Power, The Philippines (New York, 1971).

25 Quoted by Richard Falk, "Views from Manila and Washington," World Policy Journal (Winter, 1984), p. 425. The Kennan text is printed in T. Etzold and John Lewis Gaddis, Containment: Documents on American Policy and Strategy,

<u>1945-1950</u> (New York, 1978), pp. 226-28. Professor Falk's argument reiterated here is confirmed every time Congress and the State Department issue position papers on the contemporary Philippine crisis.

Chapter II

[1] V. I. Lenin, <u>Selected Works</u> (New York, 1971), p. 665. See Georg Lukacs, <u>Lenin: A Study on the Unity of His Thought</u> (London, 1970).

[2] Antonio Gramsci, <u>The Modern Prince and Other Writings</u> (New York, 1957), pp. 118-132, 164-173. Cf. Chantal Mouffe, "Hegemony and Ideology in Gramsci," in <u>Gramsci and Marxist Theory</u> (London, 1979), pp. 168-204.

[3] For a general survey and analysis of the present conjuncture and the historical background, see: <u>Liberation</u> (September 1982), official organ of the National Democratic Front, Philippines; Komite ng Sambayanang Pilipino, <u>In the Face of Adversity</u> (1982); Filippijnengroep, <u>Makibakal</u> (Utrecht, Holland, 1980); Felix Razon, "Powder Keg in the Pacific," <u>Far East Reporter</u> (New York, 1981); Philippines Research Center, <u>New People's Army of the Philippines</u> (New York, 1983).

[4] Philippines Research Center, <u>The National Democratic Front's Ten Point Program</u> (Connecticut, 1977), p. 1.

[5] Permanent People's Tribunal, <u>Philippines Repression and Resistance</u> (London, 1980), p. 206.

[6] This classic formulation was first enunciated in Amado Guerrero, <u>Philippine Society and Revolution,</u> 2nd ed., (Hong Kong, 1971), which remains the fundamental text for the principles of the Philippine national democratic struggle; it was subsequently elaborated in Amado Guerrero, <u>Specific Characteristics of Our People's War</u> (1975), and the document "Our Urgent Tasks" (1976) by the Communist Party of the Philippines.

[7] This represents the consensus in most analyses; for example, Robert Stauffer, "The Political Economy of Refeudalization," in <u>Marcos and Martial Law in the Philippines,</u> ed. David Rosenberg (Ithaca, 1979), pp. 180-218; Association for Radical East Asian Studies, <u>End of An Illusion</u> (London, 1978); and numerous articles by the historian Dr. Daniel B. Schirmer, e.g. "<u>The Philippines--Another Vietnam</u> (Boston, 1973).

[8] "The Third World Alternatives," speech before the American

Newspaper Publishers Association Convention, Hawaii, April 1980, p. 23.

9 Report of an Amnesty International Mission to the Republic of the Philippines (London, 1976), p. 56. This is corroborated further and updated in the Report of the Nov. 1981 AI Mission in its Report (London, 1982), pp. 10-28. See also International Commission of Jurists, The Decline of Democracy in the Philippines (Geneva, 1977).

10 Belinda Aquino, "The Philippines Under Marcos," Current History (April 1982), p. 162.

11 National Democratic Front, NDF Update, II (Oct. 1982), p. 5; Ang Bayan (Sept. 1982), pp. 1-4. (Ang Bayan is the organ of the Communist Party of the Philippines).

12 Aquino, p. 160.

13 See the monthly publications of the Task Force Detainees of the Philippines, Political Detainees Update; the 1981 Amnesty International Report; and TFD, Pumipiglas: Political Detainees and Military Atrocities in the Philippines (Manila, 1981); and P. M. Abinales, Militarization: Philippines (March 1982).

14 KSP Report No. 12 (Feb.-April 1982); IDOC Bulletin Nos. 8-10 (Aug.-Oct. 1980).

15 Reuben Canoy, The Counterfeit Revolution: Martial Law in the Philippines (Manila, 1980), pp. 91-94.

16 Amnesty International, The Church and Lay Workers in the Philippines (Target Sector Paper, 16 July 1982), p. 2. See also the 1982 dossier prepared by the Committee for the Promotion of Church People's Rights; J. Henry Kamm, "Philippine Nuns take the Fight to Manila Slums," New York Times (7 Feb. 1981), P. 2; The Lawyers' Committee for International Human Rights, The Philippines: A Country in Crisis (New York 1983), pp. 64-66; International Commission of Jurists, The Decline of Democracy in the Philippines (Geneva, Switzerland, 1971), pp. 26-40.

17 "Christians Under Fire: People's Apostolate versus State's Apostasy," Solidaridad (Special Issue, 1982); also issue no. 1983; Amnesty International USA Campaign Pamphlet, "Arrest, Detention and Political Killing of Priests and Church Workers in the Philippines," 1982. See also Sheilah Ocampo, "Church and State," Far Eastern Economic Review (2 October 1981), pp. 18-19; Robert Youngblood, "The Protestant Church in the Philippines' New

Society," <u>Bulletin of Concerned Asian Scholars</u> (July-Sept. 1980), pp. 19-29.

[18] "Catholic Bishops Assail Marcos Regime," <u>New York Times</u> (17 February 1983), p. A3.

[19] Leaflet entitled "Faith on Trial" published by the Committee on Promotion of Church People's Rights (Manila, 1982), p. 3.

[20] <u>IDOC Bulletin</u>, p. 11.

[21] "Filipino Theology for Liberation: A Working Paper," <u>Radical Religion</u>, II, 4 (1976), p. 9. For backgrounds, see: Bernard Wideman, "A Filipino Liberation Theology," <u>The Christian Century</u> (16 April 1976), pp. 390-93; "The Pope and the People," <u>Ibon</u> (28 Feb. 1981); Monica Sano, "The Church in the Philippines," <u>Workers Viewpoint</u> (29 Nov. 1983), pp. 11,14. For recent developments, see: Belinda Olivares-Cunanan, "Today's Challenge to Humanize the Gospel Splits the Church," <u>Mr. and Ms.</u> (2 Dec. 1983), pp. 4-9; on Cardinal Sin, see <u>Veritas</u> (26 Aug. 1984), pp. 8-10.

[22] "Some Prenotes on 'Doing Theology': Man, Society, and History in Asian Contexts," <u>The Human and the Holy: Asian Perspectives in Christian Theology</u> (New York, 1980), p. 202. On Fr. Zacharias Agatep, see <u>New Zealand Monthly Review</u> (Aug. 1983), p. 20. On the Samar priests, see <u>National Catholic Reporter</u> (4 March 1983); on the Mindanao-Sulu Pastoral Council, see <u>National Catholic Reporter</u> (16 September 1983), p. 7.

[23] <u>Program of the CNL</u> (Manila, 1984), p. 11.

[24] Ibid., pp. 18, 22-23. See also "CNL Second National Congress," <u>KSP Report No. 12</u> (Feb.-April 1982). Cf. Fifteen Religious Priests, "Some Thoughts for Reflection," <u>Philippines Update</u> (CCHRP; Washington D.C,, 1983), pp. 5-7.

[25] "Challenge to the Churches," <u>Cry of the People</u> (A report of the International Ecumenical Conference on the Philippines) (New York, 1983), p. 22. Cf. Sister Mary J. Mananzan, interview in <u>National Catholic Reporter</u> (4 March 1983), p. 10.

[26] Claver's speech is excerpted in <u>Peace Section Newsletter</u> published by the Mennonite Central Committee, XIII, 5 (Sept.-Oct. 1982), pp. 9-10. See also Claver, "The Violence of the 'Meek,'" AFSC <u>Peacework</u> (March 1978), p. 6. A telling contrast can also be shown between Claver and Bishop Julio Labayen's position as put forth in "Changing the Structures of Injustice," <u>Asia Action 41</u> (Sept.-Oct. 1983), pp. 14-17, and his speech in <u>Cry of the People</u>, pp. 2, 4.

27 See Helmut Gollwitzer, "Kingdom of God and Socialism in the Theology of Karl Barth," Karl Barth and Radical Politics, ed. George Hunsinger (Philadelphia, 1976), pp. 77-120.

28 Talk to members of the Friends of the Filipino People (Boston Chapter), Feb. 1981. In this context, I would like to recommend an analysis by "conscienticized" Christians of the government's Kintanar paper designed to suppress or neutralize the progressive tendencies in the Church: Church Trends (Jan.-Feb. 1983), p. 3.

29 "Christianity and Social Action--Three Hypotheses for Discussion," The Christian Marxist Dialogue, ed. Paul Oestreicher (New York, 1960), pp. 201-02.

30 The interview with de la Torre (31 May 1980) is excerpted in IDOC Bulletin No. 8-9-10 (August-September-October 1980), pp. 7-9, parts of which are reprinted in Peace Section Newsletter, pp. 8-9. See also an interview in FIJAR 12/13 (Summer 1981), pp. 28-31; Leon Howell, "A Parable of Oppressed Faith," Sojourner (Feb. 1980), pp. 9-10; National Catholic Reporter (7 May 1982).

31 Peace Section Newsletter, p. 8.

32 Ibid., p. 11.

33 Ibid. See also two interviews with Balweg: Roberto Z. Coloma, "A Soldier of Christ Takes to the Hills," Collegian Folio (June 1982), pp. 34-35; F.E., "The Church Has to be Revolutionary," The Irish Times (June 1983), reprinted in Mr. and Ms. (2 Dec. 1983), p. 10. In this context, compare the statements of Carlos Abesamis, "Faith and Life Reflections from the Grassroots", Alay Kapwa (1980), pp. 56-58; Karl Gaspar, "The View from the Belly of the Beast," Kalinangan (June 1984), pp. 20-21. After this chapter was written I recived Volume III issue of the KSP Kilusan on the Church entitled Signs of the Times, which I recommend to anyone wanting to explore further this subject in depth.

34 Anti-Slavery Society, The Philippines (London, 1983), pp. 91-119.

35 In the Face of Adversity, p. 32.

36 Alliance for Philippine National Democracy, The Moro People's Struggle: Documents from the Moro National Liberation Front (1979). Available from Philippines Research Center, Box 101, Mansfield Depot, CT 06268.

37 In the Face of Adversity, p. 36.

38 Quoted in The Philippines, pp. 164-165.

39 "The Kalinga Ili: Cultural-Sociological Reflections on Indigenous Theoria and Praxis of Man-Nature Relationship" in Dakami Ya Nan Dagami, ed. Cordillera Consultative Committee (Baguio City, 1984), pp. 43-48. See also in the same volume June Prill Brett, "Land Ownership and Land Use in Bontoc," pp. 28-29.

40 "Cordillera People Fight for their Land," Ang Bayan (November 1982), pp. 6-8. See also "Valley of Sorrow," AsiaWeek (5 September 1980), pp. 18-31. The latest documentation on the human rights situation in the Cordillera is International Commission of Jurists, The Philippines: Human Rights After Martial Law (Geneva, 1984), pp. 113-15.

41 "The Growing Multi-Sectoral Mass Movement of the National Minorities in the Cordillera," Human Rights and Ancestral Land: A Source Book, ed. Dept. of Anthropology, University of the Philippines (December 1983), pp. 222-32. See the whole Section IV of this excellent anthology.

42 "Large Scale Military Invasion of Kalinga-Apayao in Full Swing," Press release (5 July 1984) of the Coordinating Committee for Minority Concerns, Manila, Philippines. See also Paul Hutchcroft, "Marcos Hangs on Tight as His Grip Slips a Bit," Guardian (8 August 1984), pp. 1, 16.

43 "Murder of 50 Igorots Hit as Military Attacks," Balita (1-15 August 1984), p. 2; Philippine Trends No. 10 (July-August 1984), pp. 3-4.

44 Statement from the Kalinga-Bontoc Peacepact Holders Association, cited in Solidaridad II (October 1984), p. 8.

45 Permanent People's Tribunal, Philippines Repression and Resistance, p. 114.

46 Delia Aguilar-San Juan, "Feminism and the National Liberation Struggle in the Philippines," Women's Studies International Forum, Vol. 5, Nos. 3/4 (1982), p. 258.

47 Ibid., p. 259.

48 "Women in the Struggle," Philippine Resistance, III, Nos. 1-2 (Montreal, Canada, 1982), pp. 12-15.

Chapter III

1 See The Filipino Chronicle (1-14 May 1983), p. 4; (15-31

May 1983), p. 4; (1-7 June 1983), pp. 1, 14; Philippine News (1-7 June 1983), pp. 1, 8.

2 Robert B. Stauffer, "The Political Economy of Refeudalization," in Marcos and Martial Law in the Philippines, ed. D. Rosenberg (Ithaca, 1978), pp. 180-218. For recent commentaries, see Robert Stauffer, "The Manila-Washington Connection: Continuities in the Transnational Political Economy of Philippine Development," paper read at the Association for Asian Studies, San Francisco, 25-27 March 1983; Benedict Kerkvliet, "Possible Demise of the Marcos Regime," paper read at Northern Illinois University, 31 May-2 June 1983.

3 Ernesto Laclau, "Feudalism and Capitalism in Latin-America," in Politics and Ideology in Marxist Theory (London, 1977), pp. 15-50. See also Stephen Katz, Marxism, Africa and Social Class: A Critique of Relevant Theories (Montreal, 1980), pp. 25-106.

4 Published by Harvard University Press.

5 Ibid., p. 272.

6 Published by Greenwood Press, Westport, Connecticut.

7 An attempt to link U.S. colonial educational policy with metropolitan practice vis-a-vis Blacks and Indians has been made by Roger Bresnahan, "'Our Little Proteges': Models of American Colonial Rule," Philippine Social Sciences and Humanities Review, 43 (Jan-Dec. 1979), pp. 162-171.

8 Constantino's relevant books are The Philippines: A Past Revisited (Quezon City, 1979), pp. 250-341; and Neo-colonial Identity and Counter-Consciousness (London, 1978), pp. 25-94, 211-226. Schirmer's paper was first read at the 1974 conference of Asian Studies, San Diego, California, 14-16 June, and published as "The Philippine War and U.S. Neo-Colonialism," Perspectives on Development and Social Change, II, 7 (Cambridge, 1975). See also Jonathan Fast, "Imperialism and the Philippine Ruling Class," in The Philippines End of an Illusion (London, 1973), pp. 1-17.

9 Chantal Mouffe, "Hegemony and Ideology in Gramsci," Gramsci and Marxist Theory (London, 1979), pp. 168-204.

10 These events can be traced in the historical narratives of any study of the period: for example, Joseph Hayden, The Philippines (New York, 1942); Teodoro Agoncillo and Milagros Guerrero, History of the Filipino People (Quezon City, 1970), pp. 280-444. For a readable resume, see Belinda Aquino, "Philippines,"

The Current History Encyclopedia of Developing Nations (New York, 1982), pp. 264-268.

11 Filipinas is published by the Philippine Study Committee of the Association for Asian Studies. For a thorough review of the Marcos regime's policy toward tribal groups, see Anti-Slavery Society, The Philippines: Authoritarian Government, Multinationals and Ancestral Lands (London, 1983). Cf. Permanent People's Tribunal, Philippines Repression and Resistance (London, 1980), pp. 184-191.

12 General Emilio Aguinaldo (1869-1964), president of the first Philippine Republic, led the revolutionary army against Spain and then against the U.S. after the outbreak of the Filipino-American War in 1898. Manuel Quezon (1876-1944) was the first president of the Philippine Commonwealth (1935-1945) and the most outstanding Filipino politician during the period of American colonization. Sergio Osmena (1878-1961) was the speaker of the first Philippine Assembly and second president of the Philippine Commonwealth.

13 Emilio Jacinto (1875-1899) was the intellectual leader of the Katipunan, the revolutionary oganization which initiated the revolt against Spain in 1896.

14 The Philippine Revolution (Manila, 1969; first published in Spanish in 1931), p. 8. Mabini was the adviser to General Aguinaldo, and also served as premier and secretary of foreign affairs in the revolutionary government. He was exiled to Guam in 1901-1902 for refusing to swear allegiance to the American government.

15 Jose Rizal (1861-1896) is the national hero of the Philippines. He is considered the most important Filipino intellectual of the 19th century. His numerous writings inspired the 1896 revolution, the first anti-colonial struggle in Asia, and continues to inform Philippine political thought. See Cesar A. Majul, The Political and Constitutional Ideas of the Philippine Revolution (Quezon City, 1967); E. San Juan, Toward Rizal (Manila, 1983). The reference to "civic virtues" is found in Rizal's "Farewell Address" of 15 Dec. 1896; Majul, op.cit., p. 28.

16 The rationale of "Manifest Destiny" and U.S. annexation of the Philippines is found in McKinley's 1900 instructions to the second Philippine Commission headed by William Howard Taft, who became the first civil governor of the Philippines. It was drafted by Secretary of State Elihu Root. See Charles Burke Elliott, The Philippines to the End of the Commission Government (Indianapolis, 1917), pp. 488-489.

17 On the Philippine resistance, see the documents in Henry Graff, ed., American Imperialism and the Philippine Insurrection (Boston, 1969); William Pomeroy, American Neo-Colonialism (New York, 1970), pp. 56-98; Luzviminda Francisco, "The First Vietnam--The Philippine-American War of 1899-1902," Letters in Exile, ed. Jesse Quinsaat (Los Angeles, 1976), pp. 1-22; Stuart Creighton Miller, "Benevolent Assimilation": The American Conquest of the Philippines, 1899-1903 (New Haven, 1982).

18 For an orthodox Marxist-Leninist analysis of the Philippine formation, see Amado Guerrero, Philippine Society and Revolution (Hong Kong, 1971), More recent formulations are collected in Temario C. Rivera et al., Feudalism and Capitalism in the Philippines (Quezon City, 1982).

19 Louis Althusser, Lenin and Philosophy (London, 1971), pp. 152-165. See also Paul Hirst, On Law and Ideology (New Jersey, 1979), pp. 22-39.

20 Manuel Roxas (1892-1948), the first president of the third Philippine Republic, was one of the members of the first generation of the elite tutored by U.S. soldiers; another is Carlos P. Romulo, minister of foreign affairs of long standing. Cf. Bonifacio Salamanca, The Filipino Reaction to American Rule (Connecticut, 1968).

22 Sturtevant's book was published by Cornell University Press. Sakdalism was a peasant movement in 1930-35 directed against American administrators, Filipino bureaucrats like Quezon, feudal landlords, the clergy, and the Philippine Constabulary, the colonial police force. The uprising occurred on 2-3 May 1935. See Renato Constantino, A History of the Philippines (New York, 1975), pp. 367-370.

23 From America Is in the Heart, pp. 58-62. First published by Harcourt, Brace in 1943, it was reprinted in 1973 by the University of Washington Press.

24 The aesthetic and philosophical orientation of this reading derives from the work of Mikhail Bakhtin; see Julia Kristeva, Desire in Language (New York, 1980), pp. 124-147. For a critical interpretation of the Bulosan canon, see E. San Juan, Jr., Carlos Bulosan and the Imagination of the Class Struggle (Quezon City, 1972).

25 Among numerous examples influenced by functionalist sociology such as that practiced by the Institute of Philippine Culture administered by the Jesuit-owned Ateneo University, are George Taylor, The Philippines and the United States (New York,

1964); Theodore Friend, Between Two Empires: The Ordeal of the Philippines 1929-1946 (New Haven, 1965); and Peter Stanley's book cited earlier.

26 Towards the Restructuring of Filipino Values (Quezon City, 1972), pp. iv, 47. The more sophisticated formulations are: Frank Lynch, "Philippine Values II: Social Acceptance," Social Foundations of Community Development, ed. Socorro Espiritu and Chester Hunt (Manila, 1964), pp. 318-331; and included in Frank Lynch, ed., Four Readings on Philippine Values (Quezon City, 1964), one of the most popular and influential texts. See also Robert Fox, "Social Class," Fred Eggan et al, eds., Area Handbook of the Philippines (New Haven, 1955), I, pp. 437-467.

27 See Irene L. Gendzier, "A Critique of Modernization Theory as It Applies to Social Relations: the Place of Psychology in Modernization/Development Literature," paper read at Brooklyn College, 7 May 1979; Colin Leys, "Samuel Huntington and the End of Classical Modernization Theory," Introduction to the Sociology of "Developing Societies" (New York, 1982), pp. 332-349. For a critique of Philippine sociology practiced by Americans, see George Weightman, "Comments on the Chapter on Sociology," in Philippine Studies: History, Sociology, Mass Media, and Bibliography (Dekalb, Illinois, 1978), pp. 178-179.

28 The best example of this type of theorizing may be discerned in the writings of Dr. O. D. Corpuz, foremost ideologue of the present regime; see his "The Cultural Foundations of Filipino Politics," in Social Foundations of Community Development, pp. 407-425.

29 "Catholic Bishops Assail Marcos Regime," New York Times (17 February 1983), p. A3. See also: Report of an Amnesty International Mission to the Republic of the Philippines 11-28 November 1981 (London 1982); Resource Center for Philippine Concerns (Hong Kong), The Bitter Fruits of Militarization, No. 1, 1982; and the fortnightly publication Political Detainees Update of the Task Force Detainees of the Philippines.

30 Published for the Council on Foreign Relations by Frederick Praeger, New York, 1964.

31 Reproduction in Education, Society and Culture (London & Beverly Hills, 1977), p. 4.

32 Published by the Centro Escolar University Research and Development Center, Manila, Philippines, 1974.

33 The Good Fight, p. 149.

[34] Gregorio Zaide, Jose Rizal: Life, Works and Writings (Manila, 1961), p. 126.

[35] *Utang-na-loob* (debt inside the self) refers to "a primary debt which functions within a system of reciprocity obligations." *Hiya* (shame) and *pakikisama* (going along with the group) denote personal attitudes that regulate the Filipino's conformity to social norms of propriety, authority, etc. For a succinct description, see Frederick Chaffee, et al., eds. Area Handbook for the Philippines (Washington, D.C., 1969), pp. 171-178.

Chapter IV

[1] For the most recent sustained critique of Western Orientalism, see Edward Said, Orientalism (New York, 1978); also Byran S. Turner, Marx and the End of Orientalism (London, 1978), passim. Works referred to are: Hayden, The Philippines, A Study in National Development (New York, 1942); Gowing, Muslim Filipinos: Heritage and Horizon (Quezon City, 1979); Friend, Between Two Empires (New Haven, CT, 1965): Stanley, A Nation in the Making: The Philippines and the United States 1899-1921 (Cambridge, Mass., 1974). This statement from a government document, repeated by Marcos and other officials, typifies the tenor of the hegemonic discourse on the Moro situation: "Thus it was that while the descendants of the Filipinos in the North learned the arts of peace as a consequence of the subjugation of their ancestors, the descendants of the Muslim warriors failed to progress as a result of the victories won by their ancestors" (Office of Civil Relations, General Headquarters, Armed Forces of the Philippines, Mindanao Report, [Manila, 1973], p. 3).

[2] In Two Hills of the Same Land (Mindanao, 1978), Rad D. Silva refutes the distortions and rectifies numerous popular misconceptions shared by Steinberg and others. The MNLF Committee on Information documents the regime's genocidal impact in: Nur Misuari, "Address to the 9th Islamic Foreign Ministers Conference, Dakar, Senegal" (April 1978); "Appeal of the Bangsa Moro People to the Permanent People's Tribunal," in KSP, Philippines Repression and Resistance (London, 1981), pp. 15-22; Genocide in Bangsamoro Homeland (Tripoli, Libya, April 1983); Pata Island Report (Tripoli, July 1983); and current issues of the MNLF organ, Mahardika. For a critique of Marcos' modernizing strategy, see citations for Note 20. Also: Eduardo C. Tadem, "A Critique of Development Patterns in Mindanao," Third World Studies Discussion Paper No. 19 (April 1980); Anti-Slavery Society, The Philippines Authoritarian Government, Multinationals and Ancestral Lands (London, 1983).

[3] A recent example of popularization is T. J. S. George,

Revolt in Mindanao (Kuala Lumpur, 1980). Typical of functionalist sociologism are: Filipinas Foundation, Inc., An Anatomy of Philippine Muslim Affairs (Manila, 1971); Chester Hunt, "Ethnic Stratification and Integration in Cotabato," Social Foundations of Community Development, ed. Socorro Espiritu and Chester L. Hunt (Manila, 1964), pp. 202-31; and various articles in Peter Gowing and Robert McAmis, eds., The Muslim Filipinos (Manila, 1974).

4 "The Muslim Problem: An Analysis and A Proposed Solution" (typescript), speech delivered before the Capitol Christian Leadership, Quezon City, on 5 April 1977. Examples of patronizing attitudes are displayed in: Nick Joaquin, "Abdulmari Imao: The Filipino As Muslim," Joseph Estrada and Other Sketches (Manila, 1977), pp. 116-136; Leon Ma. Guerrero, Encounter of Cultures: The Muslims in the Philippines (Manila, 1972). See also the government's brief in Philippines Today No. 4 (June 1977).

5 Filipinengroep, Makibaka! (Utrecht, Holland, 1980), pp. 162-163, reprinted in The Moro People's Struggle (Ct.: Alliance for Philippine National Democracy, 1981). The cultural and historical background for the MNLF's orientation can be traced in Cesar Majul's writings, the most useful of which are: Muslims in the Philippines: Past, Present and Future Prospects (Manila, 1971); Muslims in the Philippines (Quezon City, 1973); "Cultural and Religious Responses to Development and Change," Sinaglahi, ed. M. L. Santaromana (Quezon City, 1975), pp. 34-48. Cf. "The Struggle of the Bangsamoro People for National Liberation," Mahardika (Nov.-Dec. 1983), 2-3. For an excellent survey of the literature and a correct necessary valorization of oral history as the sedimentation of historical consciousness, see Samuel Tan, The Filipino Muslim Armed Struggle 1900-1972 (Manila 1977). Tan's "pluralist" ambition is ironically undermined by Ibn Khaldun's hermeneutics alluded to in his introduction.

6 I have borrowed and modified the concept of hegemony from Antonio Gramsci, Selections from the Prison Notebooks (New York, 1971), pp. 55-60, passim; and expounded by Gramscians in: Chantal Mouffe, "Hegemony and Ideology in Gramsci," Gramsci and Marxist Theory (London, 1979), pp. 168-204; Anne Showstack Sassoon, "Hegemony, War of Position and Political Intervention," Approaches to Gramsci (London, 1982), pp. 94-115. On the notion of interpellation, see Louis Althusser, Lenin and Philosophy (London, 1971), pp. 121-76; Ernesto Laclau, Politics and Ideology in Marxist Theory (London, 1977); pp. 51-80.

7 Amin's theorizing is found in Class and Nation (New York, 1980), pp. 46-70. For the classic debate on stages, see Paul Sweezy et al, The Transition from Feudalism to Capitalism (New York, 1960). A recent survey is Stephen Katz, Marxism, Africa and

Social Class; A Critique of Relevant Theories (Montreal, 1980). The standard Soviet formulation is in Fundamentals of Marxism-Leninism (Moscow, revised edition, 1963), pp. 116ff.

[8] For the social dynamics in Moro society, the following may be consulted: Jeremy Beckett, "Maguindanao," Philippine Social History: Global Trade and Social Transformations, ed. Alfred McCoy and Edilberto de Jesus (Sydney, 1982), pp. 390-411; Thomas Kiefer, The Tausug: Violence and Law in Philippine Muslim Society (New York, 1972); Richard L. Stone, "Some Aspects of Muslim Social Organization," Brown Heritage: Essays on Philippine Cultural Tradition and Literature (Quezon City, 1967), pp. 90-133; Frederick L. Wernstedt & J. E. Spencer, The Philippine Island World (Berkeley & Los Angeles, 1967), pp. 502-597; and relevant selections in Gowing and McAmis, op. cit., pp. 219-224, passim.

[9] See Melvin Mednick, "Some Problems of Moro History and Political Organization, in Gowing & McAmis, pp. 16ff. By a myth of contract between the natives and the first sultan cited in certain tartibs, the Sulu sultanate justified the increase and centralization of its powers. In his authoritative history, Majul (p. 320) describes how the sultan was also a religious leader, "the shadow of Allah on earth", in his realm. "The sultan also stood as the symbol of the unity and integrity of the State. This was a fundamental principle in Sulu political life." The contract myth is challenged by a majority of traditional accounts, suggesting that it was the Muslims and their Islamic consciousness which engendered the institution of a central absolute authority (p. 322). Majul's superstructural bias needs economic contextualization.

[10] In The Philippine Islands (Cambridge, Mass., rev. ed. 1945), W. Cameron Forbes states that monthly payments of $250 were authorized for the Sultan of Sulu; $37.50 to $75 to each of the seven datus as compensation for the loss of their income from levies, tithes, etc. Forbes also enumerates Muslim women who enthusiastically endorsed U.S. sovereignty: Dayang Dayang Hadji Piandao, Sultana Jamila, Rajah Putri, Princess Tarhata, and Panglima Fatima of Tandubas.

[11] Becket, pp. 407-08. Cf. Melvin Mednick, "Sultans and Mayors," Gowing and McAmis, pp. 225-229; Reynaldo Ileto, Maguindanao 1860-1888: The Career of Dato Uto of Buayan (Ithaca, New York, 1971).

[12] The Manifesto is reproduced in KSP, Appendix V, pp. 285-287. On nation-building, see Tom Bottomore, Political Sociology (New York, 1979), pp. 99-115; Peter Worsley, The Third World (Chicago, 1964), pp. 50-92, 189-90; Barrington Moore, Jr., Social Origins of Dictatorship and Democracy (Boston, 1966).

13 On democratic and popular positions, see Ernesto Laclau, "'Socialism,' the 'People,' 'Democracy': the Transformation of Hegemonic Logic," Social Text 7 (Spring/Summer 1983), 115-19. On the political contextualization of Islam, there is practically nothing except tentative explorations by Kenneth Bauzon, "Islamic Nationalism in the Philippines Under Martial Law," paper given at First International Conference on Philippine Studies, Western Michigan University, Kalamazoo, Michigan, 29-31 May 1980. Class-reductionist research may be illustrated by Aijaz Ahmad, "Class and Colony in Mindanao," Southeast Asia Chronicle (Feb. 1982), 4-10; and Felix Razon, "Filipino Muslims and the Revolution," Philippines Information Bulletin I (March-April 1973), 17-25.

14 On the Marxist hermeneutics of space, see Fredric Jameson, "The Ideological Analysis of Space," Critical Exchange No. 14 (Fall 1983), 1-15; and the contributions of David Harvey, Henri Lefebvre, and particularly Anouar Abdel-Malek, in Richard Peet, ed. Radical Geography (Chicago, 1977).

15 "The Socialist Revolution and the Right of Nations to Self-Determination," Selections from V. I. Lenin and J. V. Stalin on National Colonial Question (Calcutta, India, 1970), p. 33. The most thorough investigation of the Marxist approaches to the national question are the two books by Horace B. Davis: Nationalism and Socialism (New York, 1967), and Toward A Marxist Theory of Nationalism (New York, 1978).

16 See Michael Lowy, "Marxism and the National Question," Revolution and Class Struggle, ed. Robin Blackburn (New York, 1977), pp. 154-56; V. G. Kiernan, "Nationalism" A Dictionary of Marxist Thought, ed. Tom Bottomore (Cambridge, Mass., 1983), pp. 346-49. For the NDF support of the MNLF, see Point 8 of the Ten Point Program (Ct.: Philippines Research Center, 1979), p. 13.

17 KSP, op. cit., p. 286. Although Asani has recorded his anti-imperialist views in "Imperialist Conspiracy in Bangsamoro Homeland" (speech to Oil Workers Anti-Monopolist World Conference, Tripoli, March 1980), I am not clear why he nostalgically lingers over the minutiae of the Sultanate bureaucracy in Moros--Not Filipinos (Tripoli, 1980), pp. 7-10. Such a tendency, which I would call the "Maranao Commonwealth Syndrome", erupts full-blown in the "Position Paper" of the Bangsa Moro Liberation Organization (August 1978) signed by Datu Salipada Pendatun and Sultan Harun al-Rashid Lucman, which begs the U.S. government to intervene on behalf of the Moro people. While in the fifties, the U.S. ruling circles didn't pay any attention to the Moros (e.g., George Taylor, The Philippines and the United States: Problems of Partnership, New York, 1964), now this superpower closely monitors the southern front; witness Larry Niksch and Marjorie Niehaus, The

Internal Situation in the Philippines: Current Trends and Future Prospects (Washington, D.C., Congressional Research Service, 1981).

18   For a narrative of the MNLF's evolution, see Lela Noble, "The Philippines: Muslims Fight for an Independent State," Southeast Asia Chronicle (Oct. 1980), 12-17. Misuari re-states the MNLF case in a manifesto submitted to the Third Islamic Summit at Mecca, Saudi Arabia, 24 Jan. 1981, in Mahardika, X (Jan-Feb. 1983), and (March-April 1983). After the failure of the 1976 Tripoli Accord, the MNLF declared on 17 April 1980 that it is resuming its fight for independence and secession; Asani, op. cit., pp. 34-37; 41-43. Cf. Frantz Fanon, "The Pitfalls of National Consciousness," The Wretched of the Earth (New York, 1963) pp. 148-205; Amilcar Cabral, National Liberation and Culture (Syracuse, 1970), p. 4, and also his "The Role of Culture in the Liberation Struggle," in Armand Mattelart and Seth Siegelaub, eds., Communication and Class Struggle, Vol. I (New York, 1979), pp. 205-212.

19   For accounts of Moro praxis and discourse, see Linda Washburn, "The Right and the Power," in Asani, pp. 27-33; Lawrence Johnson, "Time Bomb in the U.S. Empire," Mother Jones (Dec. 1979) reprinted by the Friends of the Filipino People; "The Ethnic Pot Begins to Boil," Far Eastern Economic Review (27 June 1975), 21-23; "MNLF will fight until self-rule demands are met," Philippine Times (1-15 October 1975), 5-6, 19; Tom Weber, "Guerrillas' Warning for Marcos," San Francisco Chronicle (12 Oct. 1978), 16-17; Paul Wilson, "Muslim Rebels Disenchanted with Negotiations," Philippine Times (22 Oct. 1979), 6.

20   Abdurasad Asani, "The Bangsamoro People: A Nation in Travail," Philippine Studies Conference, University of Michigan, Ann Arbor, Michigan, 2 August 1984.

21   Stauffer's paper was published by the Third World Studies Center, University of the Philippines, Dependency Series No. 31. Other relevant studies by Stauffer are: "The 'Development' of Mindanao," Pahayag (June 1975), 3-7, and "The Political Economy of Refeudalization," in David Rosenberg, ed., Marcos and Martial Law in the Philippines (Ithaca, 1979), pp. 180-218. Other critiques that elaborate similar themes are: D. Boone Schirmer, "The Jolo Massacre," Philippines Information Bulletin (April 1974), 3-12; Ernst Utrecht, "The Separatist Movement in the Southern Philippines," Race and Class, XVI (1975), 387-402; Third World Studies, University of the Philippines, "Mindanao: Development and Marginalization," AMPO (Tokyo, 1979), 24-36; Joel Rocamora, "Imperialism, the Marcos Regime, and the Economic Plunder of the Moro People," KSP, op, cit., pp. 234-52; Reuben Canoy, The Counterfeit Revolution (Manila, 1980), pp. 187-201.

22   Quoted by Horace Davis, p. 161. Kardelj complements the implication of dependency theory that only a revolutionary rupture can dismantle the circuit of metropolis-periphery as described by, among others, Hamza Alavi, "The Structure of Peripheral Capitalism" and "State and Class Under Peripheral Capitalism," Sociology of "Developing" Societies, edited by Hamza Alavi and Teodor Shanin (New York, 1982), pp. 172-94; 289-307. On the aspect of ethnicity, see Cynthia Enloe, "State Building and Ethnic Structures: Dependence on International Capitalist Penetration," Processes of the World System, ed. T. K. Hopkins and Immanuel Wallerstein (Beverly Hills, 1980), pp. 266-88; and Enloe, Ethnic Conflict and Political Development (Boston, 1973), pp. 222-23, passim.

23   "Contribution to the Critique of Hegel's Philosophy of Right," Marx and Engels on Religion (New York, 1964), p. 42. Cf. Karl Kautsky, Foundations of Christianity (New York and London, 1925), pp. 459-474.

24   Ibid. p. 136. In this context, see also Engel's critique of Feuerbach in "Feuerbach and the End of Classical German Philosophy," Karl Marx and Frederick Engels, Selected Works (New York, 1968), pp. 596-632.

25   For this section, I am indebted to the pioneering essay of Thomas Hodgkin, "The Revolutionary Tradition in Islam," Race and Class XXI (Winter 1980), 221-237. Cf. Jean-Paul Charnay, Islamic Culture and Socio-Economic Change (Leiden, 1971), esp. Chapters I, II and VI. On "Jacobin Islam" in Algeria, see Eric R. Wolf, "Peasant Wars of the Twentieth Century (New York 1969), pp. 225-230.

26   Marshall G. S. Hogson, "A Comparison of Islam and Christianity as Framework for Religious Life," Diogenes 32 (Winter 1960), 49-74. See also: Seyyed Hossein Nasr, Ideals and Realities of Islam (New York 1967), pp. 18, 97, passim; and Al Shari'ati, On the Sociology of Islam (Berkeley, 1979), pp. 116-17: ". . . in all that concerns the social system . . . the words 'al-nas (people) and Allah belong together. . . . It is only the people as a whole who are the representatives of God and His 'family.'" For a Filipino-Christian perspective on these issues, see Mindanao Sulu Pastoral Conference, Communications, No. 31 (May 1979), entire issue. On Ali Shari'ati and Mustafa as Siba'i's "socialism", see Hamid Enayat, Modern Islamic Political Thought (Austin, Texas, 1982), pp. 53-59; 144-49.

27   "The Apocalypse of Islam," Social Text (Winter 1983/84), p. 169-70.

28   Quoted in Alexandre Bennigsen and S. Enders Wimbush, Muslim National Communism in the Soviet Union (Chicago and London, 1979), p. 105; also in Helene Carrere d'Encausse and Stuart R. Schram, Marxism and Asia (London, 1969), p. 36.

29   Quoted in d'Encausse and Schram, p. 37.

30   Ibid., p. 189. Unfortunately, Western chauvinism and a bureaucratic-statist order that claims to be Marxist won out against the Muslim militants in the Communist International.

In his provocative scholarly opus Islam and Capitalism (New York, 1973), pp. 186ff., Maxime Rodinson contends that Islam is neutral toward either capitalism or socialism in its tenets, but he fails to conduct a multi-levelled analysis of the articulation of Islam with the historic national-class struggles in specific formations, especially in Third World countries undergoing a national democratic revolutionary process. However, this is an open-ended topic for further investigation.

Chapter V

1   Ernest Hemingway: A Life Story (New York, 1969), pp. 364-365. Other American literary personalities had a more constructive effect than Hemingway--for example, Sherwood Anderson, Edgar Snow--but the social-historical context of Hemingway's visit explains his "overdetermined" presence then, just as, during the Cold War era, the lecture tours of William Faulkner and Sidney Hook acquired more than just an individual resonance.

2   "Hemingway Was Here," The Language of the Street (Manila, 1980), pp. 49-64.

3   Ulrich Weisstein, Comparative Literature and Literary Theory (Bloomington, Indiana, 1973). On "influence" in comparatist discipline, see J. T. Shaw, "Literary Indebtedness and Comparative Literary Studies," Comparative Literature, ed. Newton Stallknecht and Horst Frenz (Carbondale, 1961), pp. 84-97; Jan Brandt Corstius, Introduction to the Comparative Study of Literature (New York, 1968), pp. 178-190; Claudio Guillen, Literature as System: Essays Toward the Theory of Literary History (Princeton, 1970), pp. 53-68; Robert Clements, Comparative Literature as Academic Discipline (New York, 1978), pp. 153-57. It is possible to argue, as Francois Jost does in Introduction to Comparative Literature (Indianapolis, 1974), pp. 41-61 that we should not confuse authorial influence with immanent similarity or analogy of circumstances, so as to avoid imputing to ideas of a few intellects an exaggerated determination over vast cultural processes. I agree with this viewpoint and its historical sense of heterogeneity/ plurality, but in the sphere of

analyzing the relationship between metropolis and periphery, between colonizing power and subaltern peoples, we cannot treat each entity of this dialectical complex as autonomous or separate and here I disagree with the perspectivism of Nietzschean post-structuralism--as though the Philippines has been and is now a genuinely independent nation-state such as France or the U.S. in the 19th century. Cultural studies dealing with peripheralized societies cannot ignore direct and mediated linkages with the totality of hegemonic culture which exerts a systemic pressure on the subordinate formation, even as the subject peoples invent ways of subverting, transvaluing or sublating the instruments of their subjection.

4   "The Structure of Peripheral Capitalism," in Introduction to the Sociology of "Developing Societies," ed. Hamza Alavi & Teodor Shanin (New York, 1982), pp. 181ff., passim. For a critique of dependency theory, see Stephen Katz, Marxism, Africa, and Social Class. No. 14, Occasional Monograph Series, (Montreal: McGill University Press, 1980). For the anatomy of neo-colonialism, see Jack Woddis, Introduction to Neo-Colonialism (New York, 1967); Harry Magdoff, The Age of Imperialism (New York, 1969); Pierre Jalee, Imperialism in the Seventies (New York, 1972). For the Philippine case, the standard references are: Amado Guerrero, Philippine Society and Revolution (Hong Kong, 1970); Alejandro Lichauco, The Lichauco Paper: Imperialism in the Philippines (New York, 1973); Renato Constantino, The Nationalist Alternative (Quezon City, 1979).

5   Philippine-American Literary Relations 1898-1941 (Quezon City, 1969), pp. 55ff. Cf. Gabriel Kolko, The Triumph of Conservatism (New York, 1963); Christopher Lasch, The Agony of the American Left (New York, 1969), pp. 1-60; Lasch notes that by the mid-Twenties, the socialist and populist radicalism in the U.S. was dead. A recent cogent explanation of the U.S. imperialist ethos, aside from the numerous works of William Appleman Williams, is Eqbal Ahmad, Political Culture and Foreign Policy (Washington, D.C., Institute for Policy Studies, 1980). A general description of U.S. society is Paul Baran and Paul Sweezy, Monopoly Capital (New York, 1966).

6   For the ideological orientation of the Spanish-speaking and Tagalog writers, see the following: Cesar Majul, The Political and Constitutional Ideas of the Philippine Revolution (Quezon City, 1967); Nora Jolipa, "Philippine Literary Criticism in Spanish: A Tradition of Commitment," Philippine Social Sciences and Humanities Review, XLV (Jan-Dec. 1981), pp. 333-44; E. San Juan, The Radical Tradition in Philippine Literature (Quezon City, 1971), pp. 7-60.

7   I am proposing this dialectical approach based on the Gramscian problematic of hegemony and the combined wars of position/maneuver presented in Selections from the Prison Notebooks (New York, 1971). See also Raymond Williams, Marxism and Literature (New York, 1977), pp. 108ff. On interpellation, see Ernesto Laclau, Politics and Ideology in Marxist Theory (London, 1977), pp. 100-142. For linguistic and cultural capital, see Pierre Bourdieu and Jean-Claude Passeron, Reproduction in Education, Society and Culture (Beverly Hills, 1977).

8   In 1926, Professor Cristino Jamias, a respected member of this first generation of American-trained teachers of English, wrote: "In our universities, we must emphasize mind-building. . . . Culture, which means a steady, live interest in things of the mind. . . . The tenacity to think will give us the real directors of destiny--an aristocracy of mind, an intellectual minority, unleading, unled"; quoted from "Our Absent Intellectual Minority," in L. Y. Yabes, Filipino Essays in English, Volume I (Quezon City, 1954), p. 39. The Westernization of the Filipino intelligentsia is described in the following: Romeo V. Cruz, "The Filipino Collaboration with the Americans, 1899-1902," Comment (First Quarter, 1960), pp. 10-29; Renato Constantino, "Part I" of Neocolonial Identity and Counter-Consciousness (New York, 1978), pp. 25-94; also pp. 211-226. For a survey of the theater as a colonial ideological apparatus, see Priscelina Legasto, "The Impact of American Colonial Rule on Philippine Theater," Philippine Social Science and Humanities Review, XLV (Jan.-Dec., 1981), pp. 345-70.

9   The classic text of the Thirties renaissance is Salvador P. Lopez, Literature and Society (Manila, 1940); cf. Elmer Ordonez, "Literature Under the Commonwealth," Philippine Social Sciences and Humanities Review, XXVIII (Dec. 1963), pp. 395-407. For a retrospective evaluation by Lopez himself, see his "Literature and Society--A Literary Past Revisited," In Roger Bresnahan, ed., Literature and Society: Cross-Cultural Perspectives (Manila, 1976), pp. 6-17; also his "The Writer in A Society in Crisis," Philippine Collegian (12 May 1982), pp. 4-5.

10   For a eulogistic account of Hartendorp's role, see Joy Marsella, "Some Contributions of the Philippine Magazine to the Development of Philippine Culture," Philippine Studies 17 (April 1969), pp. 297-331; also Hosillos, op. cit., Chapters III & IV.

11   Literary Theory (Minneapolis, 1983), p. 50. See the essays by Bruce Franklin and Richard Ohmann in The Politics of Literature, ed. Louis Kampf and Paul Lauter (New York, 1972), pp. 101-159; Louis Kampf, "Cultural Elitism and the Study of Literature," Criticism and Culture, ed. Sherman Paul (Iowa City, 1972), pp. 21-31. For the British inflection of New Critical elitism,

see Raymond Williams, Writing in Society (London, 1984), pp. 177-228.

12 "Certain Influences in Filipino Writing," The Pacific Spectator, VI (Summer 1952), p. 298. See also his "Writers Without Readers," Philippine Review (June 1952), pp. 16-29: literature is an "activity of the whole social organism" (p.18); "Culture can only flourish when it becomes a matter of common cooperation" (p. 21). Viray's historical sensibility suffers attenuation in his later piece "Racial Heritage," in George Guthrie, ed. Six Perspectives on the Philippines (Manila, 1968), pp. 165-97.

13 T. D. Agcaoili, ed., Philippine Writing (Manila, 1953), pp. xi, xxii.

14 "The Creative Temper, Provoked and Challenged, Triumphed," Panorama (6 Jan. 1980), pp. 26-27. See also her essay, "Literature as a Maker of National Myths," Bresnahan, op. cit., pp. 44-49.

15 "Dimensions and Responsibilities of Philippine Literary Criticism," The Literary Apprentice, XLVII (Nov. 1974), p. 63. Cold War polemics and the dogmatic elitism of the "colonial mentality" characterize most of Demetillo's criticism.

16 H. B. Furay, "The Power and Greatness of Nick Joaquin," Philippine Fiction, ed. Joseph Galdon (Quezon City 1972), p. 6; Miguel Bernad, S.J., Bamboo and the Greenwood Tree (Manila, 1961), pp. 11ff; but see Bernad's bleak prognosis for English in "Philippine Literature in English: Some Sociological Considerations," Literature and Society in Southeast Asia, ed. Tham Seong Chee (Singapore 1981), pp. 145-159. This last article contradicts and deflates Bernad's Americanizing drive in "Literature in the Philippines," Thought, 37 (Autumn 1962), p. 447. In contrast to this Platonic scholastic school is an Aristotelian trend represented by some teachers in the University of the Philippines; see Leopoldo Yabes, "A. Nudas' Telic Contemplation: A Learned and Perceptive Treatise," Carillon, XXII (Jan.-April 1980), pp. 20-22. An exception to the above Westernizing currents may be cited here: Fr. Horacio de la Costa, "History and Philippine Culture" and "The Responsibility of the Writer in Contemporary Philippine Society," in Richard Croghan, S.J., The Development of Philippine Literature in English (Since 1900) (Quezon City, 1975), pp. 319-30.

17 T.D. Agcaoili, op. cit., p. 328. For an interesting report on the USIS symposium, see Nick Joaquin, Manila: Sin City? and Other Chronicles (Manila, 1980), pp. 47-62. See also three other essays by Gonzalez: "The Filipino and the Novel," Fiction in

Several Languages, ed. Henry Heyre (Boston, 1968), pp. 19-29; "The Poetic Image in Philippine Letters," Literature and Society: A Symposium (Manila, 1964), pp. 48ff; "The Difficulties with Filipiniana," in Brown Heritage, ed. Antonio Manuud (Quezon City, 1967), p. 541: "Literary values transcend national boundaries and are to a certain extent as unpredictable as the proverbial female temper. . . . "

18   New Writing from the Philippines (Syracuse, 1966), p. 21.

19   Encyclopedia of Poetry and Poetics, ed. Alex Preminger (Princeton, N.J., 1965), p. 614.

20   Herbert Marcuse, "The Affirmative Character of Culture," Negations (Boston, 1968), pp. 88-133; Max Horkheimer and Theodor Adorno, Dialectic of Enlightenment (New York, 1972), pp. 120-67; Janet Wolff, "Culture," A Dictionary of Marxist Thought, ed. Tom Bottomore (Cambridge, Mass., 1983), pp. 109-112. For reification, see Georg Lukacs, History and Class Consciousness (London, 1971), pp. 83-222.

21   The last three terms are from Anouar Abdel-Malek, "Geopolitics and National Movements: An Essay on the Dialectics of Imperialism," Radical Geography, ed. Richard Peet (Chicago, 1977), pp. 293-308; see also his "Orientalism in Crisis," Diogenes, 44 (Winter 1963), pp. 107ff., passim. Some Third World critiques of cultural imperialism are: Frantz Fanon, The Wretched of the Earth (New York, 1968); Edward Said, Orientalism (New York, 1978); Ngugi Wa Thiong'o, Writers in Politics (London, 1981); Ariel Dorfman, The Empire's Old Clothes (New York, 1983); and the pertinent selections in the two volumes of Communication and Class Struggle, ed. Armand Mattelart and Seth Siegelaub (New York, 1979 and 1983).

22   For a sampling of American anti-imperialist writing, see Roger Bresnahan, In Time of Hesitation (Quezon City, 1981). For the itinerary of U.S. Filipinology, see the series on Philippine Studies published by the Center for Southeast Asian Studies, Northern Illinois University. A recent self-righteous defense of U.S. imperialism is Lewis E. Gleeck, American Institutions in the Philippines (1898-1941) (Manila, 1976). Note how the scholarly findings self-destruct when they are popularized in such works as: Area Handbook for the Philippines, ed. Frederick Chafee et al. (Washington, D.C., 1969); Raymond Nelson, The Philippines (London, 1968); Emily Hahn, The Islands (New York 1981).

23   "Renaissance In Many Tongues," Saturday Review of Literature, XXXIV (4 August 1951), p. 52. Donald Keene, "Native Voice in Foreign Tongue," Saturday Review of Literature (6

October 1962), p. 44. The Area Handbook cited previously propagates such fraudulent statements as: "Despite heroic attempts to sustain it, the [Tagalog] novel gradually died" (p. 140) and ". . . Except for a small group of writers producing in Tagalog, the vernaculars were seldom used for literary expression" (p. 141). Although aware of the rich and accumulating vernacular writing, Cornell University professor John Echols for the most part endorses Stegner's opinions: "The Background of Literatures in Southeast Asia and the Philippines," in George Guthrie, op. cit., pp. 133-163.

24   "The Literary View," The New York Times Book Review (12 March 1978), pp. 48-49.

25   Imelda Marcos, "Humanism: The Ideology," and Ferdinand Marcos, "Our Vision of Human Settlements," in Philippines Quarterly, 8 (June 1976), pp. 4-5, 64. The documentation on repression and militarization during the Marcos regime is voluminous. Because of space limitation, I can only cite the following: Amnesty International, Reports on the Philippines, 22 Nov.-5 Dec. 1975, and 11-28 Nov. 1981, (London, 1975 and 1981); International Commission of Jurists, The Decline of Democracy in the Philippines (Geneva, 1977); Permanent People's Tribunal, Philippines: Repression and Resistance (London, 1981); The Lawyers Committee for International Human Rights, The Philippines: A Country in Crisis (New York, 1983); Filipino People's Committee, In the Face of Adversity (Utrecht, 1983). The latest overall appraisal is Fred Poole and Max Vanzi, Revolution in the Philippines (New York, 1984).

26   Archipelago, VIII (August 1979), p. 30.

27   Ibid., p. 31.

28   E. San Juan, Bulosan: An Introduction with Selections (Manila, 1983), pp. 134-35; see also E. San Juan, Carlos Bulosan and the Imagination of the Class Struggle (Quezon City, 1972).

29   Asian Writers on Literature and Justice, ed. L. Yabes (Manila, 1982), p. 46. A massive corpus of counter-arguments have already been produced, among them: Edgar Maranan, "The Perception of Neocolonial Relations with the U.S.: Nationalism and Filipino Literature Since the 1960s," paper presented to the Second Philippine Studies International Conference, University of Hawaii, 1982; Dolores Feria, Red Pencil, Blue Pencil: Essays of Four Decades (Quezon City, 1983); Luis Teodoro and E. San Juan, Two Perspectives on Philippine Literature and Society, ed. Belinda Aquino (Honolulu, 1981). A revitalized scholarship on the vernaculars can be illustrated by the following works: Bienvenido Lumbera's contributions to Manuud, op. cit.; E. San Juan,

Introduction to Modern Filipino Literature (New York, 1974); E. San Juan, A Preface to Filipino Literature (Quezon City, 1971); Soledad Reyes, Nobelang Tagalog 1905-1975 (Quezon City, 1982); Resil Mojares, Origin and Rise of the Filipino Novel (Quezon City, 1983). The latter two titles, though crammed with bibliographic and biographical details, are flawed by the failure to rigorously theorize what exactly they are trying to achieve, partly because they operate with limited formalistic notions, and partly because they have no developed concept of a dynamic historic totality to articulate their data. This is a common inadequacy in empiricistic scholarship in the Philippines.

30 I sketch the genealogy and archive of the revolutionary cultural tradition, a sequel to my earlier The Radical Tradition in Philippine Literature, in Towards A People's Literature: Essays in Praxis and Contradiction in Philippine Writing (Quezon City, 1984). The historical context has been ably recapitulated in Teodoro Agoncillo, Filipino Nationalism 1872-1970 (Quezon City, 1974), esp. Part I, pp. 1-87F; Renato Constantino and Letizia R. Constantino, The Philippines: The Continuing Past (Quezon City, 1978). For the record, I would like to quote U.P. President Jorge Bocobo who, in the Twenties, asserted what is now generally accepted as a truism: "In what language will enduring Filipino literature be written? . . .The conclusion seems logical that the Filipino masterpiece in the world of letters, that will stand the test of centuries, will be written in Tagalog or any of the languages spoken by our people. Why is this so? Because great literature is a full-grown flower of the national soul. That soul has its habitation in the life of the common people." Quoted in Teofilo del Castillo and Buenaventura S. Medina, Jr., eds., Philippine Literature (Quezon City, 1966), p. 350.

31 Cf. Alex Magno, "Developmentalism and the 'New Society': The Repressive Ideology of Underdevelopment," Third World Studies Papers (Aug. 1983); Temario Rivera et al, Symposium: Feudalism and Capitalism in the Philippines (Quezon City, 1982). A thorough analysis of continuing U.S. economic domination is Edberto M. Villegas, Studies in Philippine Political Economy (Manila, 1983).

32 V. Voloshinov (Bakhtin), Marxism and the Philosophy of Language (New York, 1973), p. 23; cf. also P. Medvedev and M. Bakhtin, The Formal Method in Literary Scholarship (Baltimore, 1978); Ferrucio Rossi-Landi, Language As Work and Trade (South Hadley, Mass., 1983)

33 These trends, born from the crisis of institutional representation and shaped by the positional strategy to circumvent and disrupt, may be observed in the activities conducted by various

legal organizations, among them: Center for Women's Resources; Nationalist Alliance for Justice, Freedom and Democracy; KAAKBAY; Kilusang Mayo Uno; Task Force Detainees, and the Basic Christian communities.

34 This project is now being accomplished by the multifarious organizing enterprises of the New People's Army guided by the Communist Party of the Philippines; the Bangsa Moro Army led by the Moro National Liberation Front; the Cordillera Front of the Igorots; and other sectoral affiliates of the National Democratic Front in the Philippines and around the world. On the dialectic of past meaning and present significance, genesis and reception, a provocative exposition is Robert Weimann, Structure and Society in Literary History (Charlottesville, VA., 1976), pp. 18-56, 89-145.

Chapter VI

1 Quoted in Walden Bello et al., Development Debacle: The World Bank in the Philippines (San Francisco, 1982), p. 403.

2 George Simmel, Essays on Sociology, Philosophy and Aesthetics (New York, 1959), pp. 230-31; William Sharpe and Leonard Wallock, "From 'Great Town' to Nonplace Urban Realm: Reading the Modern City," Visions of the Modern City (New York, 1983), pp. 7-46; Carl Schorske, "The Idea of the City in European Thought: Voltaire to Spengler," in The Historian and the City, ed. Oscar Handlin and John Burchard (Cambridge, Mass., 1963), pp. 95-114.

3 See Roberts' important essay "Cities in Developing Societies," in Introduction to the Sociology of Developing Societies (New York and London, 1982), pp. 366-86. See also Lewis Mumford, The Culture of Cities (New York, 1970); Kevin Lynch, The Image of the City (Cambridge, Mass., 1960). One Third World study of some interest is Najib Peregrino-Brimah, Architecture for the African (Chicago, Ill., 1972).

4 Quoted in Bernard Magubane, The Political Economy of Race and Class in South Africa (New York, 1979), p. 163. See also the entries for "Geography" and "Urbanization" in A Dictionary of Marxist Thought, ed. Tom Bottomore (Cambridge, Mass., 1983), pp. 189-92; 503-4.

5 See Roman Jakobson, "Two Aspects of Language and Two Types of Aphasic Disturbances" in R. Jakobson and M. Halle, Fundamentals of Language (The Hague, 1956), pp. 55-82. For metonymic/metaphoric transformations in society, see Edmund Leach, Culture and Communication (New York, 1976), passim.

6   Nicholas P. Cushner, Spain in the Philippines (Quezon City, 1971), p. 67. Cushner draws from eyewitness accounts.

7   Based on a typed proposal sent to me by the author.

8   Renato Constantino, The Philippines: A Past Revisited (Quezon City, 1975), pp. 54-56; Teodoro Agoncillo and Mila Guerrero, History of the Filipino People (Quezon City, 1970), pp. 79-80.

9   Cristobal's piece is in Sinaglahi, ed. M. L. Santaromana (Manila, 1975), pp. 210-219. Contrast Joaquin's reductive technologism expounded in "History as Culture," The Manila Review, 11 (June 1977), pp. 22-68.

10   La Loba Negra, ed. Teodoro Agoncillo (Quezon City, 1970), pp. 2-3.

11   Ibid., pp. 45-46. See my introduction to this work.

12   See my English rendering of Balagtas' poem: Balagtas Florante/ Laura (Manila, 1977); and my commentary on it: Art and Revolution (Quezon City, 1969). Writing in 1851, Melville took occasion to stereotype Filipinos by association with the city, referring in Chapter XLVIII of Moby Dick to "the aboriginal natives of the Manillas;--a race notorious for a certain diabolism of subtility, and by some honest white mariners supposed to be the paid spies and secret confidential agents on the water of the devil, their Lord."

13   Rizal, The Lost Eden (Noli Me Tangere), tr. Leon Guerrero (New York, 1961), p. 21.

14   "On Some Motifs in Baudelaire," Illuminations (New York, 1969), pp. 155-200. Cf. Georg Simmel's thoughts on urbanism, as summarized in Essays On Sociology, Philosophy and Aesthetics by Georg Simmel, ed. K. Wolff (New York, 1959), pp. 230-232.

15   Rizal, p. 44.

16   Ibid., pp. 45-46.

17   Rizal, The Subversive (El Filibusterismo), tr. L. Guerrero (New York, 1962), p. 194.

18   The stories cited are found in Leopoldo Yabes, ed., Philippine Short Stories 1925-1940 (Quezon City, 1976) and also in E. San Juan, Jr., ed., Introduction to Modern Pilipino Literature (New York, 1974).

19   Yabes, pp. 298-308. See Rotor's collection, The Wound and the Scar (Manila, 1937).

20   See their stories in the following collections: Teodoro Agoncillo, Ang Maikling Kuwentong Tagalog (1886-1948), (Quezon City, 1949); Alejandro Abadilla et al., eds., Ang Maikling Kathang Tagalog (Quezon City, 1954); Alejandro Abadilla and P. B. Pineda, Maikling Katha ng 20 Pangunahing Awtor (Manila, 1957); Domingo Landicho, Manwal sa Pagsulat ng Maikling Kuwento sa Pilipino (Quezon City, 1974).

21   Arguilla, How My Brother Leon Brought Home a Wife and Other Stories (Manila, 1940), pp. 175-199.

22   Nick Joaquin, La Naval de Manila (Manila, 1964), p. 32. But compare Joaquin's ideas in A Question of Heroes (Manila, 1977) and relatively recent attitudes found in his numerous journalistic pieces, among them Manila: Sin City? (Manila, 1980).

23   Leonard Casper, New Writing from the Philippines (Syracuse, 1966), p. 312.

24   Ibid., pp. 381-382.

25   "Utopia, The City and The Machine," In Utopias and Utopian Thought, ed. Frank E. Manuel (Boston, 1967), p. 13. See also Raymond Williams, The Country and the City (London, 1973).

26   Nick Joaquin, Tropical Gothic (Queensland, 1972), p. 174.

27   Everyday Life in the Modern World (New York, 1971), pp. 205-6.

28   Joaquin, p. 123.

29   Ibid., p. 219. For other stories of Joaquin I cite, see his first collection, Prose and Poems (Manila, reissued 1963). For a brief treatment of Intramuros in Philippine literature, see Petronilo Daroy, "Intramuros in the Imagination of the Filipino Writer," The Manila Review, 4 (1975), pp. 36-39.

30   T. D. Agcaoili, ed., Philippine Writing: An Anthology (Manila 1953, reissued 1971), p. 314.

31   Ibid., p. 309.

32   Panata sa Kalayaan ni Ka Amado, ed. Andres Cruz (Manila, 1970), p. 188.

33 Mikhail Bakhtin, Rabelais and His World (Cambridge, Mass., 1968). Contrast the treatment of the city by American writers as discussed by David Weimer, The City as Metaphor (New York, 1966).

34 Alden Cutshall, The Philippines: Nation of Islands (Princeton, N.J., 1964), p. 74. Also Frederick L. Wernstedt and Joseph Spencer, The Philippine Island World (Berkeley and Los Angeles, 1967), pp. 142, 276-278.

35 Guerrero, Philippine Society and Revolution (Hong Kong, 1971), pp. 282-283.

36 Edgardo Reyes, Sa Mga Kuko ng Liwanag (Manila, 1966), p. 54. For the other writers I cite, see: Rogelio Mangahas, ed., Manlilikha (Manila, 1967); Federico Licsi Espino, Jr., ed., New Poems in Pilipino (Manila, 1975); E. San Juan, Jr., ed., Makibaka! Revolutionary Writing from the Philippines (Mansfield Depot, Conn., 1975); Resource Center for Philippine Concerns, Pintig (Hong Kong, 1979); Alliance for Philippine National Democracy, Jose Maria Sison: Filipino Revolutionary Fighter (Mansfield Depot, Conn., 1980).

37 Christian Science Monitor (18 September 1980), p. 836.

38 Manuel, pp. 19-20. For a historical view of the city (which draws from Lewis Mumford's classic The City in History) and an account of U.S. cities today, see Ernest Harsch, "Cities in Decay," in Life in Capitalist America, ed. S. Coontz and C. Frank (New York, 1975), pp. 13-68. The most suggestive dialectical presentation of the problematics of city life that I have found in my research is Friedrich Engels' The Housing Question (Moscow, 1970).

39 Such is the authentic dialectical comprehension of space. Recent formulations are found in Gilles Deleuze and Felix Guattari, On the Line (New York, 1983), and Fredric Jameson, "The Ideological Analysis of Space," Critical Exchange, 14 (Fall 1983), pp. 1-15. Still an inexhaustible source of insights in this field is Harvey Cox, The Secular City (New York, 1965).

40 On the revolutionary potential of the modern city, see E. J. Hobsbawm, Revolutionaries (New York, 1973), pp. 220-33. The terms "polychronic" and "monochronic" are borrowed from Edward T. Hall, The Hidden Dimension (New York, 1969), pp. 173-74.

41 Henri Lefebvre, "Reflections on the Politics of Space," Radical Geography, ed. Richard Peet (Chicago, 1977), pp. 339-352. Manila's archaic contemporaneity, if such a paradoxical phrase can

be used, can be verified and correlated with those studied by Gideon Sjoberg, The Preindustrial City (New York, 1960).

42 P. F. Kluge, "City of Dreams, City of Nightmares," Rolling Stone (15 March 1984), p. 17. For an inquiry into the literary representation of the Western urban experience, see Marshall Berman, All That Is Solid Melts into Air: The Experience of Modernity (New York, 1982). The case of Mila Aguilar has today become a celebrated test-case of the constitutional legitimacy of President Marcos's decree-making powers. It has also begun to sharply polarize the local petty bourgeois intelligentsia. On the initiative of PEN American Center (headed by Norman Mailer), PEN INTERNATIONAL in November 1984 cabled a resolution to Filipino officials demanding the release of Aguilar. The local "junta" of Philippine PEN, however, refused to consider its members' resolution to give her honorary membership (along with other political prisoners like Jose Maria Sison, Father Ed de la Torre, and others) despite a worldwide solidarity campaign for her release sponsored by luminaries like Nadine Gordimer, Paulo Freire, Arthur Miller, Adrienne Rich, Grace Paley, Toni Morrison, Gunter Grass, Denise Levertov, E. L. Doctorow, Norman Mailer, Noam Chomsky, Heinrich Boll, Simone de Beauvoir, and others. Her case continues to gain enormous international support, a "scandalous" challenge to the fascist regime.

Chapter VII

1 Philippine Trends, 11 (September-October, 1984), p. 7. Compare this assessment with that of the Congressional Research Service: Larry A. Niksch and Marjorie Niehaus, The Internal Situation in the Philippines: Current Trends and Future Prospects (20 January 1981), p. 81: "The CPP (M-L) and the NPA do not now pose a serious threat to the Philippine government." See also Far Eastern Economic Review (13 August and 13 September 1984).

2 New York Times (8 August 1984), p. A23.

3 Balita (Toronto, Canada; 1-15 September 1984), p. 19.

4 See the CPP 1969 "Programme for a People's Democratic Revolution," Annex B; and also the document "The New People's Army," Annex B in Eduardo Lachica, Huk Philippine Agrarian Society in Revolt (Manila, 1971), pp. 283-316; cf. Rectify Errors and Rebuild the Party (London, 1976). For a history of the re-established party, see Amado Guerrero, Philippine Society and Revolution (Hong Kong, 1971), pp. 36-96; also Benedict J. Kerkvliet, The Huk Rebellion (Berkeley, 1977).

5 Figures cited here are from: Liberation (March 1984),

p. 23; Ang Bayan (March 1984, June 1984); NDF Update (January-February 1984), pp. 4-5; (July-August 1984), pp. 2-3.

6   Joel Rocamora, "Turning Point: The NDF Takes the Lead," Southeast Asia Chronicle (April 1982), p. 3.

7   Walden Bello, "Election Didn't Defeat Rebel Army," Guardian (13 June 1984).

8   These operations are described in Ang Bayan (March 1983), pp. 4-5. Sources for the summary given here are: issues of Ang Bayan (15 August 1975; 29 March 1976; 29 March 1980); Dan Siegel, "NPA Gains in Philippines," Guardian (9 August 1972), p. 13; Ang Katipunan (29 March 1976; 1-15 April 1979); Filippinengroep, Makibaka! (Utrecht, 1978), pp. 142-149; Philippine Liberation Courier (29 March 1977); Ben Shandel, "Guerilla Base Grows in Philippines," Guardian (7 January 1981), p. 13.

9   Liberation (March 1984), p. 24.

10   Ka Huliau (August-September 1984), p. 10.

11   (March 1984), p. 23. For other accounts of political work, see: Samuel Bayani, What's Happening in the Philippines? (New York, 1976), p. 41; Fred Poole and Max Vanzi, Revolution in the Philippines (New York, 1984), pp. 130-166; NDF Update (September 1984), pp. 4, 6.

12   San Francisco Sunday Examiner and Chronicle (1 March 1980), p. 1.

13   Mother Jones (December 1979), pp. 39-47.

14   Economic and Political Weekly (24 November 1979), pp. 1915-1916, included in Philippines Research Center, New People's Army of the Philippines (New York, 1981), pp. 29-34. This pamphlet collects useful visitors' impressions of NPA zones, analyses, and also an NPA description of the base-building process.

15   Witeck, p. 15. Also for an update, see National Catholic Reporter (16 September 1983), pp. 28-29.

16   For a record of the most recent encounters, see NDF Update (March-April 1984). On Mao's praxis, see Eric Wolf, Peasant Wars of the Twentieth Century (New York, 1969), pp. 145-147; Edgar Snow, Red Star Over China (New York, reprinted 1968), pp. 172-181, passim; Robert Taber, The War of the Flea (London, 1970), pp. 45-58. For an attempt to reduce Mao's concept of people's war to bourgeois functionalist discourse, see Alexander

Atkinson, Social Order and the General Theory of Strategy (London, 1981). For a sample of anti-people's war scholarship, see Geoffrey Fairbairn, Revolutionary Guerilla Warfare (London, 1974).

[17] Quoted in Fifty Years of the Chinese People's Liberation Army (Peking, 1978), p. 34.

[18] See Guardian (March 1979), p. 8. For the standard revisionist apologetics, see William Pomeroy, ed. Guerilla Warfare and Marxism (New York, 1968), p. 35; 237-42.

[19] "An Interview With An NPA Cadre," People's War in the Phillippines, ed. Union of Democratic Filipinos, 2nd ed. (Oakland, CA., 1975), p. 15.

[20] Ka Huliau, p. 10.

[21] Far Eastern Economic Review (15 July 1974), quoted in Samuel Bayani, p. 41.

[22] Proletary (30 September 1906), included in Walter Laqueur, The Guerilla Reader (New York, 1977), pp. 172-178. Writing about the guerrillas in Napoleonic Spain for the New York Tribune (30 October 1854), Marx and Engels perceived the diverse, protean and slippery physiognomy of partisan bands--"the bases of an actual armament of the people"; see Laqueur, p. 159.

[23] Data on the situation in Samar based on: Filipino Support Group, Armed Struggle in the Philippines (March 1979); Philippines Research Center, New People's Army of the Philippines, pp. 46-49; Philippines Research Group, Philippines 1980 (London, 1980); FFP/AMLC, Conditions of the Filipino People Under Martial Law (San Francisco, 1979), pp. 47-54.

[24] Quoted in Laqueur, p. 241. For the African inflection of people's war in Guinea-Bissau under Cabral, see Gerard Chaliand, Armed Struggle in Africa (New York, 1969); for the Vietnamese experience, see the analysis by E. J. Hobsbawm, "Vietnam and the Dynamics of Guerilla War," Revolutionaries (New York, 1973), pp. 163-76.

Chapter VIII

[1] Permanent People's Tribunal, Philippine Repression and Resistance (London, 1980), pp. 113-14.

[2] Philippine Society and Revolution (Hong Kong, 1970), pp. 275-76. The productivist model still governs the latest

pronouncement, e.g. "Movement Fights to Free Women from Class, Gender Domination," Ang Bayan (Feb. 1985), pp. 9-12.

3   Facts and figures on the situation of Filipino women today, including a critique of Western feminism, may be found in Delia Aguilar, "Feminism and the National Liberation Struggle in the Philippines," Women's Studies International Forum, V (1982), pp. 253-56.

4   Ibid., pp. 260-61.

5   The Emancipation of Women (New York, 1966), pp. 107-08. Compare the views of Alexandra Kollontai, Selected Writings, tr. Alix Holt (New York and London, 1977), pp. 201-292.

6   Permission to reprint these letters has been given by their author.

7   Feminism in Canada, ed. Geraldine Finn and Angela Miles (Montreal, 1982), p. 253.

8   Women's Estate (New York, 1978), Chapter 5, pp. 99-122. Mitchell has also reassessed the Freud-Lacanian nexus with feminism in Psychoanalysis and Feminism (London, 1975). See also "Psychoanalysis and the Cultural Acquisition of Sexuality and Subjectivity," Women's Studies Group, Centre for Contemporary Cultural Studies, University of Birmingham, Women Take Issue (London, 1978), pp. 109-132.

9   Gabriela: Assembly Proceedings (Manila, 1984), p. 18.

10   Ibid., p. 30.

11   The Diliman Review (July-August 1984), p. 82. The path-breaking critique of dogmatic-sectarian "Marxism" is of course Sheila Rowbotham, Lynne Segal and Hilary Wainwright, Beyond the Fragments: Feminism and the Making of Socialism (London, 1979). See also Zillah Eisenstein, ed., Capitalist Patriarchy and the Case for Socialist Feminism (New York, 1979); Christine Delphy, Close to Home: A Materialist Analysis of Women's Oppression (Amherst, Mass., 1984).

12   Female, II (17 April 1984), p. 33.

13   The Diliman Review, p. 84.

14   Ibid.

15   Sunday, (12 August 1984), p. 4.

[16] See Sofronio V. Amante, "Dolores S. Feria on Women's Liberation," Diliman Review (March-April 1983), pp. 26-30.

Chapter IX

[1] Selected Correspondence (Moscow, 1955), p. 241. Cf. Raya Dunayevskaya, Rosa Luxemburg, Women's Liberation, and Marx's Philosophy of Revolution (New Jersey, 1982).

[2] Quoted in E. San Juan, Bulosan: An Introduction with Selections (Manila, 1983), p. 145.

[3] Ibid., pp. 31-38.

[4] Bienvenido Santos, Scent of Apples: A Collection of Stories (Seattle, Washington, 1967), p. 28.

[5] Ibid., p. 127.

[6] Quoted in E. San Juan, Only by Struggle: Literature and Revolution in the Philippines (Mansfield Depot, Connecticut, 1980), pp. 33-34.

[7] All quotations are from Jose Ma. Sison, Prison and Beyond: Selected Poems 1958-1983 (Manila, 1984).

[8] Maynard Solomon, ed. Marxism and Art (New York 1973), pp. 334-35, 549.

Selected Bibliography

Abaya, Hernando. The Untold Philippine Story. Quezon City: Malaya Books, 1967.

Abinales, P. N. Militarization: Philippines. Manila: Nationalist Resource Center, 1982.

Ad-Hoc Secretariat, NAJFD. Primer on the Nationalist Alliance for Justice, Freedom and Democracy. Manila: NAJFD, 1982.

Agoncillo, Teodoro. Filipino Nationalism 1872-1970. Quezon City: R. P. Garcia, 1974.

____ and Milagros Guerrero. History of the Filipino People. Quezon City: R. P. Garcia, 1970.

Aguilar, Delia. "Feminism and the National Liberation Struggle in the Philippines." Women's Studies International Forum, 5 (1982): 253-62.

Alavi, Hamza, and Teodor Shanin. Introduction to the Sociology of "Developing" Societies. New York: Monthly Review Press, 1982.

Alliance for Philippine National Democracy. Jose Maria Sison: Filipino Revolutionary Fighter. Mansfield Depot, CT: Philippines Research Center, 1979.

Althusser, Louis. For Marx. New York: Pantheon, 1969.

____. Lenin and Philosophy and Other Essays. London: New Left Books, 1971.

Amin, Samir. Class and Nation. New York: Monthly Review, 1980.

Amnesty International. Report of an Amnesty International Mission to the Republic of the Philippines, 22 Nov.-5 December 1975. London: AI Publishers, 1976. Report of an Amnesty International Mission to the Philippines 11-28 November 1981. London: Amnesty International, 1982.

Amnesty International, USA. Human Rights Violations in the Philippines. New York: AIUSA, 1982.

Anthropolgy Department, University of the Philippines. Human Rights and Ancestral Land: A Source Book. Diliman, Quezon City: University of the Philippines, 1983.

Anti-Slavery Society. The Philippines; Authoritarian Government, Multinationals and Ancestral Lands. London: Anti-Slavery, 1983.

Aquino, Belinda, ed. Cronies and Enemies: The Current Philippine Scene. Philippine Studies Occasional Paper No. 5. Honolulu: University of Hawaii, 1982.

____. "The Philippines Under Marcos: Political Decay." Paper presented at the annual conference, American Political Association, Washington, D.C., 1984.

____. "The Philippines Under Marcos." Current History (April 1982): 160-63.

____. "Politics in the New Society: 'Barangay' Democracy." Paper delivered at the annual meeting of the Association of Asian Studies, New York, 1977.

"Armed Struggle in the Philippines." Vanguard (India), 2.1 (January 1984): 12-16.

Asani, Abdurasad. Moros--Not Filipinos. Tripoli: Mahardika Press, 1980.

____. "The Bangsmoro People: A Nation in Travail." Philippine Studies Conference. University of Michigan, Ann Arbor, 2 Aguust 1984.

Asian Cultural Forum on Development (ACFOD). Philippines: Artisans of a New Humanity. Bangkok: ACFOD, 1983.

Association for Radical and East Asian Studies. The Philippines: End of an Illusion. London: AREAS, 1973.

Association of Major Religious Superiors (Philippines). Political Detainees in the Philippines. Books I and II. Los Angeles: Anti-Martial Law Coalition, 1976, 1977.

Bakhtin, M. M. The Dialogic Imagination. Austin: University of Texas Press, 1981.

Baran, Paul, and Paul Sweezy. Monopoly Capital. New York: Monthly Review Press, 1966.

____. The Political Economy of Growth. New York: Monthly Review Press, 1957.

Barnet, Richard. Intervention and Revolution. New York: New American Library, 1972.

____ and Ronald E. Muller. Global Reach. New York: Simon & Schuster, 1974.

Bauzon, Kenneth. "Martial Law in the Philippines: Paradigms of Explanation." Asia Quarterly, 2/3 (1979): 95-113; 185-202.

Bayani, Samuel. What's Happening in the Philippines? New York: Far East Reporter, 1976.

Barrett, Michele. Women's Oppression Today. London: Verso, 1980.

Bello, Walden. "The World Bank and the Economic Crisis in the Philippines." Science for the People (September/Oct. 1984): 25-28.

____, David Kinley and Elaine Elinson. Development Debacle: The World Bank in the Philippines. San Francisco: Institute for Food and Development Policy, 1982.

____ and Robin Broad. "Twenty Years of Intervention: The IMF in the Philippines." AMPO, 14 (1982): 28-31.

____ and Severina Rivera, eds. The Logistics of Repression and Other Essays. Washington, D.C.: FFP, 1977.

Benjamin, Walter. Illuminations. New York: Schocken, 1969.

Berman, Marshall. All That Is Solid Melts into Air. New York: Simon & Schuster, 1982.

Bernstein, David. The Philippine Story. New York: Farrar, 1947.

Blackburn, Robin, ed. Ideology in Social Science. New York: Vintage 1973.

____, ed. Revolution and Class Struggle. Atlantic Highland, N.J.: Humanities Press, 1977.

Bottomore, Tom, ed. A Dictionary of Marxist Thought. Cambridge: Harvard University Press, 1983.

Bourdieu, Pierre, and Jean-Claude Passeron. Reproduction in Education, Society and Culture. Beverly Hills: Sage, 1977.

Bresnahan, Roger. In Time of Hesitation. Quezon City: New Day, 1981.

____. "Our Little Proteges: Models of American Colonial Rule." Philippine Social Sciences and Humanities Review, 43 (1979): 162-71.

Broad, Robin. "The Transformation of the Philippine Economy." Monthly Review (May 1984): 11-21.

Brown, Michael, ed. "The Anatomy of Underdevelopment." The Spokesman, 28 (Winter 1973/74).

Bulosan, Carlos. America Is in the Heart. New York: Harcourt, 1946.

____. The Power of the People. Guelph, Canada: Tabloid Books, 1976.

Butler, William, John Humphrey and G. E. Bisson. The Decline of Democracy in the Philippines. Geneva, Switzerland: International Commission of Jurists, 1977.

Caldwell, Malcolm. The Wealth of Some Nations. London: Zed, 1977.

Campaign Against Military Invervention in the Philippines (CAMIP). U.S. Bases in the Philippines (brochure). New York: 1983.

Canoy, Reuben, R. The Counterfeit Revolution: Martial Law in the Philippines. Manila: Philippine Editions, 1980.

Catholic Institute for International Relations. British Companies Operating in the Philippines. Nottingham: Russell Press, 1984.

Chafee, Frederic, et al., eds. Area Handbook for the Philippines. Washington, D.C.: U.S. Govt. Printing, 1969.

Chomsky, Noam. Towards A New Cold War. New York: Pantheon, 1982.

Civil Liberties Union of the Philippines. Foreign Policy and Philippine-American Relations. Washington, D.C.: FFP, 1975.

____. A Question of National Security. Quezon City: CLU Policy Studies Group, 1983.

____. Three Years of Martial Law (21 September 1975) San Francisco: CLUP, 1976.

Communist Party of the Philippines. "Our Urgent Tasks." Unpublished typescript, 25 June 1976.

____. Overthrow the U.S.-Marcos Fascist Dictatorship, Establish a Revolutionary Coalition Government! Mansfield Depot, CT: Philippines Research Center, 1983; rpt. originally published in Ang Bayan, 15.8 (October 1983).

____. Rectify Errors and Rebuild the Party. London: Filipino Support Group, 1976.

____. "Tasks of the Communist Party of the Philippines in the New Situation." Bulletin of Concerned Asian Scholars, 5 (September 1973): 41-45.

Constantino, Renato. Dissent and Counter-Consciousness. Quezon City: Malaya, 1970.

____. The Filipinos in the Philippines and Other Essays. Quezon City: Filipino Signatures, 1966.

____. The Making of a Filipino. Quezon City: Malaya, 1969.

____. The Nationalist Alternative. Quezon City: Foundation for Nationalist Studies, 1979.

____. Neocolonial Identity and Counter-Consciousness. New York: Sharpe, 1978.

____. The Philippines: A Past Revisited. Quezon City: Tala Publishing, 1975.

____. The Philippines: The Continuing Past. Quezon City: Foundation for Nationalist Studies, 1978.

Corporate Information Center, National Council of Churches USA. The Philippines: American Corporations, Martial Law, and Underdevelopment. IDOC No. 57. (Nov. 1973) New York: IDOC-North America, 1973.

[Correspondent.] "Capitalist 'Progress' in the Philippine Countryside." AMPO, 14.1 (1982): 46-49.

[Correspondent.] "Hunger Is Their Neighbor." The Economist (13 October 1979), 58.

Corrigan, Phillip, Harvie Ramsay and Derek Sayer. Socialist Construction and Marxist Theory. New York: Monthly Review Press, 1978.

Coward, Rosalind. Patriarchal Precedents. London: Routledge, 1983.

Cox, Harvey. Religion in the Secular City. New York: Simon & Schuster, 1984.

Cranston, Alan. "Repression in the Philippines." Congressional Record, 199.58 (12 April 1973).

Cry of the People, Challenge to the Churches. A Report of the International Ecumenical Conference on the Philippines. New York: Concerned Clergy and Laity, 1984.

Davis, Horace. Nationalism and Socialism. New York: Monthly Review Press, 1967.

_____. Toward A Marxist Theory of Nationalism. New York: Monthly Review Press, 1978.

Deleuze, Gilles and Felix Guattari. On the Line. New York: Semiotext(e), 1983.

Diokno, Jose. "U.S. Policy and Presence in East Asia: An Insider's View." Address given to a conference sponsored by the Coalition for a New Foreign and Military Policy. Washington, D.C.: FFP, 1980.

Documentation Committee for Philippine Political Prisoners. Political Prisoners in the Philippines. Los Angeles: Anti-Martial Law Movement, 1975.

Dougherty, Charles. "Medical Industry Thrives, Health Care Fails." Science for the People, 13 (March-April 1981): 16-21.

Eagleton, Terry. Criticism and Ideology. London: New Left Books, 1976.

Ecumenical Movement for Justice and Peace. Katarungan 3 (March-May 1983; August-October 1983; July-August 1984).

_____. Iron Hand Velvet Glove. Studies on Militarization in Five Critical Areas in the Philippines. Geneva: World Council of Churches, 1980.

Eisenstein, Zillah, ed. Capitalist Patriarchy and the Case for Socialist Feminism. New York: Monthly Review Press, 1979.

d'Encausse, Helene Carrere, and Stuart R. Schram. Marxism and Asia. London: Allen Lane, 1969.

Enriquez, Virgilio G. Filipino Psychology in the Third World. Diliman, Quezon City: Philippine Psychology Research House, 1977.

Falk, Richard. "Views from Manila and Washington." World Policy Journal, 1 (Winter 1984): 419-32.

Fann, K.T. and Donald Hodges. Readings in U.S. Imperialism. Boston: Porter Sargeant, 1971.

Fanon, Frantz. The Wretched of the Earth. New York: Grove, 1965.

Far East Reporter. The Impact of Current United States Policy on Philippine "Independence." New York: Maud Russell, 1965.

_____. Some Current Light on the Nationalist Struggle in the Philippines. New York: Maud Russell, 1970.

Fast, Jonathan. "Imperialism and Bourgeois Dictatorship in the Philippines." New Left Review, 78 (March-April 1973): 69-96.

_____ and Jim Richardson. Roots of Dependency. Quezon City: Foundation for Nationalist Studies, 1979.

Ferrer, Ricardo, and Jose Maria Sison. "On the Philippine Mode of Production." The New Philippine Review, 1.1 (1984): 22-36; 1.2 (1984): 44-61.

Filipino Support Group. Armed Struggle in the Philippines (selections from Liberation, official publication of the National Democratic Front). London: 1979.

Filippinengroep. Makibaka! Join Us In Struggle! A documentation of five years of resistance to martial law in the Philippines. Utrecht: 1978, 1980.

First Quarter Storm. Manila: Silangan Publishers, 1970.

Foucault, Michel. Power/Knowledge. New York: Pantheon, 1980.

Freire, Paulo. The Politics of Education. South Hadley, Mass.: Bergin & Garvey, 1985.

Friend, Theodore. Between Two Empires. New Haven: Yale, 1965.

Friends of the Filipino People. U.S. Bases in the Philippines (A Position Paper). Washington, D.C.: FFP, 1978.

____ and Anti-Martial Law Coalition. Conditions of the Filipino People Under Martial Law. San Francisco: KDP, 1979.

____ . Human Rights and Martial Law in the Philippines. Oakland, CA: National Resource Center, 1977.

George, T.J.S. Revolt in Mindanao. Kuala Lumpur: Oxford, 1980.

Gillego, Bonifacio. "Our Police Force as a Tool of American Imperialism." Ronin, 1.7 (1972): 12-15.

Godelier, Maurice. Rationality and Irrationality in Economics. New York: Monthly Review Press, 1972.

Graff, Henry, ed. American Imperialism and the Philippine Insurrection. Boston: Little Brown, 1969.

Guerrero, Amado. Mao Zedong and the Philippine Revolution. Florence, Italy: II Bolscevico, 1981.

____ . Philippine Society and Revolution. Hong Kong: Ta Kung Pao, 1971.

____ . Specific Characteristics of People's War In the Philippines. Oakland: IAFP, 1979. Spanish translation by the League of Proletarian Revolution, New York, 1975.

____ . Victory to Our People's War. Montreal: Norman Bethune, 1980. Excerpt in Dare to Struggle, Dare to Win, No. 12, Mansfield   Depot,   CT: Philippines   Research   Center, 1974.

Guidote, Caridad. Imperialism and Filipino Intellectuals. Doctoral thesis, Sorbonne, 1973. (Unpublished).

Hobsbawm, E.J. Revolutionaries. New York: New American Library, 1973.

Horowitz, David. Imperialism and Revolution. London: Allen Lane, 1969.

Hutchcroft, Paul. "U.S. Bases, U.S. Bosses: Filipino Workers at Clark and Subic." AMPO, 14.2 (1982): 30-37.

IBON Databank, Philippines. IBON Facts and Figures, Nos. 1-150 (1978-84).

IDOC. "The Philippines." IDOC Bulletin Nos. 8-9-10 (August-September-October 1980).

Institute for Labor Research and Documentation. "European Multinationals in the Philippines." Philippine Labor Monitor 1 (1985): 5-69.

International Association of Filipino Patriots. "Year Eight of the Dictatorship." Philippine Liberation Courier, 4.9-10 (September-October 1980): 1, 4.

International Commission of Jurists. The Piilippines: Human Rights After Martial Law. Report of a Mission by Professor Virginia Leary, Mr. A. B. Ellis and Dr. Kurt Madlene. Geneva: ICJ, 1984.

Jalee, Pierre. Imperialism in the Seventies. New York: Third World Press, 1973.

Jameson, Fredric. The Political Unconscious. Ithaca, New York: Cornell University Press, 1981.

Johnson, Russell. Is the Philippines Next? Cambridge: American Friends Service Committee, 1970. (Mimeographed)

"The Jolo Massacre." Philippines Information Bulletin, 2.2 (April 1974): 8-10.

Katz, Stephen. Marxism, Africa and Social Class: A Critique of Relevant Theories. Occasional Monograph Series No. 14. Montreal: McGill University, 1980.

Kerkvliet, Benedict. The Huk Rebellion. Berkeley: University of California, 1977.

____. "Possible Demise of the Marcos Regime." Paper presented at Northern Illinois University, 31 May-2 June 1983.

KMU International Bulletin, I.4-5 (September-November 1984).

Kolko, Gabriel. "The United States and the Philippines: The Beginning of Another Vietnam." Journal of Contemporary Asia, 3.1 (1973): 70-84.

Komite ng Sambayanang Pilipino (Filipino People's Committee). Health--The Fruit of Struggle. Utrecht, Holland: KSP, 1983.

____. In the Face of Adversity. Utrecht, Holland; KSP, 1982.

____. Seeds of Intervention. Utrecht, Holland; KSP, 1983.

____. Signs of the Times. Utrecht, Holland: KSP, 1984.

Kuhn, Annette and Ann Marie Wolpe, eds. Feminism and Material-ism. London: Routledge, 1978.

Labor Research Association. U.S. and the Philippines. New York: International Publishers, 1958.

Lacaba, Jose F. Days of Disquiet, Nights of Rage. Manila: Salinlahi Publishing, 1982.

Laclau, Ernesto. Politics and Ideology in Marxist Theory. London: Verso, 1977.

Laqueur, Walter, ed. The Guerilla Reader. New York: New American Library, 1977.

The Lawyers' Committee for International Human Rights. The Philippines: A Country in Crisis. New York: Lawyers' Committee, 1983.

Lefebvre, Henri. Everyday Life in the Modern World. New York: Harper, 1971.

____. The Sociology of Marx. New York: Vintage, 1969.

Lenin, V. I. Selected Works. 3 Vols. New York: International Publishers, 1967.

"Let the Filipino Peasant Speak." Asian Action, 11 (November 1977): 1-20.

Levinson, G. I. Die Philippinen–Gestern und Heute. Berlin: Akademie Verlag, 1966.

Lichauco, Alejandro. The Lichauco Paper. Imperialism in the Philippines. New York: Monthly Review, 1973.

Lindsey, Charles. "Prepared Statement." Submitted to the Subcommittee on Asian and Pacific Affairs, U.S. House of Representatives, Washington, D.C., 1984.

____. "The Philippine State and Transnational Investment." Paper read at the 1984 annual meeting, American Political Science Association, Washington, D.C., 1984.

Lohr, Steve. "Twilight of the Marcos Era." New York Times Magazine. (6 January 1985): 30, 32-33, 35-36, 39, 41, 44, 46-47.

Lukacs, George. Marxism and Human Liberation. Ed. E. San Juan, Jr. New York: Delta, 1973.

Macapagal, Diosdado. Democracy in the Philippines. Ontario: Cusipag, 1976.

Magdoff, Harry. The Age of Imperialism. New York: Monthly Review, 1969.

Magno, Alexander. Developmentalism and the "New Society": Repressive Ideology of Underdevelopment. Quezon City: Third World Studies Center, 1983.

Mao Tsetung. Chairman Mao Talks to the People. Ed. Stuart Schram. New York: Pantheon, 1974.

____. Selected Readings from the Works of Mao Tsetung. Peking: Foreign Languages Press, 1971.

Majul, Cesar A. Muslims in the Philippines. Quezon City: University of the Philippines, 1973.

Marcos, Ferdinand. In Search of Alternatives: The Third World in an Age of Crisis. Manila: National Media, 1980.

Marcuse, Herbert. Reason and Revolution. Boston: Beacon, 1960.

Mattelart, Armand, and Seth Siegelaub, eds. Communication and Class Struggle. Vol. 1. Capitalism, Imperialism. Vol. 2. Liberation, Socialism. New York: International General, 1979, 1983.

Marx, Karl, and Frederick Engels. Selected Works. New York: International Publishers, 1968.

McCoy, Alfred, and Edilberto de Jesus. Philippine Social History: Global Trade and Social Transformations. Manila: Ateneo, 1982.

McKahin, George. "The Need to End Our Risky Military Ties to Manila." Rptd. Washington Post, 27 August 1978. Washington, D.C.: 1978.

Miller, Norman, and Roderick Aya, eds. National Liberation. New York: Free Press, 1971.

Miller, Stuart Creighton. "Benevolent Assimilation": The American Conquest of the Philippines 1899-1903. New Haven, Conn.: Yale, 1983.

Misuari, Nur. Political Turmoil in Manila and the Need for Caution. Progress report to the 14th Islamic Foreign Ministers' Conference, Dhaka, 6-10 December 1983. Tripoli and Tehran: Mahardika Press, 1983.

Mitchell, Juliet. Woman's Estate. New York: Vintage, 1971.

____. Women: The Longest Revolution. New York: Pantheon, 1984.

Moore, Barrington. Social Origins of Dictatorship and Democracy. Boston: Beacon Press, 1966.

Moro National Liberation Front. The Moro People's Struggle. Mansfield Depot, CT: Philippines Research Center, 1981.

Morrell, James. "Aid to the Philippines; Who Benefits?" International Policy Report, 5 (October 1979): 1-16.

____ and Severina Rivera. "The Philippines Must Not Become Another Vietnam." Newsday. (17 October 1979); rptd. by Center for International Policy, Washington D.C.

Mouffe, Chantal, ed. Gramsci and Marxist Theory. London: Routledge, 1970.

Movement for the Advancement of Nationalism. M.A.N.'s Goal: The Filipino Democratic Society. Quezon City: Malaya Books, 1969.

Movement for a Free Philippines. Life Under Martial Law: The Filipino Experience. New York: MFP, 1973.

National Action/Research on the Military-Industrial Complex (NARMIC). The Philippines: Human Rights and the Role of the United States. Philadelphia: 1978 (brochure).

National Democratic Front. "The Democratic Coalition Government." Liberation (6 March 1984): 1-4.

____. Manifesto: Unite to Overthrow the U.S.-Marcos Dictatorship! Manila: 1979. (Mimeographed).

____. The Mounting Resistance Philippines 1981. Rome: NDF International Office, 1981.

_____. NDF Update (1980-85). Utrecht, Holland.

"The New People's Army: Bracing Up for Bigger Battles." Liberation, 12.3 (March 1984): 1-26.

_____. Philippines 1979. London: Philippine Research Group, 1979.

_____. Ten Point Program of the National Democratic Front. Mansfield Depot, CT: Philippines Research Center, 1979, rptd.

National Media Production Center. Vital Documents on the Declaration of Martial Law in the Philippines. Manila: Dept. of Public Information, 1972.

National Press Club. The State of the Philippine Press. Quezon City: Foundation for Nationalist Studies, 1983.

National Secretariat for Social Action, Justice and Peace. "Support for People's Organizations Affirmed." NASSA News, 12 (June 1980): 1-10.

Nearing, Scott, and Joseph Freeman. Dollar Diplomacy. New York: Monthly Review Press, 1966.

Nemenzo, Francisco. "The Current Philippine Crisis and the Immediate Post-Marcos Future." Delivered to the Dept. of Political and Social Change and the Dept. of International Relations, Australian National University, 20 October 1983.

_____. "Rectification Process in the Philippine Communist Movement." Paper for a seminar workshop of the Institute of Southeast Asian Studies, Singapore, 17-19 Nov. 1982.

Niksch, Larry, and Marjorie Niehaus. The Internal Situation in the Philippines: Current Trends and Future Prospects. Washington, D.C.: Congressional Research Service, 1981.

Ocampo, Sheilah. "The Desperate Equation." Far Eastern Economic Review, 2 October 1981, 32-33.

Office of Civil Affairs. Towards the Restructuring of Filipino Values. Quezon City: Armed Forces of the Philippines, 1972.

Owen, Norman, ed. The Philippine Economy and the United States. Michigan Papers on South and Southeast Asia, No. 22. Ann Arbor: University of Michigan, 1983.

Paglaban, Enrico. "Philippines: Workers in the Export Industry." Pacific Research, 9.3 & 4 (1978): 2-31.

Parsons, Al. "Philippines: Rebellious 'Little Brother.'" Pacific Research, 2 (January 1971): 1-13.

Peet, Richard, ed. Radical Geography. Chicago: Maaroufa Press, 1977.

The Permanent People's Tribunal. A Brief Report. Antwerp, Belgium: KSP, 1980.

____. Philippines Repression and Resistance. Utrecht: KSP, 1981. Excerpts published in Filipino People Vs. U.S. -Marcos Dictatorship. Mansfield Depot, CT: Philippines Research Center, 1981.

Philippines Information Bulletin. Volumes I-III (1973-75).

Philippines Research Center. New People's Army of the Philippines. New York: United Labor Press, 1981.

Philippines Research Group. Philippines 1980. London, 1980.

Philippines Resource Center. Christian Responsibility and Asian Solidarity. Hong Kong: RCPC, 1979.

Pintig. Poems and Letters from Philippine Prisons. Hong Kong: Resource Center for Philippine Concerns (RCPC), 1979.

"Politics of Confrontation Continues." Philippine Report, 1 (October 1984): 1, 6-7.

Pomeroy, William. American Neo-Colonialism. New York: International Publishers, 1970.

Poole, Fred and Max Vanzi. Revolution in the Philippines. New York: McGraw-Hill, 1984.

Poulantzas, Nicos. State Power Socialism. London: Verso, 1978.

Pumipiglas. Political Detention and Military Atrocities in the Philippines. Manila: Task Force Detainees, 1980.

Quezon, Manuel. The Good Fight New York: Appleton, 1946.

Quinsaat, Jesse, ed. Letters in Exile. Los Angeles: UCLA, 1976.

Radice, Hugo, ed. International Firms and Modern Imperialism. New York: Penguin, 1975.

Razon, Felix. "Filipino Muslims and the Revolution." Philippines Information Bulletin 1 (March-April 1973): 17-25.

____. Powder Keg in the Pacific, Time Bomb in the U.S. Empire. New York: Far East Reporter, 1981.

Recto, Claro, and Renato Constantino. For Philippine Survival. Washington, D.C.: FFP, 1981.

Representative Group of Citizens. A Message of Hope to Filipinos Who Care. Manila: n.p., 1975.

Resource Center for Philippine Concerns (RCPC). The Bitter Fruits of Militarization. Hong Kong, 1982.

____. Solidaridad II (1977-1985).

Rhodes, Robert, Ed. Imperialism and Underdevelopment. New York: Monthly Review Press, 1970.

Rivera, Severina, Jim Drew and William Goodfellow. Testimony on Human Rights in the Philippines. Washington, D.C.: FFP, 1977.

Rivera, Temario, et al. Feudalism and Capitalism in the Philippines. Quezon City: Foundation for Nationalist Studies, 1982.

Rocamora, Joel, et al. "Tribal People and the Marcos Regime: Cultural Genocide in the Philippines." Southeast Asia Chronicle, 67 (1979): 1-32.

Rosenberg, David, ed. Marcos and Martial Law in the Philippines. Ithaca, New York: Cornell University Press, 1979.

Ross, Vicki. Land and Hunger Philippines, Background Paper #55. New York: Bread for the World, 1981.

Rudich, Norman, Ed. Weapons of Criticism. Palo Alto: Ramparts, 1976.

Said, Edward. Orientalism. New York: Pantheon, 1979.

San Juan, E. Bulosan: An Introduction. Manila: National Book Store, 1984.

____. Carlos Bulosan and the Imagination of the Class Struggle. 1st ed. 1972; rptd. New York: Oriole Editions, 1976.

____. "The Current Struggle Against U.S. Imperialism in the Philippines." Our Socialism, 1 (1983): 24-30.

____, ed. Introduction to Modern Pilipino Literature. New York: Twayne, 1974.

____, ed. Makibaka! Revolutionary Writing from the Philippines. Mansfield Depot, CT: Philippines Research Center, 1975.

____. Only By Struggle: Literature and Revolution in the Philippines. Mansfield Depot, CT: Philippines Research Center, 1979.

____. A Preface to Pilipino Literature. Quezon City: Alemar, 1971.

____. The Radical Tradition in Philippine Literature. Quezon City: Manlapaz, 1971.

____. Toward A People's Literature: Essays in the Dialectics of Praxis and Contradiction in Philippine Writing. Quezon City: University of the Philippines Press, 1984.

____. Toward Rizal. Mansfield Depot, CT: Philippines Research Center, 1983.

____. "U.S. Imperialism in the Philippines." Race and Class, 22 (1980); 182-89.

Sargent, Lydia, ed. Women and Revolution. Boston: South End, 1981.

Sassoon, Anne Showstack. Approaches to Gramsci. London: Writers & Readers, 1982.

Schirmer, Daniel Boone. "The Philippine American War." A talk given at the McCormick Seminary, Chicago, Illinois, 3 February 1974.

____. "The Philippines--Another Vietnam." Address given at the Community Church of Boston, 11 February 1973.

____. The Philippine War and U.S. Neocolonialism. Cambridge; Center for the Study of Development and Social Change, 1974.

____. "The Reagan Administration and the New Threat of U.S. Military Intervention." Third World Studies Discussion Paper Series, No. 23. Quezon City: Third World Studies, 1981.

____. Republic or Empire? Cambridge; Schenkman, 1972.

Seiko, Ohashi, and Endo Yoichi. "Philippines; The Election Boycott: A Vote for Unity Against Tyranny." AMPO, 16 (1984): 4-15.

Shalom, Stephen. The United States and the Philippines: A Study of Neo-Colonialism. Philadelphia: ISHI, 1981.

Siegel, Lenny. "U.S. and Marcos." Pacific Research (July-August 1973): 18-19.

Simbulan, Roland. The Bases of Our Insecurity. Manila: Balai Fellowship, 1983.

_____. U.S. Foreign and Military Policy in Asia: A Third World Perspective. Diliman, Q.C.: Third World Studies, 1981.

Sison, Jose Maria. Prison and Beyond: Selected Poems 1958-1983. Quezon City: 1984.

_____. Struggle for National Democracy. Quezon City: Progressive Publications, 1967.

Southeast Asia Resource Center. "The Philippines After Aquino, After Marcos?" Southeast Asia Chronicle, 92 (1983): 1-32.

_____. "The Philippines in the 80s--From Normalization to Polarization." Southeast Asia Chronicle, 83 (1982): 1-25.

Stanley, Peter. A Nation in the Making: The Philippines and the United States 1899-1921. Cambridge: Harvard University Press, 1974.

Stauffer, Robert. "The Manila-Washington Connection: Continuities in the Transnational Political Economy of Philippine Development" Paper presented at the Association for Asian Studies, San Francisco, 25-27 March 1983.

_____. "The Marcos Coup in the Philippines." Monthly Review, 24.11 (April 1973): 19-27.

_____. "Philippine 'Normalization': The Politics of Form," Bulletin of Concerned Asian Scholars, 12 (July-Sept. 1980): 10-18.

Steinberg, David Joel. The Philippines: A Singular and A Plural Place. Boulder, Colorado: Westview, 1982.

Sturtevant, David. Popular Uprisings in the Philippines 1840-1940. Ithaca: Cornell University Press, 1976.

Sussman, Gerald, David O'Connor and Charles Lindsey. "Philippines

1984: The Political Economy of a Dying Dictatorship." Philippines Research Bulletin (Summer 1984): 1-6.

Sweezy, Paul. The Transition from Feudalism to Capitalism. New York: Science & Society, 1960.

Taber, Robert. The War of the Flea. London: Paladin, 1970.

Tanada, Lorenzo. Nationalism: A Summons to Greatness. Quezon City: Phoenix, 1965.

Taylor, George E. The Philippines and the United States: Problems of Partnership. New York: Praeger, 1964.

Teodoro, Luis V. and E. San Juan, Jr. Two Perspectives on Philippine Literature and Society. Philippine Studies Occasional Paper No. 4. Honolulu: University of Hawaii, 1981.

Therborn, Goran. The Ideology of Power and the Power of Ideology. London: Verso, 1980.

Third World Studies Program. Political Economy of Philippine Commodities. Quezon City: University of the Philippines, 1983.

Thomas, Clive Y. The Rise of the Authoritarian State in Peripheral Societies. New York: Monthly Review, 1984.

Thomson, Charles. A Democracy Dies. Philadelphia: Philadelphia Bulletin, 1974.

"Tribal Filipinos in Agony." Tribal Forum, 3 (September-October 1982): 1-36.

Union of Democratic Filipinos. Four Years of Martial Law in the Philippines 1972-1976. Oakland: KDP, 1977.

____. People's War in the Philippines. Oakland: Pandayan, 1974.

U.S. Congress. Senate Committee on Foreign Relations. Korea and the Philippines: November 1972. 18 February 1973. Washington, D.C.: GPO, 1973.

Verdad, Juan Razon. The Philippine Crisis: Background and Perspective. New York: Far East Reporter, 1972.

Villegas, Edberto. Studies in Philippine Political Economy. Manila: Silangan Publishers, 1983.

"Violence at the Picketlines." NASSA News, 21 (April-May 1984): 5-11.

Wallerstein, Immanuel. Historical Capitalism. London: Verso, 1983.

Walsh, Tom. Martial Law in the Philippines: A Research Guide and Working Bibliography. Southeast Asia Working Paper No. 4. Honolulu: University of Hawaii, 1973.

Weissman, Steve. The Trojan Horse: A Radical Look at Foreign Aid. San Francisco: Ramparts, 1974.

Wernstedt, Frederick, and Joseph E. Spencer. The Philippine Island World. Berkeley: University of California Press 1967.

Whitehead, Guy. "Philippine American Economic Relations." Pacific Research, 4 (January-February 1973): 1-8.

Why Lt. Victor Corpus Left the AFP To Join the New People's Army. Manila: Gintong Silahis Publications, 1971.

Williams, Raymond. Marxism and Literature. Oxford: Oxford University Press, 1977.

____. The Country and the City. New York: Oxford University Press, 1973.

Woddis, Jack. Introduction to Neo-Colonialism. New York: International Publishers, 1967.

Wolf, Eric. Peasant Wars of the Twentieth Century. New York: Harper, 1969.

Wolff, Leon. Little Brown Brother. New York: Doubleday, 1961.

Worthy, William. Pampered Dictators and Neglected Cities: The Philippine Connection. Washington, D.C.: FFP, 1978.

Youngblood, Robert. "The Protestant Church in the Philippines' New Society." Bulletin of Concerned Asian Scholars, 12 (July-September 1980): 19-29.

Zwick, Jim. Militarism and Repression in the Philippines. Working Paper Series, No. 31. Montreal, Quebec: McGill University Press, 1982.

Index

Abad Santos, Pedro, 59
Activism, 78
Adorno, Theodor, 94
Aestheticism, 83, 86, 88, 97, 100, 102
African National Congress, ix
Agrava Commission, 11
Agriculture, slash-and-burn, 68
Aguilar, Delia, 154, 162–170
Aguilar, Faustino, 117
Aguilar, Mila, 126–127, 229n
Aguinaldo, Emilio, 58, 116, 209n
Ahmad, Eqbal, 13
al-Afhani, Jamal al-din, 67, 79
Alavi, Hamza, 84
Algabre, Salud, 59, 129, 152
Allegory, 189–191
Alonso, Teodora, 151
Althusser, Louis, 15, 56, 162, 179, 187
Amin, Samir, 71
Amnesty International, 2, 10, 32–33, 99
Anarcho-syndicalism, 84, 86
Anderson, Sherwood, 86, 218n
Anglo-Saxon literature, 85, 91
Aquino, Benigno, ix–x, 1, 33, 127, 178–180
Aquino, Melchora, 151
Arguilla, Manuel, 117
Asani, Abdurasad, 75–76, 215n
Asia, 27, 87, 109, 129
Asian Development Bank, 7, 23, 43, 48
Astorga-Garcia, Mila, 155, 161–163
Australia, 33, 50, 147

Authoritarianism, x, 7–8, 10–11, 20–23, 31, 34, 39, 46, 64–65, 68–69, 90, 100, 106–107, 125, 144, 151. *See also* Fascism; Martial law; U.S.-Marcos dictatorship
Avant-gardism, 88

Baker, Carlos, 81
Bakhtin, Mikhail, 102, 123, 190
Baku Congress (1920), 79
Balagtas, Francisco, 112–113, 121
Balando, Liza, 152
Balweg, Father Conrado, 29, 39, 42–43, 48–49, 103
Bangsa Moro people, 67–80, 130. *See also* Islam; Moro National Liberation Front
Barangay brigades, 32
Barros, Maria Lorena, 155–157
Barrows, David, 55
Barth, Karl, 39
Basic Christian Communities, 37, 40
Bataan Export Processing Zone, 23
Bates Treaty (1899), 70, 72
Baudelaire, Charles, 106, 114
Bauer Otto, 75
Bautista, Cirilo, 100
Bautista, Lualhati, 125
Belgium, 154
Bello, Walden, 21–22
Bell Trade Act (1946), 20
Beneria, Lourdes, 169
Benjamin, Walter, 114, 190, 192–193

255

Benevolent Assimilation, 17, 55, 85
Beveridge, Albert, 18
Black Panthers, 101
Bloc, national-popular, 75, 99, 144. *See also* United front
Bloch, Ernst, 188
Bodong (peace pact), 44, 48
Bonifacio, Andres, 114, 151
Bourdieu, Pierre, 66
Bourgeois thinking, 8, 10, 46–47, 56, 85–88, 196–197, 152–153, 155, 163–167, 185. *See also* Empiricism; Functionalism; Mechancial materialism
Brecht, Bertolt, 188
British occupation, 110, 112, 117
Brown, Norman O., 78
Buaken, Manuel, 181
Buddhism, 77
Bulosan, Carlos, 60, 100, 180–182, 189
Burgos, Father Jose, 110
Bush, Vice-President George, 2
Buss, Claude, 9
Bustamante, Governor Fernando, 110

Cabral, Amilcar, 75, 93, 149
Calvinism, 4
Camus, Albert, 109
Canoy, Rueben, 29
Capitalist development, 14, 31, 47, 72–73, 84, 112, 128. *See also* U.S. imperialism, World-system
Carino, Joanna, 48
Carter, Jimmy, 2, 25
Casper, Leonard, 90, 92–97
Castell, Manuel, 107
Castro, Father Modesto de, 113
Catholic Bishops Conference, 11, 34–35, 37
Caudwell, Christopher, 190
Cesaire, Aime, 93
Cesaro-Bonapartism, 8
Chauvinism, 45, 54, 60, 93–94, 178, 202n; male, 151–152, 155

Chico River Dam, 43, 46–48, 137, 142
Chile, 51, 101
China, 18, 24, 82, 109–110, 124, 134, 140–141, 161, 167, 173; cultural revolution, 101
Christians for National Liberation, 30, 34, 36–43
Christianity, 77, 118
CIA (U.S. Central Intelligency Agency), 5, 25–26, 88, 130, 196n
City, 105–128, 139, 145. *See also* Manila
Civil liberties, 3, 36
Civil Liberties Union, 31
Civil society, 9, 13–14, 100, 113
Class: reductionism, 30, 51, 70, 168, 173; structure, 5–6, 33, 64, 113–114, 88, 100, 103, 108, 116, 122; struggle, 15, 21, 26, 30, 42, 56, 87, 96–97, 111, 114, 123, 130, 142, 148, 157, 160, 162–163, 191, 193. *See also* Conjuncture, Contradiction
Claver, Bishop Francisco, 39–41
Coalitions, 15, 30, 108. *See also* United front
Cold War, x, 3, 13, 27, 87–89, 94, 182, 218n
Colonialism, x, 4, 69–70, 88, 107–108, 111, 151
Colorum Party, 62, 88
Comintern, 79–80
Commodification, xii, 154
Commodity: exchange, 58, 112, 123, 128, 180; fetishism, 10, 50, 91, 96, 119, 190
Common sense, 66
Communist Party of the Philippines, 30, 59, 131, 134, 136, 142, 145, 159, 170
Community, 41, 67–80, 109, 119–120
Congress of Industrial Organizations (CIO), 180
Conjuncture, 12, 30, 56, 66, 70, 82, 135, 140, 144, 180, 192
Conscientization, 34

Constantino, Renato, 54
Consumerism, 91
Contextualization, 39, 83
Contradiction, 2, 21, 26, 31, 55, 65, 73, 111, 114, 121, 157, 163, 181–182, 184, 190. *See also* Class struggle
Corazon de Jesus, Jose, 84, 101
Corpuz, Victor, 133
Cotabato-Agusan River Basin Development Project, 68
Counter-insurgency, 25, 48, 144. *See also* U.S. intervention
Crisis, 14, 46, 51, 145, 184; of monopoly capitalism, 89, 130
Cristobal, Adrian, 109–110
Crow, Admiral William, 130
Cuba, 18, 91, 161, 166, 173, 183

Dante, Commander, 133
Datu system, 72. *See also* Moro sultanate
Deconstruction, 105, 110, 175, 181, 192
Deleuze, Gilles, 83, 107, 182
Demetillo, Ricaredo, 90–91
Democracy, 4, 11, 32, 65, 78, 91, 136, 167, 172; bourgeois, 31, 56, 94
Demystification, 50–51, 181, 183
Dependency theory, 46, 53, 198n
Desire, 84, 126, 181, 184, 188
Development, 40, 43, 48, 77, 103; uneven, 49, 53, 85, 107, 124, 137, 142–144, 173
Dewey, Admiral George, 18
Dewey, John, 95
Dialectics, 12, 40–41, 47, 66, 82–83, 102–103, 108, 136, 139, 140, 145, 174, 178, 185–186. *See also* Marxism
Didacticism, 86, 113
Dimaranan, Sister Mariani, 29
Diokno, Jose, xiii, 6, 26, 65
Discourse, 9, 47, 51, 55, 65, 68, 70, 74, 84, 93–94, 96, 100, 102, 105, 174–175, 184, 212n
Dream, 190–191
Dreiser, Theodore, 89
Dulag, Macli-ing, 45

Eagleton, Terry, 89
East-West nuclear stalemate, xi
Economism, 30, 107, 153, 161, 164, 172
Economy, 7, 65, 153, *See also* Class structure; Third World formation
Ecosystem (Igorot), 47
Ecumenical Movement for Justice and Peace, 31
Education, 54–55, 85, 142–143, 148
Egalitarianism, 78, 81, 167
El Salvador, 28, 30
Elite, 7, 55, 57, 60, 97, 114, 178
Eliot, T.S., 103
Empiricism, 8, 12, 54, 93, 95, 102, 106, 136, 224n. *See also* Bourgeois thinking; Functionalism
Engels, Friedrich, 106, 160–161, 164
Engle, Paul, 88
English (literary medium), 84–86, 91, 97–98, 101, 117
Enlightenment, 56, 82, 86, 99, 101
Erlich, Reese, 138
Escandor, Dr. Juan, 2
Essentialism, 10, 92–93, 97, 174, 185. *See also* Metaphysics
Existentialism, 88, 109
Experience, 93
Exploitation, rate of, 22, 153
Export-Import Bank, 23
Export industrialization, 7, 21, 65. *See also* Development
Europe, 91, 109, 114, 155
Evangelization, 40

Falk, Dr. Richard, 27
Family, 9, 50, 64, 66, 88, 102, 121, 163–164, 169, 173
Fanon, Frantz, xiii, 46, 75, 93, 97, 179, 183
Fascism, 31, 36, 39, 82, 130, 144, 147, 157, 183
Feminism, socialist, 51, 151–175
Feria, Dolores, 157, 175
Festival, 120, 128, 187, 191

Feudalism, 108, 110, 152, 155, 157, 166, 169–170
Filipino-American War (1898–1902), ix, 5, 17, 19, 84, 86, 179, 188
Filipino: nation, xiii, 4, 101, 118; nationalism, 6
First Quarter Storm, 97
Forbes, W. Cameron, 3, 100, 214n
Ford Foundation, 49
Foreign: debt, 21–22, investment, 22–23, 32
Formalism, 87, 89, 91, 93, 100, 102
Foucault, Michel, 177, 184
Freire, Paulo, xi, 37
Friend, Theodore, 3, 67
Freud, Sigmund, 64
Frye, Northrop, 93
Fulbright, J. William, 26
Functionalism, 3, 8, 12, 54, 68, 92, 102, 210n
Fundamentalism, 100

GABRIELA, 171–172
Galiyev, Sultan, 79
Gandhi, Mahatma, 40
Gender, 49–51
Genteel tradition, 86
Geography, 140–141. *See also* Space; Territory
Gonzalez, N.V.M., 91–92
Gospel, 36, 39
Gowing, Peter, 67
Gramsci, Antonio, xi, 13, 30, 55, 66, 80, 99, 181, 184, 186–187, 198n
Greek city-state, 112
Grenada, 28
Guerrero, Amado, 124, 134, 139, 146, 152, 173
Guerilla insurgency, 88. *See also* New People's Army
Guevara, Che, 183
Guinea-Bissau, 166
Gutierrez, Gustavo, 37

Hamletting, 33, 48, 147
Hare-Hawes-Cutting Act, 66
Harrison, Francis Burton, 60, 87
Hartendorp, A. V., 86, 88

Hayden, Joseph Ralston, 3, 67
Hegel, Friedrich, 1, 192
Hegemony, xi, xiii, 6–7, 13, 32, 36, 45, 51, 53–66, 70, 74, 82–83, 91, 102, 124, 130, 139, 146, 179, 212n
Hemingway, Ernest, 81–82, 98, 103, 218n
Hernandez, Amado V., 101, 122–123, 187, 189, 192
Herrera, Trinidad, 155
Hirschman, Jack, 126
History, 79; historical becoming, 40, 180, 188; historicism, 100, 115, 118
Hobbes, Thomas, 9, 11, 102
Ho Chi Minh, 160, 185
Hofstadter, Richard, 5
Hosillos, Lucila, 85
Howells, William Dean, 98
Huk rebellion, 25, 88–89, 98, 131, 188
Human rights violations, 2, 9–10, 27, 33, 48, 147, 157–158. *See also* Militarization; Poverty
Humanism, 87, 90–92, 94–96, 99, 182
Huntington, Samuel, 8, 65, 102
Huxley, Aldous, 81

Idealism, philosophical, 95, 99, 110, 160. *See also* Metaphysics
Ideology, 9, 14–15, 36, 41, 47, 50, 53–66, 87–88, 95, 98, 108, 111, 142, 164–165, 191
Igorots, 25, 43–49, 137
Ilustrado, 55–56, 85, 88, 114, 116
Immigrants, 178–185
Immiseration, 7
Import substitution, 20
Income distribution, 6
India, 109, 112
Individualism, 92, 96, 117; Puritan, 84
Indochina, x, 23, 101
Influence, 82–83, 85–86
Institute of Philippine Culture, 4
Insurgency, ix, 98
Intelligentsia, 88–89, 97, 109, 191, 220n

International Commission of
Jurists, 2
International Monetary Fund
(IMF), 7, 33, 49, 65, 103
Interpellation, 12–13, 53, 57–59,
74, 118, 179, 182, 184
Intertextuality, xii, 45, 59, 103,
110, 186
Intramuros, 109–110, 118, 121–
122, 124
Iran, 23, 146
Irigaray, Luce, 50
Irony, 115–116, 185, 190
Islam, 67–80, 107–109, 214n,
218n; revolutionary tradition,
77–80

Jacinto, Emilio, 56, 83, 209n
Jackson, George, 83, 93
Jacob, Ave Perez, 125
Jalandoni, Magdalena, 101
James, William, 98
Japan, x, 27, 33, 87, 91;
occupation of Manila, 117,
122
Jesus, Gregoria de, 151
Joaquin, Nick, 82, 91, 100–101,
110, 112–118, 125, 190
Johnson, Laurence, 138
Joint U.S.–R.P. Military Advisory
Group (JUSMAG), 25

Kafka, Franz, 109
Kardelj, Edward, 77
Keene, Donald, 98
Kennan, George, x, 27–28
Khawarij, 78
Khidr, 80
King, Martin Luther, 43
Kinship system, 64
Koran (Qur'an), 67
Korea, People's Democratic
Republic, 24

Labor, 27, 77, 115, 128, 164, 189;
women's, 153–154, 169–170
Lacaba, Jose, 125
Laclau, Ernesto, 12, 53
La Loba Negra, 110–113, 121, 125
Land reform, 7, 137, 142, 159

Lande, Carl, 4
Landlordism, absentee, 60
Lanot, Marra, 174
Lasch, Christopher, 85
Laurel-Langley Agreement (1955),
20
Lawyers Committee for
International Human Rights,
2
Laya, Juan C., 117
Le Bon, Gustave, 113
Lee, Ricardo, 125
Lefebvre, Henri, 105, 120, 127
Legalism, 69
Legaspi, Miguel Lopez de, 107,
110, 119
Legitimation crisis, 10
Lenin, Vladimir I. 30, 74–75, 77,
81, 131, 145–146, 160–161,
184, 187
Leonard, John, 98
Lewis, Sinclair, 89
Liberalism, 9, 46, 51, 56, 68, 87,
90, 100, 163, 182
Libidinal investment, 58
Locke, John, 9, 32
Lodge, Henry Cabot, 18
Logic of identity, 71
Lowell, Robert, 88
Lukacs, Georg, 122, 186
Luxemburg, Rosa, 75, 177
Lynch, Frank, 3
Lynch, Kevin, 107

Mabini, Apolinario, 56, 83, 209n
MacArthur, Arthur, 24
McCarthyism, 89, 182
Machiavelli, Nicolo, 8
McKinley, William, 18–19, 85,
109n
McNamara, Robert, 106
Magbanua, Teresa, 151
Magsaysay, Ramon, 200
Mahan, Admiral, 18
MAKIBAKA (Free Movement of
New Women), 50, 156–157
Malaka, Tan, 79
Malcolm X, 93, 179
Malnutrition, 7
Mangahas, Rogelio, 125

"Manifest Destiny," 3, 19, 56, 85, 209n
Manila, 106–128, 135
Mao Zedong, 124, 139–140, 146, 159, 174, 183
Maranan, Aida, 173
Maranan, Edgar, 125
Marcos, Ferdinand, x, xii, 1–3, 13–14, 21, 31–32, 129, 153
Marcuse, Herbert, 94
Martial law, 21, 31, 47, 155–157
Marx, Karl, 12, 18, 67, 78, 96, 178, 185
Marxism, 30, 34, 36, 40, 69–70, 74, 78–79, 81–82, 95–96, 100–101, 103, 107, 139–140, 142–143, 145, 148, 164–168, 187–189, 191. *See also* Conjuncture; Contradiction; Dialectics
Mass media, xi, 102, 129
Materialism, mechanical, 30, 141, 161, 164, 172, 186
May, Glenn, 54
Melville, Herman, 226n
Merchant capital, 73, 107, 111
Messianism, 36, 45
Metaphysics, 8, 40, 90, 95–97. *See also* Idealism
Metz, Johannes, 41
Mexico, 109–110
Middle East, 24
Militarization, 3, 32, 35, 44, 102, 144. *See also* Human Rights violations Martial Law; U.S.-Marcos dictatorship
Military Bases Agreement (1947), 25
Mission civilizatrice, 2, 85, 98
Misuari, Nur, 69–70, 74
Mitchell, Juliet, 172
Modernism, 82, 87–88, 93, 113
Modernization, 8, 13, 21, 43, 47, 54, 65
Montesquieu, Louis, 32
Moro National Liberation Front, 31, 44, 68, 71, 73–74, 77, 80, 130, 215n, 216n
Moro sultanate, 71–73, 214n
Mother Goddess, 121

Movement for a Democratic Philippines, 157
Mumford, Lewis, 107, 119
Muzzafar, Manafi, 79
Myth, 92, 117, 121

National Council of Churches, 35
National Democratic Front (NDF), 1, 11, 15, 30, 36–37, 45, 49, 130, 143, 147, 158, 173
Nationalism, 21, 75, 101, 162, 172, 198n
Nationalities, 31, 45, 157, 178
Nation state, 73, 75, 219n
Neo-colony, 19–20, 26, 31, 51, 53–66, 83–84, 89, 101, 155, 158, 164–165, 172, 184, 219n. *See also* Third World formation
New Criticism, 88–99
New People's Army (NPA), 5, 11, 30, 46, 49, 129–150, 156, 158–160, 186
New Patriotic Alliance (BAYAN), viii, 15
New Society apologetics, 9–10, 36, 64, 91, 94, 155, 160
New Testament, 39
New Zealand, 50, 154
Nicaragua, 23–24, 28, 39, 124, 146, 173
Nixon administration, x
Nolasco, Cynthia, 127, 172
Norway, 154
Nuclear plant, 23
Nuclear war, 24–25

Objectivity, 95
O'Brien, Edward J., 88
Obscurantism, 94
Ocampo, Hernando, 117
Ocampo, Satur, 125
Oligarchy, 4, 58, 86, 125
Orcullo, Alexander, 2
Order, 8
Orientalism, 67–68, 82, 98
Osmena, Sergio, 209n

PAKSA (Writing for the People's Progress), 99
Palestine, 28

Pan-Islamism, 79–80
Pareto, Vilfredo, 8, 102
Paris Peace Conference, 19
"Parity rights," 19
Parpan, Mariflor, 47
Parrington, V.L., 100
Paterno, Pedro, 116
Patriarchal order, 121, 164, 172–175
Patronage system, 5, 14, 31
Pax Americana, 3
Paz, Dr. Remberto de la, 2
Pecheux, Michel, 15
PEN International, 99, 229n
Pentagon, 26
People's Tribunal (Permanent), 76, 158
People's war, 44–45, 48, 124, 134–149, 160, 184. *See also* National Democratic Front; New People's Army; Revolution
Perry, Commodore, 18
Phallogocentrism, 174
Phenomenology, 93
Philippine Commonwealth, 87, 100
Philippine National Economic Council, 22
Philippine Writers League, 81, 87, 101
Pilar, Marcelo del, 83
Pluralism, 64, 175
Positivism, 95
Pound, Ezra, 121
Poverty, 6, 23, 33
Power, 66, 137; dual, 30, 135, 142
Pragmatism, 25, 99–100
Praxis (practice), 12, 14, 30, 37–38, 40, 75, 80, 86, 96, 103, 126, 141, 169–170, 178
Presidential Assistance on National Minorities (PANAMIN), 44, 46
Productive force, 75
Proletarian art, 95, 102, 123, 125, 148, 183, 186
Propagandist reformers, 82, 187, 192
Prophetic faith, 41, 120, 186, 189

Prostitution, 50, 153, 158, 173
Protestant conscience, 111, 118
Puerto Rico, 18

Quezon, Manuel, 57–60, 66, 209n

Rabelais, Francois, 123
Racism, 54, 66, 85, 99, 170, 181, 202n
Rationality, 9
Realpolitik, 27
Reagan administration, x, 2, 25, 32
Reason, 126, 174
Reception, 82–83
Recto, Claro, 101, 191
Re-feudalization, 53, 64
Reification, 64, 90–92, 94, 96, 119, 122, 173, 180, 185
Religion, 33–43, 71, 77, 100, 214n
Religious persecution, 35, 110–112
Renaissance *virtu,* 84, 113
Representation, 69, 71, 84, 88, 101
Repressive de-sublimation, 94
Reproduction of the relations of production, 15, 56, 64, 83, 85–87, 169–170. *See also* Conjuncture; Hegemony; Praxis
Rerum Novarum (Pope Leo XIII's encyclical), 37
Resistance, national-popular, 11, 48, 69, 73, 178, 180
Ressentiment, 109
Revisionism, 131
Revolution, 12, 40, 79, 86, 88, 116, 130, 136, 141, 143, 146, 155, 160, 181, 187–188; tradition of, 40–41
Reyes, Edgardo, 125
Reyes, Isabelo de los, 84, 101
Reyes, Narciso, 117
Rhetoric, 107–108
Richards, I.A., 97
Rizal, Jose, 56, 58, 66, 83, 97, 101, 114–116, 121, 125, 187, 189, 192, 209n
Roberts, Bryan, 107

Roman Catholic Church, 33–43, 110–111
Romero, Archbishop Oscar, 37
Romulo, Carlos P., 183
Rosaldo, Renato, 55
Rosca, Ninotchka, 109
Rotor, Arturo B., 117
Roxas, Manuel, 210n
Roy, Ajit, 138

Saguinsin, Father Ed, 40
Sakdalista, 88, 116, 129, 152, 188, 210n
Said, Edward, 55
Salgado, Pedro, 12
Salonga, Jovito, 69
Salvaging, 3, 179
Samar, 146–148
Sancho, Nelia, 155, 157–158
Santayana, George, 98
Santos, Bienvenido, 182–183
Santos, Epifanio de los, 101
Santos, Lope K., 83–84, 101, 117
Sartre, Jean-Paul, 96
Schirmer, Daniel, 54
Schiller, Friedrich, 192
SEATO, x
Secession, right to, 74, 77
Sedimentation, 53
Seignous II, George, 25
Self-determination, 45, 49, 67–80, 153, 175
Semiotic excess, 63. *See also* Discourse; Festival
Sexism, 49–50, 160–175
Seward, William, 5, 18
Shakespeare, William, 91
Silang, Gabriela, 151, 171
Simmel, George, 106–107
Sin, Cardinal Jaime, 1–2, 11, 26, 34, 37
Sison, Jose Maria, 103, 125, 133, 184–191
Sivanandan, A., 13
Social Darwinism, 54, 85, 122
Socialism, 39, 79, 88, 130, 160, 165–166, 184, 191
Socialist Party, 59, 131
Sociology: of knowledge, 66; urban, 107

Solarz, U.S. Representative Stephen, 5, 130
Soliman, 109, 111
South Africa, ix, 30
South Korea, 51
Soviet Union, 24–26, 28, 161
Space, 127–128, 181–182, 184
Spain, 18, 72–73, 82, 83, 108, 116, 118, 151; absolutism, 39, 56
Spanish-American War, 14, 85
Spengler, Oswald, 106
Spirituality, 43
Stalin, Joseph, 75
Stanley, Peter, 3, 54, 67
State: apparatus, 3, 9, 31, 55–56, 69, 84–86, 99, 181; corporatist, 102; national security, 21; neo-colonial, 6, 70, 72, 144; neo-fascist, 13–14
Stauffer, Robert, 76
Steinbeck, John, 89
Steinberg, David Joel, 4, 67–68
Stegner, Wallace, 98
Strategy, counter-hegemonic, 75
Structuralism, 93; post-structuralism, 105, 219n
Sturtevant, David, 59
Subject, 15, 57, 57, 65, 178–179; position, 57, 59, 65, 71, 74, 92, 102, 184
Subjectivism, 66, 109
Subjectivity, 50, 70, 149, 174–175
Sullivan, William, x, 15
Superstructure, 71. *See also* Hegemony; Ideology
Surplus extraction, 22, 71–72
Symbolic Order, 63, 175
Syquia, Serafin Malay, 183

Taft, William Howard, 64, 87, 99, 209n
Tagalog, 88, 99, 117
Tancangco, Luzviminda, 173
Task Force Detainees (Association of Major Religious Superiors, Philippines), 2, 10, 31, 34–35
Taylor, George, 3, 65
Tayug uprising, 60–63
Technocrats, 21, 32, 43, 60, 65, 99, 109, 137

Territory, 74, 77, 123, 140
Theology: of liberation, 39, 78; of struggle, 36
Theoretical production, xii, 105
Third World formation, 3, 9, 12, 33, 51, 64–65, 69, 83, 87, 98–99, 136, 158, 172, 219n
Thomas, Clive, 3
Tiempo, Edith & Edilberto, 90
Tolentino, Aurelio, 83, 117
Torre, Father Edicio de la, 39, 41–42, 125
Torres, Camilo, 37
Torture, 3. *See also* Human Rights violations
Totality, 8, 51, 64, 71, 83, 117, 123, 139, 187
Tourism, 49–50, 153, 155, 158, 173
Tradition: populist, 100, 102; radical, 82
Transcendentalism, 88
Transnational corporations, 7–8, 20, 22, 26, 47, 69, 122, 126, 143, 147, 155, 178
Tributary formation, 71, 108
Trilateral Commission, 27
Trilling, Lionel, 87
Tripoli Agreement, 69
Tutelage, 5, 54–56, 58, 85–87, 98, 179, *See also* Neo-colony
Twain, Mark, 17, 98

Umma, 70
Unite, Amado, 122
United front, 145–146, 161, 171–172, 183
United Nations, 17, 99; Human Rights Commission, 2
United States: academic scholarship, 4; aid, xi, 2, 32, 53, 130; banks, 22; bases, x, 2, 4–5, 23–26, 53, 130, 133, 153; foreign policy, x, 23–24, 85; House of Representatives, x; imperialism, 4, 18–19, 23, 27, 38–39, 46, 53, 69, 84–86, 99, 101, 106, 122, 131, 144, 152, 155, 159, 162, 177–179, 187; intervention, 3, 11, 24, 48, 72, 84, 116, 132–133, 136, 160, 179, 197n; Marcos dictatorship, 17, 30, 85, 102, 109, 125, 129–130, 134, 136, 144, 152–153, 156, 161, 172, 178–179; pacification campaign (1899–1913), 72, 98; Senate, ix; "special relations" with Philippines, x, xii, 53

Universalism, 91, 97
Universality, 78, 178
Urdang, Stephanie, 168
Use-value, 71
Utopia, 105, 116, 119, 120, 149, 188

Value system, 9, 64–65, 212n
Vanguard, revolutionary, 75, 80, 139, 187
Vatican Council (Second), 36
Vernacular writing, 83–84, 98, 100–101
Veyra, Jaime de, 101
Vietnam, 24, 31, 48, 65, 82, 101, 156, 161, 177
Villa, Jose Garcia, 86, 90, 100, 117, 190
Villegas, Edberto, 21
Violence, 13, 39–40, 43, 48, 179, 195n
Viray, Manuel, 89–90, 122

Wages, 7, 22
Wallerstein, Immanuel, 77, 99
War: of movement, 14, 30, 55; of position, 15, 30, 55, 181
"Warm body" export, xiii, 154, 178
Weber, Max, 102, 106–107
West Germany, 49, 154
Wideman, Bernard, 142
Will, national-popular, 77, 88, 102, 142
Williams, Raymond, 105
Witeck, John, 137, 141
Wolfe, Thomas, 89
Women: combatants, 50; oppression of, 49–50, 151, 175. *See also* Chauvinism; Sexism

World Bank, 21–22, 27, 33, 43,
    48–49, 53, 65, 103, 106, 125,
    137
World-system, capitalist, 53, 55,
    72, 77, 89, 99, 106, 122, 130,
    163, 180, 191

World War II, 20, 88, 106, 117,
    119, 121–123

Yugoslavia, 193

Zimbabwe, 124

About the Author

Educated at the University of The Philippines and Harvard University, San Juan is the author of several classic studies of Philippine literature: *The Radical Tradition in Philippine Literature; Carlos Bulosan and the Imagination of Class Struggle;* and *Toward a People's Literature,* winner of the 1984 Catholic Mass Media Award and the 1985 National Book Award from the Manila Critics' Circle. A study of the Philippine writer Nick Joaquin is forthcoming. San Juan is presently writing a book on the inter-relations of art, ideology, and discourse.

San Juan is Professor of English and Comparative Literature at the University of Connecticut, Storrs. He is a member of the International Brecht Society, Pen American Center, Modern Language Association, and the Institute of Culture and Society. He is also an editorial contributor to *Socialist Politics* and *East Wind.*

Women's Work
Development and the Division of Labor
by Gender
Eleanor Leacock, Helen I. Safa
& Contributors
304 PAGES   PHOTOS   BIBLIOGRAPHY   INDEX

Transnationals and the Third World
The Struggle for Culture
Armand Mattelart
192 PAGES

Beyond Revolution
A New Theory of Social Movements
Daniel A. Foss and Ralph Larkin
Introduction by Stanley Aronowitz
"The most important book on social movements since
Alain Touraine."
— Stanley Aronowitz
192 PAGES

Marxism
The Science of Society
Kenneth Neill Cameron
"A refreshingly jargon-free introduction to Marxism."
— *Library Journal*
240 PAGES

The Politics of Education
Culture, Power, and Liberation
Paulo Freire
"Here speaks a teacher who lives life, a revolutionary
with hope."
— Change
240 PAGES   PHOTOS

Women and Nutrition in Third World Countries
Sahni Hamilton, Barry Popkin
& Deborah Spicer
160 PAGES

The Struggle for Rural Mexico
Gustavo Esteva
320 PAGES

Spiritualist Healers in Mexico
Kaja Finkler
272 PAGES

Class, Power, and Austerity
The New York City Fiscal Crisis
Eric Lichten
Introduction by Stanley Aronowitz
256 PAGES

Escape from Auschwitz
Erich Kulka
Foreword by Herman Wouk
192 PAGES   PHOTOS

Applied Anthropology
An Introduction
John van Willigen
320 PAGES   PHOTOS

In Her Prime
A New View of Middle-Aged Women
Judith Brown, Virginia Kerns
& Contributors
240 PAGES   PHOTOS

Political Anthropology
An Introduction
Ted C. Lewellen
Foreword by Victor Turner
160 PAGES   PHOTOS

Women and Colonization
Mona Etienne, Eleanor Leacock
& Contributors
352 PAGES   PHOTOS

Sex and Class in Latin America
June Nash, Helen I. Safa
& Contributors
352 PAGES   PHOTOS

Bergin & Garvey Publishers, Inc.
670 Amherst Road
South Hadley, Massachusetts 01075
(413) 467-3113